# TURNER

## A LIFE

*James Hamilton*

**Hodder & Stoughton**

Frontispiece: *Self-Portrait*. Oil on canvas, *c*. 1799. Turner Bequest, Tate Gallery, London

First published in 1997
by Hodder and Stoughton
A division of Hodder Headline PLC

British Library Cataloguing in Publication Data

ISBN 0 340 60623 1

Designed by Behram Kapadia
Typeset by Hewer Text Composition Services, Edinburgh
Printed and bound in Great Britain by Mackays of Chatham PLC
Hodder and Stoughton Ltd
A division of Hodder Headline PLC
338 Euston Road
London NW1 3BH

*For*

*K. A. T. E*

*with love*

"The only secret I have got is damned hard work."
– *J. M. W. Turner to Miss Fawkes*

# Contents

# List of Illustrations

## Second Section – Portraits and Miscellaneous

## Colour Section

# TURNER'S FAMILY TREE

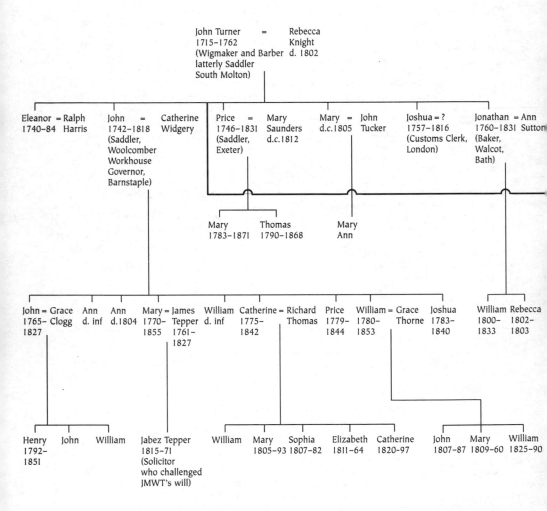

John Turner = Rebecca
1715–1762 Knight
(Wigmaker and Barber d. 1802
latterly Saddler
South Molton)

Eleanor = Ralph    John = Catherine    Price = Mary    Mary = John    Joshua = ?    Jonathan = Ann
1740–84 Harris    1742–1818 Widgery    1746–1831 Saunders    d.c.1805 Tucker    1757–1816    1760–1831 Sutton
    (Saddler,    (Saddler, d.c.1812    (Customs Clerk,    (Baker,
    Woolcomber    Exeter)    London)    Walcot,
    Workhouse    Bath)
    Governor,
    Barnstaple)

Mary    Thomas    Mary
1783–1871    1790–1868    Ann

John = Grace    Ann    Ann    Mary = James    William    Catherine = Richard    Price    William = Grace    Joshua    William Rebecca
1765– Clogg    d. inf    d.1804    1770– Tepper    d. inf    1775–    Thomas    1779–    1780–    Thorne    1783–    1800–    1802–
1827    1855    1761–    1842    1844    1853    1840    1833    1803
    1827

Henry    John    William    Jabez Tepper    William    Mary    Sophia    Elizabeth    Catherine    John    Mary    William
1792–    1815–71    1805–93 1807–82    1811–64    1820–97    1807–87 1809–60 1825–90
1851    (Solicitor
    who challenged
    JMWT's will)

Drawn up from published and unpublished research by John Parsons,
Rosalind Turner, Selby Whittingham and the author

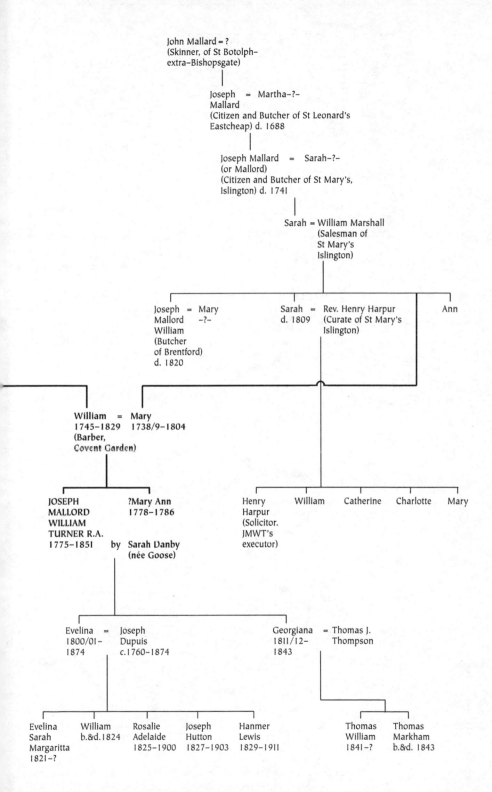

John Mallard = ?
(Skinner, of St Botolph-
extra-Bishopsgate)

Joseph = Martha-?-
Mallard
(Citizen and Butcher of St Leonard's
Eastcheap) d. 1688

Joseph Mallard = Sarah-?-
(or Mallord)
(Citizen and Butcher of St Mary's,
Islington) d. 1741

Sarah = William Marshall
(Salesman of
St Mary's
Islington)

Joseph = Mary          Sarah = Rev. Henry Harpur          Ann
Mallord   -?-          d. 1809 (Curate of St Mary's
William                         Islington)
(Butcher
of Brentford)
d. 1820

William = Mary
1745-1829  1738/9-1804
(Barber,
Covent Garden)

JOSEPH          ?Mary Ann          Henry    William  Catherine  Charlotte  Mary
MALLORD          1778-1786          Harpur
WILLIAM                             (Solicitor.
TURNER R.A.                        JMWT's
1775-1851    by  Sarah Danby       executor)
                 (née Goose)

Evelina = Joseph          Georgiana = Thomas J.
1800/01-  Dupuis           1811/12-   Thompson
1874      c.1760-1874      1843

Evelina   William    Rosalie    Joseph    Hanmer          Thomas    Thomas
Sarah     b.&d.1824  Adelaide   Hutton    Lewis           William   Markham
Margaritta           1825-1900  1827-1903 1829-1911       1841-?    b.&d. 1843
1821-?

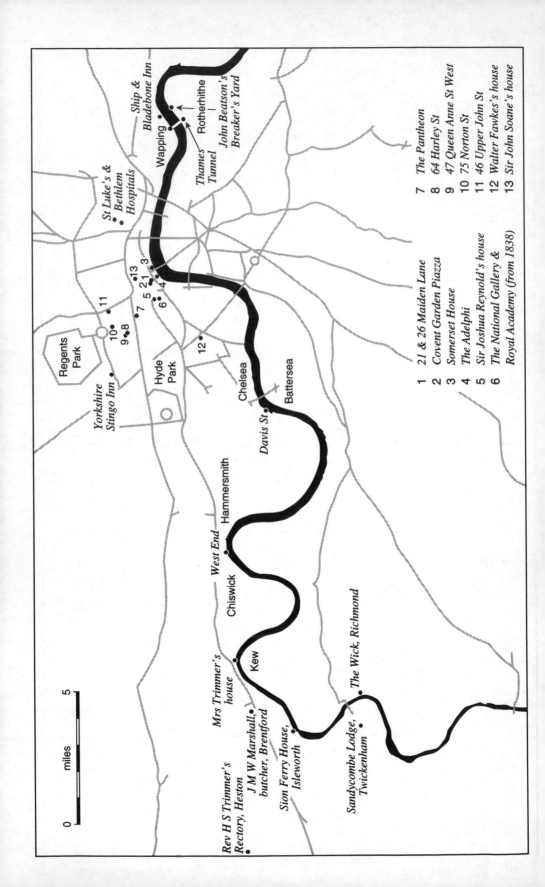

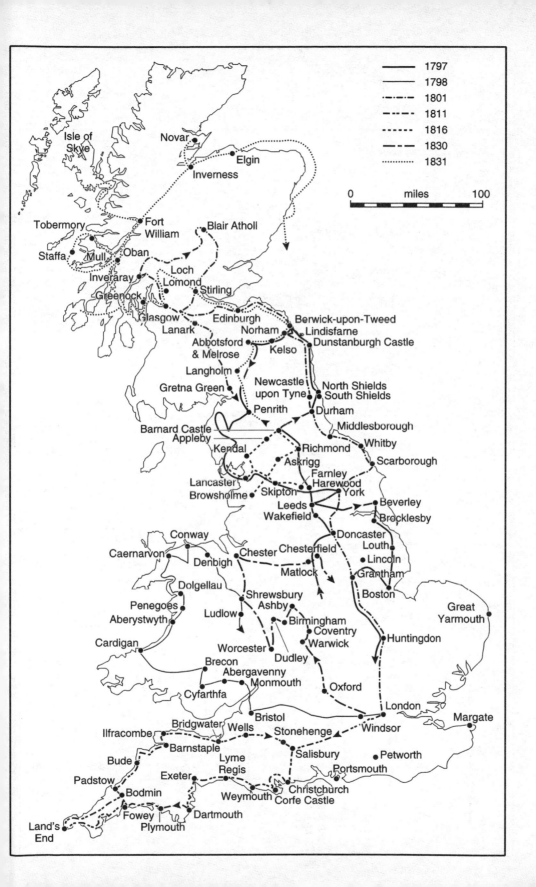

| | |
|---|---|
| ———— | 1797 |
| ——— | 1798 |
| —·—·— | 1801 |
| —··—··— | 1811 |
| ------- | 1816 |
| —·—·— | 1830 |
| ·········· | 1831 |

0        miles        100

Isle of Skye

Novar

Elgin

Inverness

Tobermory

Blair Atholl

Fort William

Staffa

Mull

Oban

Inveraray

Loch Lomond

Greenock

Stirling

Glasgow

Lanark

Edinburgh

Berwick-upon-Tweed

Norham

Lindisfarne

Abbotsford & Melrose

Kelso

Dunstanburgh Castle

Langholm

Gretna Green

Newcastle upon Tyne

North Shields

South Shields

Penrith

Durham

Barnard Castle

Appleby

Middlesborough

Kendal

Richmond

Whitby

Askrigg

Scarborough

Farnley

Lancaster

Harewood

Browsholme

Skipton

York

Leeds

Beverley

Wakefield

Brocklesby

Conway

Doncaster

Louth

Caernarvon

Chester

Chesterfield

Denbigh

Lincoln

Matlock

Grantham

Dolgellau

Boston

Penegoes

Shrewsbury

Ashby

Aberystwyth

Ludlow

Birmingham

Great Yarmouth

Cardigan

Worcester

Coventry

Warwick

Dudley

Huntingdon

Brecon

Abergavenny

Monmouth

Oxford

Cyfarthfa

London

Bristol

Margate

Bridgwater

Wells

Ilfracombe

Stonehenge

Windsor

Barnstaple

Bude

Lyme Regis

Salisbury

Petworth

Padstow

Exeter

Portsmouth

Bodmin

Weymouth

Christchurch

Land's End

Fowey

Dartmouth

Corfe Castle

Plymouth

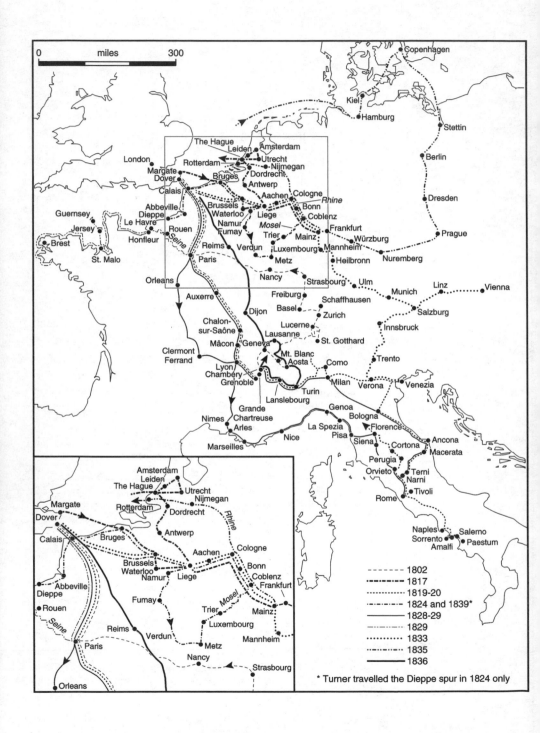

miles
0        300

Copenhagen
Kiel
Hamburg
Stettin
Berlin
Dresden
Prague
The Hague
Leiden
Amsterdam
London
Utrecht
Margate
Nijmegan
Dover
Rotterdam
Dordrecht
Bruges
Antwerp
Calais
Aachen
Cologne
*Rhine*
Abbeville
Brussels
Bonn
Dieppe
Waterloo
Liege
Coblenz
Frankfurt
Guernsey
Le Havre
Namur
Würzburg
Jersey
Rouen
Fumay
*Mosel*
Mannheim
Nuremberg
Brest
Honfleur
Trier
Luxembourg
St. Malo
*Seine*
Reims
Verdun
Heilbronn
Paris
Metz
Ulm
Orleans
Nancy
Strasbourg
Auxerre
Freiburg
Munich
Linz
Vienna
Schaffhausen
Dijon
Basel
Zurich
Salzburg
Chalon-
sur-Saône
Lucerne
Innsbruck
Mâcon
Lausanne
St. Gotthard
Clermont
Ferrand
Geneva
Lyon
Mt. Blanc
Trento
Chambéry
Aosta
Como
Grenoble
Milan
Lanslebourg
Verona
Venezia
Turin
Grande
Genoa
Bologna
Chartreuse
Nimes
La Spezia
Florence
Ancona
Arles
Nice
Pisa
Siena
Cortona
Macerata
Marseilles
Perugia
Orvieto
Terni
Narni
Rome
Tivoli
Naples
Salerno
Sorrento
Paestum
Amalfi

Amsterdam
Leiden
The Hague
Utrecht
Margate
Nijmegan
Dover
Rotterdam
Dordrecht
Calais
Antwerp
*Rhine*
Bruges
Aachen
Cologne
Brussels
Bonn
Waterloo
Liege
Coblenz
Namur
Frankfurt
Abbeville
Fumay
*Mosel*
Dieppe
Rouen
Trier
Mainz
*Seine*
Verdun
Luxembourg
Reims
Mannheim
Paris
Metz
Nancy
Orleans
Strasbourg

- - - - - - 1802
-·-·-·- 1817
··········· 1819-20
-··-··- 1824 and 1839*
———— 1828-29
—·—·— 1829
·········· 1833
—··—··— 1835
———— 1836

* Turner travelled the Dieppe spur in 1824 only

# Acknowledgements

D)ozens and dozens of people, living and dead, have helped me to write this book. Along with every other admirer of Turner, I am inestimably grateful to the generations of artists, critics and art historians who, since the 1850s, and increasingly since 1975, have pieced together the minutiae of Turner's life with little active help from the subject himself. One by one – led in recent years by Martin Butlin, Evelyn Joll, John Gage, David Hill, Eric Shanes and Andrew Wilton – they have shown us all how to *enjoy* Turner.

I would like particularly to thank Dr Patricia Allderidge, Michael Ashcroft, Stephen Astley, Julian and Isabel Bannerman, Susan Bennett, Joe Borelli and Pam Pearce, Liz and Maurice Bott, Richard Bowden, Sylvia Brown, Vivienne Brown, Dr Christopher Buckland-Wright, Harry Buglass (who drew the maps), Geremy Butler, Andrea Cameron, Diana Chardin, Emma Clarke, Dennis Cole, the late Mrs Susan Cowdy, Jane Cunningham, Judith Curthoys, Nicholas Danby, Jim Davies, James Dearden, Judy Egerton, the Earl of Egremont, Jane Farington, Dr Robin Ferner, Sallie Fewlings, Marjorie Gibbs, Anne Goodchild, Ronald Graham-Clarke, Francis, Mary and Edward Greenacre, Veronique Gunner, Jean Hackett, Patrick and Caroline Hamilton, Linda Hammond, Camilla Hampshire, Hugh Hanley, the Earl of Harewood, Colin Harrison, Professor Francis Haskell, David Holmes, Nicholas Horton-Fawkes, Marilyn Hunt, Dr Frank James, the late Philip Jebb, Stan Jenkins, William R. Johnston, Valerie Kedge, Elyse Klein, Alice Laird, Nicholas Lee, Dr Robert Leon, Brian Liddy, David Linnell, Professor Harold Livermore, Nigel and Virginia May, Irena McCabe, Alison McCann, Michael McIntyre, Tony Marsh, Betty Matthew, Gayle Mault, Frances Maxwell, Stewart Meese, Corinne Miller, Julie Milne, Griselda Munro Ferguson, Ian Murray, Grania Normanby, Susan Palmer, John Parsons, Colin Penman, Christine Penney, Audrey Price, the late John Price, Margaret Reynolds, Sgt. Chris Richford, Mark and Diana Roberts, Nicholas Savage, Carol Seagrove, Chantal Serhan, Wendy Sheridan, Alison Sproston, Anthony and Julia Stanton, Anne Steinberg, John Thackray, Wynne and Diana Thomas, Sir Michael Thompson, Dr John Thornes, Professor Kelsey Thornton, Joyce Townsend, Dorothy Turner, Richard Walker, Joanna Wallace, Elizabeth Waller, Penny Ward, Ian Warrell, Barbara Wheeler, John T. Williams, Victoria Williams, Roger Wootton, Tim Wormleighton, Doris Yarde and Percy Young for generous help, advice and information, freely given.

# Acknowledgements

Others deserve special thanks, for encouragement, for reading my text in whole or part, for trying to correct my naturally wayward sense of direction, and in one case for taking me to the Tate Gallery at an early and impressionable age: David Blayney Brown, Ann Chumbley, Richard Cohen, Francis Dixon, Rowland Eustace, Dr John Gage, Thomas, Elinor and Marie Hamilton, Angela Herlihy, Carol Johnson, Evelyn Joll, David Lindley, Roland Philipps, Eric Shanes, Rosalind Turner and the late Patsy Wills. Rowland Eustace, Eric Shanes and Andrew Wilton all read my text thoroughly and constructively. My final thanks are to J. M. W. T. and K. A. T. E. for all this and practically everything else.

James Hamilton
Warwick, 1996

# Further Reading

This book is a life of Turner, and cannot therefore also be a picture book, or a detailed art history. Readers are encouraged to find some or all of the following books in which Turner's works are extensively reproduced, and his art discussed in detail.

Martin Butlin & Evelyn Joll: *The Paintings of J. M. W. Turner*; 2 vols, Yale, revised edition, 1984.

John Gage: *Colour in Turner – Poetry and Truth*; Studio Vista, 1969.

John Gage: *The Collected Correspondence of J. M. W. Turner*; Clarendon Press, Oxford, 1980.

John Gage: *J. M. W. Turner – "A Wonderful Range of Mind"*; Yale, 1987.

Luke Herrmann: *Turner Prints – The Engraved Work of J. M. W. Turner*; Phaidon, 1990.

David Hill: *In Turner's Footsteps*; John Murray, 1984.

David Hill: *Turner in the Alps*; Geo. Phillip, 1992.

David Hill: *Turner on the Thames*; Yale, 1993.

David Hill: *Turner in the North*; Yale, 1996.

Graham Reynolds: *Turner*; Thames & Hudson, 1969.

Eric Shanes: *Turner's England 1810–38*; Cassell, 1990.

Eric Shanes: *Turner's Human Landscape*; Heinemann, 1990.

Andrew Wilton: *J. M. W. Turner – His Art and Life*; Fribourg, 1979.

Andrew Wilton: *Turner in his Time*; Thames and Hudson, 1987.

# Introduction

The young man makes deep unwavering contact with his audience and with the world. He has a fashionable white linen stock wrapped two or three times around his neck, and tied with a knot. His pale waistcoat and dark shirt are generously cut, and over all he wears a brown woollen coat with a pronounced collar. These are stout but stylish outdoor clothes, the habit of a gentleman traveller. He has generous lips and his hair is trim, powdered and ruffled into shape for the purpose of the portrait.

Quite as interesting as the facts the portrait gives us are insights it chooses to conceal. Being full face, we are shown nothing of the profile or mass of the sitter's nose or chin, nor of his height, nor any clue about who he is, where or how he lives, or what he does. All we can say for certain is that gazing straight at us is a good-looking young man, evidently well provided for, with rare poise and enviable confidence. This is a self-portrait, painted by Turner around 1798 when he was twenty-three or twenty-four years old.

Turner was highly self-conscious from an early age about his physical appearance. As other portraits show, he had a prominent and fleshy nose and a jutting chin. None of this is revealed in the self-portrait. He was short, and as the son of a barber came from a class expected to dress and pamper the rich, rather than to parade good looks and breeding itself. At the time that this portrait was made, Turner's surroundings were a cramped painting room in a dark, narrow, noisy street below Covent Garden Piazza in London.

The self-portrait also restricts our access to the subject's eyes, which are cast behind a deep shadow that lies across his face like a highwayman's mask. Very few portraits catch Turner's eyes; those which are not in profile tend to show him looking down, or away, his eyes shy of direct contact. The examining gaze of the portrait painter Turner found hard to bear. Avoiding people, his eyes were for the landscape and for the sea. Landscape did not stare back. To look out most clearly on landscape, the painter has best to shade his eyes, and through eyes shaded by a strong overhead light is precisely how Turner looks out on us in the *Self-Portrait*.

Turner was propelled by a fierce desire, fuelled by overwhelming talent and physical resilience, to reveal to himself and to others the personality of the British and European landscape and the moods of the surrounding seas. He kept no diary, but the many sketchbooks he used at home and on his travels are intensely autobiographical. He jotted in them names and dates, materials and prices, methods and intentions among the countless thousands of landscape and marine studies that were the sketchbooks' primary purpose. Open any page and, though the order may be random and the reception sometimes poor, Turner the man and painter broadcasts on wavelengths that we can pick up if we try. The sketchbooks give clues to his techniques through colour recipes and paint dabs; to his itineraries in the lists of places written out in advance of a journey; to his income and expenditure; to his struggles to master the theory of perspective well enough to teach it to students; and to his further struggles to improve his public speaking technique. They show his obsessions not only as a painter of landscape, but as a poet fighting for a line and throwing his pencil away in frustration when the line eludes him. And they show his state of body and mind – recipes for medical treatments and studies of genitalia and copulation jostle for space alongside harbour views, ships in full sail and other subjects.

Before the sketchbooks were available to study at the beginning of the twentieth century, a seedbed of colourful legends grew up around Turner. These were watered by the potent mixture of his precocious talent, his popular acclaim and his extreme ambition as a young man, his determination to exhibit paintings grandly but to be correspondingly guarded about himself and his private life. As a result there grew a temptation to map his life by anecdote, which is about as useful as mapping the ocean floor by the evidence of the islands that rise to the surface. Modern scholarship is rapidly weeding the seedbed, but nevertheless there are instances where Turner's tendency to mystify has been aided and abetted by later generations. In one case, Turner hides behind the mask of a precise portrait of an unknown man drawn probably in the 1820s by Cornelius Varley using a patent graphic telescope. The portrait has appeared on book covers, frontispieces and in exhibitions as a likeness of Turner, but comparison of the bone structure of the head with accepted portraits and with Turner's own death mask reveals it to be of somebody else altogether. Using it so widely is like writing a book about Orson Welles and putting Marlon Brando's picture on the cover.

Two examples of the special biographical insights that the sketchbooks bring will suffice for now. The first reflects their importance to Turner as sources for his paintings. Most probably in 1820, when he had just returned from six months in Italy, he made numbered labels for the sketchbooks and stuck one of these, with a title indicating the contents, on the spine of each book. Many of these labels are still in place. The only reason for labelling them on the spine was so that Turner could put them in order on shelves in his studio. This innate tendency for tidiness, which reveals itself also in other parts of his life, is a quality which has never been properly recognised. Instead, our attitude towards Turner's domestic arrangements have been coloured by anecdotal and partisan reports of the squalor at his house in Queen Anne Street in the five or so years before his death, when he was already an old and sick man and not really living there anyway.

The second insight concerns the intensity at which Turner worked on his travels. Sitting in a public coach waiting at some Italian pass or French village, he would take out his sketchbook and start to draw the church on the hill; then, without apparent warning, the coachman cracks his whip and the party sets off; Turner's pencil slips and the view of the church on the hill breaks up in a skittering of uncontrollable pencil marks. Trying nevertheless to draw as the coach trundles off, Turner makes one or two pages of zigzaggy drawings of goodness knows what until he has to give up for the time being.

Over more than sixty years, Turner travelled thousands of miles to seek the landscape out. He was drawn overwhelmingly to coasts – at Margate, Folkestone, the Cornish peninsula, the north-east of England. The rub of the land with the sea electrified him, and he observed their union from the cliff, the beach, the pier or from a small boat. On longer sea journeys he would draw coastal horizon after horizon as his ship sailed slowly by. In some sketchbooks he would make perhaps five or six horizons one above another on a page. When one looks at them one breathes the ozone that energised him.

Between the years 1790 to 1817 Turner came to know Britain as few others of his period; only the Wesleys or the agriculturalist Arthur Young rival him, and Turner was as concerned as they with the people who had created the landscape and who lived by it. There are few paintings and drawings by Turner that have no human figures or other traces of the passing presence of people. He gave voice to the collective memory of the form and shape of Britain through extended series of watercolours painted expressly to be engraved and widely circulated. These series of more than two hundred works, made over a thirty-year span, are the heart of his purpose. From 1817, Turner's eyes moved also to Europe, where he travelled nearly every year until 1845 when he could manage it no longer.

The fashions of the day, and conflicts within him and without, led Turner also to historical and literary landscape, echoes of the Grand Manner that had preoccupied the preceeding generation of painters. He was born in 1775 and so lived at a time of profound change, when revolutions in America and France were throwing doubt in Britain on the rule of kings. Painters responded to such extensive social turbulence with the swagger and heroic gesture of the Grand Manner. When Turner died in 1851, the expanding railway network and the Great Exhibition reflected an unquestioned certainty in trade, science and enterprise. Painting had moved into detail – the well-trimmed interior, the social anecdote, the high local colour. In the seventy-six years of Turner's life, the western world moved from anxiety to certainty, and became modern.

Turner himself, however, moved the other way. The confident, arrogant young man of the 1800s became in the late 1840s a shuffling, muttering outsider who took increasingly to drink. Though known in every household as a great artist, Turner in his last years was written off by his public as a sad shadow of the genius who had once painted the *Shipwreck* and *The Fighting Téméraire*. To the world he had died before his time.

# Prologue

## 27th April 1775

Between one and three in the afternoon, a remarkable phenomenon, representing in a most beautiful manner three suns, was distinctly seen.

Thus, the *Annual Register* described the two hours of spectacular solar effects that had been seen on 27th April 1775 from Chatham Barracks and Bexley in Kent to Flamstead Hill fifty miles to the north-west in Hertfordshire.[1] About halfway between Flamstead and Chatham, in Maiden Lane Covent Garden, J. M. W. Turner had, probably, just been born. The exact date of Turner's birth is unknown, but it was a strange, auspicious moment when, around the likely date, his countrymen experienced a spectacular solar halo strong enough to warrant a full-page engraved diagram in the *Gentleman's Magazine*.[2] Solar haloes are reasonably common; but this one appeared at the time of birth of the greatest painter of sunlight that the world has ever known.

Nearly three weeks later, despite "blighting fogs and frosty nights; and scarce any rain for 30 days,"[3] William and Mary Turner wrapped their baby up and took him out of Maiden Lane to be christened at St Paul's Church in Covent Garden Piazza.

# ONE

# Maiden Lane and Brentford

## 1775–1790

William Turner, the baby's father, had rural, distant roots. He had come, no more than ten years earlier, from the deep west of England, from the small country town of South Molton at the foot of Exmoor in Devon. His own father, John Turner, had been a wig-maker and barber in South Molton, and one of sufficient status to be entrusted with the care and teaching of boy apprentices by the Church Wardens and the Justices of the Peace of the parish.[1] When John Turner died in 1762 he left tidy provision for his wife and seven children.[2] Two sons at least, John and William, were grown up by this time. The eldest son, John the younger, was bequeathed all of his father's working tools, his best suit, hat and wig, and a guinea, with the expectation that he would follow in his father's footsteps. In the event it appears that John Turner the younger became a saddler and later a wool-comber and poor-house guardian.[3] William, who had been born in 1745, received only "my white coat" and a guinea payable when he became twenty-one. The five other children, Eleanor, Price, Mary, Joshua and Jonathan, were also bequeathed a guinea each, payment to be delayed until their twenty-first birthdays. South Molton was suffering a serious population decline in the late 1760s and early 1770s through the gradual weakening of the market for the heavy cloths such as serges and felts that were a speciality of the town.[4] This may have been the spur which prompted William to take his white coat with the guinea in its pocket and make for London. He settled just off Covent Garden and following his father's example set up in business as a barber and wig-maker.

Mary Marshall, J. M. W. Turner's mother, came from a family of London butchers. They can be traced as far back as her maternal great-great-grandfather, John Mallard, a skinner from St Botolph-extra-Bishopsgate.

His son, Joseph Mallard (d. 1688), lived at St Leonard's, Eastcheap on the edge of the highway down which the cattle from Essex and beyond were driven for slaughter and sale at Smithfield. Joseph Mallard's son, Mary's grandfather, another Joseph Mallard (d. 1741),[5] gained his freedom from apprenticeship in 1697, and was described when he died as a "Citizen and Butcher". At the same time, according to the spelling in his will, he and his family became Mallord, and this form generally, though not consistently, applied from then on. Joseph Mallord moved with his family north and west out of the City to the clearer air of the salubrious parish of St Mary's, Islington, and diversified his wealth and invested in property. At his death he owned four houses in Wapping and four acres of marsh land at Barkingside, north of Redbridge. His only surviving child, Sarah, who married William Marshall, an Islington salesman, stood to inherit all this, and to pass it on in turn to her four children, Joseph Mallord William, Sarah, Mary (b.1738 or 1739) and Ann.[6]

When William Turner and Mary Marshall met around 1770, William, slim, healthy, chatty and eager with an engaging Devon brogue, was in his mid-twenties. Mary has been described as a housekeeper, a sufficiently vague, meaningless but polite term for a single woman in her thirties.[7] Both were well over the normal age for first marriage in the late eighteenth century, and for Mary the end of her marriageable and child-bearing years was approaching. Her elder sister Sarah had already married, and her elder brother had moved away from Islington to follow his grandfather's trade of butcher in the prosperous community of New Brentford.

William and Mary, as proudly named an English coupling as any might be, married at St Paul's Church, Covent Garden on 29th August 1773. In applying at Lambeth Palace for a licence to marry without banns, William swore that he was a twenty-eight-year-old bachelor, Mary a thirty-four-year-old spinster, and that he had lived for the "four weeks last past" in the Parish of St Paul, Covent Garden. Although this was a marriage between property-owning citizenry and the deracinated working trades, it was a marriage of free choice and optimism. William the barber had landed Mary the solid London citizen's granddaughter; Mary, the older woman with little hope of inheriting any share of her grandfather's estates, and rapidly receding chances of marriage, had found William the plucky, hard-working young man from a far county.

According to the only surviving physical description of him, written after William Turner's death:

> he was ... spare and muscular, with a head below the average standard, small blue eyes, parrot nose, projecting chin, and a fresh complexion indicative of health, which he apparently enjoyed to the full. He was a chatty old fellow and talked fast; and his words

acquired a peculiar transatlantic twang from his nasal enunciation. His cheerfulness was greater than that of his son, and a smile was always on his countenance.[8]

If we can rely on the fact that William Turner was a cheerful, smiling gossip, he would have been the right stuff for the barber's trade, which has always required cheerfulness, flattery, and the ability to engage customers' interest for as long as it takes to cut their hair.

Knowledge of the character and appearence of Turner's mother is even thinner, and heavily embellished by hearsay. Turner's first biographer, Walter Thornbury, built his picture of Mary Turner around the sometime existence of an unfinished portrait of her by her son, "one of his first attempts". Thornbury writes:

> The portrait was not wanting in force or decision of touch, but the drawing was defective. There was a strong likeness to Turner about the nose and eyes; her eyes being represented as blue, of a lighter hue than her son's; her nose aquiline, and the nether lip having a slight fall. Her hair was well frizzed ... and it was surmounted by a cap with large flappers. Her posture therein was erect, and her aspect masculine, not to say fierce.[9]

This portrait has not been traced – and Thornbury had not seen it – so we can only take his uncorroborated account at face value. To his description of this fierce, masculine, erect figure, Thornbury adds that Mary Turner had been "a person of ungovernable temper". This was a trait that, in part, her son inherited.

William took Mary to live in rooms at the south-west end of Maiden Lane, number 21, where he had been a tenant since Lady Day, 25th March. The house was part of a line of dwellings built on the edge of the site of Bedford House, demolished in 1707. Maiden Lane is about halfway between the Strand and Covent Garden Piazza, and runs parallel to both. Unlike their wide, light-filled expanses, it was then narrow, noisy and dark. Running east–west it was pretty much in shadow, and quite apart from the rubbish its inhabitants threw out, it collected muck from the market when it rained and backwash from the rudimentary sewers. Its name derived from the fact that it was the place where prostitutes lingered.[10]

The Turners' rooms were rented from the auctioneer Joseph Mooring, who had used the building for sales and exhibitions. In 1765 and 1766, Mooring had let them to the Free Society of Artists,[11] and from 1769 the Incorporated Society of Artists had used it as a school of painting, drawing and modelling. In the basement was William Wootten's Cider Cellar, a drinking place described in 1750 as a "midnight concert room,"[12] "to which you descended by ladder to the concert-room, which, in another house, would have been the kitchen, or the cellar; and the fittings of the place were rude and rough."[13]

This rowdy house in Maiden Lane was, nevertheless, a sensible place for a barber and wig-maker to be. One hundred yards to the north, around London's flower and vegetable market, was a community of shops, stalls, coffee houses and other businesses selling all the human frame required in the hinterland of two of London's great theatres. These, the Theatre Royal Covent Garden and the Theatre Royal Drury Lane, each attracted two thousand or more people nightly in the season, from the rich and noble to the pecking poor, a great pulsating unremitting throng in search of entertainment, glittering lights, laughter, company, active oblivion and barbering.

The theatres had their essential and their satellite trades – the managers, the actors and actresses, the scene painters and shifters, sellers of food and drink, porters, drivers, sedan chairmen, sweepers and ostlers all adding to the vivacious street life. Another hundred yards to the north was Long Acre, a road rattling then with the workshops of coach and trunk makers, the centre of Britain's mechanical transport industry and its dependants, forges, ironmongers, coach painters, colourmen and print dealers. The same distance to the east, in Bow Street, magistrates sat to hand sentence down to murderers and swindlers who came to court with small armies of chanting supporters. Minor felons such as Filch, the boy pickpocket in *The Beggar's Opera* of 1728, were dealt with: "Where was your post last night, my boy?" asks Mrs Peachum. "I ply'd at the Opera, madam; and considering 'twas neither dark nor rainy, so that there was no great hurry in getting chairs and coaches, made a tolerable hand on't. These seven handkerchiefs, Madam."[14]

Frightening and potentially violent though it was, London west of Temple Bar was tightly knit and its people interconnected. Though the Incorporated Society of Artists had left Maiden Lane in the early 1770s, having been swallowed up by the new Royal Academy of Arts, artists and architects lived and worked in considerable numbers in the area bounded by Long Acre in the north and the Strand in the south. The area remained the focus of their livelihoods, the place where they met, talked, made friends, fell out and had their hair dressed.

In Maiden Lane and the parallel Henrietta Street alone, artists were a significant element of the population. Between 1763 and 1777 artists who lived at various addresses in Maiden Lane included William Burgess, James Butler, Thomas Hearne, William James, Henry Jouret, James Nixon ARA and the engraver Benjamin Thomas Pouncey. George Burgess had a Drawing Academy at number 33. In Henrietta Street lived the engraver

William Dickenson and the painter Samuel Hieronymus Grimm. Even if only Hearne, Nixon and Grimm are remembered today, the others all had their ambitions and contributed to the atmosphere of the area. Others in neighbouring streets at this time were Edward Dayes, John Flaxman and Thomas Hudson.

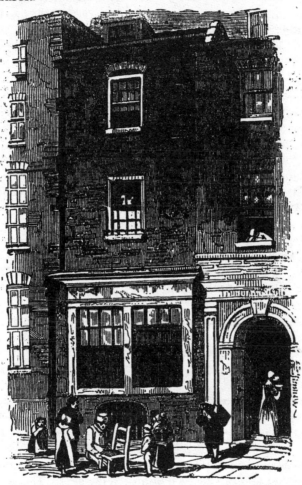

*Turner's birthplace.* From *The Illustrated London News*, 10th Jan 1852.
This may depict 26 Maiden Lane, where the family later moved.

On 14th May 1775 William and Mary Turner's child was baptised with his maternal uncle's names: Joseph Mallord William.[15] The tradition begun and maintained later in his life by J. M. W. Turner himself, puts his birth date exactly three weeks before the christening, 23rd April, St George's Day – a good day for a true patriot to choose, after some reflection, to be born upon. If the traditional birthdate is correct the very cold weather might explain the unusually long gap between the child's birth and his baptism. But there is no good reason why we should accept it, for high infant mortality rates prompted god-fearing parents to have their children christened promptly. The baby's three strong names suggest that his parents had ambitions for the child, and wished to signal his firm connection above all to his mother's family. A Devon-born barber's son he may have been, but he was also descended from a line of London citizens and property owners.

From Lady Day 1776, when the baby would have been barely crawling, the Turners ceased to pay Poor Rates in Maiden Lane. This has been taken to suggest that they had moved out of the parish, but it is equally possible that they remained where they were and the rate was paid by their landlord. William Turner's name reappears in the Maiden Lane Poor Rate register at Lady Day 1795, where he is listed as living on the north side of the lane, at number 26, directly opposite his former address. We know from other sources that by 1795 the family had been living in Maiden Lane for at least five years, and at number 26 for at least four, without having been listed in the Poor Rate books.[16] This narrows down their putative absence from Maiden Lane to between September 1778 and April 1790.[17] There is also circumstantial evidence, below, that the family was already living at 26 Maiden Lane by 1782 or 1783, so there are no firm grounds to suggest that the Turners ever left.

William Turner could never have been short of customers if he was any good at cutting and dressing hair. Periwigs, the full-bottomed wigs whose tails flowed over the shoulders of the rich and noble in the early eighteenth century, had long gone out of fashion. Hogarth's satirical engraving *The Five Orders of Periwig* (1761) had signalled the killing off of the full-bottomed wig by making it and its wearers into a laughing stock. Although the first layer of Hogarth's joke likens the periwigs to architectural orders, his visual subtext compares them to unarousable genitalia. In their place, a fashion for smaller wigs and natural male hairstyles developed. In Sheridan's *The Rivals*, first performed in 1775, Fag the elegant servant advised strongly against his master wearing a wig. "None of the London whips of any degree of *ton* wear wigs now," he said.[18]

The return to natural hair in men and the fashionable loathing of the hairy chin must have brought plenty of work for William Turner. Barbers shaved their customers, trimmed and curled their hair and wigs and sold perfumes and wig powder. William Turner may also have been a puller of teeth and a low-grade surgeon, for the trades went together. Serving leaders of fashion in London's centre of artistic gathering and display, law-giving and gossip, his customers included a heavy proportion of artists, theatrical people and men of influence and connection.

Hairdressing was, when Turner was a boy, an item for news and jokey chit-chat. New hair fashions brought an influx of foreign hairdressers to London. *The Times* reported in January 1785: "The friseurs of Paris are pouring in daily; a post coach, with six inside, and ten outside, arrived at Charing Cross a few days ago – without luggage."[19] The trade supplied its most plentiful by-product to a fringe of the art world. Exhibiting both at the Society of Artists and the Free Society of Artists in the 1770s, regularly enough to make it a significant activity, were a dozen people who made embroideries and pictures out of hair and called themselves "Workers in Hair". Mary Lane, for example, exhibited thirty various works in hair, including landscapes after Hollar and Claude, at the Society of Artists from 1770 to 1777. Other practitioners were Mr Nodder of Panton Street, Mrs Putland, John Turmeau and the industrious Passavant family.

There is no reason to doubt that William Turner was a successful part of this busy world of service, and it is possible to make a guess at what he earned. James Boswell gives a clue to this in his "Scheme of Living", written out on his arrival in London in November 1762. He planned to have his "hair dressed every day, or pretty often, which may come to £6 [for the year]."[20] This suggests that Boswell budgeted fourpence to fivepence a day for the service, perhaps more when trimming was required. The figure is corroborated by Charlotte Burney who, in a letter to her sister Fanny in April 1780, reports that for a night out at the Pantheon an acquaintance had paid her hairdresser 9d, "and yet thought it 3d too dear!"[21]

If these figures represent, as they must, a standard charge, William Turner, serving say four customers an hour, might expect to take between eleven and sixteen shillings a day; much more if he employed assistants. If he worked on his own for six days a week, this suggests his weekly income might have been around £4 or £5, or £240–£280 per year. Given extra profits of sales of scents and preparations, dentistry and surgery, and bags of trimmings for the "Workers in Hair", he might take home at least £300 a year. This makes a tidy income, something like £15,000 in late 1990s money, and suggests that there is no case whatsoever for believing that William Turner was poor, as has traditionally been assumed. In a near contemporary text, Edward Dayes remarked significantly that as a barber William Turner "conducted a decent trade".[22]

One regular customer whom William Turner visited at home was Humphrey Tomkison, a jeweller and goldsmith who practised in Maiden Lane from 1768 to 1777 and then from 1779 to 1784 one hundred yards away in Southampton Street at the eastern end of Maiden Lane.[23] Tomkison's son, the Soho piano-maker Thomas Tomkison (?1764–1853), approved in 1850 what was effectively an affidavit claiming that his father was the first to discover that young William Turner had an unusual talent:

On one occasion, Turner brought his *child* with him; and while the father was dressing my father, the little boy was occupied with copying something he saw on the table ... On being shown the [boy's] copy, my father said, "your son never could have done it." He had copied a coat of arms from a handsome set of castors, which happened at that time to be on the table.[24]

The boy might have been no more than eight or nine – suggesting that this may be 1782 or 1783 – and if Tomkison's memory was accurate his preceding remark that the Turner family "lived in Maiden Lane, a corner house in a little court", suggests that they had already moved to number 26, which was on the corner of Maiden Lane and by a little enclave within the buildings on the north side, Hand Court.

In 1785 William and Mary Turner sent William their son, then aged ten, away to live in New Brentford. Thornbury, quoting from now lost but probably genuine manuscript recollections of the engraver Edward Bell who had known Turner, says that this was "in consequence of a fit of illness". Whose illness it was is not clear. It has generally been assumed that the family's putative youngest child Mary Ann was mortally ill, but this idea has the weakness of being one assumption built upon another.[25]

Old Brentford, down towards Kew Bridge, had been described in 1765 as "the ugliest and filthiest place in England" on account of the ramshackle huts on the riverbank opposite the new gothick Kew Palace then being built for the Prince of Wales.[26] New Brentford, however, built in the mid-eighteenth century a mile or so away to the west, was on the edge of an area of market gardens and orchards interspersed with fine houses. Walking the distance of about two miles from New Brentford north to Ealing, John Yeoman, a farmer and potter from Somerset who travelled to London in the 1770s, passed

five Esquires' seats, one Bishop, one Duke's and the Princess Amelia House [i.e. Gunnersbury House]. So I leave the reader to judge the pleasantness of our walk and, where there was no gentleman's seat, it was gardeners' gardens with fruit trees all in full bloom, which make it like the seat of paradise.[27]

Turner's uncle and namesake, Joseph Mallord William Marshall, was by now established as a butcher in New Brentford. His house and shop were on the north side of the Market Place, next to the White Horse Inn, backing on to the River Brent, and it is likely that the boy lived there for about a year. Thornbury tells us that he went to a school run by John White in Brentford Butts, just beyond the Market Place.

In the mid-1780s, Old and New Brentford happened to be the place where a new revolutionary movement in education was just beginning. Mrs Sarah Trimmer (1741–1810), a writer for children and a passionate believer in the availability of education for all classes of young people, was a Brentford woman who set up Sunday schools at St George's Chapel, Old Brentford, in 1786. Within two years, these schools were attracting 300 boys and girls.[28] In 1787 Mrs Trimmer founded the Brentford School of Industry for girls, teaching reading, writing and home crafts such as embroidery and dress-making. There was nowhere better in all England in 1785 than Brentford for the education of young people.

This extraordinary and energetic woman lived with her large family on the north of Kew Bridge, Old Brentford. Her two younger sons, John and Henry, went to John White's day school.[29] Her husband, James Trimmer, was the owner of successful brick kilns on the bank of the river at Kew Bridge. He was well known in the town; his bricks had built most of New Brentford. Among his professional contacts was the Brentford mason and builder, Thomas Hardwick, who, with the Trimmers, was among the subscribers to the building of St George's Chapel, Old Brentford in 1766.[30]

Sarah Trimmer came from an intellectual background, having grown up amongst artists and writers. Her father, Joshua Kirby (1716–74), had been an Ipswich artist who became one of Gainsborough's closest friends and patrons. The early landscapes and portraits by Gainsborough that Kirby owned at his death descended to Sarah, and hung in her Brentford house. When she was thirteen, her father wrote and published *Dr Brook Taylor's Method of Perspective Made Easy* (1754), a highly influential attempt to render a complicated system of perspective into manageable form for a thrusting generation of literate artists. Shortly after this book appeared, the Kirbys moved to London, where Joshua taught perspective in the St Martin's Lane Academy. He was close friends with Hogarth and Reynolds, knew Dr Johnson, and rose to be President of the Incorporated Society of Artists (of Maiden Lane). He came to know Lord Bute, who introduced him to the Prince of Wales, later George III, to whom he taught perspective, and in due course the Prince of Wales made Kirby Clerk of Works for his new palace at Kew.

In this influential role, Joshua Kirby was closely in touch with building development opportunities over the river in Brentford. He was the architect of St George's Chapel, to which James Trimmer and Thomas Hardwick subscribed, and using his connections with the Incorporated Society of Artists must have been involved in commissioning or at least obtaining for the church Zoffany's painting of *The Last Supper*.[31]

Within the limited confines of Covent Garden, Strand and Soho, an area of about half a square mile, everybody in the artistic, literary and theatrical worlds knew everybody else, or knew of them. Indeed, it was devilish difficult to get away. During one party at Joshua Reynolds's house in Leicester Square, at which Joshua Kirby and Sarah were present with Samuel Johnson, an argument arose about a certain passage in *Paradise Lost*. Young, ambitious and scholarly, Sarah Kirby whipped a Milton from her pocket and there and then located the passage in question, settling the argument.

This anecdote comes from the introduction written by Rev. Henry Scott Trimmer to his mother's *Life and Writings*. It will naturally have been enlarged and buffed up by the passage of time and family pride, but nonetheless, as Henry Scott Trimmer continues:

> Doctor Johnson was so struck with a girl of that age making this work her pocket companion, and likewise with the modesty of her behaviour upon this occasion, that he invited her next day to his house, presented her with a copy of his Rambler, and afterwards treated her with great consideration.

Henry Scott Trimmer goes on to record that his mother competed for a Premium at the Society of Arts (later the Royal Society of Arts), and obtained a prize for the second best drawing.

> This knowledge of drawing which she had acquired when young, became very useful to her when she was a mother, as it enabled her to amuse her children in their infancy, and likewise to direct them afterwards in the exercise of this talent in that way.[32]

While having the courage and character to set up Sunday schools in Brentford, Sarah Trimmer wrote educational texts for children which explained the natural world, and the central place of God in creation. She also wrote reading primers and a series of volumes of stories from the Bible. This strong literary circumstance gave an intellectual backbone to the teaching of children in Brentford. Although she had moved to Brentford on her marriage in 1762, Sarah Trimmer remained in touch with London art circles, and was in a position to help a bright child in a family stricken by "a fit of illness". She knew, for example, the painter Henry Howard (1769–1847) who painted her portrait in 1798, and who became a close friend both of Turner and Henry Scott Trimmer.

Sarah Trimmer published her own philosophy of education in 1792, which includes the observation:

> And if there be other [poor children] whose bright genius breaks through the thick clouds of ignorance and poverty, reason and humanity plead in their behalf, that they should be indulged with

such tuition as may enable them to advance themselves, by the exertion of their abilities, to a higher station, and fill it with propriety.[33]

Turner's father was not a man to shy away from telling anybody who might be interested that he had a very bright boy who already showed talent in drawing. As a busy barber, he had every opportunity to regale his captive audiences with accounts of his family life, and he is known to have told Thomas Stothard "My son, sir, is going to be a painter."[34] He displayed his son's drawings round the shop, and sold them for one to three shillings each, so it could not be long before news of the Covent Garden barber's clever boy who painted, and who might do very well, would reach the ear of people who were of a mind to help him. A busy barber's shop is the perfect information exchange.

Turner's earliest surviving exercise as an artist is in the copy of *Picturesque Views of the Antiquities of England and Wales* by Henry Boswell, now in Hounslow Libraries. He was encouraged to colour in the plates in this album by a friend of his uncle, a Brentford brewer, John Lees, who paid him twopence a time.[35] This is the boy's first known encounter with such an extended series of landscape views, and colouring seventy of them opened his eyes and imagination, and filled his pocket. They also encouraged him to look at the sky, a habit which, he recalled as an old man, continued to earn him good money:

> When I was a boy I used to lie for hours on my back watching the skies, and then go home and paint them; and there was a stall in Soho Bazaar where they sold drawing materials, and they used to *buy* my skies. They gave me 1s 6d for the small ones and 3s 6d for the larger ones. There's many a young lady who's got my sky to her drawing.[36]

His examination of the plates in *Picturesque Views* was soon followed by a long journey in which he was able to see new landscapes unfolding slowly in front of him. Sarah Trimmer had ten surviving children when Turner was in Brentford. Of her two youngest, John was Turner's age and Henry Scott three years their junior. But John Trimmer was a consumptive, and Henry and an older sister Elizabeth showed signs of the condition as children. To speed their convalescence, Sarah Trimmer took Elizabeth, John and Henry to attend doctors in Margate and to benefit from the sea air.[37] A handful of drawings of Margate town and surroundings by Turner survive from around 1786, and we should consider the possibility that the Trimmers encouraged Turner to travel to Margate with them. The traditional explanation for the existence of these drawings is that Turner's father sent his son to school in Margate, "moved by I know not what reason".[38] John Trimmer died of his consumption in 1791, but Elizabeth and Henry survived, the latter remaining Turner's lifelong friend and becoming, ultimately, one of his executors. Though it remains circumstantial, a Trimmer connection gives a base of reason, and a motive force, to the nature of Turner's formative months in Brentford and Margate.

After his Brentford and early Margate period there were other ways by which Turner's talent was fostered. Thornbury reported that the print-seller and engraver J. R. Smith of Long Acre employed him with another promising boy of his age, Thomas Girtin, to put watercolour washes onto prints. Ruskin, however, understood Turner's first drawing master to be the inebriate, wayward history painter Mauritius Lowe (1746–93), who lived in squalor with his family in Westminister, and who had been befriended by Dr Johnson. Lowe's chaotic life, in "a room all dirt and filth, brats squalling and wrangling, up two pairs of stairs, and a closet ... the repository of all the nastiness and stench and filth, and food, and drink, and – ..." led to his early death. Though a promising painter, Lowe was in no state to give Turner consistent drawing lessons.[39] What neither Lowe, nor Girtin nor other younger artists had was the special lucky London vantage point in which to show their work, William Turner's barber's shop. Here, collectors such as Humphrey Tomkison, F. J. Du Roveray, a stockbroker and picture dealer, and the influential physician Thomas Monro bought the boy's drawings and remembered his name.

Turner was well aware of his talent by the time he was twelve or thirteen, and was already becoming practised in the art of making money out of it. He learned how to look by observing the quotidian in Covent Garden market, the Long Acre carriage works, the colour grinders, the print shops and the life of the street. The River Thames, with its traffic and the opportunities this brought for Turner to study and handle rigging and experience boats and ships at work, was only 400 yards south of Maiden Lane. He began to learn all he knew about ships and the sea during his boyhood, and learned too about picture-making by copying engravings and the work of established artists including Edward Dayes, Michael Angelo Rooker and Paul Sandby.

Many of the drawings he made at this time show that Turner was rapidly becoming competent at perspective. Architecture was a recurring subject in his earliest surviving sketchbooks of 1787 and 1789, where there are studies of Radley Hall, Lambeth Palace and other buildings with the perspective lines ruled in. On one page there are notes reminding himself of the names of the architectural orders "Tuscan/Doric/Corinth".[40] These studies continued to the end of the 1780s, when Turner was fifteen years old, and living with his Uncle Joseph and his wife Mary who by 1789 had moved from Brentford to Sunningwell near Abingdon. This relationship, which evidently remained warm for more than thirty years, introduced Turner to the architecture of Oxford, a lifelong source of inspiration and subject matter for him.

The skill of his perspective exercises, and Turner's conscientious attitude to them, reflects the hard practical experience that he was beginning to receive in architects' offices. The first architect we know he worked with is Thomas Hardwick (1752–1829), the man commissioned in 1788 to repair Inigo Jones's church of St Paul, Covent Garden. Hardwick was the son of the Brentford mason builder of the same name. This independent link with the Trimmers of Brentford, and Hardwick's Covent Garden connection, adds yet more vigour to the integrated network of contacts and friendships for the astute and ambitious young Turner which the Covent Garden barber's shop catalysed and Brentford confirmed.

Thomas Hardwick the Younger was by the late 1780s a fully fledged architect with a silver medal in architecture from the Royal Academy and two years' experience studying in Rome and other continental cities. He had been a pupil of Sir William Chambers when the latter was working on the construction of Somerset House. The exact details of Turner's involvement with Hardwick are not known, though he did make a squared-up drawing of the church of St Mary the Virgin, Wanstead, Essex, which was completed to Hardwick's designs in 1790. Thornbury notes that Turner made a watercolour of the church for the architect which, with other early work, Hardwick kept.[41] Other architects who employed and taught Turner included James Wyatt (1746–1813) and Joseph Bonomi the Elder (1737–1808).[42]

Thomas Hardwick's son Philip (1792–1870), who became another of Turner's long-standing friends and an executor, followed his father into architecture. He told Thornbury:

> Mr [Thomas] Hardwick ... not desiring to enslave the boy for seven years ... went to Hand Court, and informed the barber ... that the boy was too clever and too imaginative to be tied down to a severe science. He recommended him to be sent as a student to the Royal Academy, for the purpose of qualifying himself for the profession of an artist.[43]

William Turner's barbering may not have provided enough money to pay for an apprenticeship, but there are two independent reports that suggest that he came into a bequest in the 1780s. Thomas Tomkison recalled in 1850 that:

> a gentleman died who had been long under Turner's razor, and left him a legacy of £100. The moment my father [Humphrey Tomkison]

heard of this he begged Turner to allow him to dispose of the £100 for the benefit of the boy by articling him to Malton, the distinguished architectural draughtsman of that day – this was done accordingly.[44]

According to Thornbury, quoting Henry Scott Trimmer's son Frederick, the bequest amounted to £200, "with which sum he placed out his son with an architectural draughtsman, who, seeing some of his productions subsequently, said, 'He is not indebted to me for this.'"[45]

The evidence of William Turner's relative prosperity as a barber makes the existence of the legacy more credible. Money follows energy; it always has. Visible hard work against heavy odds opens the way for constructive and surprising generosity. It also sets a very potent example for a child, and was probably the most valuable legacy that William Turner the elder left his son.

So the small world of architectural and perspective studies in London recognised young William Turner's talent and took him under its wing. Hardwick taught the subject, so did Thomas Malton the Younger (1748–1804) who held an evening class in Conduit Street from 1783 to 1789 as did the brothers Thomas and Paul Sandby. Thomas Sandby was Professor of Architecture at the Royal Academy during Turner's youth, and as a student of architecture the boy would have been expected to attend his course of six lectures on the rise of architecture, the classical orders and so on.[46] That Turner was an unusual pupil is evident from the story that he insisted on putting reflected light into the windows he drew onto an architect's study. The architect told him to paint the panes an unvarying grey, and the bars white. "But it will spoil my drawing ..." the boy riposted.[47] All of these teachers lived and worked within fifteen minutes' walk of Maiden Lane. In later life, Turner himself "used to say", according to Thornbury, when reference was made to a school where Sandby taught, "But my real master, you know, was Tom Malton of Long Acre."[48]

There is the clear inference in this emphasis on Malton that the Sandbys taught him too.

These advances did not happen one after another, but in parallel, with an increasing momentum as Turner's potential became recognised. Among the barber's other customers who took a particular interest in the boy's progress was the Rev. Robert Nixon (1759–1837), curate of Foot's Cray near Sidcup. Nixon was an amateur who exhibited watercolours at the Royal Academy from 1790. With young Turner's watercolours pinned up round the shop, and the boy himself working in the background, Nixon urged him to come to meet John Francis Rigaud RA, a painter of historical pictures and portraits. Rigaud was Visitor of the Academy Schools at the time, the equivalent of the Admissions Tutor.[49]

To be received as a student at the Royal Academy Schools at Somerset

House, a young artist had to enrol for a term as a probationer and satisfy the members of the Academy Council that he could draw satisfactorily from the plaster casts of antique sculpture kept in the Academy. Six drawings, one only by each of the six applicants including William Turner, were shown to the Academy Council by the Keeper, Agostino Carlini, on 11th December 1789. Sir Joshua Reynolds, the President, was in the chair, and around him were Sir William Chambers and the painters William Hodges, James Barry and John Opie.

This was the last intake of students which Reynolds approved before he resigned on 23rd February 1790. It was also the first step that took Turner towards his career as an Academician. For the rest of his life, the Academy was to be his work place, meeting place, market place and club; the place where he learnt his art and where he taught it; where he made friends, admirers and enemies; where he diverted, impressed and shocked his public; and which he filled, year in, year out, with canvases that would be increasingly incandescent with light. The Royal Academy was twenty-one years old to the day, and Turner fourteen. They began, now, to grow up together.

# TWO

# "...an eye for nature..."

## 1790–1798

At fifteen and sixteen, William Turner was a taut, mumchance lad who preferred drawing to people. He spoke little in adult company, and was self-conscious about his height: he grew to be about 5 feet 4 inches. What stands out in a sensitive self-portrait miniature painted in 1791 is the boy's enormous wide eyes, his fringe and luxuriant shoulder-length hair, well kept and elegantly curled by his father.

Turner had to be persuaded to paint the miniature. He said it was "no use taking such a little figure as mine, it will do my drawings an injury, people will say such a little fellow as this can never draw."[1] Such early professional concern for his reputation shows a self-awareness which echoes and re-echoes during Turner's life. It is yet more evidence of his determination to excel in drawing – by which here he meant watercolour – at a precociously early age. Having slipped into the Royal Academy on Reynolds's final intake of students, he just caught Sir Joshua's last days as an effective teacher and leader of artists. The President was rapidly losing his sight, and was as deaf as a post, but nevertheless he was revered as the personification of their studies by artists of Turner's generation, and blessed for his generosity and even-handedness. The attitude that he offered by example to students was "an implicit obedience to the *Rules of Art*, as established by the practice of the great masters".[2] Hard work and humility in front of great art of the past was a prerequisite, and as he preached, so he practised.

His stern but sensible attitude underpinned the studies of William Turner and his generation, whatever their ultimate ambitions might have been. Potential history painters, portraitists and landscape artists all went through the same course of instruction in drawing; no one was taught to paint. Turner's signature first appears in the incomplete registers of the Plaster Academy on 21st July 1790, though he had spent a probationary year there in 1789, drawing from the plaster casts and working towards his full admission as a student. Thereafter, until 10th October 1793, Turner signed in 137 times.[3] He was evidently a highly diligent and conscientious student who took to heart Reynolds's observation that

> a facility of drawing, like that of playing upon a musical instrument, cannot be acquired but by an infinite number of acts ... And be assured, that if this power is not acquired when you are young, there will be not time for it afterwards: at least the attempt will be attended with as much difficulty as those experience who learn to read and write after they have arrived at the age of maturity.[4]

Turner had been an enrolled student at the Royal Academy Schools for exactly a year when Reynolds delivered his fifteenth and final Discourse on 10th December 1790, urging his students above all to study the works of Michelangelo. Among his many gifts, Reynolds was a great, if often inaudible, teacher who subtly paced the ideas and advice he wished to offer. He expressed satisfaction in his final Discourse that he had not attempted to foster in students *"newly-hatched unfledged* opinions ... I have pursued a plain and *honest method*; I have taken up the art simply as I found it exemplified in the practice of the most approved painters." This solid warning to young artists against following whim, fashion and novelty was the artfully-laid prelude to what must be his central sentence to his audience, and perhaps the central idea of the Discourses. With the fifteen-year old William Turner sitting in front of him, Reynolds then said: "Eh? ..." The audience suddenly lost the thread of the Discourse. The speaker probably carried on oblivious for a sentence or two, but there had been a terrific crash, probably owing to a weakness in the building, and the floor of the lecture room began to move. Reynolds's audience was rapidly leaving, some shrieking that the building was going to collapse. No collapse took place, so gingerly at first, the members of the audience returned to their seats.[5] Reynolds dusted himself down, cleared his voice, and resumed:

> The great, I may say the sole, use of an academy is, to put, and for some time to keep, the students in that course, that too much indulgence may not be given to peculiarity, and that a young man may not be taught to believe that what is generally good for others is not good for him.

These sober words, underlined by the drama of the evening, were to underpin Turner's lifelong relationship with the Royal Academy, the place where he later recalled he had spent "the happiest perhaps of my days".[6]

The painter and illustrator Thomas Stothard (1755–1834), a man who had himself passed through the Royal Academy Schools in the late 1770s, recalled that as students both he and Turner had in their time taken advantage of Reynolds's invitation for them to work in his studio in Leicester Fields (now Square) copying paintings there.[7] Reynolds's own collection of Old Masters included Rubens's *Moonlit Landscape*, Poussin's *Landscape with Orion* and Rembrandt's *Susannah*. There were paintings and drawings by artists from the Venetian, Bolognese, Roman and Florentine schools, and Dutch and French paintings and drawings. These and Reynolds's own finished and unfinished portraits, plaster casts, and prints picked up on his travels, filled the walls and cupboards of his house. It was a rich conglomeration of rare and wonderful relics of a great life, and an enthralling place for any young artist to be at the threshold of his own.

Reynolds's career as a portrait painter was over by the time Turner was of an age to benefit from his studio presence. So if the boy did visit Reynolds's studio, the house in Leicester Fields will have been a dusty echoing shell which he could explore without the blind and deaf old man seeing or hearing him, and where he could run his eyes and hands at will over the machinery and rigging of the portrait painter's art. There was an exhibition gallery and an octagonal painting room, designed to Reynolds's specifications, lit from above by a single high window. In the centre was a raised throne set on castors so its position could be adjusted, and sitters posed with red or yellow cloth-covered screens beside them to throw reflected light back onto their faces.[8] All this tangible, evocative paraphernalia may have raised Turner's enthusiasm for portrait painting, but it will certainly have shown him the value to a professional artist of his own private gallery, his own art collection, and the importance of being self-sufficient and socially aware.

That Turner had had some kind of youthful association with Reynolds is suggested by the presence in Turner's studio of a small watercolour view of the Thames from Richmond Hill, *c.* 1790.[9] This was Reynolds's view, the scene from the back windows of his country house, The Wick, painted perhaps by the young Turner, or by a contemporary. The graceful bend of the river with extensive wooded landscape beyond was to become a leitmotif in Turner's art, and for twenty years or more a developing symbol for a host of poetic and visual allusions. As Reynolds's view, the one that the old man loved but could no longer see, it stands as a symbol of the young William Turner's reverence and affection for the Past President of the Royal Academy.

In April 1790, Turner's watercolour *Archbishop's Palace, Lambeth* was accepted for exhibition at the Royal Academy. That the work of a student, particularly a fifteen-year-old, should be selected was rare enough; but that the same picture should show the titular subject being part obscured by a shadowy foreground inn was risky. Clearly, however, Turner's observation of townscape had showed him how buildings overlap and butt up against one another, rather than standing in misleading isolation as they did in architects' presentation drawings. Turner's *Archbishop's Palace, Lambeth* is a naughty little picture, maddeningly well painted, and nothing to do with what he was being taught at the Academy. The light tonality and detailed attention to all the nuances of the buildings – the chimneys, the coping stones, the brickwork, the curiously observed porch on the right – all go to demonstrate, on the other hand, Turner's attentiveness to his architectural training, and to Sandby and Malton's teaching. There is no clue given in the Royal Academy catalogue for 1790 that exhibit no. 644 was painted by a juvenile, and by his reported remarks on his self-portrait evidently Turner preferred to keep the fact that he was short, plain and youthful to as limited a circle as possible.

Turner had personal connections with the Archbishop's Palace at Lambeth, and with St Mary's Church, whose tower pokes up above the middleground building in the watercolour. A good friend and neighbour, the musician John Danby of Henrietta Street, Covent Garden, had married Sarah Goose at St Mary's only two years earlier. We might also add that his own father, perhaps accompanied by his mother, had gone to the Palace in 1773 to apply for a licence to marry. The delicate anecdotal human narrative that the pair of lovers walking out together in the foreground gives to the picture is of a kind that would recur again and again in future watercolours; and if there are any further personal inferences to be drawn from the picture, they are of the kind that would have amused family and friends. It may be no coincidence, then, that Turner gave this early watercolour to John Narraway, a leather dresser and gluemaker of Bristol, who was an old friend of his father.

Turner's education as an artist was running on a number of fronts in the early 1790s. He followed the standard Academy tuition of drawing from casts of antique sculpture, in preparation for the Life Class, which he entered on 25th June 1792. In addition, he made imaginative illustrations to literature, continued to copy prints and drawings of landscape by his elders, and drew in the manner of Gainsborough, Richard Wilson and Dutch seventeenth-century landscape painters. His knowledge of Gainsborough was particularly striking, and may be connected to his suggested access to Mrs Trimmer's collection in Brentford. He learnt how to make engravings, showed great diligence in improving his technique of drawing architecture, and listened to the advice of his elders. Through the evidence of two self-portraits made at the beginning and end of the decade, Turner had more than a passing interest in becoming competent in portraiture, and must have taken lessons in it. All this was available to every other ambitious artist of his generation; but what stands out in Turner's case is the breadth of his interest, and his dogged refusal to specialise. At all times he kept a weather eye open for opportunities to make money out of his art.

Turner also had access to some of the most extraordinary impromptu performances of classical literature of the day. The great scholar Richard Porson (1759–1808), who like Mauritius Lowe wasted his life in drink, enthralled audiences in the Cider Cellar in Maiden Lane in the 1790s with long recitations from Shakespeare, Homer and Pope.[10] Only a step away from his home, and free, these recitations may have been – we cannot say they were – an early oral source for the deep knowledge of the classical world that Turner gathered throughout his life, and for his enthusiasm for it.

In September 1791 Turner travelled from London to Bristol for his first recorded visit to the city. He stayed with the Narraway family in Broadmead, a wide, straight street running due east from the north-east corner of Bristol city walls. Narraway is a deep-rooted north Devon name; many are listed in births, marriages and deaths in Barnstaple in this period.[11] If the friendship between William Turner and John Narraway had been of long standing, as it must for Turner to have entrusted his only son to him, then it is likely that they had come to know one another in north Devon, and that they were both part of the Barnstaple and South Molton diaspora of the 1760s and 1770s.

Broadmead was one of the points of arrival for travellers from London. Climbing down from their coaches they found themselves in a place more like a long square than a street, surrounded by rambling one- and two-storey houses, some tiled, some thatched, most built about two hundred years earlier. By the 1790s, two centuries of weather and rain, hard knocks and shoddy repair had worn the buildings of Broadmead into a ramshackle decrepitude. There were seven inns in the 200-yard-long street and over forty other businesses of such variety that the arriving or departing traveller could find pretty well all he needed for his immediate aid and welfare on the coach-step.

William Matthews, printer and editor of the New Bristol Guides for travellers was enterprisingly located in Broadmead. But beside him and the butcher, baker and umbrella-maker, the emphasis was on ancillaries of the livestock trade – John Anthony the Saddler and Bristlecutter; Perrin & Bence the Curriers; Thomas Tucker the Hay Weigher; and John Narraway the Leather Dresser. With the making of glue, soap and leather goods, Broadmead had particular smells of its own, which mixed mischievously with the stink from the city's twenty odd glasshouses: 'From the continual smoke arising from them, [these kept Bristol] constantly darkened and in dirt, while the inhabitants are almost suffocated with noxious effluvia.'[12] On Tuesdays and Fridays a hay market was held in Broadmead, adding to the din and vitality.

Coming into all this urban activity, Turner will have felt quite at home.

We shall never know whether he was sent to the Narraways by his father or he went to stay with them of his own accord, but Turner's own inner drive and singleness of purpose makes it likely that the combination of bed and board with family friends, and some of the most dramatic scenery in Britain, made it an expedition that he could eagerly propose, and his father not readily refuse him. Though he did so reluctantly, it was for the Narraways that Turner drew his *Self-Portrait* miniature.

From the surviving sketches and finished watercolours it is clear that Turner was as energetic as he was opportunist. He listed "12 views of the River Avon" in a surviving sketchbook, and made some of them, as if he thought that he might be able to sell the idea to a publisher of engravings, or sell some to local gentry.[13] He scrabbled up and down the rocks in the clear air on either side of the Avon Gorge, half an hour's walk from Broadmead, to such an extent that the Narraways nicknamed him "The Prince of the Rocks".[14] His viewpoints take the extremes. They are either vertiginously high or dramatically low. He spirals down to the River Avon in a view east from the high tower of Cook's Folly, and then, looking the other way from the Folly, he transports the viewer through a screen of trees to the Welsh coast as far as the eye can see. Hot Wells is taken from below at an acute angle; and even the south porch of St Mary Redcliffe, in a watercolour worked up later at home, is shown as a clattering geometry of piers, porches and flying buttresses. The adventure of these youthful views is staggering, and his enjoyment in making them immediately infectious.

Nothing can adequately prepare a traveller for a first sight of the Avon Gorge, then or now. At any state of the tide in the summer or autumn it is a most exotic landscape, with lush forest, precipices and a narrow track clinging to the side of the winding river. It is comparable in dramatic effect to riverscapes in northern India, Africa or the virgin rain forests of South America. The clear air, curves and diagonals of the Avon Gorge had a cleansing effect on Turner. He could see for miles from the eyrie he discovered at Cook's Folly, but by getting him out of the sinks of Covent Garden and Bristol it can only have given him time to think, to examine his opportunities and to look out into the distance.

Despite being short in stature, Turner had a slim, lithe build, masses of energy and an enviable physical fitness. He could walk for miles without flinching, and did so.[15] Later in the 1790s he would walk the forty-mile round trip from Covent Garden to Bushey, Hertfordshire, and back "to make drawings at half-a-crown a piece, and the money for our supper when we got back home."[16] Turner's obituarist in the *Annual Register* of 1851 remarked that the artist could cover

20 to 25 miles a day, with his baggage at the end of a stick, sketching rapidly on his way all good pieces of composition, and marking

effects with a power that fixed them in his mind with unerring truth at the happiest moment.[17]

His physical energy was mixed with an extraordinary degree of inquisitiveness as to what things looked like and why, whether they were in the open country or part and parcel of urban squalor. The same *Annual Register* obituarist wrote also that Turner was

> always on the alert for any remarkable phenomenon of nature. He could not walk London streets without seeing effects of light and shade and composition, whether in the smoke issuing from a chimney-pot, or in the shadows upon the brick wall, and storing them in his memory for future use.

Turner was chronically optimistic and opportunist. Grubby, damp and noisy surroundings in Covent Garden and Bristol, full of the "litter" which fascinated him, were an opportunity for him to understand local colour, and provided a basis for the expression of his later experiences of industrial Warwickshire, Yorkshire, Shropshire and South Wales. Living with a mother and her alleged "ungovernable temper", he learnt how to merge silently into the background. As it is also for birdwatchers and spies, invisibility is a primary requirement for the painter of landscape and everyday life. Being the only son of a thrifty, financially cautious but entrepreneurial father, Turner quickly learned the value of money and how to make it, save it and spend it without drawing too much attention to himself.

Sitting at the top of Cook's Folly, aged sixteen, Turner was looking out at the most dramatic view he had yet experienced. Though Brentford may have been a kind of paradise, and the sea in the bay at Margate might have been whipped up into good fulsome storms while he was there, only the Avon Gorge in the September light gave him height, depth, distance and crystal clarity all at once. He had coloured miscellaneous engravings of picturesque views in an antiquarian volume while he was living at Brentford, but his 1791 Bristol drawings were his first expression of the experience from a high point of the motion of the engine of the air.

Early in his student career, Turner began to make friends among young artists of his own age. He had already met Thomas Girtin (1775–1802), who was developing into another ambitious and talented watercolour painter, and at the Academy his friends included Henry Aston Barker (1774–1856) and Robert Ker Porter (1775–1842). These boys were "great companions and confederates in boyish mischief" in the Schools.[18]

Henry Barker had just arrived in London with his father from Edinburgh. The pair came to the capital with a big idea: Robert Barker (1739–1806), who had coined the word "panorama" to describe the 180- or 360-degree view from the top of a hill or other vantage point, had exhibited in Edinburgh and Glasgow his *View from the Top of Calton Hill, Edinburgh*. This was received by *The Times* with "the most flattering applause and encouragement" when it was first shown in 1788. Father and son came to London with the hope of making a similar success in the south. Theirs was a simple plan, though expensive to realise. They took out a patent for the idea, which they described as "singular, instructive and pleasing", and urged the public to hurry to see it at 28 Haymarket "as from the confined scale this piece is on, but few can see it at one time, the lovers and encouragers of art, and the curious in general, should not therefore delay the inspection."[19]

The *Panorama* rivalled the *Eidophusikon*, a dramatic show of moving pictures, light and sound effects invented by the painter Philippe de Loutherbourg, that had enthralled London society in recent seasons. We can be sure that Turner, Girtin and Ker Porter saw both the *Panorama* and the *Eidophusikon*; indeed Porter's own appetite for such spectacular media was sufficiently whetted to prompt him to start building his own career in panoramas, which took him to Scandinavia and Russia. Girtin too went on to make a vast panoramic view of London, which he christened with another exotic portmanteau name, the *Eidometropolis*. The Barkers pressed on with their original initiative, creating a *Panorama* of London from a viewpoint on the southern bank of the river from the roof of Albion Mills at Blackfriars Bridge. This opened in 1792, and led to their taking premises of their own in Leicester Fields the following year where they showed many subsequent productions.

The Barkers' *Panoramas* had on average 10,000 square feet of canvas,[20] so as well as providing entertainment, they also gave painters an extra outlet for their labour. While the fashion was at its flood, panoramas generated a new audience for art, one which in turn fed the market for watercolours and oil paintings, and encouraged the subscription sales of landscape engravings. They were six parts art and four parts theatre, and for those who produced them, an extension of theatrical scene painting.

Stage painting in the established London theatres had always been a staple source of income for painters. Philippe de Loutherbourg (1740–1812), who came to England from Alsace and Paris in 1771, soon found work as a stage painter for David Garrick, and became the most influential and inventive stage designer of the day. Turner took some of the opportunities that the theatre offered, and from late March to early July 1791 painted scenery with a fellow student, William Dixon, at the Pantheon Opera House in Oxford Street. Reflecting the long hours of work against the clock, Turner earned about four guineas a week with extras for overtime for seven weeks' work, a generous enough sum for a sixteen-year-old boy.[21] The special taste that panoramas and stage painting encouraged in Turner was the early experience of visual drama on a very large scale, and of the long horizontal format that came to be characteristic of him in his mature years.

Turner's professional connection with the Pantheon makes his watercolour *The Pantheon the Morning after the Fire* all the more poignant and personal. Early on 14th January 1792 a fire started behind the stage. The resident caretaker smelled smoke, but before he could reach the fire it had taken hold. The building burned "with great fury" until about the following noon:

> Before any engines were brought to the spot, the fire had got to such a height, that all attempts to save the building were in vain. The flames, owing to the scenery, oil, paint, and other combustible matter in the house, were tremendous, and so quick in progress, that not a single article could be saved.[22]

Turner was on the spot the next day. He made pencil sketches of the interior and exterior which he worked up into a pair of watercolours which are unified by their common low viewpoints, but are otherwise dissimilar in mood. Turner sold the interior view to his early teacher of architecture and perspective, Thomas Hardwick, who was a professional rival of the Pantheon's architect, James Wyatt. It shows precarious towers of tottering brickwork with two men picking over the rubble of Wyatt's great creation, as if they were contemplating the decline and fall of the Roman Empire among the ruins of the Forum. Shafts of sunlight stream in through the gaping windows on the remains of this Roman pastiche.

Turner's exterior view is by contrast jaunty and matter-of-fact. The drama of the fire is told directly by the gestures and attitudes of the bystanders. One fire-fighter tries to turn off a standpipe; another chucks away a bucket of water; a third with a warning bell on a stick over his shoulder oversees the mopping up amid coils of flaccid hose pipes. Then there are tired firemen walking slowly out of the ruins of the building; an officer of the militia describing the events to a couple of curious passers-by; and a group of gloomy tradespeople chewing the fat on the right. It is a freezing cold morning. The firemen's water dripping off the building has formed icicles on the cornices, while a small boy blows on his fingers to keep his hands warm.

The differences between the two *Pantheon* drawings, the obverse and reverse of the same subject, demonstrate Turner's extreme versatility, and his acute sense of propriety of subject. With these, as with *Archbishop's Palace, Lambeth*, he took the initiative to rewrite the rules of urban topography, moving eighteenth-century anecdote into sober nineteenth-century narrative. Turner showed his watercolour *The Pantheon the Morning after the Fire* at the Royal Academy exhibition in May 1792. At that time the scandal of the fire was still topical, as it was probably no accident.[23] The picture never sold.

Turner's other exhibit at the Royal Academy of 1792 was a watercolour view of Malmesbury Abbey,[24] worked up from sketches made on his 1791 expedition.[25] This is painted in a much more orthodox picturesque manner, with trees growing up in the ruins of the abbey, a shaft of light coming though an archway, and a pig or two kept in thatched sties in the abandoned aisles. As a pair, the two watercolours are head to head in their approach – the modern matter-of-fact of the Pantheon fire contrasted with what had already become, in the short history of watercolour in Britain, the "traditional" manner of Paul Sandby, Edward Dayes or Michael Angelo Rooker. This was a calculated way for Turner to show potential patrons the wide range of his talents.

Over the next two or three years, Turner continued to exhibit water-colours at the Academy. Once the exhibition had opened in late April he set off on his travels. This pattern – painting in the winter and travel in the summer – would continue for most of his life. In May and early June 1792 he returned to his base with the Narraways in Bristol, and pressed on across the Severn estuary to Chepstow and into South Wales, towards the view he had seen from his perch on Cook's Folly the previous year. He went up the Wye Valley, past Tintern Abbey, and on via Llanthony Abbey north-west to Builth Wells and Rhayader.

His goal was the falls of the River Mynach at the foot of Plynlimmon. Turner was now, with his pony and sketchbooks, in the heart of the Cambrian Mountains, further from home than he had ever been. Aberystwyth and Cardigan Bay were just over the hill. His sketchbook records interest in his work from Mr Clithero of New Ormond Street and Mr Clutterbuck, who was to pay 2½ guineas for a view of Llanthony Abbey, and Mr Brydges who perhaps commissioned a view of Skyrrid Mawr near Abergavenny.[26]

The purpose of this journey, and others in the early 1790s, was to experience, practise, look, sketch, remember – and earn. Turner was interested in everything, the wide landscape itself, the natural and man-made features within it, the lives and work of the people he came across, and the towns and villages they had built up around them. On his journeys in the early 1790s Turner also went to Oxford and Windsor, to Guildford, to Hereford, Worcester and the Midlands, and to Canterbury, Rochester and Dover. He always made careful preparations, and planned his routes, distances to be covered, places to stay and presumably the coach services well in advance. When he was in Herefordshire in 1793 he drew a map of the country around Great Malvern with notes of the miles to be covered from "Mr Arrowsmith's house". Before he left for Derbyshire on his 1794 journey, somebody wrote out five pages of directions, distances and lists of sights to be seen in the sketchbook he took with him.[27] Another friend did the same job for him the following year before his second journey to South Wales.[28] Such careful preliminaries not only reflect the importance of these journeys for Turner – their expense in terms of time and money, and the essential repayment with good saleable work – but they reflect also his methodical and prudent cast of mind, Turner's own sensible stewardship of his great talents, and his way of making his friends work for him.

He made a particular bee-line for architectural subjects, whether ruinous or in active use, for they offered twin challenges. One was the physical challenge to reach and see for himself buildings that he had been told about or knew from engravings; and the other was to put to use the practical skills that he had been taught by architectural draughtsmen. Only out in the field – on his own – could he explore the actuality of scale, mass, and of light on masonry. A note on the back of a small unfinished study of a tree and a tower, shows Turner looking carefully at tonality: "In the shadow the Stones the same. Some Umber and S[ap] Green – The Broken part umber and Bister, the distant part a Blue Green Sap and B[ister]."[29]

He worked fast. Rather than sit in front of a ruin or a church for hours on end drawing every detail, he would take advantage of the fact that most architecture is symmetrical, and that one side of a gothic window generally echoes the other. With practical common sense, he would draw only half, or part of the building, making written or drawn notes of irregular detail, and then move on to the next subject or point of view. "The same only all Plain" is written on one drawing.[30] Although he had firm control of his hand, his architectural training encouraged him to take short cuts where he could, and use a ruler to make sure he had got a tower dead straight.[31] From raw material gathered in the field, Turner made his finished watercolours at home.

In the later eighteenth century, Wales, the Lake District and Scotland had become favourite destinations for tourists. Turnpikes and new regular coach services were extending inland travel to far-flung places. A diary of one traveller's journey into Wales from London in July and August 1792 throws light on the relative ease of travel in the period. So close is it indeed to the spirit of Turner's own wide-eyed intelligence, and to what is known of his travels at this time, that it was first published as Turner's own diary.[32] The unknown traveller had watercolour and landscape poetry in mind as he climbed on his horse up a hill overlooking the Conway Valley:

... nothing very interesting from the Road ... till we reach the summit which overlooks the Vale of Conway here the swelling hills

Turner prepares for a journey. Some notes written out for him in the 1795 "South Wales" sketchbook. TB XXVI. Turner Bequest, Tate Gallery, London.

folding as it were over each other & beautifully gradating till they blend softly into the Horizon all blue & tender grey tints irradiated in the summit in the distances by the setting sun wch bears the Hills in the foreground that overhang the River Conway quite in Shadow.

A later passage speaks breathlessly of clouds seen from the summit of Cader Idris:

> tinged with the most beautiful pearly tints – the whiter parts clear beyond expression – the way down much more craggy – & rugged – & dangerous than going up – returned after dark perfectly fatigued & satisfied with the grandest scenery I ever beheld.

Here is a lay traveller's spontaneous and unsolicited expression of his joy at picturesque travel, the journey being undertaken in order to experience the view. It is he, and men and women like him, who created the graded market for paintings and engravings, that artists such as Turner were determined to make money from. For his part, Turner was hardy enough to disregard the real discomforts of travel, the long hours on bumpy roads, the cramped carriages, the bad inns. Though he was promoted to the Life Class of the Academy in June 1792, he was off on his travels again soon enough, certainly to Surrey and possibly on to Kent later in the summer and again in the autumn. One impetus for this perpetual motion was his decision to enter an open competition that year for a Premium from the Society of Arts, the organisation that had encouraged Sarah Trimmer's youthful efforts forty years earlier. He applied under Class 190, for the best drawing of landscape by persons under twenty-one, and submitted a view of Lodge Farm, near Hambleton, Surrey.

Turner heard he had done well in the competition late the following March when he and four others of his age were invited by the Committee to present themselves at the Society's rooms in the Adelphi at 11 a.m. on Wednesday 17th April 1793 to prove their abilities by making a drawing under "the inspection of the committee".[33] This they did, successfully, and Turner won not money, but a small silver medal in the shape of an artist's palette with a gold rim. This medal, inscribed with his name and date, was the Society's highly prestigious and sought after Greater Silver Palette.[34]

The Society for the Encouragement of Arts, Manufactures and Commerce had been founded by William Shipley in 1754 to act as a forum for the stimulation of natural talent in Britain and the Colonies. It spread its net exceedingly wide, offering Premiums, or medals and cash awards, for innovation and successful experiment in the fields of mechanical invention, discoveries in chemistry and mineralogy, geographical exploration, improvements in husbandry, and excellence in what it called "The Polite Arts". This was the category that Turner entered.[35]

The guiding ideal behind the Premiums was to enlarge Britain's productive capacity, to find practical solutions to problems which slowed down industrial growth, so that Britain would have the edge over France in world and commercial influence. The Premiums for the Polite Arts as awarded in 1793 were all, except one, for drawing and engraving, under-lining the Society's intention to promote practical skill which might also be diverted to map-making, surveying or mechanical drawing for the nation's commercial or military advantage. Turner was proud of his Greater Silver Palette. He kept it in its velvet mount safely in a drawer where it turned up after his death.[36] It was his first and last official award of any kind, and the first token of official recognition of his talents.

By his constant travelling Turner seemed to be painfully aware of the brevity of life, the need to be ahead of the game, and the importance of being recognised. When he sat still he was either looking out over landscape, sitting at his drawing board in the Academy Life Class, or in his room in Maiden Lane. He remembered, and marked well, James Barry's command to students at his lecture "On Colouring", given in February 1793: "Go home from the Academy, light your lamps, and exercise yourselves in the creative power of your art, with Homer, with Livy and all the great characters, ancient and modern, for your compa-nions and counsellors."[37]

On Friday evenings in the winter, Turner worked by lamplight with Thomas Girtin and one or two others copying drawings, watercolours and engravings in the collection of the distinguished and well-connected physician Dr Thomas Monro (1759–1833). Monro, who lived in Bedford Square and, from 1794, at 8 Adelphi Terrace, had a passion for old master paintings, for prints and particularly for watercolour which he collected by the armful. Dozens by Hearne, Rooker, Dayes, Cozens and many other painters of greater or lesser talent hung in his house, and he had yet dozens more in folios. He was himself an amateur sketcher, as was his friend and neighbour John Henderson, and together the pair added to their collections the work of their young protégés which they bought at the rate of 2s 6d or 3s 6d an evening and a bowl of oysters.[38] It is not clear when this arrangement began, but Monro may have been one of the purchasers from Turner's father's shop, and he and Turner had known each other at least as early as 1793 when Turner made a watercolour of Monken Hadley, Hertfordshire, in which a Monro property appears.

The artist and diarist Joseph Farington RA (1747–1821) recorded that he had been told that "Dr Monro's house is like an Academy in an evening. He has young ones employed in tracing outlines made by his friends etc. Henderson, Hearne etc lend him their outlines for this purpose."[39] Though other artists also worked in Monro's rooms, Turner and Girtin, it seems, were the two regular attenders. This went on for about three years, from six until ten on Fridays. It was an efficient little production line. According to what Turner and Girtin told Farington a few years later, in a suspi-ciously simplistic account of a double-act, "Girtin drew in outlines and Turner washed in the effects."[40]

Turner did not need Monro's instruction, but he did need the companionship and the gossip that the evenings brought. And he knew which side his bread was buttered: 2s 6d or 3s 6d an evening and a bowl of oysters was a very good return for doing what you enjoy, and would probably be doing at home anyway. Turner was learning how to please influential men, and he yet knew few who were as wealthy or as well-connected as Monro and Henderson. Being polite to Monro would lead to further introductions, as surely Turner anticipated. And of course it was not an "Academy", far from it – somebody talking to Farington had used that word as an idle simile, "... it's *like* an Academy"; and Farington had studiously passed it on as fact.

Turner's first notice in the press came at his fifth Royal Academy showing in 1794. The *St James's Chronicle* spoke of the "great precision in the outlines" of his watercolours, which are "well chosen and well coloured".[41] This year there was no setting out of his stall to show the range of his abilities in watercolour, as there seems to have been in 1792. These watercolours, one waterfall and four crumbly ecclesiastical architectural subjects, were skilful and calculated exercises in the manner of Edward Dayes, "great precision in the outlines," as the critic said, being just about right. A week or so later the *Morning Post* commented that three of Turner's drawings:

> are amongst the best in the present exhibition; they are the productions of a very young artist, and give strong indications of first-rate ability; the character of Gothic architecture is most happily preserved, and its profusion of minute parts massed with judgement and tinctured with truth and fidelity. This young artist should beware of contemporary imitations. The present effort evinces an eye for nature, which should scorn to look to any other source.[42]

This is a thoughtful and progressive piece of criticism. Noticing Turner's "strong indications of first-rate ability", the writer goes on to warn him against following other artists too closely, and to use his own eyes and brain when looking at nature.

If Turner had had such a thing as an order book, it would have been full of commissions in the mid and late 1790s. For him, entrepreneurship was innate. Two sketchbooks in use when he went to South Wales and the Isle of Wight in 1795 each have a list inside the cover headed "Order'd Drawings" – Viscount Malden of Hampton Court near Leominster, Herefordshire, five views; Sir Richard Colt Hoare of Stourhead, four; John Landseer, eleven, to be engraved; and others for Messrs Lambert, Mathews, Laurie, Mitchells and Kershaw. He had been doing so well that as a juvenile he had to have Trustees to administer his savings. It was also at this time that he may have expanded his working space by moving into rooms adjoining 26 Maiden Lane, in the rear area known as Hand Court. These two buildings were integral, not separate addresses, but Turner may also have gained his own staircase.

In the mid-1790s something happened to Turner's watercolour painting. The *Morning Post*'s criticism of 1794 seems, on the face of it, to have been one of the factors that moved him on from making clever and elaborate exhibition watercolours in the manner of his elders, into paintings of air and light. A fundamental change took place between *The Interior of the Ruins of Tintern Abbey* (exh. 1794),[43] and two years later *St Erasmus and Bishop Islip's Chapels, Westminster Abbey* (exh. 1796).[44] The former is brilliant, precise, but empty; the latter is so filled with veil upon veil of light and air and the sober march of shadows that it quite hums with pleasure. In the foreground Turner painted a tombstone inscribed WILLIAM TURNER NATUS 1775, a quiet but clear way of drawing attention to his new adulthood at the exhibition which opened on the very day of his twenty-first birthday.

This new manner blossomed through Turner's increasingly muscular technique. The intensity of *Transept of Ewenny Priory, Glamorganshire* (exh. 1797)[45] is heightened by the artist scratching at the surface in places with his fingernail to allow the rough white of the paper to show through. This self-licensed freedom of the pigment was pushed to new extremes in the following three years, when Turner went to the north of England (1797) and into north Wales (1798) once again, and leapt off into the new century. The act of finishing a painting in the orthodox manner had become irrelevant; instead Turner allows the paint to float across the white paper, as a cloudscape will float across a landscape. The burst of sunlight from *Llanberis* (c. 1799–1800)[46] shows Turner's true eye for nature, scorning to look at any other source, as the *Morning Post* had suggested.

But there was another medium for Turner now – oil. He first exhibited an oil painting, *Fishermen at Sea*, at the Royal Academy in 1796. He had been experimenting with the medium for three or four years before he was able to bring it to an exhibitable standard. One of the earliest attempts, c. 1793, *Watermill and Stream*,[47] reflects both his eagerness to consider the mainstream medium of his contemporaries, and to study the art of the distant or recent past. There were any number of ways he could see old master paintings. Reynolds's collection had been open to those students who wanted to see it; Mrs Trimmer had her Gainsboroughs; Dr Monro owned Old Masters, as did Turner's growing group of patrons of the 1790s, whose houses he visited on his travels. The London sale rooms and art dealers' shops were a further rich source. One important opportunity he had among many was the showing of the collection of the Duke of Orleans, which the art dealer Thomas Slade had bought and displayed in

London in the spring of 1793. This included Rembrandt's *The Mill* and *Rest on the Flight to Egypt*, and other Dutch and Flemish paintings.

There is an anecdotal report that gives some idea of the beginning of Turner's enthusiasm for oil. The antiquary and artist the Rev. James Douglas (1753–1819), who had been a chaplain to the Prince of Wales since 1787, saw Turner painting at the back of the Maiden Lane shop when he called to have his hair dressed.

[He] ingratiated himself into the young artist's favour, [and] was allowed an inspection of a number of his paintings and drawings on paper – for, I believe, he had never then painted on canvas. Mr Douglas was so struck by the talent exhibited by young Turner, that he took him immediately under his patronage, and shortly after his acquaintance with him invited him to his house at Rochester, where he encouraged him to exercise his talents [in oil on canvas] by painting from nature.[48]

James Douglas was just one of the highly curious people who had seen Turner's exhibits at the Royal Academy in the 1790s, and were itching to know more about him. The satirist and critic John Williams, who wrote under the name of Anthony Pasquin, said in the *Morning Post*, reviewing the 1797 Royal Academy exhibition:

We have no knowledge of Mr Turner, but through the medium of his works which assuredly reflect great credit upon his endeavours, the present picture [*Fishermen coming ashore at sunset, previous to a gale*; now lost] is an undeniable proof of the possession of genius and judgement.[49]

A writer in the *St James's Chronicle*, perhaps the same as remarked on Turner's conservatism three years earlier, mused in 1797 that "there is mind and taste in everything the man does – and yet he is not [a member] of the Royal Academy."[50]

Another interested layman was Thomas Green, a Suffolk barrister who had enough money to avoid practising the law and to enjoy books and exhibitions instead.[51] He first came across Turner in the 1797 exhibition, and told his diary: "Particularly struck with a sea view by Turner ... I am entirely unacquainted with the artist; but if he proceeds as he has begun, he cannot fail to become the first in his department." Two years later, Green was still impressed, but probably little the wiser about the character of the man:

... again struck and delighted with Turner's landscapes ... he has given a depth and force of tone [to *Caernarvon Castle*, watercolour] which I had never before conceived attainable with such untoward implements. – Turner's views are not mere ordinary transcripts of nature: he always throws some peculiar and striking *character* into the scene he represents.[52]

Interestingly, these are two of the very few references to *painting* in the published extracts from Green's diary, and it is a clear measure of the particular impact that Turner had made upon him.

By the summer of 1796 Turner seems to have made himself ill, and he did not travel far, spending some weeks painting in Brighton and Margate. Then the next summer, 1797, he was off again, this time to the north of England to carry out commissions for Lord Yarborough at Brocklesby Park, Lincolnshire, and to Leeds for the Hon. Edward Lascelles, of Harewood, who gave Turner his first commissioned landscape subject in oils, a pair of views of Plompton Rocks. Then he went on down to Surrey to make some paintings for Thomas Monro's friend the collector William Locke of Norbury Park just north of Dorking. At some point in this period Turner had a painful fall that kept him more or less restricted to Covent Garden for a time. In a letter to his friend Rev. Robert Nixon he wrote: "I have unfortunately fell again[st] the Pavement on my knee, so hurt that I cannot walk to Lewisham for fear of inflamm."[53]

One could call all this travelling madness, an obsession, and so perhaps it was. No artist compares with Turner for mileage covered in England over this period. A walk to Lewisham seems to have been routine. But it is clear too that something else drove him, a supreme love of doing what he did, an unswerving and justified confidence in his abilities, and the knowledge that if he carried on in this way he would never be poor.

England in the 1790s was run on patronage. Everybody in the aristocracy, "the great, who live profusely" as Daniel Defoe had described them, knew everybody else, were related, or at least knew where and how they lived and what their prospects were. One rung down, "the rich, who live plentifully", the network was just as tight. These two categories embraced some of the most extraordinary and inventive men of the age. They included the 3rd Duke of Bridgewater whose enterprise and vision created mines and canal systems; the Earl of Egremont whose philanthropy led to improvements in the efficiency of agriculture; Sir Richard Colt Hoare the banker; Walter Fawkes the Yorkshire farmer, agricultural innovator and reforming politician; and William Beckford the fabulously wealthy writer, traveller, builder and fantasist. All these men were at one time or another in the 1790s or early 1800s direct patrons of Turner.

And one patron led to another – Thomas Monro, very small fry by comparison, introduced Turner to William Locke, through whom he built a contact with Locke's intimate friend John Julius Angerstein, underwriter, founder of state lotteries and art collector. The London networks had threads spreading into the shires, into and among the great houses owned by these powerful men. Through Richard Colt Hoare, Turner came to know William Beckford and Sir John Fleming Leicester, a highly influential figure in the north-west, and owner of Tabley Hall, Cheshire. In Yorkshire and the north-east the invisible network of friendships and political and marriage alliances brought together Walter Fawkes, Edward Lascelles, Lord Darlington, Lord Yarborough, Spencer Stanhope and Thomas Lister Parker. Turner was born without connections into a barber's shop where influential men were captive under the razor. They held no fears for him; he had seen them with their wigs off. The networks that his father developed gave Turner the example and all the opportunities he needed to foster his talent and play the field. As a direct result of his success at selling himself, Turner could confide to Joseph Farington in October 1798 that "he had more commissions at present than he could execute and got more money than he expended."[54]

Some of the money he earned he spent on good clothes. Those he wears in the *Self-Portrait* of around 1798 show that he bought with an eye to quality, and the respect that fashionable dress would bring him. There is a practically endless list in the "Dolbadern" sketchbook of 1799, of his projected needs for the summer trips of that year to Wales, Somerset and Lancashire:

> 3 coats; 4 waistcoats – white; 5 breeches; 4 underwaistcoats; 6 cotton stockings; 2 silk stockings – black; 8 cravats; 3 pocket handkerchiefs; 3 boots; 3 shoes; 4 coloured waistcoats; 6 shirts; 2 welch stockings; 1 white silk stockings; 1 silk handkerchief; 1 great-coat; 1 overalls; 1 black waistcoat.[55]

Though too reserved in nature ever to be a fully blown dandy, Turner knew that handsome clothes were an effective passport to patronage. The sheer quantity of stuff he packed could also suggest a need for security.

As further opportunities to cultivate potential patrons, please his friends and to make money, Turner gave drawing lessons. This was standard practice in the period; an ability to sketch was as essential a talent then as the ability to take snaps with a camera has been in the late twentieth century. He charged 5 shillings a lesson, according to Farington,[56] and seems to have continued to teach for ten or more years from the mid-1790s. The letter to Robert Nixon, quoted above, is written on the back of an ink and wash drawing by Nixon of an archway which Turner has annotated and returned: "Get all the shadows in Ink – except *the sky Blue and Ink*. The Arch wash with Bistre after this Shadow of Ink."

Although he kept on friendly terms with influential Academicians such as Joseph Farington, John Hoppner and Thomas Lawrence, none of them could seriously be called his friends. His real friends in the 1790s seem to have been consistently on the fringes of the world of painting, polite amateurs or musicians, people with comfortable houses, happy families, friendly, undemanding, motherly men and women able and willing to accept Turner as they found him.

Central among these people were William Wells and his family of Knockholt, near Sevenoaks, and Robert Nixon of Foot's Cray who had been one of Turner's trustees. Turner went on painting expeditions with both Wells and Nixon, and though stage coaches were readily available, Turner would regularly walk down to see them and think little of it. William Wells (1762–1836) was an occasional exhibitor at the Royal Academy and, in 1804, became one of the founders of the Society of Painters in Watercolour. He and his family had a town house in Mount Street, where Turner retreated in the late 1790s "as a haven of rest from many domestic trials too sacred to touch upon".[57] This sideways remark was written years later by Wells's daughter Clara, and may refer to the angry presence of Turner's mother at home. The Wellses clearly felt an affectionate concern for Turner; Clara Wells added that "Turner loved my father with a son's affection; to me he was an elder brother."

[Turner] usually spent three or four evenings in every week at our fireside, and though very much more than half a century has elapsed, I can still vividly recall to mind my dear father and Turner sketching or drawing by the light of an Argand lamp, whilst my mother was plying her needle, and I, then a young girl, used to read aloud some useful or entertaining work.[58]

It is quite clear that where Turner was happy, relaxed and not feeling threatened by circumstances, he would open up and become as much fun as a merry uncle. Indeed when he stayed with the Wellses at Knockholt, he was just that. On one occasion he encouraged the children to dabble their fingers into cakes of red, blue and yellow and pad them about on the foreground of an uncompleted watercolour. After a while Turner cried out "Stop!" and using the resulting mess as a basis, turned it into a landscape with imaginary forms in the foreground.[59] Clara remembered him as a "light-hearted, merry creature" who romped about noisily with her younger sisters: "When I went into the sitting-room, he was seated on the ground, and the children were winding his ridiculous long cravat round his neck; he said, 'See here, Clara, what these children are about.' "[60]

Wells's and Nixon's sketching parties included other Academicians and mutual London friends on the fringes of the intelligensia. Robert Nixon regularly attended meetings at the Royal Society, the neighbour of the

Royal Academy in Somerset House, where lectures on scientific topics and current discoveries were given. The Royal Academy, Royal Society and their third neighbour in Somerset House, the Society of Antiquaries, were the most influential information exchanges in London, many steps up from the barber's shop.

Other close friends of the 1790s outside the world of painting were the musician John Danby (1757–98), his wife Sarah and their three young daughters who lived in Henrietta Street until they moved north to 26 Upper John Street around 1797. Danby was a highly prolific and popular composer of light music, with a strong bass voice which earned him 5-shilling engagements in the chorus at Drury Lane. His glees and catches were memorable and hummable, and widely known through performances at Vauxhall and Ranelagh. Three collections of his songs were published during his lifetime. Danby was a Roman Catholic, and also wrote religious music, mainly for performance in the chapel of the Spanish Embassy, Manchester Square, where he was organist. He was nearly twenty years older than Turner, of some standing in the London musical world, being a member of the Royal Society of Musicians and a Catch Club prizewinner.[61]

There is ample evidence in Turner's sketchbooks for his love of music and his affinity for it from the 1790s, and John Danby may have been a catalyst for this. Studies of pipers and dancers, transcriptions of songs, even snatches of musical notation appear from time to time. Songs which he picked up at the theatre stuck in the back of his mind, and he wrote out the words of one, "The Friar" from the pantomime *Merry Sherwood*, in the back of a sketchbook in 1802.[62] He owned, and may have played, a flute which was found in his house at his death.[63] In 1798 Danby became seriously ill, and eventually lost the use of his limbs. The night that a benefit concert was given for him in May 1798, Danby died at home in Upper John Street, leaving Sarah pregnant and with three young daughters.[64] By the time of John's death, Turner had been closely drawn in to the Danby family circle. Perhaps eighteen months or two years after Sarah had given birth to John's posthumous child, Turner made Sarah pregnant again.[65]

Developing connections and worldly success began inevitably to draw down criticisms and rivalries upon Turner. A dyspeptic account of one weekend at Foot's Cray in spring 1798 is given by Stephen Rigaud (1777–1861), the son of J. F. Rigaud RA, and himself an aspiring, though much less successful, painter two years younger than Turner. The first criticism that Rigaud makes is that Turner refused to accompany the sketching party to church on Sunday, but instead spent the time painting water-colours indoors; the second that he refused to contribute to the cost of the wine for the picnic on the following day's sketching trip – but his reported words "No, I can't stand that" could just as clearly mean that Turner did not like to drink during the day when he was working, or that he simply did not like wine. Farington reported much later that Turner did not like French or Swiss wines, "his constitution being bilious".[66]

Another piece of backchat came from the portrait painter John Hoppner RA (?1758–1810), who told Farington in January 1798 that he had seen two oil paintings in Turner's studio, one a rainbow landscape, the other a waterfall, and that they appeared to be by "a timid man, afraid to venture".[67] But when he saw these paintings, which Turner was preparing for the Academy, they would have been unfinished, with none of their surface detail. Between Hoppner's first view of them and the opening of the Academy exhibition in late April, these two paintings were transformed by further work. *Buttermere* has a tight and sophisticated construction, the rainbow's semicircle tipping stylishly over to the left, beginning its course in front of turbulent clouds and mountains, but ending it captured as a reflection in the lake. Sunlight flows under the rainbow with a liquefaction that Rubens, but none other, might have achieved. *Morning among the Coniston Fells* may be more conventionally influenced by Salvator Rosa or Gaspard Poussin, but timid it is not. The wind blows fiercely across the upper levels; the shepherds have difficulty in controlling their sheep; and the mountainside is an accomplished jumble of rock, tangled trees and water.

When these paintings were exhibited, a critic in the *Oracle* went so far as to say that: "W. Turner has a variety of Picture worthy of the attention of the *Cognoscenti*. He takes a distinguished lead in the present Exhibition, and rises far superior to our expectation on forming an opinion of his previous works."[68]

Gradual and irreversible changes were now beginning to take place in Turner's life. Though he was twenty-three, a year below the age limit, he put his name down for election as Associate of the Royal Academy. This was his challenge to the Academy; to recognise formally the new talent that had erupted at its gates. He entered his name for the vote, and in early June 1798 left for Bristol and Wales. Once again he stayed with the Narraways, this time for two weeks, and from the account left by Ann Dart, John Narraway's niece, he brooded noticeably during the fortnight. Was he debating with himself his chances for election as an ARA; was he considering his position with Sarah Danby? He borrowed a pony from his uncle – which he never returned or paid for – and went into Wales. His destination was Snowdon and the surrounding area, where Richard Wilson had been born, and the landscape that provided the mainspring for Wilson's art. Turner recalled years later that he had been searching for Wilson's birthplace, at Penegoes, near Machynlleth, and so perhaps he had.[69] The watercolour studies painted in front of the landscape of Wilson reflect the newly coursing energy in his life, a lately acknowledged impatience with the neat and ordered picturesque view in favour of a direct emotional response from within the subject itself.

He was in Wales "alone and on horseback ... Much rain but better effects" as Farington, probably quoting Turner himself, expressed it,[70] for seven weeks. On his return, Farington assured Turner of his support for an Associateship, having earlier lobbied Thomas Lawrence RA and William Hamilton RA to vote for him. Turner then left London again, now to go north to Lincolnshire to paint the mausoleum that James Wyatt had designed in Lord Yarborough's grounds. On his return, he lobbied further support, and so obsessed was he with the idea of becoming an Associate, he was not averse to offering inducements:

> [Turner] requested me to fix upon any subject which I preferred in his books, and begged to make a drawing or picture of it for me. I told him I had not the least claim to such a present from Him, but on his pressing it I said I would take another opportunity of looking over his books and avail myself of his offer. – Hoppner, He said, had chosen a subject at Durham.[71]

Farington continued to assure Turner that he would be safely elected, and urged him not to consider (as Turner was) leaving Hand Court and Maiden Lane until he had got still more money behind him, despite the fact that his present rooms were small, dark and unsuitable for a painter.[72] But there were bitter factions at the Academy at this time, and Farington got his forecast wrong. Turner lost by four votes in the second ballot, to Martin Archer Shee and Charles Rossi. Whatever disappointment he might have felt he kept at least from Farington, saying merely that "he had no title to so much favour."[73]

It was at about this time, when he was considering the various pressures upon him, his ambitions and commitments, that Turner examined himself closely and painted the self-portrait of his young maturity. Here, Joseph Mallord William Turner gazes right out at the world. He has cut off his locks of childhood, and his eyes are boldly emphasised by strong, even exaggerated shadow from his brow. He is dressed soberly, but there is amplitude and quality in the cloth. Disappointment at the Academy elections would only be temporary. He is deeply confident, looking firmly out onto the world which he would come to articulate. "*This*," he seems to say, "is who I am. This is what I can do. But this is not what the world shall see of me."[74]

# THREE

# "Turner, a young artist..."

## 1798–1802

Academicians did not talk much about students as a rule, except to complain. They complained in 1796 about loitering around the Academy;[1] and two years later the Council voted to exclude students from all the Academy apartments, except the Plaster and Life rooms, on account of "some irregularities".[2] There was a general feeling of unease, even rowdiness, where young men with very little talent or hope of advancement in the arts packed the teaching rooms, causing a state of affairs that was "little calculated to do honour to the institution".[3] As the example of Sir Joshua Reynolds began to fade into history, rot in the teaching rooms set in.

The war with France, the expense, the worry of it, the fear of invasion, had very quickly rebounded onto artists and their livelihoods. Acts of Parliament which suppressed individual freedom – Treasonable Practices and Seditious Meetings (1795) and the Combination Act (1799) – passed in the heat of the war with France, became law and removed liberties that Britons had taken for granted. Abraham Raimbach, then a young and hopeful artist engraver, recalled "the abject and almost expiring state to which the fine arts had been reduced."[4] Aware of the destitution that so often faced artists, the Prime Minister, Pitt the Younger, exempted them from the new income tax he had levied to pay for the war. Large paintings of history, literature and myth were just no longer selling. Even Farington, no history painter he, tells us that he had to react to this change in events and taste: "I have been employed three days on small canvases of select subjects, as I am induced to think pictures of a small size will be saleable, being convenient for many."[5]

Turner's success, apparently against the flow of the times, startled his elders. There is an unconcealed note of amazement in Farington's record when Turner boasted to him that he had "60 drawings now bespoke by different persons".[6] With the wind being taken out of the sails of the older generation, Turner pressed the advantage. The calculating side to his character emerges in an illuminating entry in Farington's diary. Here, Turner assessed his current situation aloud to Farington, and balanced his responsibilities to his parents against those to himself and his career prospects: "W. Turner called on me ... He talked to me about his present situation. He said that by continuing to reside at his Father's he benefitted him and his Mother: ..." but, on the other hand, "he thought he might derive advantages from placing himself in a more respectable situation [i.e., a better address than Maiden Lane]."[7]

Of Turner's contemporaries, one of the most active and certainly the most talented was Thomas Girtin. By the autumn of 1798 Girtin had travelled widely in Britain. He too was beginning to make influential friends among some of the same collectors as patronised Turner, and was exhibiting at the Royal Academy to great effect. The *True Briton* predicted in 1799 that "Mr Girtin will stand very high in professional reputation."

By early 1799 gossip was having it – as relayed by Hoppner to Farington – that Edward Lascelles was beginning to play one artist off against the other, "to set up Girtin against Turner" as candidates at the Academy. The roots of the matter were complex, and ranged from the personal to the political. On the one hand Girtin, who had begun to give Lascelles painting lessons, appears to have had more natural charm than Turner, and Lascelles simply liked him more. On the other hand, Turner may already have become friendly with Walter Fawkes, a gentleman collector on the edge of Academy social circles, who was widely known for his democratic sympathies. "Mr Fawkes holds republican principles," Farington reported, "the Lascelles family are quite aristocrats."[8] We shall learn more about Fawkes in later chapters, but the point to be made now is that Fawkes and Lascelles were neighbours in Yorkshire with a long history of family feuding, and also determined political rivals. Lascelles's brother Henry was Tory MP for York, while Fawkes was an active Whig, speaking publicly in the county, and, in 1796, offering himself as a parliamentary candidate for York against Henry Lascelles.

Turner had first visited Lascelles's Yorkshire house, Harewood, in the summer of 1797, shortly after Lascelles had bought his watercolour *St Erasmus and Bishop Islip's Chapels, Westminster Abbey*. It is likely that both he and Girtin were at Harewood together at this time, and sketched together in the park.[9] Turner did not return to Harewood – he may not have been invited back, although Lascelles continued to buy his work until 1808 – while Girtin proceeded to come and go, to travel with and teach Lascelles, and to enjoy his direct patronage and friendship.

Thomas Girtin, clubbable, amenable and charming, if inclined to enjoy the wild life of the taverns, was serious competition for Turner. So too was the young painter John James Masquerier (1778–1855). He had been born in Chelsea of French parents, but in 1789 the family returned to Paris, where, despite the early terrors of the French Revolution, the boy seemed somehow to find the opportunity to study drawing at a school near the Tuileries. The Masqueriers escaped back to England in 1793, and the boy went on to become a student at the Royal Academy Schools. Such a romantic boyhood as his cannot have failed to impress his contemporaries. His own sociability and easy talent, combined with his awe-inspiring early experiences, gave him added edge, and the confidence to mingle with ease amongst potential patrons. The poet Thomas Campbell described Masquerier as "a pleasant little fellow with French vivacity".[10]

Girtin and Masquerier were two amongst many highly ambitious and entrepreneurial young artists at work in London in the late 1790s, each as talented as they were energetic and able. Not only did they aim for the highest standards in their arts, but a common principal intention was to make money and achieve fame out of it. Another was John Constable, a year younger than Turner, a tall, handsome fresh-faced unworldly youth brought up in the shadow of a Suffolk mill. By early 1799 he had settled in London, across the Strand in Cecil Street, a hundred yards from Maiden Lane. Others with similar ambitions included Henry Barker and Robert Ker Porter, the traveller and watercolourist George Chinnery (1774–1852), the architect and topographer John Buckler (1770–1851), and the traveller and watercolourist William Daniell (1769–1837). The common factor between these young men, some of the young lions of their day, is not so much their talents as artists but rather their ability, their physical and mental stamina and in many cases the sheer bravery that carried some of them so far away on their travels. Masquerier braved the French Revolution; Ker Porter went to Russia; Chinnery to India and China, Daniell to India, and Buckler extensively around the British Isles to make drawings, watercolours and, later, engravings of important buildings.

Although with a two-hundred-year perspective we may see Turner as the leading spirit in this cult of adventure among young artists, he was in fact only one of a significant and competitive pack. There are enough recorded contacts amongst them to reveal an extensive network of social and professional inter-relationships. Masquerier was Hoppner's pupil; Turner knew both Hoppner and Masquerier, and indeed sat for a portrait by the younger man around 1800. Chinnery was a fellow student with Turner in the Plaster and Life Academies. William Daniell emulated Turner's watercolour technique, and was happy enough to tell Farington of it,[11] while Buckler, like Turner, was employed by Sir Richard Colt Hoare, and worked later with Turner himself on Whitaker's *History of Richmondshire*. When Turner crossed the threshold of the Academy as an aspirant Associate, he may have noticed John Constable making his way to the Academy Schools.

Disappointing though his failure to be elected ARA in November 1798 will have been, Turner knew that another opportunity would come along the following year. He was in the meantime able to display his art in a new and highly influential circle, having been commissioned in 1798 by the Clarendon Press in Oxford to make full-size watercolours for engraving and publication on the University Almanack, or calendar. Almost every year, from 1799 to 1811, it was a Turner view of Oxford that was posted in University offices and quadrangles, and this, a neat evolutionary movement from his platform in his father's barber's shop, brought him yet more recognition and a further power base.

The nature of Turner's activity over the twelve months between the 1798 Associates' election and the next suggests transparently that he determined to put all his cunning and his powers of political acumen into making quite sure he would not fail again. The most important person to have on his side was Joseph Farington. This tall, thin, bendy figure, with a pate as bald and shiny as goose fat jelly, was his generation's scribe, the author of what were already voluminous diaries recording all he came across in the world of culture and politics. He was no trend-setter; his own pen, ink and wash drawings had the air of having been made twenty years earlier, and that was how he preferred it to be. Farington could be an influential friend, but also, as was later to prove, a difficult enemy.

The inducement that Turner had offered Farington in October 1798 would not go away. He and Turner called on one another from time to time, Turner worrying endlessly to the point of obsession about becoming an Associate of the Academy. During one conversation in May 1799 Turner told Farington that J. J. Angerstein had offered him 40 guineas, way over the asking price, for a watercolour of Caernarvon Castle; that William Beckford wanted him to go to Fonthill to make some views; and that Sir Richard Colt Hoare wanted more views of Salisbury Cathedral from him.[12] He made it crystal clear to Farington that he was getting work from those who mattered.

Turner continued, however, to worry about his address. Would living in Maiden Lane damage his chances? Would it not be better if he found somewhere more fashionable? Farington seems to have equivocated on the point, advising him this time not to tie himself down with a house of his own with all the expenses that that entailed, but, if he were determined on moving, to rent for the time being. The biggest problem that Turner had was not so much that the address was unfashionable, but that he just did not have the space in Maiden Lane to carry out all the work he had on commission, let alone to make oil paintings of exhibition scale and standard. The light in that smoky and overcrowded part of London was poor, as Constable was finding: "I paint by all the daylight we have, and that is little enough. I sometimes see the sky, but imagine to yourself how a pearl must look through burnt glass."[13]

If he was to be successful in the 1799 Academy election, Turner had not only to put up a very good showing at the coming exhibition, but also to have plenty of influential friends who would vote for him. So when Farington and Robert Smirke called once again for tea, Turner returned to the subject of a gift of a watercolour for Farington. This time the older man could not politely refuse, though he kept a distance, and Smirke made the choice. Smirke chose a view of Lodore in the Lake District for Farington, and for himself – for the gift was now extended to Smirke – a view of Richmond in Yorkshire.[14] To achieve the success he sought, it was essential that Turner not only kept his friendships in trim, but also remained close at hand and continually in touch with what was going on at the Academy. At the risk of offending a rich and influential patron he refused Lord Elgin's offer to accompany him to Greece and Turkey that year to make drawings of the remains and the landscape. At any other time Turner might have gone, and come to an arrangement with the patron over his fee. As it was, Turner demanded the high figure of £400, and balked at Elgin's insistence that all the drawings be included in the price. So Turner stayed in England, where he had to be.

At the Royal Academy exhibition of 1799 Turner showed four oil paintings and seven watercolours. In their subject matter, composition and painting techniques they displayed the wide range of Turner's abilities at this crucial time in his career. With these eleven pictures Turner, the man who had failed to become an Associate only six months earlier, fired a highly public broadside straight at the eyes of the Academy. One of the oil paintings was a broadside quite literally: *The Battle of the Nile, at 10 o'clock when the L'Orient blew up, from the Station of the Gun Boats between the Battery and Castle of Aboukir.*

News of Nelson's victory off the coast of Egypt reached London within days of the battle on 1st August 1798. It was a thrilling moment, evidence not only that Britain had found Napoleon's weak spot, but also that in Nelson the nation had a flamboyant naval hero who could at last bring results. Turner's painting is lost, and no record of its appearence has survived. It is likely, however, that in choosing to paint this subject at such a crucial moment in his own career Turner was deliberately taking issue with a constituency of artists and their patrons to whom the depiction of naval engagements was stock-in-trade. He himself had never painted such a subject before, and it was the first time he had attempted a painting of a piece of contemporary history. At the 1799 Academy exhibition the Battle of the Nile was the subject of four other paintings. Turner might well have suspected – if gossip had not told him – that the subject would come up like an expected exam question, and that Robert Cleveley, Nicholas Pocock, John Thomas Serres or Philippe de Loutherbourg, four widely respected painters of marine battles, might attempt it.

The great victory at the Nile remained high in the public mind for months afterwards by a series of spectacular recreations by other artist-entrepreneurs. The Barkers opened a panorama depicting the event, and another William Turner, a painter and coachmaker from Shoreditch, opened a theatre off Fleet Street, which he called the *Naumachia*, especially constructed for the re-enacting of sea battles. His opening battle was a one-and-a-half-hour long rendering of the sequence of events at the Nile.[15] At the Royal Academy Robert Cleveley (1747–1809) and Nicholas Pocock (1740–1821) performed to type, both putting in two paintings of the battle, and giving them titles of essay length. One of Pocock's, for example, read: *View of the French line of Battle in the Bay of Bequires, with the approach of the British Squadron under Rear Admiral Lord Nelson to the attack on the evening of the glorious 1st August 1798.*

Cleveley and Pocock were old salts in their fifties, whose annual offerings of sea battles and other maritime subjects were eagerly awaited and predictable. Pocock had been a seaman himself, a ship's captain who had regularly crossed the Atlantic, and had taken part in sea battles. He could be relied upon to get his flags, rigging and maritime detail right, to the great pleasure of other old sailors among his audience. He always ensured that, whatever the state of the battle, his ships could be clearly seen.

The quality that is immediately apparent from the title of Turner's contribution is that the young artist presents his audience with a single precise moment in the battle, the dramatic turning point at ten o'clock when the French ship of the line *L'Orient* exploded, as seen from one of the gun boats nearby – and the position of the gun boats is fairly precisely given too. This all suggests that Turner was working from an eye-witness report, or an abstract of a published description. Press reports of the picture were not wholly encouraging. The *London Packet* said that

> Mr Turner has compleatly failed in producing the grand effect which such a spectacle as the explosion of a ship of the line would exhibit. He has moreover mistook the colouring of such an eruption – the reflection should be red, but the vitreous flame should be bright and prismatic in its tints.[16]

Although Turner's compositions were already paying due homage to the Old Masters and to the work of senior painters, he was developing a manner of arranging objects on his canvases that had a disturbing edge to it. In his *Harlech Castle*, another oil painting exhibited in 1799, classical composition comes head to head with industrial reality. Turner's painting shows a small shipyard where the hull of one ship on the stocks is shown clearly in silhouette, but three others at least are jumbled one behind the other at the water's edge.

This cluttering, particularly of shipping, reflects landscape or seascape as it is. Only the painter can decide whether or not to pick apart a conglomeration of objects presented to his eye and place them with individual clarity. Shipping subjects have always had an in-built critical audience of old stagers who know the way a three-master should be rigged, and taking this extraordinarily touchy subject head on, and with increasing boldness, Turner came to show, for example in the *Bridgewater Seapiece* (1801), how ships move with the swell. There was also another audience whom Turner respected, the ordinary Briton, who was as aware of the dangers of the sea as any citizen of the twentieth century has been aware of the dangers of traffic on the roads. Any common man who had so much as walked along a beach in the 1790s could "read" Turner's marine paintings and feel the danger of the ungovernable motion of the sea. The artist whom Turner always acknowledged as his mentor in sea subjects, the seventeenth-century Dutch painter Willem van der Velde the Younger, had the imagination to paint the sea and its motions as they were, and not to try to tame them. Picking up a mezzotint after one of van der Velde's marine paintings, Turner said to Henry Scott Trimmer with emotion years later: "Ah! That made me a painter."[17] He might have added that in four places he had known from his childhood – the Pool of London, Brentford, Bristol Docks and Margate – he had watched boats at work, and that had made him a painter too.

The annual Royal Academy exhibition, selected by a small committee of Academicians, opened each year at the end of April with a grand dinner. In 1799, the dinner was, according to *The Times*, one of the largest the Academy had ever held.[18] It was a gorgeous, glittering and glorious occasion, the 200 guests only being properly accommodated when an extra table had somehow been rushed in. A good time it certainly was, but it was also a political rally.

The guest of honour in 1799 was HRH Edward, Duke of Kent, the fourth son of George III. The Duke, who was Commander-in-Chief of the forces in British North America, came in the full dress uniform of the Royal Fusiliers, accompanied by his ADC. Cheers were given, toasts drunk and as the light fell and the candles were lit, patriotic songs were sung. The President, Benjamin West, toasted the Duke; the Duke toasted the assembly before him; and then the Duke called the party to drink "to success to the Arms of the Archduke Charles". Here was one military leader inviting a clear demonstration of loyalty for another, from a gathering of artists and their friends whose own private divisions between republicanism and monarchy were marked. But this evening the gathering was toasting the success of Austrian allies against a common enemy, and the Duke received a show of loyalty "with the most lively acclamation". By inviting, not for the first time, a Royal Duke, along with an archbishop, some earls, knights and a representation of the "Visitors and Amateurs of Fine Arts", the Academy placed itself firmly within the fabric of establishment British life. This was the nature of the organisation, with its customs and ceremonial, that Turner wished fervently to join as a full and participating member.

The 1799 exhibition was the second in recent years in which artists were allowed to append lines of poetry to their canvases. These were printed in the catalogue and may also in some cases have been painted onto the frames to acknowledge the poetic nature of painting. There were many profound artistic and poetic reasons for paintings to be read with poetry in mind; the two arts were seen to be complementary, the one providing colour, place and atmosphere, the other movement, time and language. In 1798 only seventeen out of about five hundred exhibitors had taken the new opportunity to quote poetry, and Turner was one of them. He saw additional opportunities for self-advertisement, and slammed the advantage home by adding four or five lines of Thomson and Milton to the catalogue entries of five of his paintings. Until 1798 the Academy exhibition catalogue gave single line entries, thus:

136 *Moonlight, a study at Millbank*  W. Turner.

The inclusion of lines of poetry inevitably blew this neat typography apart, and drew the eye immediately to the entries for Turner's paintings. Thus, they stand out on the catalogue pages like beacons.

Turner's contributions to the 1799 exhibition were received with encouragement. The Academy this year was on course of recovery after two scandals. In 1797 a faked secret colour recipe allegedly used by Titian and Tintoretto was peddled to gullible senior Academicians by an amateur painter, Mary Ann Provis. As a result the Academy became the butt of jokes, focused in a satirical engraving by James Gillray. As if this were not enough, the Academy had also passed through the painful, long drawn out and very public process of expelling its Professor of Painting, James Barry RA, ostensibly because he had time and again vilified the Academy and its members in his lectures and in print. Barry also had republican sympathies, and they underlay the reasons for his expulsion. The Academy was looking desperately for good publicity, which the royal presence, the extreme professions of loyalty, and the lavish banquet helped significantly to provide. *The Times* declared that the 1799 exhibiton was

allowed by the best judges to contain, this year, more collective merit than it displayed in the last two seasons. It may not be necessary to

193 Portrait of the Hon. Mrs. Ferguson  —  *M. A. Shee*
194 Portrait of Mrs. Anderson  —  *J. Fairbone*
195 Portrait of the Earl of Inchequin  *J. Hoppner, R. A.*
196 Morning amongst the Coniston Fells, Cumberland  *W. Turner*

————— " Ye mifts and exhalations that now rife
" From hill or ftreaming lake, dufky or gray,
" Till the fun paints your fleecy fkirts with gold,
" In honour to the world's great Author, rife."

Milton Par. Loft, Book V.

197 A cottage near Ramsgate  —  *L. J. Coffe*
198 Portrait of an artift  —  *J. Opie, R. A.*
199 Portrait of a child of the artift  —  *Mrs. Bell*
200 * Landfcape  —  *T. Taylor*
201 Portrait of a cocking fpaniel  —  *S. Edwards*
202 A view of Lambeth, with a group of barges, from the Horfe-
    ferry road  —  —  *D. Turner*
203 A landfcape, morning  —  *R. Freebairn*
204 Portrait of the Hon. Mrs. Stephenfon  *S. Woodforde*
205 A man's head, a ftudy  —  *T. Clarke*
206 Fruit  —  *T. Johnfon*
207 Portrait of Mr. Bafing  —  *T. Maynard*
208 * Infant care  —  —  *H. Afhby*
209 Lion and tiger fighting  *J. Ward*
210 Portrait of Lady Ann Lambton and children  *J. Hoppner, R. A.*
211 Portraits of Devonfhire cattle, in the poffeffion of Sir Henry
    Mildmay, Bart.  *S. Gilpin, R. A. Elect.*
212 Generous fchool boys, or the collection for a foldier's widow
    *W. R. Bigg, A.*
213 Portrait of a dog  —  *J. Northcote, R. A.*
214 Portrait of the Countefs of Oxford  *J. Hoppner, R. A.*
215 Portrait of Mr. J. Trotter  *W. Beechey, R. A. Elect.*
216 Woodman and gypfies  —  *J. Ward*
217 Landfcape, evening  —  *J. Phillips*
218 A landfcape  —  *J. Phillips*
219 The Son of Man, in the midft of the Seven Golden Candle-
    fticks, appearing to John the Evangelift, and commanding
    him to write.—For the New Abbey at Fonthill.—Rev.
    1ft chap. v. 13.  *B. Weft, R. A.*
220 Richard III. in his tent the night preceding the battle of
    Bofworth, approached and addreffed by the ghofts of
    feveral, whom, at different periods of his protectorfhip
    and ufurpation, he had deftroyed  *H. Fufeli, R. A.*
221 Portraits of Mr. Wedderburn's children  *W. Beechey, R. A. Elect.*
222 Portrait of Mr. Bird  —  *A. J. Oliver*

Page from Royal Academy exhibition catalogue, 1798. Barber Institute Library, University of Birmingham.

observe that the boasted discovery of a preparation, by which it was supposed that the professors of the Venetian School prepared their canvases, has failed in producing the effects proposed, and that the generality of our artists now rely on their own skill and experience, in giving to their productions force and brilliancy of colouring.[19]

The exhibition also had good attendances in 1799, swelling the Academy's coffers and putting the past behind it. Calculating from admission charges received, more than 61,000 people attended, paying 1 shilling per head (more than twice the price of a good haircut) and 28,000 catalogues were sold.[20]

For a new artist, this was a good time to break into the Academy. Change had come in the acknowledgement of literature as an integral part of painting; and the Provis affair had shown some older artists, such as Rigaud, Smirke and Stothard, in a bad light, creating ideal conditions for a new, uncontaminated artist to break in. The new confidence of the Academy reflected the confidence of the nation as victories over Napoleon seemed to be gathering momentum. It was a particularly potent sign that Turner's work was singled out for praise in *The Times* report of the 1799 annual dinner alongside established artists such as Hoppner, West and Beechey: "TURNER, a young artist, who distinguished himself last exhibition by a variety of excellent pieces, continues to support the reputation he has acquired."

The apparent ease with which Turner was able to adapt his manner to the styles of artists of the recent and comparatively distant past brought him further notice, and enabled him smoothly to make the work of Vernet, Wilson, Rosa or Claude contemporary again. He performed these favourite old tunes divinely, never making pastiches, always extending the perceived range of his model artist's style, and always cleverly keeping a step ahead both of his elders, and of those who collected old masters. Turner also found that the best way of assimilating an understanding of the style of an old master was to paint in his manner.

This playful chameleon tendency was extraordinarily disarming, and had the effect of seducing the collector, catching him off guard. An old Irish dilletante bachelor, Andrew Caldwell, was breathless in admiration for Turner when he first began to notice his paintings. Caldwell had for years kept up a correspondence with an Irish bishop, Thomas Percy, Bishop of Dromore, and in 1802 expatiated grandly to his ancient friend about a new young painter he had just discovered. At the time of writing Caldwell was seventy and Percy seventy-three, so even through such dim old eyes talent would out:

A new artist has started up, one Turner; he had before exhibited stained drawings, he now paints landscapes in oils; beats Loutherbourg and every other artist all to nothing. A painter of my acquaintance, and a good judge, declares his pencil is magic; that it is worth every landscape painter's while to make a pilgrimage to see and study his works. Loutherbourg, that he used to think of so highly, appears now mediocre.[21]

The one old master who posed so strong a challenge that Turner professed he could never win it, was Claude, the seventeenth-century Frenchman whose lyrical evocations of ancient Roman places and events had captivated English travellers on their journeys around Italy in the mid-eighteenth century. By 1800 the compositions of Claude had moved beyond the walls of aristocratic picture galleries and into the vernacular fabric of English art and landscape design. Turner's own personal experience of Claude led to what was reportedly a highly emotional outburst in front of *Seaport with the Embarkation of the Queen of Sheba*. The owner of the picture, J. J. Angerstein, had invited Turner to see it, and left the young man alone with it for a while. The lambent light, the slow, rhythmic march of the architecture and the quiet hum of absorbed activity in Claude's painting clearly held Turner in thrall. Angerstein's return to the room and his first quiet words to his guest broke the spell. Turner became awkward, agitated and suddenly burst into tears. "Whatever's the matter? Why are you crying like that, my boy?" said Angerstein. "Because I shall never be able to paint anything like that picture!"[22]

This highly charged moment, privately shared between Turner and the gentle cultivated man old enough to be his grandfather, must have moved Angerstein too. When the experience was gradually sublimated into the watercolour *Caernarvon Castle*, exhibited at the Royal Academy in 1799, Angerstein gave Turner 40 guineas for it. This figure was fixed by the buyer himself, and "much greater than Turner would have asked", as Farington put it.[23] There was surely no reason for Angerstein to have done this if it was not natural generosity and the willingness to acknowledge the intensity of the private moment that had passed between the two men, and to salute Turner's young and evolving genius.

In May 1799 Turner had another opportunity to look deeply into Claude. William Beckford, already a patron of Turner, had just bought the pair of paintings *The Landing of Aeneas* and *Landscape with the Father of Psyche Sacrificing to Apollo* which had come to England from the Altieri Palace in Rome. The pictures, and the story of their recent escape from Rome to England in advance of the approaching French army, had become of such celebrity in London when Beckford's purchase was announced that connoisseurs and artists came in crowds to see them at his house in Grosvenor Square. Turner was among them. Again Claude brought a lump to his throat, and again he experienced the same mixed feelings of inadequacy and delight. Farington reported Turner's exasperation: "He was both pleased and unhappy while he viewed [*Sacrifice to Apollo*], it seemed to be beyond the power of imitation."[24] Discreet displays of emotion in front of supreme works of art could do Turner no harm at all. It revealed – whether intentionally or not – the sensitive and vulnerable nature beneath the surface of this ambitious and politically aware young man.

Turner was by now confident enough of his own dexterity to describe his manner of painting in watercolour to Farington, and undoubtedly to others in his circle too. Significantly, he did not speak of his technique of oil painting in the same way. There was a straightforward reason for this – his technique at this time did not differ from anybody else's, and he certainly did not get himself involved at this stage in his life with crackpot ideas like recipes for cod-Venetian colouring. By 1799 Turner was most widely known as a watercolour painter, having made about three hundred finished watercolours, and having exhibited only eleven oil paintings.

In watercolour, for Turner a much more physical process at this period than oil painting, he was continually experimenting, and told Farington as much over a cup of tea in Hoppner's garden in Fulham. Other artists – Opie, Fuseli and Sawrey Gilpin – were there too, so it might be reasonably supposed that they were part of the discussion of his novel technique: "Turner came to tea. He told me he has no systematic process for making drawings. He avoids any particular mode that he may not fall into manner. By washing and occasionally rubbing out, he at last expresses in some degree the idea in his mind."[25] A few months later, Turner spoke again about his watercolour manner to Farington. Fervently criticising the mechanical dabbings of John "Warwick" Smith and others, he told Farington that he himself had no settled process, but drove the colours about on the paper until an image emerged that expressed the idea in his mind.[26]

In these two snatches of conversation Turner is describing a new intuitive approach to his medium, one in which real physical contact with the colour and the paper is the first essential. He was decidedly not secretive about it. For Turner, the fingernails and fingertips were as capable of creating expression in paint as any brushes. This reveals his openness of mind towards painting, a refusal necessarily to subscribe to any of the many theories of art, published or unpublished, that were current at the time. In "driving" the colours about the paper, Turner is also expressing his own driven nature, and the driven nature of much of his subject matter – clouds, wind, waves – natural power that Claude never chose to represent.

Turner spent the summer and early autumn of 1799 out of London. He had watercolours to paint for William Beckford, which took him to Fonthill in Wiltshire, and in September he went north to Lancashire to make another series of commissioned drawings. Fonthill was the living obsession of William Beckford, who at the age of nine had inherited enormous wealth from his father, the owner of Jamaican sugar plantations and a one-time Lord Mayor of London. The younger Beckford had been born with a wild eye and mind. He had written on dreams and dream-travel, he composed a parody history of art, and in, allegedly, a single sixty-hour sitting wrote – in French – *Vathek*, a novel about a Caliph who could kill with a glance. When he was a boy, his father's old friend Lord Chatham was exasperated enough to refer to him as "all air and fire".

Beckford became a compulsive collector with an apparently bottomless purse, though the purchase of the Altieri Claudes gave him cause to reflect on the massive amounts of money he was spending. Given the opportunity to improve his father's house, Fonthill Abbey, he pulled it down and in 1796 with the architect James Wyatt he set about creating the most astonishing gothick palace the world had ever seen. The façade was 350 feet long, the tower 225 feet high, and the main internal vista through the central octagon became after further alterations 312 feet long.

This most awe-inspiring of great houses was in course of building at great speed, day and night, when Turner came to stay. There was noise, and smell, and incessant activity. "It's really stupendous the spectacle here at night," Beckford himself wrote at a later stage,

> The number of people at work at night, lit up by lads; the innumer-
> able torches suspended everywhere, the immense and endless
> spaces, the gulph below; above, the gigantic spider's web of scaffold-
> ing – especially when, standing under the finished and numberless
> arches of the galleries, I listen to the reverberating voices in the
> stillness of the night, and see immense buckets of plaster and water
> ascending, as if they were drawn up from the bowels of a mine, amid
> shouts from subterranean depths, oaths from Hell itself, and chanting
> from Pandemonium.[27]

Turner, however, was not overawed; indeed he seems to have been unmoved by the whole grandiose affair. Although careful pencil studies of the tower under scaffolding and a small pencil sketch of some men lifting blocks of stone with a tripod survive, Turner was not attracted by all this activity, and on the evidence of the watercolours kept well away. His finished pictures show the building from great distances over the Wiltshire Downs, and set it in a landscape that it significantly fails to dominate. Unfinished watercolours of Fonthill, however, show Turner experimenting with effects of intense light through loosely applied washes of colour.[28] It may be that during this visit Beckford and Turner discussed the *Plague of Egypt* that Turner was to paint for him, an angry subject to hang in the company of the placid Altieri Claudes. Such a violently passionate biblical subject was not yet part of his stock-in-trade. The seed of the painting which became *The Fifth Plague of Egypt* (exh, 1800)[29] and which began to fruit in Beckford's company, had been planted a few years earlier. Turner and Beckford, during an earlier conversation, may already have discussed the possibility of such a commission, according to a note in a sketchbook of

1795,[30] and this led to Turner making some dynamic pencil studies of Moses parting the Red Sea, and Moses standing on a rock with the tribes of Israel behind him.[31] On the tiny pages of this calf bound sketchbook – 5¼ × 3⅛ inches – Turner moves the pencil about, using his finger to rub the graphite into a shiny grey mist, and casts dry red pigment across the image of the terrible sea swamping the Egyptian armies. Taking its place in the sketchbook among views in Wales, and other small figure studies, this is precisely the kind of inspirational image-making on a minuscule scale that makes Turner Turner. And further, the idea of painting a *Plague of Egypt* on the scale of the Altieri Claudes gave Turner a particular jolt that was in a few months time to have a radical effect on the way he managed his career as a painter.

After three weeks at Fonthill Turner packed up his coloured waistcoats, cravats and stockings and travelled via London north to the refreshingly prosaic ambience of Lancashire. He had been invited there at the instigation of the collector Charles Townley of Towneley Hall, Burnley, to travel around the district of Whalley west of Burnley making drawings of the monuments and remains. Turner's drawings were to form the basis of engraved illustrations to a history of Whalley then being written by the local vicar and antiquary Dr Thomas Dunham Whitaker. If the commission was an important one for Whitaker, for Turner it was another workaday job. But it did give him the means to travel once again into north Wales, and to paint in Snowdonia.

It was now almost exactly a year since he had last been in Snowdonia. Then, he had the coming ARA elections on his mind. This year that imponderable was accompanied by considerations of his future accommodation. He could no longer stay in Maiden Lane; he was now so inundated with commissioned work that the back extension of his parents' house in Hand Court was quite unsuitable. Further, if he were to paint a *Plague of Egypt* to accompany Beckford's Claudes the painting must be four feet by six at least to match the Claudes in scale and to have any hope of providing an effective foil to them. As his oil paintings to date had been nowhere near that in size – three feet by four seems to have been the standard maximum – we must draw the conclusion that this was about as big as he could go on canvas in Hand Court. He was sure enough of his own talent and worth to have no technical worries, but nevertheless to pull off a performance to hang next to Claude was like going on stage at Drury Lane opposite Mrs Jordan as Rosalind. *The Plague* had to be a breath-taking picture. He had no particular worries about his future income, and seems now to have felt that this was the time for him to take the plunge and move.

There was another, private reason for this decision. The disturbing atmospheres created by his mother's aggravated temper were coming to a head, and she was being freely spoken of in the parish as a lunatic. Asking advice of Farington, Turner looked about for rooms of his own. He considered some lodgings in George Street, Hanover Square, which Farington thought would make a very good situation.[32] But a fortnight later he had looked at rooms on the other side of Oxford Street, 64 Harley Street, which he had been offered at between £50 and £55 a year. Farington thought they sounded all right for an aspirant ARA: "If the lodgings were desirable, the situation is very respectable and central enough."[33] So that seems to have been that. By comparison with Maiden Lane, the rooms were clean, fresh and new, and Turner took them. By mid-November he had moved in.

Travelling around Britain, developing his friendships, getting involved with Sarah Danby, politicking on the fringes of the Academy, all these activities had benefits on the side. They took Turner away from the domestic stresses at 26 Maiden Lane, which, by the early months of 1799, must have been getting seriously out of hand. Thomas Monro, Turner's teacher-client and confidant, was by profession a mad-doctor, the owner of Brooke House, a private lunatic asylum in Hackney. He was also the Visiting Physician to Bethlem Hospital, and in that role was one of the most powerful and influential figures in the world of madness. At the very least in conversation with Monro Turner could hear about the advice he gave on the treatment of George III, and hear about what he and his father should do about his mother. There were only two options for Mary Turner – private treatment, or treatment at one of the two London asylums open to patients on payment of a bond, St Luke's and Bethlem Hospital.

During the course of 1799, Mary Turner's condition worsened. If he had chosen to do so, Monro could have recommended he take Mary in as a patient at Brooke House, but somebody would have had to pay. The family's treatment of Mary Turner when at last she was committed to a mad hospital, St Luke's, in Old Street in November 1799,[34] was shabby to say the least. We may assume that St Luke's was firm in its condition that people who had been mad for more than twelve months might not be admitted for treatment, so until 1799 Mary may not have been considered ill enough or was not enough of a nuisance. She had two parish bond holders,[35] but the names of her husband and son are absent from the documents.

In the same month in which he moved to a fashionable address north of Oxford Street and in which his mother was committed to a lunatic asylum, Turner became an Associate of the Royal Academy. He won, by the wide majority of ten votes to three, the single vacancy contested on 4th November by nineteen candidates. He immediately joined the social Academy Club and began to attend their dinners.

Turner's rooms in Harley Street were part of a development which the Duke of Portland had begun with Robert Adam as his architect some twenty-five years earlier. The streets were laid out on a formal grid pattern with Portland Place as its spine and Park Crescent and Cavendish Square at its northern and southern extremities. It was a neat, elegant private estate behind iron gates, a world away from the rowdy society of Covent Garden with its seventeenth-century street patterns, narrow streets and dark corners. It was an astute move for Turner, for the area was the home of moneyed collectors and connoisseurs, and on the edge of the country. Where thieves and prostitutes lurked in Covent Garden, in the Portland Estate potential patrons fluttered invitingly at their doorways like butterflies on a bush. Standing on his doorstep, Turner could see, looking right, new London, new houses with walls ripe for pictures; looking left he could see at the far end of the street the lower slopes of Primrose and Haverstock Hills.

There was, however, one major disadvantage. The painter John Serres had the use of a parlour in the house, and a room on the second floor. The parlour was by custom communal, and, in Farington's words Turner "much objects to it [Serres's presence] as it may subject him to interruption."[36] The root of the problem was not specifically Serres's presence, but the complications that might ensue from it. Serres was in a miserable marriage, and needed a bolthole. His wife Olivia and their two baby daughters lived nearby at 81 Wimpole Street. Olivia was highly promiscuous, subject to delusions, and was rumoured to be having an affair with the pioneering colour chemist George Field of Berners Street. It may have been tough on Serres, but the last thing Turner needed at this time, when he was ready to concentrate in better rooms on an important new body of work, was to be a shoulder for another man to cry on. In the event, poor Serres's life began to fall apart. He moved to cheaper accommodation in Berners Street, and eventually separated from Olivia.[37]

The first oils Turner painted in his Harley Street rooms were not celebratory landscapes or works reflecting the joy of being alive. There is a dark mood in both *The Fifth Plague of Egypt* and *Dolbadern Castle* which he also exhibited in 1800, that had not appeared before in his work. Both paintings are about bondage – the former depicting one of God's ten responses to Moses's cry "Let my people go!"; the latter a bleak, friendless landscape dominated by a jutting tower and a rocky overhang. In the foreground of the latter are some soldiers and a half-naked figure whose hands are bound behind his back. This is an image of a castle in Snowdonia that Turner had seen and sketched the previous autumn, and it was exhibited with five lines of anonymous verse reflecting on the imprisonment at Dolbadern of the thirteenth-century prince Owain Goch:

> How awful is the silence of the waste
> Where nature lifts her mountains to the sky.
> Majestic solitude, behold the tower
> Where hopeless OWEN, long imprison'd, pined
> And wrung his hands for liberty, in vain.

Below the rotting, solitary tower is a cameo of physical cruelty. The sentiment of the poem underlying the painting, with its cry for liberty, would not have been lost on those fellow artists and Academy visitors who opposed the new curtailments on freedom in Britain. But alongside these grave political developments, there were two starkly important personal situations that could – one might indeed say should, for he was a sensual human being – have affected Turner's feelings and behaviour at this period. The first was his affair with Sarah Danby, and the birth of their daughter, Evelina, in late 1800 or 1801.[38] Over the preceding few years Turner had from time to time written down lines of verse, usually his own, but sometimes half-remembered snatches of things he had read or heard at glee concerts or at the theatre. His affair with Sarah, and perhaps also his observations on the strife between John and Olivia Serres, provoked these lines:

> Love is like the raging Ocean
> [?Wind] that sway, its troubled motion
> Woman's temper ever bubbling
> Man the early bark which sailing
> In the unblest treacherous Sea
> When Cares like Waves in fell succession
> Frown destruction oer his days
> Orwhelming ... [?crews] in [?traitrous] way
> Thus [?thru] life we surely tread
> Recr[e]ant poor or vainly wise.
> Unheed[ing] seeks the bubble Pleasure
> Which Bursts in his [?Grasp] or flies.[39]

But equally close to home was Mary Turner's lunacy. She had not been cured by a year at St Luke's, and after one or two days' grace was taken across the road to be admitted to Bethlem Hospital for Lunaticks. Mary Turner was committed to Bethlem Hospital not by her husband or son, but by her brother-in-law, Joshua Turner. Joshua, one of William's younger brothers, was a storekeeper at the London Excise Office, and lived only a few hundred yards from the hospital at Grasshopper Court, Whitecross Street, off Finsbury Square.[40] This proximity may explain why Joshua signed the committal papers, but there is no further indication that Mary's husband or son wanted to have anything to do with her at all. They do not appear in the documents even as holders of a bond to finance Mary's treatment. This act (£100 down, plus 20s per week while she was curable; £200 down and 22s 6d per week once incurable) was performed by Robert Brown, an upholsterer of Bedford Street, Covent Garden and Richard Twemlow, a peruke maker of Air Street, Piccadilly. On the documents these men are described as "F" for friends. Twemlow had also been a bondholder for Mary when she was at St Luke's.

Joshua confirmed in his petition to the President, Treasurer and Governors of Bethlem Hospital that Mary had been "disordered in her senses about 9 months, was not so before, is in a healthy condition, has not attempted Mischief, is strong enough to undergo a course of Physic, but is Poor and an Object of your Charity".[41] The declaration about mischief meant that she had not behaved in a dangerous or harmful way towards people or property. On the point of Mary's mental condition, the Bethlem authorities were either being seriously misled, or, knowing her medical history, had turned a blind eye. The senior official whose eye would have had to be blind to the real situation was Dr Thomas Monro.

Treatment at Bethlem changed according to the season. In the winter, when Mary Turner was admitted, patients were locked in their cells, where they slept on straw, for fourteen or fifteen hours a day. Dr Monro believed that cures could be sought not necessarily through the use of medicine, but that "seclusion, diet and moral management" were "of the first and most essential importance".[42] Mary Turner will have been seen by Monro on her admission to Bethlem, but not necessarily to any great extent thereafter.

In the summer months, from May to September, the patients were treated by the hospital apothecary and keepers with blood-letting, and with courses of medicines that made them vomit and defecate. Although patients were no longer subjected to mocking visits by crowds in search of entertainment, as they had been until the 1760s, they lived in a building that was already on the verge of collapse, with insufficient foundations, and a roof too heavy for its walls to bear. Structural piers had in many cases been cut away to make storage areas. The floors were rarely level; wide fissures ran up the walls; and shops and houses clustering round the building took light and fresh air away from the inmates.[43]

It was to such conditions, and to casual care, incessant noise and stench of damp straw, blood and filth, that the Turner family committed Mary. Though her son had plenty of money to spare, the family seems to have made no attempt to ensure Mary received more than the most basic care. The normal maximum length of stay for a patient at Bethlem was twelve months, unless the patient had recovered sooner, when he or she was discharged "uncured". Mary Turner was discharged uncured on 26th December 1801, but it seems that she never left the hospital. Instead she was readmitted to the Incurable Department on 2nd January 1802. By this time life had moved on. Her son had set himself up in rooms in fashionable Harley Street, and her husband was sharing a house a few hundred yards away at 75 Norton Street with the mother of her son's child. The family could not or would not have Mary back. She remained in the hell-hole of Bethlem Hospital for nearly two and a half years until her death on 15th April 1804.

Turner's driving ambition was to fulfil his vocation as an artist. Although there is not one reference to Mary in his surviving correspondence – though this is incomplete – there are hints of her in his notebooks, which suggest that he may not have suppressed his feelings for her entirely. The "Dinevor Castle" sketchbook has small studies of struggling figures, related to the bound captive in *Dolbadern Castle*, and these may be sublimations of his mother's trials.[44] In his "Egyptian Details" sketchbook there is a drawing of a writhing figure that may conceivably suggest that he visited his mother, and made a sketch of a fellow patient.[45] Besides these, only a light pencil sketch profile of an old woman in a mob-cap, made around 1794, remains as a possible, and unproveable, acknowledgement that this tragic, bewildered figure had ever passed across Turner's life.[46]

Turner's happiness at becoming ARA was certainly not complete, but nevertheless being established in rooms in Harley Street with his father and lover round the corner and his mother out of sight, Turner could get on. He was effectively living at two addresses, using the Harley Street rooms to work in, but giving 75 Norton Street as his address in the Academy catalogues from 1801. This practice of keeping at least two separate addresses going lasted until the day of his death. Turner was considered enough of a celebrity, tomorrow's man, for George Dance RA, the current Professor of Architecture at the Royal Academy, to draw a profile of him in 1800 for his *Collection of Eminent Characters*. He was now the bread-winner of what passed for a family, and his father, aged fifty-five, had no financial imperative to carry on his work as a barber. Turner, however, had need of a studio assistant to help him stretch and prime the canvases he was coming increasingly to use, and to run errands. He also needed somebody he could trust not to gossip about him in inns and coffee houses, and who would not be a constant drain on his resources. To the son, the father was a readily available and reliable candidate.

The increase in size of Turner's oil paintings was continuing apace, with the commissioning in 1800 by the Duke of Bridgewater of the five feet by seven feet canvas *Dutch Boats in a Gale: Fishermen Endeavouring to put their Fish on Board*. Like the *Fifth Plague* for Beckford, this was also a pendant for an existing old master, Van der Velde's *A Rising Gale*, in the Duke's own collection. The supply of pendants, that is paintings to hang together in balance or contrast, was beginning to bring Turner considerable income. Beckford had paid 150 guineas for *The Fifth Plague*, and the following year Bridgewater paid 250 guineas for his painting. That he was eager to paint such pictures, which would by definition be the subject of vigorous comparison, illuminates Turner's willingness to learn from old masters, as Reynolds had taught him. It was also a challenge, and evidence of Turner's confidence that his old master mentors would themselves encourage him to higher things. Though Turner's painting was made to hang adjacent and at right angles to Bridgewater's Van der Velde, it was the only modern painting in a gallery hung also with Claude, Van Dyck, Gaspard Poussin, Cuyp and Nicolas Poussin.[47] That Turner was, in 1800, aged twenty-five, seen to be suited to such company is a sure measure of the esteem in which his work was now held.

The Bridgewater Seapiece is the next surviving oil painting after Fishermen at Sea in which Turner wrestled with the depiction of a large expanse of marine swell, and with an equally active skyscape. The sky in the earlier painting is a fretted mist, and acts as no kind of foil to the sea. In The Bridgewater Seapiece, on the other hand, there is a palpable unity between sky and sea that has not appeared in Turner's oil painting before. Undoubtedly this was to an extent generated by the example of the Van der Velde; but it also suggests that in his larger studio Turner could stand back from his oil painting in a way that had never been possible for him before. By comparison, the largest oils he painted before the move to Harley Street, the pair Plompton Rocks, made in about 1798 for Edward Lascelles, are banal and frieze-like in composition suggesting that Turner painted them with his nose up against the surface.

Between the receipt of the commission for The Bridgewater Seapiece and the end of April 1801, Turner had completed this work and another very large canvas, a biblical subject, The Army of the Medes Destroyed in the Desert by a Whirlwind – foretold by Jeremiah. Nothing is now known of this latter picture, and it is probable that Turner painted it out in the 1830s, and that it is now underneath The Vision of Jacob's Ladder.[48] Both the Bridgewater painting and The Army of the Medes had, in their different ways, drawn excited crowds at the Academy, and both broke new ground for Turner and his public reputation. The Bridgewater Seapiece, as the Monthly Mirror reported, "has with the justest claims, become a peculiar favorite of the spectators."[49] Fuseli said it was the best picture in the exhibition, and agreed with no less a figure than Benjamin West that this new ARA had done "what Rembrandt thought of but could not do."[50] Although this was probably a bit of flattery, another influential collector, Charles Oldfield Bowles, went further and told Turner personally that his exhibits of 1800 and 1801 were the best landscape paintings that had been shown publicly for forty years, "since the Niobe".[51]

The Army of the Medes, which followed The Fifth Plague of the previous year in biblical subject matter and explicit violence posed some puzzles for Royal Academy visitors. One seems to have been overheard complaining that the painting was "all flags and smoke",[52] while the turbulent obscurity of the storm that Turner evoked led the Star to suggest that "there is so much trick in the execution that we doubt much of its chief beauties could be retained in a print."[53] This remark is a lightning flash, and shows that Turner's work had now reached the stage where it was natural for critics to muse aloud about its suitability for reproduction in the medium of engraving or mezzotint. Turner had been working for publishers of engravings for some time, but his contracts in these cases were to produce portfolios of specific views, for example the Oxford Almanack subjects, that an engraver could reasonably transpose into engravings. To have publishers approach him to engrave a particular oil painting on the commercial judgement that it would have a wide appeal was quite another thing. In the event such a discussion did not take place to practical effect until 1805, but clearly publishers were waiting quietly for Turner to produce the right painting for wider public consumption. The published remark in the *Star* may be the only relic of a series of engravers' and critics' conversations debating the commercial wisdom of publishing an engraving of *The Army of the Medes*.

This painting sunk back for thirty years into the piles of canvases stacked up in Turner's studio. That its impact had been particularly strong, however, is shown by a passage published, and perhaps written, as much as ten years after its Academy exhibition:

[Turner's] *Whirlwind in the Desert* astounded the connoisseurs, who after contemplating at proper distance an embodied violence of atmosphere that seemed to take away one's senses, found themselves, when they came near, utterly at a loss what to make of it, and as it were smothered in the attempt.[54]

After expending all this emotion in paint, and delivering both large paintings to the Royal Academy on time, Turner and his father needed to escape London. In the summer of 1801 they went their separate ways, William the elder travelling to Walcot, near Bath to see his elderly mother, and William the younger to Scotland. The younger William was suffering from exhaustion after the physical and intellectual effort of thinking out and painting these two great pictures. He complained of being "weak and languid" to Farington,[55] and a few days later spoke of "imbecility". This is "weakness, feebleness of mind or body" in Dr Johnson's definition, but "imbecility" was also already defined as a degree of mental defect of less degree than idiocy. With his mother in Bethlem Hospital, something which Farington may not have known about, we should not rule out the possibility that Turner was using the word with consideration, and that he did not only mean that he was physically exhausted. He was also a father, or about to be, for Sarah was well into her pregnancy or already the mother of Evelina.

Turner left for Scotland in late June, apparently with a man called Smith, from Gower Street.[56] It was not unusual for Turner to take a travelling companion on his longer trips, though sometimes they fell by the wayside or remained invisible and silent witnesses. Smith seems to have been one of those who faded out; certainly, despite his evident illness, Turner must have been a driving and exhausting companion. He was away from London for about two months. He travelled via York to Norham Castle and Berwick-on-Tweed, and thence to Edinburgh where he stayed a week, leaving on 18th July. He continued west from Edinburgh, via Glasgow, and then north-west along the side of Loch Lomond towards Inverary and Loch Awe. This was the only available route, the one taken by the few hardy English travellers who had prospected the gateway to the Scottish Highlands after the Jacobite Rebellions. Two of these had been Samuel Johnson and James Boswell in 1773; and another, in 1788, was Joseph Farington who provided Turner with "directions to particular picturesque places".[57]

With Farington's guidance and encouragement, Turner will certainly have travelled with enthusiasm, despite the difficulty of the roads north of Glasgow. These were the remains of military roads which, fifty or more years after their construction during the Jacobite Rebellions, had already fallen into disrepair.[58] The prevailing weather on the trip, little sunshine, not much rain, no storms, cool though not cold, and cloudy in general,[59] were ideal conditions for travelling, the kind of sightseeing weather that any long distance traveller would envy.

Although he had one major commission to attend to, from the Duke of Argyll, Turner did not go to Scotland in 1801 primarily to satisfy the fancies of others. He took at least eight sketchbooks with him, and these he filled with quick pencil sketches made as if from a coach or from horse-back, and a group of atmospheric studies in watercolour. Turner paid close attention in his studies this time to the people he came across on the journey – fishermen and women, other travellers and townspeople – but the most significant product was what Ruskin later named the "Scottish Pencils", a set of elaborate pencil drawings, most about twelve by eighteen inches, of which sixty or so survive.[60] These drawings with their wealth of topographical, incidental and tonal detail were made on the spot, directly in front of their subjects. They are what might be termed "foundation" drawings, considered ruminations on the way land or rock masses behave in particular light and weather effects for Turner's own use in the future. Some have touches of yellow, many have white highlights; all are on paper toned down with what Turner later revealed to be an inventive mixture of indian ink and tobacco water.[61] That these drawings knocked about his studio for years thereafter is clear from their rubbed and dog-eared state; and that he continued to use them as reference points and *aides-mémoire* in later paintings of massy landscape is evident from the watercolour *Loch Fyne, Argyllshire* (exh. 1815), among others.

Meanwhile, Turner's father was in Bath. William Turner the elder, accompanied by his brother Joshua, travelled to see their mother. Rebecca

Turner had been living for the past year with her fifth child, Jonathan, who had become a baker and biscuit maker in the Somerset village of Walcot. She might have died at any time, and the two brothers will surely have expected that this would be their last sight of their mother. It is possible that they were summoned to Walcot by Jonathan.[62] Rebecca was known by the family to have a cosy amount of money to hand. When she left Devon in April 1800, where she had lived for years with her youngest child Mary, she had (according to Mary) £201 in cash and IOUs, along with some silver, books, and an expensive check coat and gown, a calamanco.[63] The cash alone represented a reasonable year's income, the equivalent of say £15,000–£20,000 in the 1990s. Rebecca told William (according to William)[64] that her things were to be shared equally between her children after she was gone. Although William and Joshua went to Bath with the object of saying farewell to their mother, this need not exclude a natural desire of the brothers to secure their inheritance.

When Turner was in Scotland the Academician Francis Wheatley died. This caused a vacancy in the ranks of Academicians, and on his return to London in late August Turner had plenty of time to devise a campaign to be elected to the senior rank at the February elections. He found, however, that his most valuable ally, Joseph Farington, was out of town, on his own northern tour. Turner called at his house five times in the following months to leave or receive messages,[65] before Farington returned in late January 1802. During Farington's absence, two further Academicians, William Tyler and William Hamilton, also died, thus increasing the Royal Academy's opportunity to re-invigorate itself.

In early February 1802 Farington and his friends came to the conclusion that they would vote for Turner, John Soane the architect and the sculptor Charles Rossi to fill the three vacancies. And, despite the additional candidacy of the Italian born architect Joseph Bonomi ARA, that was precisely how the voting went. William Turner became a Royal Academician elect on 12th February 1802.

# FOUR

# Royal Academician: "Confident, presumptuous — with talent"

## 1802–1806

J oseph Mallord William Turner's first recorded act after his election as Royal Academician was to call the next day on Joseph Farington.[1] Handshakes, claps on the shoulder and embraces of congratulations and thanks will naturally have been exchanged between the tall Farington and stocky young Turner. Farington, whose influence and insider knowledge made him one of the power-brokers of the Academy, would have been justly proud of his nursing to election the young man whose work now took its natural place bedside the old masters, hanging between Claude at Fonthill Abbey, and, in the Duke of Bridgewater's Gallery, with Claude to his right, Van der Velde to his left, and Poussin, Cuyp and Van Dyck nearby. Taking such company, Turner was now widely accepted to be the great hope for the future of painting in England.

As recorded later by Farington, their conversation moved straight to the practical subject of painting, a subject which, from the lips of a modern master, was well worth listening to:

> [Turner] paints on an absorbing ground prepared by Grandi and afterwards pumissed by himself. It absorbs the oil even at the fourth time of painting over. When finished it requires three or four times going over with mastic varnish to make the colour bear out. He uses no oil but Linseed oil. By this process he thinks he gets air and avoids any *horny* appearance.[2]

Sebastian Grandi, the man Turner now employed to prepare his canvases, was a colourman who had once ground colours for Reynolds.[3] His "absorbing ground" was prepared in a smelly, complicated process at his workshop in Long Acre. "Take the bones of sheep's trotters," he wrote, "break them grossly & boil them in water until cleared from their grease, then put them into a crucible, calcine them, & afterwards grind them to a powder."[4] To his clients' specifications, Grandi applied "dead colour", that is, a flat mosaic of colour patches in a chalky absorbent medium over a rough sketch of the subject. The dead colours were organised to lie beneath and enliven the surface colours applied by the artist.

Turner saw his oil paintings as considered and technical objects of manufacture into which much time, money and physical effort was invested. The absorbent ground was well rubbed down with pumice to give a matt finish into which the paint would key well. Then pigment was applied, mixed with a light linseed oil which did not clog. The linseed oil enabled the colour to flow, and was thin enough to allow Turner to work up the image again and again to an increasing depth of luminosity. To finish, three or four coats of a gummy varnish were painted on to enliven the colour, to lift the tonality and to give the painting a healthy glow. This was the "air" that Farington suggests that Turner aimed at, and which had given Turner such a mixture of joy and agony when he had seen it so effortlessly achieved in the paintings of Claude. It was the antithesis of the dry, callus-like, "horny" surfaces that were all too common in the oil paintings of amateur and minor professional artists who paid insufficient regard to the technical side of making a painting.

Turner's father watched Grandi carefully when they were together in his son's studio.[5] Preparing canvases was to become his job, to save the "firm" some money. Turner had the greatest respect for the medium of oil on canvas, for the cost of materials and for the industry involved in creating each painting. He wasted very little, indeed at this period almost half the oil paintings he made were exhibited in the highly selective, exacting and exposed surroundings of the Royal Academy. Turner did not use oils for casual or reckless experiment; his forum for experiment was the more economical medium of watercolour on paper. For Turner to embark on an oil painting was a step of some moment, undertaken with a sober professional attitude, a regard for the financial outlay and the certain expectation of success.

In early 1802 he had four major paintings on the stocks, two seascapes, and a biblical and a mythological subject. They, and a group of new watercolours of Scottish subjects, fresh reflections of his recent tour, were due for display at the Royal Academy from late April, and had taken up the greater part of his time and energy since September. It was of the utmost importance to Turner that he should get these paintings right, as this would be his first appearance at the Royal Academy as a full Academician. The range of his subject matter and approach this year was characteristically daring. Both seascapes, *Fishermen upon a Lee-Shore in Squally Weather* and *Ships Bearing up for Anchorage*, depict moments of maximum danger that Turner had witnessed, and which he expressed also in the technical precision of the titles. Somewhere down on the south coast he had seen a small boat in trouble, and had rapidly sketched events as they unfurled by the second.[6] These drawings became his raw material.

The other two oils, *Jason* and *The Tenth Plague of Egypt* also represented dangers to life and limb, but these were dangers abroad and distant in time, set in the language of the old masters. *The Tenth Plague* – the death of the first born – is staged in front of a noble Poussinesque backdrop, lit by a sidelight falling onto towers and crenellations that have both an Etruscan and a medieval European aspect. A terrifying storm with rolling clouds comes in from the left, bending a tree and underscoring the despair of the foreground women with their dead babies. There is nowhere a storm quite like this in Poussin, though there is more than a passing resemblance in the lie of the architecture to Poussin's *The Saving of the Infant Pyrrhus*.[7] Both paintings touch upon mortal dangers to children, a subject which as a father himself Turner had cause to reflect upon.

The range of subject matter and medium that Turner brought to the 1802 exhibition suggests that he was struggling to decide where he was to go as an artist, where his loyalties lay, and how he should best use his time and strength. There are widely differing pictorial attitudes between the *Plague* and *Jason*, and the two marines with their close observation of the movement of light, air and water. If this struggle was formalised in 1802 on the gallery wall, it raged within the pages of Turner's sketchbooks. Within the compass of a few pages, Turner would sketch a mountain range giving colour notes, make pencil studies of a castle or country house, and then go on swiftly to groups of classical figures, the skeleton of a classical composition, or a note of the layout of an old master painting. All these tendencies occur together in the tiny calf-bound "Dolbadern" sketchbook,[8] which contains two compositional sketches from Poussin, drafts of poetry and various lists.

The sketchbooks Turner bought were flash accessories, generally expensively calf-bound with a leather spine, one or more brass clasps and occasionally gold tooling on the covers. His contemporaries, elders and patrons could not fail to be impressed by them as he brought them out to make notes or to discuss a picture. Now that he was a full Academician, Turner added further style to his status. He began to sign his exhibited work "J. M. W. Turner", a reference with a much more impressive and dignified ring than the ordinary "William Turner" with which he had previously signed his watercolours. He was "William Turner" when he signed his letter to the Academy Council accepting the Academicianship in February 1802,[9] but "J. M. W. Turner" in the minutes at his first appearance as a member of the Council at the end of the year. He was never, so far as we know, referred to in his family or outside it, as "Joseph".

There were practical reasons for this change of style. There were a lot of "Turners" about. Charles Turner, later to become the distinguished engraver, had been a popular student at the Academy Schools since 1795;[10] and another William Turner had been admitted as a sculpture student in 1801.[11] In the 1790s, George Turner ran Turner's Drawing Academy at 24 Charing Cross, from which address emanated to public exhibitions further members of the Turner tribe, Sophie Turner[12] and "Master Raphael Turner, aged 7½".[13] And then there was William Turner the theatrical entrepreneur, whose Naumachia was such a success around the time of the Battle of the Nile and beyond. To run ahead, William Turner ("of Oxford", 1789–1862) was to enter the scene in 1807 to complicate matters further. There is little wonder that J. M. W. Turner wished to keep his distance with a defensive prow of sharp initials at one end, and a proud stern, RA, at the other. The first exhibited oil painting that Turner signed as "J. M. W. Turner" was *Ships Bearing up for Anchorage*, bought by Lord Egremont.

It was at about this time, too, that Turner made it quite clear that his middle name was Mallord and not "Mallard". His mother's family had originally been Mallards, and although his grandfather's generation was patently Mallord, the spelling wavered over the years. J. M. W.'s birth certificate was mis-spelt "Mallad", and his Uncle Joseph was buried in Sunningwell as a "Mallard".[14] The "Mallard" spelling must always have been present in his family consciousness, as he signed himself with a drawing of a duck from time to time.[15] And no doubt it amused him greatly to be called "Mall*ord*" by all those grandees around the Royal Academy.

In mid-April 1802, as he was preparing his paintings for transport to exhibition at Somerset House, Turner's grandmother died in Walcot at the home of her son Jonathan. News of this filtered through to the London Turners within a week or so,[16] and it caused William Turner the elder to look quickly to his interests. Father and son might already have known that the old woman had in her last months become an enormous financial and emotional burden to Jonathan and his family. But despite the effort that the brothers William and Joshua had made to travel to Bath the previous summer, and despite their mother's spoken assurances, it looked as if the two brothers in London were in danger of being cut out of the will. First of all there was a difference of opinion about how much money Rebecca Turner had had when she left Devon for Bath in 1800. Her daughter Mary claimed she had left Devon with £201 and various effects.[17] Jonathan, however, had insisted that "when she came to my House she had one hundred and sixty pounds & if she had lived much longer she would have Expended all she was worth." Then, darkly, Jonathan added:

Mother give me all, but her clothes is for sister Mary & if there is no dispute between you Four Brothers which is not in want I will freely give up the fifty to Mary. But if there is I can keep it all I have not sent to London [i.e. to William and Joshua] Nor neither shall I. It was Expensive enough last Summer ... I have had a Sick House a long Time. My wife has been very ill with the Fatigue Oblige to give it up for Mother was so very Heavy that brought her almost to the grave with her and the little boy has been very ill likeways.[18]

Jonathan had suffered all the hard work and distress of having an old parent in his house, needing constant attention for months, and affecting everybody's health and goodwill. "She has been great Expense. Trouble and fatigue I would not go through it again for Double her property. She has been helpless this half year & lastly I have had people to sit up with her at Night."[19] If Jonathan were to be believed, there was probably not very much money left, and clearly Jonathan thought that he deserved to have it. But the other brothers were not having this, William being the most insistent that they get their rights or resort to law. William, indeed, behaved like a turkey cock, apparently taking advice from lawyers at Doctors Commons.[20] The bullish attitude of John, the elder son, by now the governor of the Barnstaple Workhouse, was representative of them all: "... perhaps we may meet altogether there [Bath] to put a finish to it – for I am resolvd. to Push the Matter to the last extremety shod. he prove tardy and will not dilly dally with him."[21]

Though he may not have considered the estate to be worth much – a fifth of his grandmother's residue was less than the price he could get for a watercolour – Turner will have been party to conversations about the affair. On his father's side he came from a family of self-made, hard-working craftsmen and petty bureaucrats – John the saddler turned woolcomber and workhouse governor, William the barber, Price the saddler, Joshua the customs clerk and Jonathan the baker. These were not lucrative occupations, but this generation of Turners all held jobs which carried with them a certain respectability in a limited social circle. The prospect of inheritance from their mother's estate was probably the only chance of unearned extra money that any of them were ever likely to have, and with it they might expect a mildly enhanced social cachet. This was one of the roots of character that J. M. W. Turner had inherited. His mother's family, on the other hand, had an entrepreneurial spirit in trade. They came from the citizen class, later diversified into property, and married into commerce. The Mallord Marshall ethos was for making money without limit by their wits and through opportunity. In Mary Turner, however, this was a strain that had become touched by the expression of a furious temper, and by madness.

In the weeks following his grandmother's death, Turner was preparing to travel to France and Switzerland, his first trip beyond his own shores. One fundamental political event was now dominating the thoughts of the nation, and it set Turner's mind racing with plans for the coming months. In March 1802 a peace had come into force between Britain and France. It had been signed at Amiens the previous October, and one important effect was that France and northern Europe were no longer closed to the free movement of British travellers as they had been for a decade.

This new opportunity caused a sudden rush of English men and women of all kinds across the Channel. Many were artists, too long cooped up in England with no access to the treasures of Europe and its extremes of landscape and townscape. Abraham Raimbach, who was himself part of the rush, wrote an extensive and colourful account of the exodus:

> ... the eager curiosity of Englishmen to visit the scenes of revolutionary horrors and eventful changes that had taken place in the interim greatly added to the ordinary interest of a journey to Paris ... It would be difficult to convey an idea of the *rush* that was made to the French capital by persons of every class who had the means of transit in their power.[22]

Turner's first priority was not to see Paris but to experience the dramatic Alpine landscapes that he had heard so much about, and at least to touch Italy. It was a canny way of avoiding the heat and crush of Paris in the summer, getting the best weather for travelling in Switzerland, and escaping the bore of bumping into too many Englishmen on holiday. He set off on 15th July 1802 – this date is given by Farington in his diary, with a clear indication that Turner knew precisely where he was going: "Turner sets off for Paris tomorrow on his way to Switzerland."[23] He did not travel alone. His companion was Neweby Lowson, a County Durham man of his own age, part of the landed social network of the north of England.[24] The referee for Turner's passport was Lord Yarborough, and according to a note published years later, Yarborough and "two other noblemen" subscribed to send Turner off "to study on the Continent the works of the great masters."[25]

The weather in the Channel had been turbulent and windy for at least a week before the pair set off. Raimbach had crossed from Brighton to Dieppe on 8th July, and had had a very rough crossing in which he had been drenched to the skin.[26] Turner's expedition nearly ended in disaster before it had barely begun. The packet boat was forced by heavy seas to wait outside the harbour bar at Calais. Turner, however, eager to land as soon as possible, appears from vivid sketches he made on the spot to have transferred to a pilot boat which was nearly sunk in the rough weather and confusion. His only recorded comment on the event is the laconic note – written it must be said three or four years later – "Our landing at Calais. Nearly swampt," beside a sketch for the painting *Calais Pier* (exh. 1803).[27]

On arrival in Paris, the companions spent 32 guineas on a cabriolet[28] to carry them south, and hired a Swiss servant. These relatively luxurious travel arrangements were not of the kind generally characteristic of Turner, but this time the three "noblemen" were paying. We can piece together the route they took, and the effect it had on Turner, through the sketchbooks and by picking a way through the entries in his diary where Farington records later conversations with Turner.[29] It took the party four days to travel 280 miles to Lyons on the post carriage route (what is now the N6) via Auxerre, Chalon-sur-Saône and Macon.[30] Turner sketched on the way – at Sens, Joigny, Auxerre, Avallon[31] – but they were in a hurry and had a specific object in view, so did not linger.

After the long descent down to the valley of the River Saône at Chalon, Turner saw something to remind him directly and overwhelmingly of home. The Saône at Chalon, and south along the flood plain towards Tournus and Macon, is slow, wide and dotted with small islands. Then – as now – it was an essential and placid thoroughfare for the boats which traded at the many small quays between Chalon and Lyons. The Saône flooded, it receded, it was home to heron and a habitat of willows and alder. It was an intimate, fluid universe in precise and parallel harmony with the Thames at Brentford, Isleworth and Richmond. Turner made a sketch of Tournus and the river in his book,[32] and kept it for possible use later.

After three expensive days and nights in Lyons – "Lyons very dear, 8 livres for a bed"[33] – they travelled on towards Grenoble, "about a day's journey".[34] Here were the largest mountains that Turner had experienced, steeper and more "sublime" than anything Wales or Scotland had provided him with. Constant in the distance as they travelled in the late July sun were the Alps. Grenoble is at the southern end of the Grande Chartreuse, a valley about five miles wide with precipitous limestone cliffs on either side, like a massively overwhelming Dovedale. The sketches that Turner showed later to Farington were, in words which probably echo Turner's own, "abounding with romantic matter".[35] It is apparent from his sketches that as he came nearer to the mountains, Turner's excitement rapidly increased, as the drawings tend more to completeness, and sometimes go across onto double-page spreads.

From Chambéry, at the head of the Grande Chartreuse where the valley narrows, the trio travelled about the Alps. Turner drew all the way. They went up the valley of the Arve from Geneva to Bonneville and Chamonix, and from there made expeditions up the mountain Montenvers to the great glacier the Mer de Glace; then to the Petit St Bernard Pass beside Mont Blanc, across the Italian border and down into Aosta. Aosta was a revelation: it is a Roman city on a square grid plan, with the remains of a Roman theatre, a city wall, a great gate, an arena and a grand imperial arch dedicated to Emperor Augustus after whom the city is named. Though the mountains are a perpetual presence in Aosta, it was, and remains, an imperial city with ruins on a grand scale. Turner can have seen nothing like it outside Piranesi's engravings and the watercolours of J. R. Cozens.

Then the party sped north again through the Grand St Bernard Pass into Switzerland to Martigny, and on up the Rhône Valley. At Lake Geneva they turned east towards Interlaken, Grindelwald and the Reichenbach Falls. As well as landscape, he observed the local people, watched processions, and had lots of fun – Turner came back with a sexy water-colour of two naked women in bed together.[36] They sang songs as they drove along the valleys wild: this one, from the 1798 Covent Garden production of *Merry Sherwood*, Turner wrote out (with mild textual errors) in a very shaky hand, presumably as the cabriolet was trundling along:

> I am a friar of Orders Grey
> Down in the valley I take my way
> I pull a blackberry thorn or hip
> Good store of venison fills my scrip.
> My long bead roll I merrily chant
> Wherever I go no money I want
> A cheerful cup is my Matin song
> And the Vespers bell is a bowl, ding dong.
> Then after supper of heaven I dream
> But that is a fat pullet and clotted cream.
> By self denial I mortify
> With a dainty bit of a warden by.
> I am clothed in sackcloth for my sins
> With old sack wine I am lined within.
> No lord or squire or Knight of the Shire
> Lives half so well as a holy Friar.[37]

Turner and Lowson were in Switzerland in high summer. This was the extremely prudent and thoughtful plan decided upon before they left England. They knew they would see the Alps in the best possible weather, with the dangers of ice and snow eliminated. The rocks would be bare, the precipices hard, sheer and deep, the grass green, the sky blue and the storms quick and powerful. For a painter in search of new experiences, there could be no better time to see the Alps than in August and September.

Their engagement of a Swiss servant before they left Paris was another piece of good sense. They paid him 5 livres a day,[38] and undoubtedly chose a Swiss for his local knowledge, his presumed skill in the mountains, and his value as an interpreter. In 1802 the Swiss were generally well disposed towards the English for their defiance of Napoleon, but nevertheless a friendly Swiss servant would tend to ease any difficulties likely to be encountered between nationals. To keep their expenses to a minimum the party had to bargain, "or imposition will be the consequence",[39] and here the servant was worth his weight in gold, for Turner had little French and no German.

The party returned to Paris on 27th or 28th September. Farington reported that Turner was unimpressed with the landscape of France: "The Country to Lyons very bad, – and to Strasbourgh worse".[40] That this did not seem to appeal to Turner in retrospect may be due to his excited memory of the Alpine scenery while driving back to Paris; on the other hand he may have been thinking of the poor physical condition of the people and country after the Revolution. Through the filter of Farington's notes it is clear that Switzerland lived up to Turner's expectations, despite a distinct critical edge to his remarks in which he made staunch comparisons with mountain landscapes that he himself had seen in Wales and Scotland:

> The lines of the Landscape features in Switzerland rather broken, but there are very _fine parts_.[41]

> The Grande Chartreuse is fine; – so is Grindelwald in Switzerland. The trees in Switzerland are bad for a painter, – fragments and precipices very romantic and strikingly grand. The Country on the whole surpasses Wales; and Scotland too, though Ben [Arthur?] may vie with it ... The Great fall at Schaffhausen is 80 feet, – the width of the fall about four times and a half greater than its depth. The rocks above the fall are inferior to those above the fall of the Clyde [which Turner had seen only a year previously], but the fall itself is much finer ... The weather was very fine. He saw very fine Thunder Storms among the Mountains.[42]

This topographical beauty contest was directly related to the perceived quality of real landscape when compared with those painted by Salvator Rosa, Nicolas Poussin, Gaspard Dughet or Claude Lorrain. Their works were considered to be lodestones of style. Further, when Farington reports that the weather was "very fine" he does not mean that it was sunny all the time, but that for the painter there were good lights and darks, dramatic cloud and atmospheric effects with, as he adds, thunder and lightning of sufficient quality to inspire breathtaking paintings. "Very fine" weather could have meant, and probably did mean at times, "very bad".

These comments were made by Turner to Farington when the pair met in the Louvre. That they deal almost entirely with Turner's direct perceptions of landscape is highly significant, and show how dominant in his mind these recollections are. Because Europe had been closed for so long, Turner was practically alone among artists of his age in experiencing the Alps. The excitement, the mature objective engagement by Turner with his experiences, and his thoughts of how he could make use of them in the future, blows clearly through Farington's diary.

Paris was packed during this summer of uneasy peace. "On the Boulevards a free tide of human beings flowed on in a continued stream, fluttering in all the gay colours of the rainbow, and harmonised and softened by the glowing tints of the setting sun."[43]

Pausing only, let's say, to sell the cabriolet, Turner made his way to the Louvre, where Napoleon had assembled treasures looted from royal and aristocratic collections in France, Italy and Austria. On the cornice of the Louvre, the French had inscribed the words *Les fruits de nos victoires!* These included works by Titian, Veronese, Poussin, and other artists whom Turner had long admired and seen in brief sallies in England, but could now see on the grandest possible scale. Not for nothing did the French authorities realise the powerful propaganda value of the Louvre and let foreigners freely in at the expense of the locals. Raimbach gave a rather naïve interpretation of this political act: "Strangers in particular had much reason to be gratified by the extraordinary facilities of viewing these wonders so liberally afforded them, on the mere showing of their passports, and even on days when the inhabitants themselves were not admitted."[44]

Turner had come to this great palace of art fresh from the sublime landscapes of the Alps, from whose sharp, clear heights he had, for the first time, looked into Italy. The sight of line upon line of vast Italian paintings down the length of the Grande Galerie held him firmly in the eye. His own extensive pictorial and written notes deal with the paintings one by one, and restrict themselves to technical and pictorial qualities. In this, he is precisely complemented by Abraham Raimbach, whose record takes the broader, touristic view:

> On ascending the staircase ... you enter the spacious saloon ... Here
> burst upon the astonished sight the gorgeous work ... of Paolo

Veronese, *The Marriage of Cana*; together with the *St George* by the same great artist; the *St Peter Martyr* of Titian; the *Conversion of St Mark* by Tintoretto ... It would be a vain effort on my part to enter into a detailed account ...[45]

But this is precisely what Turner does, in notes closely written in tiny handwriting from page edge to page edge.[46] Turner's eye is taken most firmly by Titian, but he writes also about Guercino, Domenichino, Poussin and Ruisdael, and makes studies with colour notes of some of the paintings. Turner describes Titian's *Entombment* as "among the first of Titian's pictures as to colour and pathos of effect".

The expression of Joseph [Turner means here Nicodemus] is fine as to the care he is undertaking, but without grandeur. His figure, which is clothed in striped drapery, conveys the idea of silent distress, the one in vermilion attention, while the agony of Mary and the solicitude of Martha to prevent her grief and view of the dead body, with her own anguish by seeing, are admirably described ... Mary is in blue which partakes of crimson tone, and by it unites with the bluer sky. Martha is in striped yellow and some streaks of red, which thus unites with the warm streak of light in the sky. Thus the Breadth is made by the three primitive [i.e. primary] colours breaking each other, and are connected by the figure in vermilion to the one in crimson'd striped drapery, which balances all the breadth on the left of the picture by its brilliancy ... The flesh is thinly painted, first by a cold colour over a Brown ground, so that it is neither purple nor green; some red is used in the extremities, and the lights are warm.[47]

The dominant theme in this series of notes, and others in the same book, is the effect on Turner of the *colour* in these old master paintings. Although he examines composition and character in other notes and sketches, his close examination of colour, and of the way the paintings were made, gives an indication of his priorities. As a man determined that his life's work should emulate the old masters, Turner is above all concerned to take this unique opportunity to discover how their paintings were physically put together, and how the artists deployed their colour. This was knowledge he could not gain from studying prints.

Turner spent at least a fortnight in Paris. The whole of the Royal Academy's democratic tendency seemed to be on holiday there at the time. Of the other English artists in Paris we know from Farington that he met Fuseli, John Opie, Martin Archer Shee, Masquerier and Benjamin West,[48] while Raimbach adds Thomas Phillips, Thomas Daniell, John Flaxman and many others to the list.[49] Turner, with Fuseli and Farington, also met the French painter-revolutionary J. L. David, a dangerous man to cross, "of a very black & swarthy complexion – & his right cheek is much swelled ... David is not we are told of an agreeable disposition."[50] In the pause as Napoleon increased his grip on power in France, the summer of 1802 was a long, hot, tense *vernissage*.

On his return to London, Turner set himself some daunting physical and intellectual tasks. From the studies in the nine or more sketchbooks he had filled on the journey he distilled information, feeling and memory to begin or continue the production of half a dozen canvases to be finished in time for hanging at the Academy in late April 1803. As with his production for the Academy in earlier years, the 1803 group was prompted by a mix of experience and events, and the directive of Turner's own personal taste.

One, with the scene-setting title *Calais Pier, with French Poissards preparing for Sea: an English packet arriving*, is a drama-documentary, fact and fiction rolled into one. It shows a moment in the sickening swell that Turner later claimed to have experienced himself as one boat was trying to land, and two to set sail. Although it is also an evident pun on the French word for "fish", the title carries an undisguised insult: "*poissard*" in the 1790s meant "pick-pocket", being derived from the French word "poix" meaning "pitch", because "things stick to his fingers."[51]

*Calais Pier*, based on observation and experience, is conceived as a piece of dramatic sea painting every bit as thrilling as Van der Velde or Ruisdael. Turner had already criticised Ruisdael's "inattention to the forms which waves make upon a lee shore embanked" in his Louvre sketchbook, and *Calais Pier* gave him an opportunity to show that he had the eye and instinctive understanding of the sea to make a convincing and truthful interpretation of wind-blown waves within an engaging narrative.

Two further canvases were distilled from drawings Turner had made in the Alps. Both show the moment when the tip of Mont Blanc appears thirty miles distant above the mountains of the Haute Savoie in the Arve Valley at Bonneville. This first sighting of their goal is as dramatic in its own way as the fearsome situation off Calais Pier had been. The cast of the landscapes overall is brown and green, summery and bucolic with resting shepherds and sheep. Only the distant icy summit gives the hint of reality, the suggestion that we are now in a dangerous, uncertain landscape. That two such similar paintings should have been painted at about the same time suggests that Turner may have hovered uncertainly over them. The one which he called *Châteaux de St Michael, Bonneville, Savoy*, he continued to work on, and hesitate over, well after the exhibition had closed. Appearing strangely uneasy as to how to proceed with the painting, Turner wrote to its eventual purchaser, Samuel Dobree, in June 1804: "... may I ask once more 'am I to put out the cloud in the Picture of Bonneville?' If you can drop me a line decide[d]ly yes or no this Evening or tomorrow morning it shall be as you wish."[52] The spirit of Poussin is evoked in these two Savoy landscapes, and this may explain Turner's apparent attack of nerves over them. Poussin's example was of such a magnitude, and his following among collectors and critics so complete, that to flaunt his manner, to break his rules, to say boo to Poussin in any disrespectful way whatsoever was to court critical disaster. To show homage to Poussin, while noisily breaking rules elsewhere, was, however, the smart way to proceed.

With the example of Claude the young artist was on similarly hallowed ground. Nevertheless, here Turner moved with speed and skill. His *Festival upon the Opening of the Vintage of Macon* is both a glorious homage to Claude, and a refracted amalgam of mixed memories, his lifelong remembrance of the Thames palmed gently into his recall of his own arrival in the Saône valley. The subject is not, however, Macon, but Tournus, the town just up river, which Turner had sketched from high ground, and had mistakenly inscribed "Macon". In *Macon* Turner makes us look, for the first time in his surviving exhibited oil paintings, directly at the sun. But by the artist's subtle trickery, the eye cannot stand it for long, as it can never stand looking at the sun in reality. Look once, and the disc of Turner's sun is shapeless and broken in two; look again and there is a small tight white circle high within the upper patch, painted in three segments – a dab, a wipe and smoothly flat. So strong is the light around it that this small abstract white disc actually rejects the eye and bounces it away onto ethereal tresses of light and off into the tinted clouds.

The distant pimply hills that Turner gives us in *Macon* are of a kind that he will have seen disappearing as he travelled away from the blue Burgundian Hills on the last stage for the Alps. They are also echoes of the hills that Claude painted at his horizons, being a feature of the landscape on the road between Pisa and Rome that Claude knew well, but which Turner had not yet seen. But the most compelling reference in the painting is to the view of the Thames from Richmond Hill, and more precisely the view from the back door of Sir Joshua Reynolds's house. A close reading of the title of Turner's painting shows that this is the opening of the vintage *of* Macon, not *at* Macon. Given the care with which Turner constructed his titles, for example "*Poissards*", and the importance to him of language and literature, the role of that slim preposition should not be underestimated. So in terms of geographical location, we are in the land of artifice, midway between the valleys of the Thames and the Saône. Signalling further the fact that this is artifice motivated by the shock of *déjà vu* when Turner first saw the Thames-like Saône, Turner adds a group of dancing figures, possibly based on the dancing group in Poussin's *Bacchanal before a Herm* that had been at Bryan's Gallery in London in 1795.

Turner's fifth oil painting at the 1803 Academy exhibition was the gentle

*Holy Family*. Here are echoes of Giorgione or Titian, in figures of an enchanting humanity and calm. Evidently this was painted with an eye fresh from the Louvre, but further, painted as it was at the time in Turner's life when he had become a father, *Holy Family* may also be read as a reflective family statement. Another striking canvas of this period, *Venus and Adonis*, is more troubling; indeed Turner may never have exhibited it. Its composition is directly based on Titian's *Death of St Peter Martyr* which we know Turner saw in the Louvre, but in place of the main figures Turner has painted Adonis with his back to us, and a naked Venus with her face masked by his head. At their feet is a cast-down Cupid. For a young artist with ambitions to old master status this is an extraordinary performance, and hideously unsettling. In the story from Book 10 of Ovid's *Metamorphosis* Venus has been wounded by Cupid's arrow and falls in love with the beautiful huntsman, Adonis. Venus wants him to stay with her, and hunt easy prey, like hare or deer. Adonis, however, wants to go and hunt the wild boar. With no personal features given to either Venus or Adonis we are led on to see this picture both for what it is, and also as a *roman à clef*: Turner, like Adonis, was not content with easy prey, but would go off and leave his women and hunt wild boar.

By now, Turner's public reputation hung on a continuing series of outstanding watercolours, and one oil painting after another with subjects so varied that they defied categorisation. All that could be predicted about Turner's brilliance was that it was unpredictable and that he would take every opportunity to surprise, to shock, to enchant and to transport. And given the chance – as his first use of lines of verse in the 1798 RA catalogue demonstrates – he would make quite sure his name was very heavily underscored.

A few weeks before the predictably unpredictable Turner set off for France in the teeth of a Channel gale, his good-natured friend Thomas Girtin returned quietly to England from Paris. The lives of Turner and Girtin, though exactly parallel in time, geography and profession, had, otherwise, deeply running contrasts which have been exaggerated over time. Turner's conduct of his private life gave cause for concern in retrospect at the beginning of Victoria's reign. Girtin, on the other hand, was happily and conventionally married to an Islington goldsmith's daughter in 1800, and, for the first few months of the marriage, lived with his wife's parents. The couple had a son, neatly, just over a year later. Thornbury called Girtin's father-in-law "a rich liveryman of the Goldsmith's Company, who was fond of Art", and so he may have been.[53]

Girtin got on well with the influential collector and amateur artist Sir George Beaumont (1753–1827), and, as he had with Edward Lascelles, travelled with him around the picturesque spots of north Wales, and sold pictures to him. Girtin's son later described his father to Thornbury as "almost ascetically temperate, and his taste always inclined to the refined and elegant",[54] qualities which have always gone down well with the landed gentry. A social backlash, however, was developing against Turner. Having been an early supporter, speaking highly of *The Bridgewater Seapiece*,[55] Beaumont began to dislike Turner now, being jealous of him as an artist.

Turner had a whirlwind's energy, while Girtin coughed a great deal, and had a bad chest. He suffered from asthma, which may have developed into consumption, and this led to his early death. Girtin was a painter of highly accomplished, limpid watercolour views, his *White House, Chelsea*[56] becoming an icon of tranquillity and reflected emotion even in his short lifetime. Unlike Turner, however, whose approach to painting in watercolour was physical, opportunistic and chromatic, Girtin's watercolours are tranquil, generally low-toned, and calm as a milch-cow.

But Girtin had a dream. He dreamt of working on a scale even greater than Turner's. Where the latter remained content to confine his pyrotechnics within the borders of a picture frame, Girtin dreamt of theatrical scale, and had the will to make sure his dreams were realised. Following in the footsteps of the Barker family, Girtin made studies for, and saw to completion, his panorama of London, the *Eidometropolis*. During the six months he spent in France, November 1801 to May 1802, he made drawings, watercolours and etchings for a similar speculative panorama of Paris. Girtin's London panorama opened in Spring Gardens soon after he returned in the summer of 1802. The *Eidometropolis* was advertised in *The Times* as being of 1,944 square feet.[57] Thus, if it was about ten feet high, it would have been nearly two hundred feet long, arranged in a long curve or circle. This was a monumental physical effort for an asthmatic to contemplate, even with extensive assistance.

The Paris panorama was not to be. Girtin died in November 1802, and Turner followed his coffin to its grave in St Paul's Church, Covent Garden. No doubt the work of overseeing and installing the *Eidometropolis* had hastened his end. He and Turner were close friends, opposites in temperament who had attracted one another, and had shared experiences. There is no record of Girtin's view of Turner's work, but of Girtin, Turner said of a watercolour even then in the British Museum: "I never in my whole life could make a drawing like that; I would at any time have given one of my little fingers to have made such a one."[58]

If, as Thornbury claimed,[59] Turner did say in later life "had Tom Girtin lived, I should have starved," he, Turner, was being characteristically kind to the memory of a fellow artist, uttering an emotional response, which of course had no basis in fact, but was generous enough. But Turner did say, and with justification, "We were friends to the last, although *They* tried to separate us."[60]

"*They*" were some parts of the social and artistic establishment. Farington gave a clue to the way the fault-lines ran in the remark to his diary quoted in Chapter Three: "Hoppner told me Mr Lascelles as well as Lady Sutherland are disposed to set up Girtin against Turner [as an ARA in the Academy elections] – who they say effects his purpose by industry – the former more for genius – Turner finishes too much."[61] "Effects his purpose by industry", here, means lobbies and politicks among Academicians a great deal, activities which in a well-rooted, mature art-courtier may be expected. From a precocious young man whom many could remember as a pupil at the Academy Schools it was, to the establishment, an unedifying sight. Thus Turner put people's backs up, and generated antagonism against him. The loss of Girtin, the loss of the only young artist on the horizon whose talents could hope to keep Turner in check, was a grievous disappointment. For many in the establishment the wrong artist had died.

Beaumont's dislike of Turner developed over the years into open warfare. By 1803, he was beginning to show signs of turning against the younger man. He criticised Turner's foregrounds as being "comparatively blots"[62] and remarked of *Macon* that "its subject was borrowed from Claude, but the colouring forgotten."[63]

Beaumont was a land-owning baronet with Leicestershire acres and a house in Grosvenor Square. He liked to have young artists and writers about him, and to be constantly in the swim. He was a collector in the grand manner, having bought Claude, Rubens and Rembrandt, and having commissioned paintings from the living artists he befriended. Not only paintings did he collect, but people too, inviting them warmly for weeks together to his country house, Coleorton, near Leicester. He had nevertheless an uncomfortable habit of carelessly dropping them when they ceased to interest him, as Thomas Hearne reflected ruefully: "Beaumont sweeps away those Artists who at the time are not his Objects."[64] Beaumont gave his opinions on what was good taste and what bad, freely and without fear, but with considerable favour, and took upon himself the role of moral policeman to the world of taste. He told Farington that he would "never scruple to express [his] opinion because . . . it is proper to do so when bad taste is prevailing."[65]

Another influential figure was Sir Francis Bourgeois (1756–1811), a well-connected painter, collector and traveller who had, in his time, been Court Painter to the King of Poland. He and Turner remained good friends, but nevertheless he called Turner "a little reptile" when the pair had a loud argument after an Academy Council meeting at the end of 1803. Turner snapped back, "Well then, you're a *great* reptile, with ill manners!"[66] This kind of bad-tempered behaviour was beginning to get Turner a reputation. He seemed to be rapidly evolving from the amenable young aspirant, eager to impress at the Academy, into somebody rather more trying. Even

Farington began to turn against him. "His manners," Farington recorded, "so presumptive and arrogant were spoken of with great disgust." A few days later he distilled his view further. Listing the characteristics of some fellow artists, he wrote of Turner: "confident, presumptuous – with talent."[67] Another of the irritated elders was Ozias Humphrey (1742-1810) the miniature painter who complained of "the arrogant manners of the new member of Council and the Academy ... more like those of a *groom* than anything else; no respect to persons or circumstances."[68]

This arrogance, in the eyes of his elders, was one of Turner's great personal problems. Advised by Thomas Stothard to thank all those who had voted for him at the 1802 elections for Academician, Turner said he would do nothing of the kind. "If they had not been satisfied with his pictures, they would not have elected him. Why, then, should he thank them? Why thank a man for performing a simple duty?"[69] This story may be apocryphal, but, whatever the case, in the event sense prevailed. Someone or something did persuade Turner to write and thank his peers, for the Royal Academy Council Minutes record on 19th February 1802: "Read a letter from Mr Wm. Turner Academician elect, expressing his thanks to the President of Academicians, for his Election."

About a mile away from Somerset House as the pigeon flies, a brave new exhibiting society was forming itself. Boldly called the British School, it had rented rooms in Berners Street, just north of Oxford Street. This was a direct and calculated threat to the Royal Academy. Its patron was the Prince of Wales, whose artistic set, centred at St James's Palace, was itself a social rival to the court of the King and Queen.

The Royal Academy relied heavily for patronage on George III and Queen Charlotte and their court, and as a result of the overt factionalism within its walls, lost no opportunity to remind the court of its collective loyalty. Examples abound throughout the 1780s and '90s of the Academy Council minting commemorative medals for the King, and sending the Royal Couple heartfelt loyal greetings – for the King's recovery from madness in 1789; for his birthday; for his escape from an assassination attempt in 1800. In sucking up in this way, the Academy was looking after its own interests, for Somerset House was leased to it by the King who could, theoretically, throw them out. For all its artistic excellence and its royal connections, the Academy was geographically isolated from the new money of the Portland, Grosvenor and Bedford Estates. Somerset House was cramped, noisy and expensive, crowded too with offices of government, and cheek-by-jowl with the rooms of the Royal Society and the Society of Antiquaries. It was hemmed in to the south by the river and to the north by the city and Covent Garden, while fashion had moved a mile north and west.

In setting up in Berners Street, the British School, with its resonantly patriotic title, was bound to draw off patronage from the Royal Academy. Its founders were the Irish artist William Ashford, and two men with marital infidelities on their minds, George Field and John Serres. The aim of the British School, as proclaimed in its first catalogue, was to be the home of a "perpetual exhibition and sale of the Original Works of Modern Artists". As a commercial art warehouse, open throughout the year, it would challenge the Academy's monopoly. When works sold, at 5% commission to the School, they could be removed by the purchaser and replaced by the artist with others, and, further, dealers could buy, keep their purchases on the walls and sell them on once more. This was a radical departure in the manner of exhibiting contemporary art, a brash, market-led intrusion into the genteel world of Academy exhibiting practices. Its finance came from the three directors, its patrons, proprietors and ex-hibitors. Five hundred and one works are listed in the catalogue as being exhibited in 1803, so the premises were substantial, and the outlay of capital and goodwill considerable. A few Royal Academicians exhibited, and some notable dead artists were wheeled in as make-weights – Reynolds, Wright of Derby, Wilson, for example – but Turner did not show.

The British School failed almost immediately. Farington later reported that Field told him that "the exhibition was broken in consequence of the pecuniary embarrassment of Serres, for whom Field and Ashworth became responsible to the amount of £1,000."[70] This was less than fair. The cause was in fact the failure of Serres's marriage with Olivia, her rumoured liaison with George Field, and the crippling financial burden of the settlement agreed between these three when Serres and Olivia parted. On the back of the indenture is Serres's despairing pencilled note "Not of such is the Kingdom of Heaven."[71] Contrary to Farington's report, the British School was torn apart not by the lack of ready money, but by the overabundance of sex.

The participants must all have known that the whole venture was doomed before it ever began, and one wonders how they could, leg-ally, have proceeded. Turner's absence from the whole thing may reflect his care as a new member to keep on the right side of the Royal Academy; but it may also suggest that having had some domestic dealings already with Serres he knew all along that the British School was a school for scandal and would fail.

All the evidence suggests that Turner had a calculated career plan at this time. No sooner had he been elected to the rank he had coveted, Royal Academician, than he removed his mask of geniality and clubbability. From being good-natured about his first failure to be elected ARA, and his transparent tactic of giving watercolour inducements to influential new friends, Turner's mood changed and he became bad-mannered and difficult in some eyes, coarse and money-grubbing in others. He also quickly found himself in a position of great power in the Academy, being propelled by current rules straight onto the Academy Council in January 1803. The following April he was elected onto the Hanging Committee to decide the content and appearance of the next exhibition.[72]

Further, he began to set about building his own gallery. This might not have been so significant had Turner been a rich collector or an established artist. Private patrons and picture dealers all over London had galleries of their own; Count Truchsessian had opened a new gallery in 1804 with modern top lighting; Reynolds had had one, as had Gainsborough. But for a new Academician, whose talents the Academy had itself nurtured, and from whom it might expect some degree of loyalty, this was going too far. The Royal Academy had been established not only as a place where artists might meet and students be taught, but also as a place where they would exhibit together and benefit from the mutual strength of a well-established and financially secure institution, to replace the scattering of little exhibiting societies around London. Nevertheless display at Somerset House was poor; the pictures were crowded on the walls, and there was absolutely no guarantee that an artist's work would be fully visible. In building his own picture gallery, Turner would eliminate all those disadvantages and be able to show his work in optimum conditions.

Turner's house, on the corner of Harley Street and Queen Anne Street, had a back garden with outbuildings, about 1500 sq. ft. in all. Turner bought the lease of these for £350 in 1802,[73] and by 1803 appears in the rate returns as the named rate payer for the address as a whole, indicating that he had eased out the other tenants.[74] Having the money to build already saved up in stocks, he set to work to create a gallery whose measurements Farington gives as seventy feet long by twenty wide.[75] This must be a misunderstanding as Turner had not, by 1804/05 got nearly enough unsold paintings to fill such a large space. Further, a plan c.1809 shows the total site beyond the house to be only 38 feet 5 inches by 40 feet 10 inches. On this plan, an "outbuilding" 16 feet 1 inch by 36 feet 11 inches transverse to the site is marked, and this may be the gallery.[76] This was the first step Turner took in extending his property ownership beyond his own immediate domestic needs. Throughout his life it was to be followed by further property dealing which brought him income, anxiety and extra work.

Turner could not paint at Harley Street when the builders were in, so in the meantime he worked in the Keeper's rooms in Somerset House.[77] His architectural training gave him all the experience he needed to undertake the design and oversee the construction or conversion of the building. It also gave him the necessary contacts in the building trade, knowledge of the best sources of bricks, timber, slate and labour – and we should not forget that his great friend Henry Scott Trimmer was a brick-maker's son.

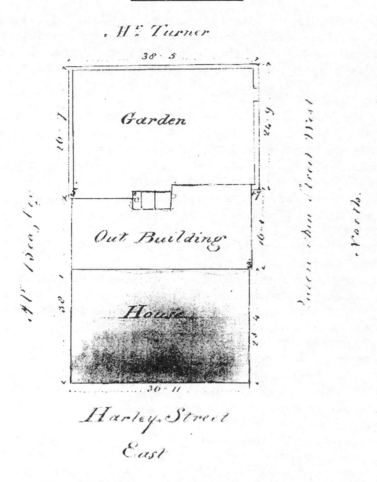

Plan of Turner's property at 64 Harley Street, *c.* 1809.
Howard de Walden Estates.

Turner's experience as a practising artist and exhibitor will naturally have taught him the necessity of strong floors and good access for heavy frames and paintings, both in and out, a high doorway onto the street, and enough turning space to allow paintings to be manoeuvred. A gallery of this relatively modest kind would have taken ten or eleven large paintings, [78] and some smaller ones besides. It was an ideal exhibiting space, which Turner could easily fill at this stage in his career, and where the British School had just failed, Turner's venture had every chance of success.

Turner was preparing to open his Gallery, and to receive acclaim and money from the world of art, when his mother died in Bethlem Hospital on 15th April 1804. Although she had been married at Covent Garden and her son was christened there, Mary was not taken back to St Paul's Church for burial.[79] To all appearances Mary Turner had effectively been left to rot by her successful son and lucky husband. Shortly after Turner's own death family gossip had it that Mary's son never visited her, "and that she died of a broken heart".[80] That is to say of misery, probably a normal end for Bethlem inmates.

Patrons and fellow artists soon beat a path to Turner's Gallery, the latest private gallery in town. Farington's diary, and some of the few letters which survive from the middle of 1804, show that Turner was assiduous in inviting fellow artists and potential purchasers to see his paintings. The diplomat Lord Auckland was invited, though he does not appear to have bought anything,[81] and the quietly spoken and modest city banker Samuel Dobree came and bought, four or five times.[82] Ozias Humphrey RA, despite his earlier fury at Turner's bad manners, was a visitor,[83] as were Sir John Leicester and Lord Yarborough who tussled over the ownership of Turner's *Macon*.[84]

The ownership of a gallery gave Turner the added confidence to bargain with the prices of his pictures, and, dangerously, the sense of security to play one patron off against another. The episode of the sale of *Macon* is evidence of this. Leicester had made Turner an offer of 250 guineas for the painting when it was first shown at the Academy, and the following year, when it was being exhibited in Turner's Gallery, 300 guineas. This was the price Turner had asked the year before, with no takers. By now the picture was well known in the art world; it had been acclaimed and already had a literature. So Turner increased the price to Leicester to 400 guineas. This piece of hard dealing annoyed Leicester, a rich and powerful collector, not used to bandying words, still less haggling, with artists, and he pulled out. Soon after this, Turner sold *Macon* to Lord Yarborough, one of the patrons of his 1802 continental trip, for 300 guineas. It was now common knowledge that Turner could be undiplomatic when it came to pricing his work. He persistently asked the Marquis of Stafford, the heir of the Duke of Bridgewater, for an additional 20 guineas for the frame for the *Bridgewater Seapiece*, when he had already been paid a handsome 250 guineas for the painting itself.[85]

In August 1804, Henry Scott Trimmer moved from a curacy in Suffolk to the living of Heston, Middlesex. Since 1798 Trimmer had been a Classics scholar at Merton College, Oxford. He graduated in 1802, the year Turner featured Merton College Chapel on the Oxford Almanack, and moved from Oxford to Suffolk. We do not know whether the long-standing friendship between him and Turner was part of the impetus, or whether it was just an added pleasure, but whatever the case, during the course of 1804 Turner rented Sion Ferry House at Isleworth, half a mile south-east of Heston on the north bank of the River Thames. In the same year, Turner's father, Sarah and her children, vacated 75 Norton Street.[86]

Turner had, in May, provoked by his rudeness a bitter row at an Academy Council meeting with Joseph Farington. He was being continually criticised as a bad influence on younger artists, and this had probably got at him: "A certain artist has so debauched the taste of the young artists in this country by the empirical novelty of his style of painting that a humorous critic gave him the title of *over-Turner*."[87] Turner had been spoiling for a fight, and perhaps the opening of his Gallery had emboldened him, made him obnoxiously cocky, some may have said. The row began when Turner came in late and took Farington's seat when Farington and others had left the meeting to discuss an agenda item in closed session. Farington was furious when he and the others returned:

[Turner] had taken *my Chair* & began instantly and with a very angry countenance to call us to account for having left the Council, on which moved by his presumption I replied to him sharply & told him of the impropriety of his addressing us in such a manner, to which He answered in such a way, that I added His Conduct as to behaviour had been cause of Complaint to the whole Academy.[88]

This was at least the second fit of bad temper that Turner had shown to his Academy Council colleagues. Behaviour of this kind was evidently something he had in common with his late mother. Undoubtedly as a direct result of this exchange, Turner attended no more meetings of the Council, even though his term of office on the Council still had six months to run. He did not turn up at the King's birthday dinner and other formal and social Academy meetings. Instead, he went down to Isleworth and worked in the sun up and down the Thames, painting from the bank, from a boat on the river and in the surrounding country. He came back now to painting in oils in the open air, as he had done in the Kent beech woods in 1799. During these summer months his style became less confused, less dynamic and gestural, returning instead to a mood of calm reflection, and to subject matter of the eye rather than the imagination. Beginning, and leaving unfinished, nearly two dozen canvases of Thames subjects suggests also that Turner was becoming more relaxed with his materials, less tight with his money.

After overseeing the first season at his Gallery and departing so abruptly from Royal Academy affairs, the calm of the Isleworth riverside was like paradise. It also had echoes of his boyhood in Brentford, about half a mile downstream. The sketchbooks which Turner filled at this time suggest that at Isleworth he had deep and extended musings on the classical world, particularly of Virgil, Homer and Shakespeare. In addition to the limpid watercolours with their Claudean and Poussinesque intertwining of art and nature, there are in one particular sketchbook lists of stories from classical literature that might suggest subjects for paintings: the Meeting of Pompey and Cornelia; the Parting of Brutus and Portia; Cleopatra in her Barge; Jason arriving at Colchis; Ulysses at Chrysa; Ulysses with Chryseis; Dido and Aeneas; Nausicaa; Latona and the Herdsmen; Phaeton's Sisters; Pan and Syrinx; Salamacis and Hermaphroditus; Pallas and Aeneas; the Return of the Argo.[89]

Perhaps Turner had brought books with him to Isleworth, perhaps not. But the depth of his re-engagement with the classical world and classical thinking during the course of these few months suggests that he had somebody to talk to, to have conversations and readings with. The only possible candidate, and one who was by now living ten minutes' walk away, is Henry Scott Trimmer. Knowing as he must have done of Trimmer's move to Heston, how natural and inevitable it would be for Turner to get in touch there and then with his old friend.[90] All previous writers on Turner have followed Thornbury in suggesting that Turner and Trimmer met for the first time in Kew or Hammersmith in 1806. It is clear from the preceding chapters that their friendship must have been of long standing, and as a consequence Trimmer had the opportunity to play a central role in Turner's development as a classical painter. There is every possibility that Turner and Trimmer also met in the intervening years, particularly when Turner was at Merton and other Oxford colleges preparing his Almanack watercolours.

During these middle years of the decade, Turner paused from the obsessive travelling which characterises the period up to 1802, and which begins again in 1816. He did travel in these middle years, but it was less hectic than before, concerned more with reflection, renewal and growing maturity than with discovery. The Napoleonic War had once again closed Europe, and Turner avoided Scotland and Wales by choice. The landscapes he saw now – in the West Country, the south coast, Cheshire, Yorkshire – were not mountainous, but coastal, pastoral, riverside, moor and heathland. He began gradually to regroup his energies, to take stock of what he had achieved to date, and to find ways of focusing public recognition and to profit from his art. The period between 1803 to 1816 is the one in which Turner opens his own art gallery, feels secure enough in London to set up a series of second homes beyond its borders – one of which he designs and builds for himself – and engages in business partnerships with engravers to distribute his work more widely.

Turner's pastoral river landscapes and his ruminations on classical subjects around 1804 and 1805 should also be considered in the light of the contemporary martial mood in the country. England, now feeling the constant threat of French invasion, was a country under extreme tension. The Defence of the Realm Act of 1798 had called upon every parish in the land to detail the number of able bodied men they could supply to take up arms, and send the returns to the government. The 1798 survey was repeated in 1803. Such surveys were not undertaken lightly or silently; they were administratively complex and became the talk of the inn and the market place. "Boney" and his army was seen by no Briton as an idle threat, but one to be taken seriously, soberly and with resolve. The immediately visible effect of this was the publication of large numbers of mocking cartoons threatening death to Napoleon, patriotic comment in newspapers and broadsheets, and the formation of local militias in every shire and borough of the country. Troop movements, exercises, and the sight of soldiery from one part of the country popping up in another became a commonplace. Day-to-day life in Britain in the two or three years before Trafalgar was extraordinary.[91]

Turner made his own comment on the situation in a painting exhibited at the Royal Academy in 1804. What to all appearances is a typical Turnerian seascape with a small rowing boat in the swell making its way towards a conglomeration of shipping, is titled *Boats carrying out Anchors and Cables to Dutch Men of War in 1665*. The title would only have been known to those who had paid sixpence for the catalogue; to anybody else it was just a shipping subject. It took 170 years for Turner's message to be noticed, when it was interpreted by A. G. H. Bachrach, who pointed out that Turner was trying to illuminate the similarities between what he saw as the generally complacent attitude of the British in 1804 and the situation in 1665. Then, the Dutch, having been defeated at sea off Lowestoft, began to refit their fleet until they were able to return and harry the British navy in 1666 and 1667. In 1804, Bachrach suggests, the British were similarly unaware of the significance of events across the Channel.[92] But if Turner *was* issuing a warning statement in this painting, it was mute, and, so, virtually useless. Even the contemporary press seems to have missed the point. The *Sun* said: "Why the scene before us should be placed so far back as 1665, it is difficult to conceive, except by referring to that affectation which almost invariably appears in the work of the Artist."[93] There is instead a clear possibility that there was an element of tease here, that Turner was setting up a coded historical reference and wondering if anybody would understand it.

When Turner reopened his Gallery for the 1805 season it contained, *inter alia*, three furious new paintings of cataclysm and disaster – *Shipwreck*, *The Deluge* and *The Destruction of Sodom* – as if he had changed the code of his historical reference and chosen another more blatant approach. Of these paintings, Turner had conceived *The Deluge* at least by 8th May 1804, when he is referred to as "engaged upon a very large picture of the Deluge, which he intends for the exhibition next year".[94] If the *Dutch Men of War* was indeed a discreet reference to the dangers besetting Britain in the early years of the Napoleonic Wars, the three large paintings of storm and destruction exhibited in 1805 can be seen as a further reflection of the national mood of anxiety and distress in no uncertain terms. At about five feet by eight each, these were considerable works, with a massive physical and emotional impact.

One of the paintings, *The Deluge*, was probably begun as a commission which in the event was never delivered.[95] *Shipwreck* was soon reserved by Sir John Leicester and prepared for hanging in the gallery he was building at his new London house, 24 Hill Street.[96] Having failed to get hold of *Macon*, Leicester's quick action in reserving *Shipwreck* suggests that he hoped to forestall difficult behaviour on Turner's part.

*Shipwreck* was also seen at the Turner Gallery in 1805 by the entrepreneurial young engraver Charles Turner (1773–1857). He and J. M. W. Turner shared a deeply sprung energy, an eye for the strong, emotional image, and a shrewd grasp of what would have public appeal. They were both famously bad-tempered. Charles Turner had known his namesake for some years, certainly since he, Charles, had become a student at the Academy in 1795. In a teasing but in the circumstances wry and self-referential gesture, Charles had drawn a grumpy portrait of his friend and inscribed it "A sweet temper". The pair had many mutual friends – J. J. Masquerier, Abraham Raimbach, Augustus Wall Callcott – and as an ambitious publisher and engraver it was Charles Turner's business to create and foster friendly contacts with his fellow artists. There was another thing they had in common: both were physically odd, J. M. W. stocky, jowly, no oil painting; Charles club-footed.[97]

It is very likely that the agreement between the two men to make a mezzotint engraving of the painting had already been reached before *Shipwreck* was first shown to the public. Charles referred in the print prospectus to "that celebrated picture of *A Shipwreck*". In cooking up the wording between them, Charles and J. M. W. Turner used salesmen's hyperbole to raise interest, assuming, on past form, that by the time the print had been announced, it would indeed be "celebrated". The fact is, however, that when the Turner Gallery exhibition ended there had been no press reports of *Shipwreck*, indeed no known published comment on the 1805 Turner Gallery exhibition at all. This was the first time, since Turner had become involved with the Royal Academy, that he had failed to show there, and for him not to do so and to exhibit only in his own gallery, will have been widely read as a snub. The silence in the press may reflect some kind of conspiracy, as the Academy habitually cornered some papers by taking advertisements in them and not in others.[98] Quite soon after he had sold the painting J. M. W. Turner drafted a letter to Leicester asking for his permission to retain it for a few months in order for it to be engraved.[99] This was no particular hardship for Leicester, as his gallery at Hill Street had not yet been built.

The first great wave of national rejoicing during the opening years of the Napoleonic Wars began early in November 1805 when the papers began to announce the victory at Trafalgar. On 22nd December, Nelson's flagship HMS *Victory* appeared on the horizon at the mouth of the River Thames and the next day dropped anchor off Sheerness. Momentarily, rejoicing turned to mourning as Nelson's body, removed from the rum-filled coffin in which it had floated since his death, was transported to Greenwich for the lying-in-state. HMS *Victory* immediately became an object for sight-seers, Turner among them. He hurried down to Sheerness, with a sketch-book in his pocket,[100] to make notes for what would be his second grand account of contemporary history, to be painted and shown when that history was still fresh in the minds of those who had helped to make it.

Turner talked to the men about the battle, got from them a precise chronology and information about who was where and who did what, made studies of uniforms, studies of the ship and what survived of its rigging and its relative position at the height of the battle. He was assiduous in his efforts to make sure that he heard precisely what happened. He must himself have climbed the jury-rig, for he made a pencil study from high up. The notes Turner made reveal the way his eyes roved about the ship, and how he talked to the men, collecting more detailed character information than he would ever need. He will not have revealed who he was, so to the sailors he would just have been an engaging gent who poked questions about the battle at them and scribbled notes into a little book.

Undress a red jacket; sometimes a red fancy shirt.
[Here a pencil sketch of a Marine.]
  Lt Williams middle s[ize] small, dark eye, small rather pointed nose. 5'8"
  Mr Atkinson, square, large, light hair, grey eye, 5'11".
  Mr Holm [?] Middle. Young. dark eyes. rather small good teeth 5'9"
  Mr Adam [?] broad, rather tall and dark. 5'10"
  Boatswain: dark arched e'brow, forward chin, sharp hooked.
  C[aptain] Hardy wore B[lack?] gaiters. 4 sailors carried some officer down about the time L[ord] N[elson] fell, on his left arm. Someone forwarded to help him. A marine to every gun stands aft 8 others. C[aptain] Hardy rather tall, looks broad full faced but sharp nose and fair, about 36 years. Marshall, young, long [pig]tail, round face, proud lips. 5'2"

When his painting *The Battle of Trafalgar, as seen from the Mizzen Starboard Shrouds of the Victory*, was first exhibited in an unfinished state at Turner's Gallery in May 1806, it upset all the expected rules of marine composition, and upset or at best confused the artist's public. Joseph Farington could not see the point: "His picture of the Battle of Trafalgar . . . appeared to me to be a very crude, unfinished performance, the figures miserably bad."[101] A young woman, Betsey Wynne, unknown to Turner, voicing the direct opinion of the amateur connoisseur, wrote in her diary: "I went to see Turner's picture of the battle of Trafalgar, it is confused and pleased me not."[102]

The viewpoint is high up in the mizzen mast, on the beam of its to'gallant sail, giddily out over the sea on the starboard side, and at precisely the level of the French sniper who is in the act of firing at Nelson. Taking poetic licence, or at least the licence to shrink time and to depict both the act and its immediate aftermath, Turner shows Nelson already slumped to the deck as the shot rings out from the Frenchman's barrel. The disorder and noise of war as revealed here is, to a late twentieth-century eye, oddly familiar. Now, given the presence of the video camera in conflict, we know that chaos disjoints clarity. Events cannot wait for classic composition to unfurl, a fact fully appreciated by Turner.

This painting of the battle was not the only depiction of HMS *Victory* that Turner painted in the months after Trafalgar. A further homage to the great ship, exhibited years later as *Portrait of the Victory, in Three Positions Passing the Needles, Isle of Wight*, is a marine fantasy, a homage to *Victory* seen in full sail from port, from starboard and dead ahead.[103] Like Van Dyck's *Triple Portrait of King Charles I*, here are three aspects of a hero, in this case the hero of Trafalgar sailing in the Channel in a fresh wind and patchy sunlight.

One of the visitors to Turner's Gallery this season was Walter Ramsden Hawkesworth Fawkes (1769–1825), the owner of a house in Grosvenor Place and a large estate in Wharfedale near Otley in Yorkshire. Fawkes had known Turner probably since the 1790s, and having himself visited the Alps may have advised Turner on his itinerary. Having already bought watercolours of Swiss subjects from Turner, Fawkes was sufficiently impressed by him to buy *Portrait of the Victory*. Fawkes was deeply patriotic, and prepared to do something about his views in the political arena. He had been a school friend of the reformer Francis Burdett, and had begun in politics as an honest independent, with a sense of history and a feeling for the common man. In May 1796 he put himself forward for nomination as an MP for Yorkshire with the words: "I am connected with no party; I am equally unknown to ministry and opposition; my country's good is my only aim; the only qualifications I can boast of, are my honest intentions and my entire independence."[104] Being advised at that time not to stand against his neighbour, the Tory Henry Lascelles who had vast sums of money at his disposal, Fawkes withdrew from the 1796 election. In 1798 he formalised his political affiliations by joining the Whig Club, and in 1802 did stand for Parliament unsuccessfully against Lascelles.

Fawkes was a rare human being, in which were combined candour, practicality, humour and an awareness of the common good. He also had a good eye, and the money to indulge himself as a collector. Though he bought paintings by Ruisdael, Guercino, and other old masters, Fawkes was also a careful judge of contemporary painting. By the time he met Turner, he had already commissioned pictures from William Hodges, William Anderson and John "Warwick" Smith. He and Turner had much in common. They shared a doughty patriotism, and a hatred of tyranny. If at times Turner's expression of his views on liberty were somewhat elliptical, as in *Dolbadern Castle*, Fawkes had the directness of a Yorkshire-man. He spoke his mind freely and eloquently at public meetings, and having pledged support for the war with France, set up the Wharfedale Volunteers in 1803 from his tenantry and neighbours.[105]

Fawkes and Turner had both achieved wealth recently, Turner through his hard work, intelligence and skill, Fawkes through his father's lucky inheritance from a distant cousin. Walter Fawkes came from a heavily inter-married Yorkshire family which had ramifications throughout the county. His grandfather had been Walter Ramsden (d. 1760), and plain Mr Ramsden would have been Turner's friend too, were it not for two successive bequests whose sole purpose was the need to keep property intact and a name going. In the first bequest, the grandfather, Walter Ramsden, assumed the addi-tional surname Hawkesworth to inherit from his mother's father, Sir Walter Hawkesworth Bt (d. 1734/5), and to live at Hawkesworth Hall, near Guiseley. His only son, Walter Ramsden Beaumont Hawkesworth (1746-92), received by the second bequest in 1786 Farnley Hall and widespread estates, provided he bolted the name Fawkes onto his already well extended troupe of names. This Walter Hawkesworth's benefactor was his great-grandmother's sister's third son, Francis Fawkes (1707-86).[106] By 1786 Walter Hawkesworth was the father of five sons and two daughters, a healthy enough prospect for the continuation of any name.

Francis Fawkes the benefactor was an extraordinarily rich man, so for Walter Ramsden Beaumont Hawkesworth to assume his surname was little hardship. Before his death, Francis Fawkes had set the modernising of Farnley Hall in train by commissioning in about 1774 the fashionable York architect John Carr to build a new wing onto the gloomy Jacobean house, which was stuffed with Civil War relics.[107] In the six years that were given to Francis's heir as owner of Farnley Hall, Walter Ramsden Beaumont Hawkesworth Fawkes continued the employment of John Carr, and saw to virtual completion the building of a sparkling new mansion overlooking a wide prospect of Wharfedale. At his death in 1792, this great house and fortune passed in turn to his eldest son, Turner's future friend Walter Ramsden Hawkesworth who himself added Fawkes to his surname by Royal Licence in December 1792.

The extent of his inherited riches did not turn Fawkes away from his political principles. It was this amiable staunchness, the determined democrat in Fawkes, that particularly attracted Turner. Their thoughts ran along similar lines, expressed in January 1806 when Turner exhibited his painting *The Goddess of Discord* at the opening exhibition of the British Institution. *The Goddess of Discord Choosing the Apple of Contention in the Garden of the Hesperides* was the first of the series of paintings with themes from Greek myth that Turner exhibited since he escaped to Isleworth in 1804. The message of the painting is allusive, and its sources are muddled, but during the year or so after it was exhibited Turner wrote in a notebook he reserved solely for poetry his "Ode to Discord" which follows the imagery of the painting closely:

> Discord dire sister of Etherial Jove
> Coeval hostile even to heavenly love
> Unasked at Psyche's bridal feast to share
> Mad with neglect and envious of the fair
> Fierce as the noxious blast thou cleav'd the skies
> And sought the Hesperian Garden golden prize.
>
> The Guardian Dragon in himself an host
> Aw'd by thy presence slumber'd at his post
> With vengeful pleasure pleas'd the Goddess heard
> Of future woes and then her choice preferred
> The shiny mischief to herself she took
> Love felt the wound and Troy's foundation shook.[108]

This portentous piece of word-smithery is the first time Turner had worked a literary idea together in verse and painting. Turner muddles his sources in the poem,[109] but this is less important than the fact that both painting and poem were made as Britain plunged yet deeper into war with France. In the Greek myth, the Goddess of Discord, Eris, took the apple marked "For the Fairest" from the Garden of the Hesperides, and threw it among the wedding guests to cause confusion. This wedding riot led to the Trojan War. Turner's painting, following on from his "warnings" of 1804 and 1805, is a plea in the language of Poussin and the setting of the landscape of Switzerland, for peace and freedom and for national watchfulness in a time of war.

Fawkes himself had an honourable pedigree as a wakeful guardian dragon. He was a colonel in the West Yorkshire Militia of 1797, before he raised the Wharfedale Volunteers. Even as Turner was exhibiting his painting Fawkes wrote to the Whig politician Thomas Creevey: "Why, my dear fellow, I have been a Whig, a *Great big* Whig all my life, ever since I was a reasonable being, in defiance of *advice*, or *persecution*, of hostility of every kind, I have stuck to my text."[110] Some years later, Fawkes encapsulated his own yearning for freedom and reform in his booklet *The Englishman's Manual* (1817): "The Reformers of England proclaim that those principles are hourly violated, which their ancestors established with so much industry and toil – principles which they upheld in the closet and the dungeon, in the senate, the field, and on the scaffold."[111]

Fawkes's parliamentary ambitions were triggered again when Parliament was dissolved in October 1806. Henry Lascelles, the younger brother of Turner's erstwhile patron Edward, had paid insufficient attention since he was returned for Yorkshire in 1802 to growing unrest in the West Riding woollen industry. In the spirit of mutual good neighbourliness, Fawkes and Lascelles exchanged letters of polite mutual esteem when the former decided to stand against the latter for one of the two available seats, but then the gloves came off.[112]

There were three candidates fighting for the two seats, Lascelles and William Wilberforce being the sitting members. Lascelles's supporters accused "the Friends of Mr Fawkes" in election leaflets of attempting to "Disturb the Tranquillity of the County". Fawkes, having received great acclaim at a meeting at the Cloth Hall in Leeds, urged his supporters to a "Continuance of active Exertions in his Favour." In the meantime, Fawkes's supporters had been working hard in Sheffield, rousing Lascelles's supporters to yet further effort. One of Fawkes's policy platforms was the abolition of the slave trade, a passion he shared with Wilberforce. He published a letter to the Yorkshire electors, which included the assurance that "The Slave Trade ... has ever had my deepest Abhorrence; nor will I yield in strenuousness, however I might in Efficacy, to the chief patron of its Abolition – Mr. Wilberforce himself." Lascelles, who was heavily criticised during the campaign for neglecting the cloth workers, lost the seat to Fawkes.[113]

Walter Fawkes remained in Parliament only for a matter of months. The 1806 Parliament, the shortest recorded, lasted until its dissolution the following April. Fawkes, who had been dangerously weakened financially by the expense involved, did not stand again. The seats were contested in 1807 by Wilberforce, Lascelles and Lord Milton, heir of Earl Fitzwilliam, and Lascelles lost once more.

As the fever of the 1806 election raged about the nation, Turner took his own first step to protect his imagery and to spread it more widely. He had already created a large body of work which had been distributed in the *Oxford Almanack* and the *Copper-Plate Magazine* by engravers such as John Walker and James Basire. His name had first appeared on the credit line of a published landscape engraving in 1795. Most of these engravings had been made from watercolours specifically painted by Turner on his national tours for the marketable value of the *view*. A growing public demand called for control, and a system. Turner's oil paintings were becoming well known and sought after even before their paint was dry, and his Gallery attracted connoisseurs and the curious alike. Turner's solution to the problem of broadcast and control was to create a formal record of his images, selected and grouped by himself, which he would etch onto copper for a professional printmaker to finish off with aquatint and to print. To ensure that the prints were of the best, he, J. M. W. Turner, would oversee the printing process to ensure quality.

Part of the credit for this venture is traditionally given to Turner's old friend William Wells of Knockholt, on the reasonable grounds of Wells's daughter's recollection of the events nearly fifty years later. But memory plays tricks, and we should take with some caution Clara Wells's assertion that Turner "required much and long continued spurring" before he could be urged to undertake the project. Turner was far too worldly wise, experienced, ambitious and protective of his work and freedoms to need to be introduced to such an idea by Wells or anybody.

Clara Wells recalled that her father had nagged Turner for weeks to do something about protecting his images:

> I remember over and over again hearing him say – "For your own credit's sake Turner you ought to give a work to the public which will do you justice – if after your death any work injurious to your fame should be executed, it then could be compared with the one you yourself gave to the public." Turner placed implicit confidence in my father's judgement, but he required much and long continued spurring before he could be urged to undertake Liber Studiorum.[114]

It is unrealistic to think that Clara Wells could have remembered accurately for nearly fifty years so long and involved a sentence as that she attributed to her father. But it is significant that the motive, as expressed by Clara, was first to enhance Turner's credit, his fame, and secondly to protect the integrity of his images. After William Wells had been going on about it long enough, Turner slapped the table at Knockholt, apparently in October 1806, and said (according to Clara): "Zounds, Gaffer, there will be no peace with you till I begin. Well, give me a sheet of paper there, rule the size for me, tell me what subject I shall take." Clara goes on to suggest that her father arranged the subjects under the headings that Turner came to adopt, Pastoral, Architectural, Historical, Mountainous, Marine and Epic or Elevated Pastoral. This claim goes a bit too far, but it does suggest that there had already been much conversation between the two men at Knockholt about how the project might proceed.

Turner was well aware of the practice of Claude, who had created his

*Liber Veritatis* ("Book of Truth") to protect his images from copyists and corruption. The *Liber Veritatis* had begun to find a wider public in the 1770s when John Boydell published Richard Earlom's series of mezzotints of the images. So, determinedly echoing Claude's example and emulating Boydell's entrepreneurship, Turner set about the task of selecting and making a record of those images that he felt spoke the clearest, and which he particularly wanted to be more widely known. In homage to Claude, Turner invented the grand latinate title *Liber Studiorum* (literally, "Book of the Studios") for his venture.

Turner was between homes when he stayed with the Wellses in October 1806. He was by now leaving Sion Ferry House in Isleworth and preparing to move to a rented house 6 West End, Upper Mall, Hammersmith. Like Sion Ferry House, this was directly on the river, but, being just off the Great West Road, was not so isolated, was convenient for scheduled carriage services into London, and about a two hour walk from Harley Street.

The River Thames was the lifeline Turner needed to keep him in touch with London, and, conversely, the barrier that kept London away from him. Throughout his life the river had had a magnetic attraction for him, and he found it impossible to stay away for long from its even flow. He rowed on it, fished in it and, by now, already had his own sailing boat.[115] Affluent enough now to stay away from London *and* earn his living, Turner could indulge his love of fishing and sailing where the water was freer of pollution and traffic, and the wind unhampered by the buildings and bridges of the capital.

West End, Hammersmith must have seemed on the face of it to have been in an idyllic spot. "It was of a moderate but comfortable size, and its garden, intersected by the Church Path, extended to the water's edge. The house, a white one, with another house at its side, was on the north of the Church Path."[116] The church, half a mile away to the west, was St Nicholas, Chiswick, where Hogarth had been buried. The same distance further west lay Lord Burlington's elegant Chiswick Villa, and around the corner from Turner's house was Hammersmith Terrace, where Philippe de Loutherbourg lived. In social terms, West End had a similar cachet to Harley Street, as Farington observed: "The Society in the vicinity of Hammersmith Terrace was spoken of as being sociable and neighbourly so as to render a residence there very desirable."[117]

But whether or not Turner knew it at the time, his living there could only be temporary. In December 1806 work began directly behind the house on the construction of the West Middlesex Water Works. Had there been meadows and market gardens nearby, as Finberg suggests,[118] they will very soon have been torn up. The three acres of land behind Turner's house were being excavated throughout 1807 and 1808 into two large reservoirs, with brick buildings to house a pair of 20 horsepower steam engines.[119]

There will have been no peace, and certainly no contemplative solitude for a fisherman painter, with lighters coming backwards and forwards constantly to moorings near his house to take away the spoil, and labourers' hutments, and armies of men with shovels and barrows singing, cursing, digging and whistling by day, and drinking, carousing and womanising by night. Little wonder, then, that within six months of moving to Hammersmith, Turner was actively making arrangements to move on and reorganise his life yet again.

On 2nd December 1806 he bid £95 at auction for a freehold estate with a cottage and half an acre of land at Lee Clump near Great Missenden, Buckinghamshire,[120] and on the following 4th May he completed a deal to buy for £400 a few acres of land at Twickenham.[121] These were first steps in a complicated property operation that enabled him to sublet 64 Harley Street; to create a new entrance for his Gallery around the corner in Queen Anne Street; to take shares in an adjacent house, 44 Queen Anne Street; to build a house for himself and his father in Twickenham; and to find somewhere secluded for Sarah Danby and her daughters to live.

---

*SMALL COMPACT & DESIRABLE*

# FREEHOLD ESTATES AND COTTAGES,

## *BUCKS.*

---

# PARTICULARS

*OF A VERY DESIRABLE*

## *FREEHOLD ESTATE,*

CONSISTING OF

### A SMALL FARM HOUSE,

*WITH NEW-BUILT RANGE OF STABLING,*

AND

### About FIFTY ACRES of

## Arable, Meadow & Wood Land,

LATE IN THE OCCUPATION OF

JOHN FRANKLIN, RICHARD DWIGHT & the Widow GINGER,

*BUT NOW IN HAND;*

LIKEWISE

## A FREEHOLD BRICK HOUSE,

WITH

## *FARM-YARD, COW-HOUSE, BARN, GARDEN,*

### And THREE CLOSES of LAND,

*In a Pleasant PART of the COUNTY of BUCKS,*

### AT POTTER'S ROW,

One Mile from MISSENDEN, Five from AMERSHAM, Six from WYCOMBE,
and Five from WENDOVER;

AND

### Three Freehold Cottages, Garden, & Orchard,

*At LEE CLUMP;*

WHICH WILL BE SOLD BY AUCTION,

### *BY MESS^{RS}.*

# *HOGGART & PHILLIPS,*

## (SUCCESSORS TO MR. SMITH)

*At GARRAWAY'S COFFEE-HOUSE, CHANGE-ALLEY, CORNHILL,*

On TUESDAY, the 2nd of DECEMBER, 1806,

AT TWELVE O'CLOCK,

IN FIVE LOTS.

---

Particulars may be had at the *Crown, Amersham; White-Hart, Missenden; Greyhound, Chalfont St. Peter's;*
*Red-Lion, High-Wycombe; Red-Lion, Chesham; White-Horse, Wendover;* at *Garraway's;* and of
Messrs. *HOGGART & PHILLIPS,* No. 62, *Broad-Street, near the Royal-Exchange.*

Sale particulars for the property that Turner bought at Lee Clump, near Great Missenden in 1806. The property is the final one listed. Private collection.

# Various Degrees of Friendship

## 1806–1811

A young Scot, David Wilkie, arrived in London at the end of May 1805. He was exactly ten years younger than Turner, and, having blown straight into the probationer class at the Royal Academy on the strength of his folio of drawings, moved up to a full studentship in the December 1805 intake. He came to the Academy in the following wind of the sensation he had caused in Edinburgh that same summer with his uncomfortably vivid and mimetic painting of country fun in Fife, *Pitlessie Fair*. This he had promptly sold, and so paid for his venture to London.

Wilkie was a tall, slim, fresh-faced young man, with a broad smile, a kiss curl at his forehead, and an engaging Scots drawl. He was the son of a Fife minister, well brought up and personable, who had spent a childhood and youth observing ordinary people at work and play. His perceptive understanding of change and movement in human relationships, of passing gesture and expression drew him naturally to multiple figure subjects, narrative and low-life. No artist with such a flair for story-telling and the ability to catch character and incidental detail had been seen in London since Hogarth.

Wilkie lost no time in painting another picture of ordinary life which would exhibit the full range of his extraordinary talent. His contribution to the 1806 Royal Academy exhibition was *The Village Politicians*,[1] a small painting of a group of hobbledehoys arguing about politics in a run-down inn. "There was no getting in sideways or edgeways," Haydon reported of the crowds that stood in front of it.[2] That *The Village Politicians* should appeal with such immediacy to so many people, suggests that by introducing low-life painting of exquisite quality to the Royal Academy for the first time, Wilkie was reawakening a genre whose potency had been dormant. Hogarth, the closest comparable figure to Wilkie, had died four years before the Academy's foundation, and Teniers, the artist whom Wilkie had described as going to the height of human perfection in art, was a long dead old master. Of living artists, only Morland came near to the spirit of Wilkie's subject matter, but where Morland painted generalities, country life for the wealthy to wax nostalgic over, Wilkie showed his audience life as he really saw it. In the exhibition of 1806, Wilkie touched a nerve that confirmed that the real power was with the people. "Young man, that is a dangerous work," Fuseli told him. Amazed – or so it appeared – at his success, Wilkie, wide-eyed, repeated "Dear, dear, it's jest wonderful."[3]

Although Parliament had not yet been dissolved when the 1806 Royal Academy exhibition opened in late April, Pitt's Tory government was tottering. The men who argued over a newspaper article in Wilkie's painting were the representatives of precisely those who would attend political meetings of the kind that Fawkes and Lascelles were to address in the months to come. The light-handed braw young Scot deftly paralleled the changing mood with an artistic sea-change that he himself had begun to effect.

For the first time in his career Turner may have been rattled by the success of another artist, particularly as Turner was already well aware of the genius and popularity of Teniers. Now a famous man, rich and sought after, the rate of Turner's rise to fortune had taken some knocks. With some delight, therefore, Beaumont and his friend Lord Mulgrave discovered the new young Wilkie who was a sure-fire antidote to the manner and manners of Turner. Before *The Village Politicians* was finished, Beaumont and Mulgrave went to see it, and "so electrified with it [were they], that they each gave him a commission, one for *The Blind Fiddler*, the other for *Rent Day*." Haydon continued: "Wilkie was now up in the high life, and if a young man wanted to be puffed at dinners until Academicians were black in the face, Lord Mulgrave and Sir George were the men."[4]

Wilkie's instant popularity caused Turner to take stock. It is all too easy to read a knee-jerk reaction into his move in response to what has been described as Wilkie's "challenge" at the Royal Academy of 1806. But if it was a challenge over which Turner had brooded, he responded ultimately with coolness and notable aplomb and played two aces the following year. In the first, he exhibited half a dozen new landscapes and seascapes at his own gallery in Queen Anne Street. These included in particular the extraordinary picture *Walton Bridges* whose twin parabolas arc boldly just above eye level across the painting, reminiscent in their lighting of Canaletto and William Marlow but in their composition of nobody at all but J. M. W. Turner RA.

Down by the river at the Royal Academy, however, Turner played his second ace, taking Wilkie on at the "low-life" game with a painting which raised the stakes of the genre to a new level of sophistication and humanity. Turner neither made nor implied jokes at the expense of his subject, nor displayed any form of sentimentality towards them. Where Wilkie makes a kind of enclosed box-like theatre for his composition, Turner creates a space through which light and air can flow freely from front to back, and in which the main plot – the blacksmith arguing (mildly) with the butcher – only marginally dominates the sub-plots of workman-like activity in the background, the conversation between the ponies on the right and the idle drama of the cock, hens and chickens on the left.

Like Wilkie's *Village Politicians*, Turner's painting tells a small story. But the main thread of its narrative remains firmly locked within its title, *A Country Blacksmith disputing upon the Price of Iron, and the Price charged to the Butcher for shoeing his Pony*, and thus it is a narrative by implication only. Indeed a writer in the *Monthly Magazine*, misunderstanding the title's role as a scene setter rather than a scene describer, felt that the full title was "rather too much to express in a picture, nor is it reasonable to expect that such a story should be clearly told on canvas."[5] Where the Wilkie was topical in generalities, Turner's painting is topical in the particular, and sets a very small local incident against a current national issue, the recent tax on all iron products made in Great Britain, which directly affected the price of iron in the village smithy. With the word "price" so dominant in the title, we can be certain that Turner meant his painting to be topical.

Had Wilkie not appeared on the scene when he did, Turner's *Country Blacksmith* would probably have remained unpainted. If it did nothing else, Wilkie's sudden entrance reminded the world of taste and fashion that here was another manner of painting that was ripe for revival, and the gallop began to satisfy it. Turner took the genre up with paintings such as *The Unpaid Bill* (1808), *The Garreteer's Petition* (1809) and *Harvest Home* (c.1809). Although Turner was to lose interest in low-life painting after a few years, other artists, principally William Mulready and Edward Bird, built long careers on it.

In reacting to the impulse of Wilkie, Turner was not only picking up a dropped stitch by showing that he could paint genre as well as – better than – anybody. If there is a touch of the competitive pedant in his attitude towards Wilkie's work at this time, this was not personal to a fellow artist, but directed instead, through his painting, towards an enemy. Turner will have soon known that Wilkie's contribution to the 1807 Academy was commissioned by Beaumont, so he had every reason to want to blast it off the walls with a work of his own.

Beaumont had continued his systematic programme of rubbishing Turner's exhibition pictures with an attack in 1806 on *The Goddess of Discord*. Of this he made the snide comment that it appeared to him to be the work of an old man who still had ideas but had lost the ability to express them. None of his remarks had been published, and all were probably made off the cuff. But consistent and stretched as they were over a few years, we might accept that in recording them, Farington was doing so accurately, and with some measure of relish.[6] Turner had already become, inevitably, dinner party gossip. With Farington as host, Beaumont and some others tore him apart, and not for the first time: "We passed a very sociable evening. We had a strong conversation on the merits of Wilson as a landscape painter and the vicious practice of Turner and his followers was warmly exposed."[7]

Beaumont considered himself to have an opinion on landscape painting because he did a bit himself. His friends told him he was good, but they also let it be known that his paintings were too small and their subjects too trifling for serious consideration. There is an inevitability about the fact that of Turner's most virulent and persistent critics, the chief of them, Sir George Beaumont and later on the Rev. John Eagles, were indifferent landscape painters with high opinions of themselves. In Beaumont's case, however, where he failed as an artist, he succeeded as a patron and as an encourager of the young. For this we should be truly grateful, for as well as taking Wilkie up, he was an early supporter of the young John Constable, Haydon and Girtin.

The ace that Turner played at the Academy of 1807 has echoed throughout his career and since, and gave Turner's œuvre a perceptible roundness and humanity. Adjacent to *The Country Blacksmith* in the cramped arrangement at the Academy hung Turner's second contribution to the exhibition of that year, *Sun rising through Vapour: fishermen cleaning and selling Fish*. The deeply felt tranquillity of this painting was thoroughly at odds with the paintings of deluge and war of the two previous years.

Dr Johnson had defined "vapour", *inter alia* as "fume, steam"; and over the past twenty or twenty-five years experiments with oxygen, hydrogen and steam by Joseph Priestley, James Watt and others had extended Johnson's definition by demonstrating the reality and the variability of the air we breathe. By giving a name, *vapour*, to the stuff that his sun is rising through, Turner is articulating the existence and palpability of the medium that pervades the canvas from the picture plane to the rising sun. With the piles of fish, and the chattering people on and offshore, Turner graphically evokes the sounds and smells of the morning, from the smell of the fish to the sound of the morning gun going off from the stern of the far distant ship. The gun brings a further element into the painting, time – for the sound of the gun is travelling across the still waters, and in a second or two will remind these people that the day has started.

As a rallying point, Turner was now beginning to attract the admiration of younger artists. Despite his response to Wilkie, it is evidence of the young Scotsman's good sense and equanimity that Wilkie did not generate an enmity with Turner, as he may well have been encouraged to do. At a dinner party in Albany, off Piccadilly, soon after the 1807 Academy exhibition had closed, some of the guests parroted Beaumont's belittling opinion of Turner's work – that you could make nothing out, that Turner couldn't paint, and that de Loutherbourg was superior to him. Henry Thomson RA disagreed – he said he would rather have a sketch by Turner than all de Loutherbourg had ever done. Wilkie was present, Farington noted,[8] "and concurred in giving a preference to Turner".

These were some of the early moments of a friendship and understanding between Turner and Wilkie that was to be lifelong and mutual. It blossomed about 1810, and culminated in Turner's expression of his grief at Wilkie's death in 1841, in the painting *Peace – Burial at Sea*. Turner remained initially critical of Wilkie; he seems to have thought that Wilkie was capable of a great deal more than popular low-life painting, and of pandering to royal and aristocratic patronage and flattery. Turner expressed his feelings in a piece of rhyme scrappily written out in a sketchbook, which directs his blame at "Flattery", a clear reference to Beaumont:

> Coarse Flattery, like a Gipsy came
> Would she were never heard
> And muddled all the fecund brains
> Of Wilkie and of Bird
> When she call'd either a Teniers
> Each Tyro stopt contented
> At the alluring half-way house
> Where each a room hath rented.[9]

Turner's friendship with the painter Augustus Wall Callcott (1779–1844) also began to ripen in this decade. Callcott was three years younger than Turner, and shared with him the burden of the opprobrium of Sir George Beaumont who, from 1806, was publicly lumping both of them together as "the white painters". This was a meaner jibe then than it may appear, for Beaumont was criticising the high tonality of their pictures, the light, local colour and atmosphere that so clearly marked Turner's work out, and which Callcott had also adopted. Beaumont himself approached whiteness from an angle peculiar to his generation and kind; his own personal love was the colour brown. He seriously recommended to Constable that the colour of "an old Cremona fiddle" was just the thing for the prevailing tones in a landscape painting; and at another time he mused to Constable, when the two were painting together in the country, "Do you not find it difficult to determine where to place your *brown* tree?"[10] To which Constable replied that he never painted a brown tree.

An additional, perhaps the root, reason for Beaumont's attack on Callcott, was that the latter refused to be set up by Beaumont and his fellow Directors of the British Institution as an alternative to Turner, a malleable rival who would dance to their tune and paint the kind of pictures which would be acceptable to connoisseurs. These men were the old guard, hanging on into a new century whose taste perturbed them, and whose fashions they took determined action to attempt to control. In his diary for 1805, Callcott and some friends "all seemed to agree [the British Institution] had the appearance rather of desiring to get the patronage into its own hands than to benefit the arts."[11]

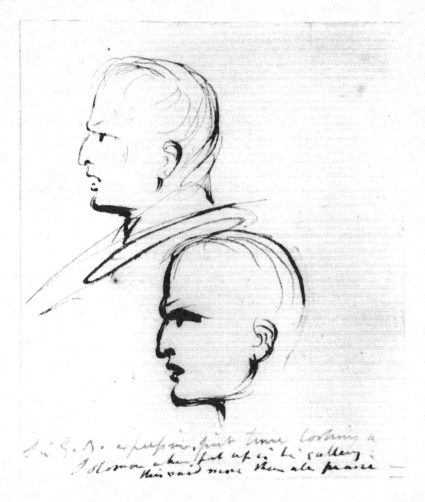

Benjamin Robert Haydon: *Study of Sir George Beaumont looking at a picture.* Pen and ink, 1814. Tate Gallery, London.

The British Institution was the child of the connoisseurs. Set up in 1806 in the former Shakespeare Galleries in Pall Mall, it challenged the Academy in being controlled by collectors rather than artists. Its exhibitions settled into the pattern of British artists in the winter and old masters in the summer, and it wooed artists' support by organising competitions with cash prizes and other inducements, which the Academy did not do. Callcott and Turner were thrown together in their wish to keep a distance from the British Institution, and the younger man's staunchness in sticking by his friend strengthened their relationship. Turner, however, was broad-backed and experienced enough to shrug it off, "too strong to be materially hurt by Beaumont's attacks".[12]

In December 1807 Turner was elected unopposed to the post of Professor of Perspective at the Royal Academy. As Professor, he was expected to give an annual series of lectures on perspective, a subject upon which he had now to display his authority as a theorist. He needed to find a copy of Joshua Kirby's *Perspective Made Easy*, and so perhaps at this time he borrowed one from Kirby's grandson, Henry Scott Trimmer, for Trimmer's copy turned up in Turner's library after the artist's death.[13] There is a hint that Turner began to get cold feet about teaching. He started to improve his shaky knowledge of perspective theory, beginning a thorough course of reading from ancients such as Pliny the Younger, from Renaissance mathematicians and architects, Guidobaldo del Monte, Vignola and others, and from the moderns, Thomas Malton, Dr Brook Taylor and Joshua Kirby. His practical application to the great task facing him led him to remove himself from London in order to devise his approach to the subject.

In the summer of 1808 he travelled north to Tabley House in Cheshire where he had been invited by Sir John Leicester to paint two views of the house and grounds. In the three sketchbooks used at Tabley, besides studies of the park, there are careful drawings of the lighting arrangements for a picture gallery, notes on the arrangement of paintings, some pencil studies of curtaining and moulding round pictures, and snatches of music. Among these is the notation for the music that came to be attached to Ben Jonson's lines "Drink to me only with thine eyes".[14] Having completed his gallery at Hill Street, Sir John Leicester was now actively contemplating a second, at Tabley House. Turner's experience as a picture gallery designer will have been valuable to him, and it is inconceivable that they did not discuss the subject. There are further written notes in the books that show that Turner was actively thinking about perspective, the nature of seeing, and trying to analyse why it is that light can distort as well as clarify.

Ideas came to him as he sat fishing. Fishing, to Turner, was the greatest relaxation in the world, an opportunity to be still, to reflect, and allow light and air to circulate the tired corners of his brain. Like Isaak Walton, Turner

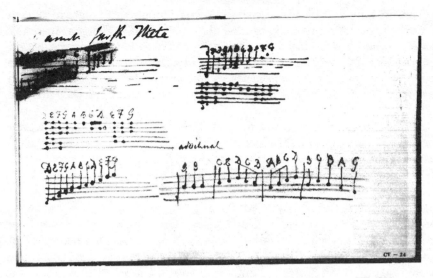

Musical notation, from the 'Tabley 3' sketchbook, 1808. TB CV.
Turner Bequest, Tate Gallery, London.

was a "Brother of the Angle", who, as Walton did in *The Compleat Angler*, could echo in his attitude to the brotherhood Sir Henry Wotton's encomium that angling

> was an employment of his idle time, which was then not idly spent . . .
> a rest to his mind, a cheerer of his spirits, a diverter of sadness, a
> calmer of unquiet thoughts, a moderator of passions, a procurer of
> contentedness; and that it begat habits of peace and patience in those
> who professed and practised it.[15]

For Turner it had yet added value. Sitting quietly on a river bank he was connected to the landscape through his rod and line, and was for an hour or so part of its mechanics, its rhythm. With his shadow falling behind him so as not to make the fish suspicious, he was also, *ipso facto*, looking out over the river in the direction of the sun and seeing the sun's activity among the clouds, its reflection on the water and the nature of its passage through the sky. From about this date on, his notebooks have many quick pencil studies of sky, sun and cloud with notes about momentary passing colour. His paintings too are alive with examples of what it is that reflection does to sunlight, from the white double reflection of a yellow sun in *Sun rising through Vapour*, to the vivid slash of white sunlight on the middleground sea in *Fishing upon the Blythe-Sand* (exh. 1809).

Turner's friend the painter Henry Thomson RA was staying at Tabley at the same time, and he told Callcott (who told Farington) that Turner's time there "was occupied in *fishing* rather than painting".[16] Using Tabley as a base, Turner went on a fishing trip into Wales, as far as Corwen on the River Dee. Sitting with his rod on the river bank he wrote what must have been fairly spontaneous observations of what light does to a white object – perhaps the float on the end of his own fishing line – bobbing on the water:

> A white body floating down a River the Dee altho ... the whole surface from the Water which had on its inclined plane [?] a dun cloud reflected, yet on the same tint the reflection of the White Body had not any light or white reflection but on the contrary had its reflection dark.[17]

These preparatory years, the three years between Turner's election as Professor and his first course of lectures in 1811, were also those in which he confirmed his friendships with two rich, cultivated men, and succeeded in aggravating a third. At the same time he came more fully to know the landscapes which these men were creating on their estates, and to express the artifice of landscape management through the reality of paint.

Fawkes's Farnley and the Earl of Egremont's Petworth, both of which Turner first saw within a short space of time in 1808 and 1809, became, in succession, homes to him for his three mid-life decades. There are remarkable correspondences between both Fawkes and Egremont, Farnley and Petworth, and, it follows, between Turner's attitude, output and behaviour during the extended weeks spent at these two estates. At Sir John Leicester's Tabley House, however, Turner was not so readily welcome. Not only did he disappear for long periods to fish in Wales on his 1808 visit, but he also sent a bill to his host for some gratuitous "Instructions in Painting".[18]

The friendships between Turner and Fawkes and Egremont had taken perhaps six or seven years to mature. Turner had known Fawkes since the 1790s, and his first known contact with Egremont was in 1802 when the Earl bought *Ships bearing up for Anchorage*. Since buying this picture, Egremont kept up the relationship, buying many paintings, and inviting Turner up to his northern estates at Cockermouth, and down to those in the south at Petworth in 1809. There are conspicuous links between Fawkes and Egremont themselves which go deeper than their shared passion for modern painting, and deeper too than their political differences. Egremont was a Tory, and in 1806 had pledged himself to Henry Lascelles's cause against Fawkes by letter.[19] What brought Fawkes and Egremont together, however, professionally if not socially, was their common concern for the improvement of their estates, for the modernisation of their agricultural practices, the strengthening of the quality of their cattle, and the welfare of their tenants.

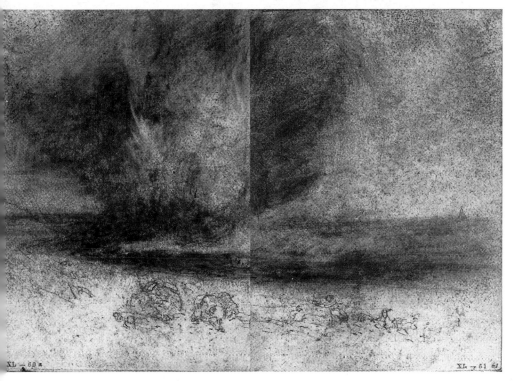

Study for *Parting of the Red Sea*. Pencil with red pigment, *c.* 1798. 'Dinevor Castle' sketchbook, TB XL. Turner Bequest, Tate Gallery, London.

*Sequence of drawings of a boat in trouble*. Pen and ink, *c.* 1800–02. 'On a Lee Shore 1' sketchbook, TB LXVII Turner Bequest, Tate Gallery, London.

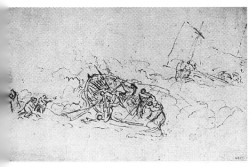
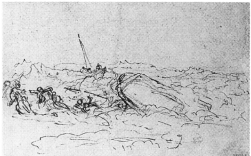

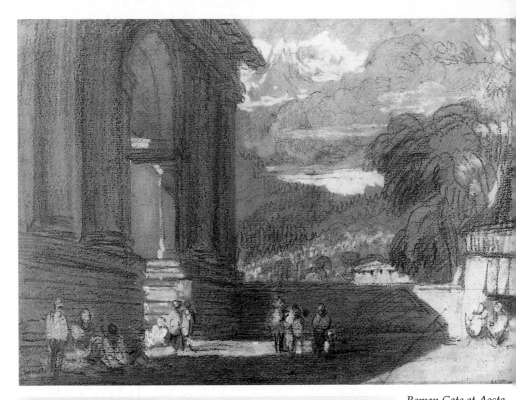

*Roman Gate at Aosta.*
Pencil, charcoal and
chalk, 1802. 'Grenoble
sketchbook,
TB LXXIV. Turner
Bequest, Tate Gallery
London.

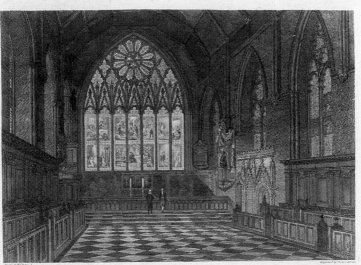

INSIDE VIEW of the EAST end of MERTON COLLEGE CHAPEL.

*The Oxford Almanack,*
1802. Ashmolean
Museum, Oxford. Th
interior of Merton
College Chapel is
engraved after Turne

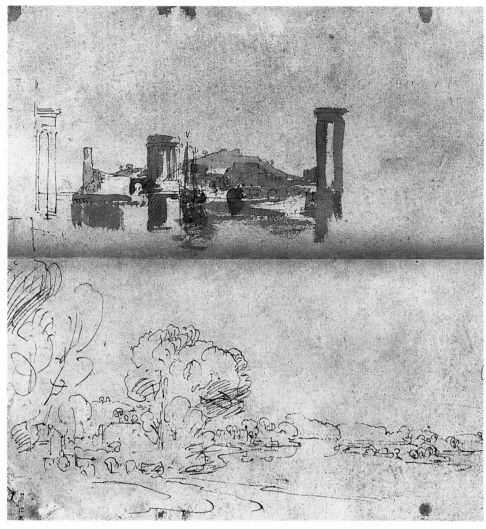

*Group of classical buildings, with a view on the Thames.* Pen and ink and wash, 1805. 'Studies for Pictures Isleworth' sketchbook, TB xc. Turner Bequest, Tate Gallery, London.

*Studies of Sandycombe Lodge.* Pencil, *c.* 1810–11. 'Windmill and Lock' sketchbook, TB cxiv. Turner Bequest, Tate Gallery, London.

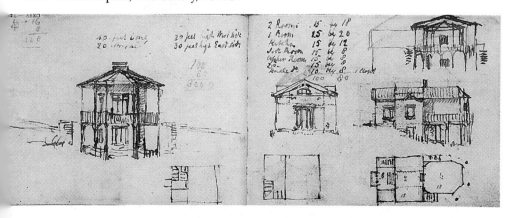

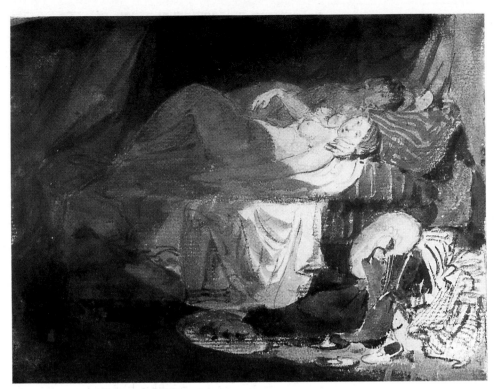

*Two women in bed.* Watercolour, 1802. 'Swiss Figures' sketchbook, TB LXXVIII. Turner Bequest, Tate Gallery, London.

*Erotic figure subjects.* Pencil and pen and ink, *c.* 1805–10. TB CCCLXV-A Turner Bequest, Tate Gallery, London.

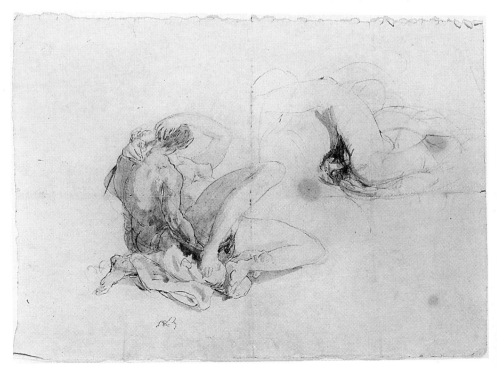

*Venus and Adonis.* Oil on canvas, *c.* 1803–05. Private collection.

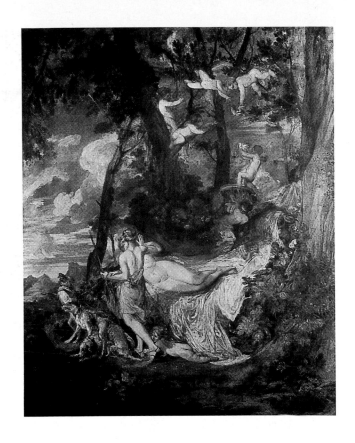

*Seated nude.* Pencil and watercolour, *c.* 1804. 'Academies' sketchbook, TB LXXXIV. Turner Bequest, Tate Gallery, London.

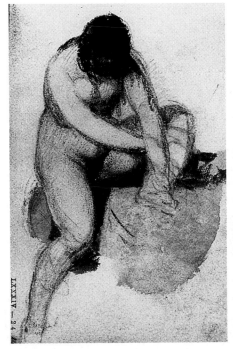

*Writing serpent with figure.* Pencil, *c.* 1810. 'Windmill and Lock' sketchbook, TB CXIV. Turner Bequest, Tate Gallery, London.

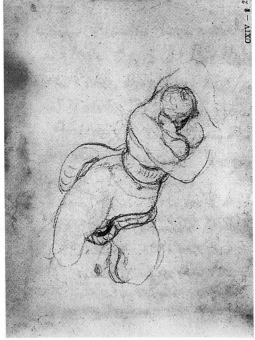

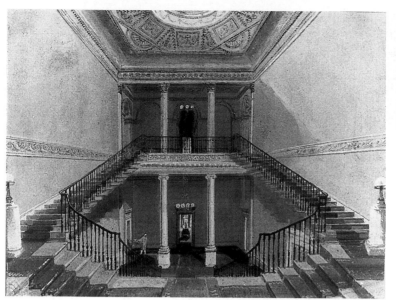

*The Staircase, Farnley Hall.* Watercolour, *c.* 1818. Private collection: photograph Courtauld Institute of Art, London.

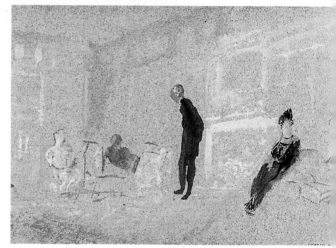

*The Vicar on the Hearthrug, Petworth.* Watercolour, 1830s. TB CCXLIV. Turner Bequest, Tate Gallery, London.

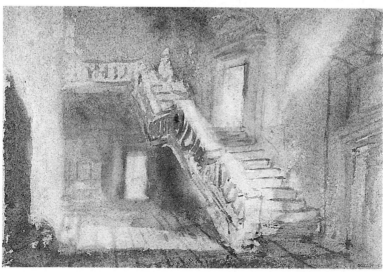

*The Old Library Staircase, Petworth.* Watercolour, 1830s. TB CCXLIV. Turner Bequest, Tate Gallery, London.

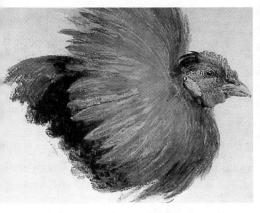

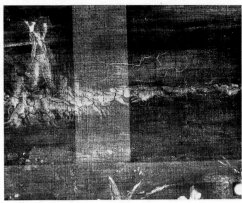

*Head of a Gamecock.* Pencil and watercolour, *c.* 1818. Leeds Museums and Galleries (City Art Gallery).

X-ray detail from *Raby Castle.* Oil on canvas, 1818. The Walters Art Gallery, Baltimore.

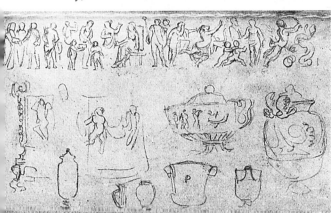

(Left) *Details drawn in the Vatican.* Pencil, 1819. 'Vatican Fragments' sketchbook, TB CLXXX. Turner Bequest, Tate Gallery, London.

(Below left) *Reference sketches of Italian sites, drawn from engravings.* Pen and ink, 1819. 'Italian Guide Book', TB CLXXII. Turner Bequest, Tate Gallery, London.

(Below) *Unsteady drawings made in a moving coach.* Pencil, 1828. 'Marseilles to Genoa' sketchbook, TB CCXXXI. Turner Bequest, Tate Gallery, London.

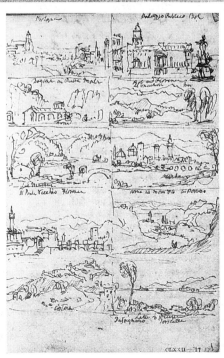

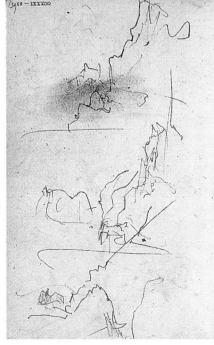

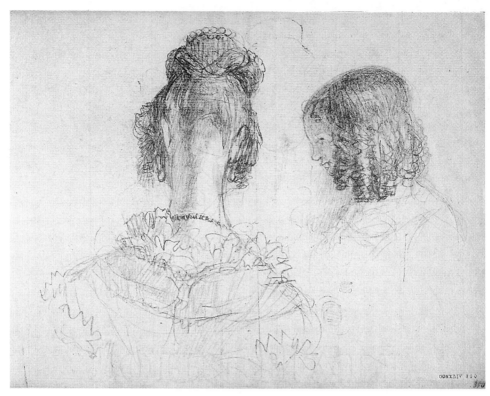

*Coiffures.* Pencil, *c.* 1827–35. TB CCCLXIV-350. Turner Bequest, Tate Gallery, London.

*Lovers.* Watercolour, 1830s. 'Colour Studies 1' sketchbook, TB CCXCIb. Turner Bequest, Tate Gallery, London.

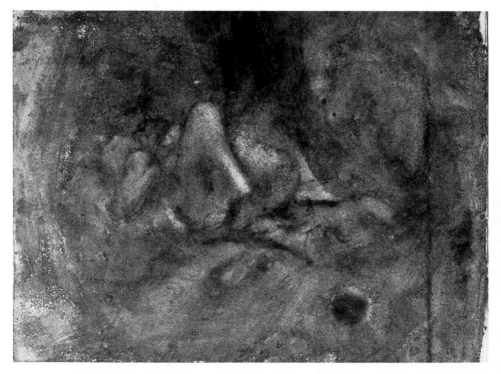

Fawkes developed his 15,000 acres of Wharfedale in a manner which showed benevolence and understanding for the needs of his tenants, and a methodical approach to the husbanding of his land. He was a co-founder of the Otley Agricultural Society, an organisation which aimed to bring local farmers together in a drive to increase efficiency of land use and production. He was a successful breeder of shorthorn cattle, which after the Napoleonic Wars carried his reputation into Europe, and his work as an amateur zoo keeper led him to introduce zebra on his land.[20] For his part, Egremont's breed of Sussex cattle had, by 1798, reached a quality that the agriculturalist William Marshall believed had set a standard for the country to look up to "for the point of excellence".[21]

Turner's friendship with Walter Fawkes blossomed in 1808. Although he may have visited Farnley earlier, Turner's regular visits seem to have started in 1808, directly after his visit to Tabley. This was his most likely arrival date, because it followed almost immediately the removal of painters' ladders and scaffolding from the inside of the new wing of the house.

In August 1808 Fawkes settled a £200 bill for extensive interior decorations, including three coats of paint for the enormous new entrance hall, and decorative murals elsewhere.[22] We may perhaps see this as a signal, at least to Fawkes himself, that now he had done with Parliament he would concentrate his efforts on Farnley, and bring it to a pitch of perfection as the home for his large family and growing art collection. For Fawkes, the best thing about London, now, was the coach to Leeds. It is tempting to think that Turner's first visit to Farnley took place at the first convenient moment after this great springclean both of Fawkes's house and of his life. Turner will then have seen Farnley Hall at its very best, and be welcomed by Walter Fawkes as an honoured visitor and a good, firm friend.

When Turner first saw Farnley Hall the building was an exciting and invigorating collision of two totally incompatible architectural styles. The old Jacobean manor had heavily mullioned windows with long narrow leaded panes of glass, low ceilings, dark oak beams and panelling. The floorboards were wide, creaky, and the source of sudden updraughts; the levels various and puzzling with odd rooms and unexplained corners, and all crammed with miscellaneous relics of the English Civil War.

Although the view to the south over Wharfedale was – still is – glorious, expanding from east to west for miles along the track of the sun, the principal view from the manor was to the east, overlooking the stables. That was fine to catch the rising sun and to check up on the ostlers, but as a prospect it was dull. The manor was built two hundred years before any coherent thought was given in England to landscape design, and to the placing of houses for full topographical effect. Its situation was, instead, a relic of the placement of fortified castles on high ground, overlooking property for the purpose of boundary defence rather than the enjoyment of its extent. The Lascelleses of Harewood had been the Fawkeses' neighbours to the east since the sixteenth century. They were even then greater landlords than the Fawkeses, traditionally Royalist in the Civil War when the Fawkeses were Parliamentarian, and well connected to the court. The families went to law over a boundary dispute in the 1740s, in a case that dragged on for five years.[23]

In commissioning John Carr to transform the manor house, the forebear Francis Fawkes had shown himself to be a modern man. He put the old dispute behind him, and, with cool symbolism, also re-oriented his house, turning his back on the Lascelleses and their lands. In an additional piece of lucky irony, John Carr was married to a Lascelles, and came to Farnley fresh from designing Harewood House and other great houses on the York plain. Although Carr and his client were discussing the commission as early as 1774, work on the new house does not seem to have begun until 1786, the year Hawkesworth inherited. Construction was largely finished by 1790 when the final bill came in.[24]

Carr's masterstroke at Farnley is his management of the internal spaces, particularly the theatrical transition from the compressed rooms of the old manor house to the airy lightness of the new. The main entrance remained in the old house, and so, on Turner's first visit, he would have passed initially through this gloomy interior. From the staircase landing of the old house, however, he would then have entered through a dark narrow link corridor at first-floor level, suddenly, into a brightly lit, forty-five-feet-high, central hall sporting its new, fresh coat of paint. The contrast from the claustrophobic old building to the physical impact of wide lighted space is violent. Ahead, the main staircase runs away centrally downstairs and curves upstairs also to right and left within a lacelike banister. Carr places the visitor immediately on the architectural centre stage at his arrival, making him look, as does an actor in a theatre, across at the columned gallery above and at the pit below. For an artist of Turner's sensibility, architectural understanding and dramatic appreciation this must have been a magnificent and memorable arrival.

At the bottom of the grand staircase the banisters curve away gracefully until their line is swallowed up by an inlaid motif on the newel post. Ahead is the saloon. Here there will have been more theatricality laid on for Turner's arrival. Into the shadowy room he walks, making his way with his host around the furniture and past the dark bookshelves and pictures on one side and another. Fawkes opens the new shutters, which flap against each other as they fold. Immediately the light flows in from the wide, low valley of the Wharfe, like water through a sluice. From the eminence of the new house, the full extent of the valley is laid out before Turner. The further hillside, perhaps a mile away, seems near enough to touch, the details of the houses, trees and animals being clearly visible to a sharp pair of eyes on a fine day. The landscape is of a small scale, undemonstrative tenor, domestic and tamed, quite at odds with the landscapes of Scotland, Wales or Switzerland that Turner had seen over the past ten years. The one curious aspect of the view from the ground floor of Farnley Hall is that the River Wharfe, whose windings dominate the traveller's approach to Otley from Leeds, is practically invisible – there is one small flash of reflected light from the river surface down to the left, but that's about it.

Otley is a long, dark, stone town, with a main street that jerks right and left between the buildings, shaking the traveller well until he is spilled out onto the road west to Ilkley. Where Farnley Hall has a benign dominance of its surrounding landscape, in Otley, a mile away, the hills strike back. Lowering over the town from the south is the firm line of Otley Chevin, whose shadow is a constant presence in winter, and whose shoulder, in summer, leans across unpleasantly like a protection racketeer. The turning to Farnley from Otley is tight and easily missed. Pass it and after half a mile the traveller is out in the wide open lonely spaces of Blubberhouses Moor where the land falls quickly away to the west and the weather is constantly at the turbulent edge of change. In so small an area, the country around Farnley is eccentric and lively to the point of caprice.

But it was not the landscape alone, nor Farnley Hall, that attracted Turner and kept him coming back again and again. It was also the character of Walter Fawkes, whose perceptive eye, radical conversation, ease of living and expansive, generous nature, made Turner feel unreservedly welcome, and put no social pressures upon him. He could come and go as he pleased, take part in family activities or not as he chose, and paint where and what he liked.

The summer after this first encounter with Farnley, Turner had another social and architectural experience of comparable intensity and of as lasting an effect. Having invited him to paint at Cockermouth in Cumberland, Lord Egremont called Turner down to make a preliminary visit to Petworth in preparation for a proposed painting of the house and estate. Petworth, like Otley, is a small town on the edge of a long river valley. And like the Wharfe at Otley, the River Rother below Petworth also runs west to east. Here, however, the similarities end, for the approach to Petworth on the London road runs by the long estate wall, and the profile of the house with its encircling park and lake acts as a kind of shield for the town to its east. Petworth House is a part of its town, where Farnley Hall is a distant outpost.

Moving about the house, guided, let us suggest, by Egremont himself, Turner will have been taken to the Oak Hall. This modest rear entrance lies behind the long, west-facing dining-room with its faded white panelling, swags of fruit and vegetable carving by Grinling Gibbons, family portraits and a magnificent view over the park. Then up the staircase in the Oak Hall, two flights, and through a long room down a narrow corridor to a further door. Through this door, Turner and Egremont come into a high light well, the light falling gloomily even on a bright afternoon through some unseen baffle. This is another narrow space, the right-hand side being filled entirely by an enormous staircase, a curiously overlarge and overbearing feature of so constricted a space. Already, to reach this point, they have climbed fifty, sixty stairs, and must by now be quite high in the building; but in terms of orientation, the new arrival is totally confused.

They climb the stairs and Egremont opens the door at the top. As he does so, the light in the room, its concentration, its colour – all these are explosive, painful, as Turner's eyes adjust from the gloom in which he has been submerged for the previous few minutes. This is the Library, high, wide, long, every dimension in firm opposition to those of the corridors along which Turner and Egremont have just padded. And ahead an arched window fifteen feet high by nearly as many broad brings in the light from the north and east, and looks out (or did then) over a tennis court, a fountain and the soaring 140-feet-high spire of the Church of St Mary the Virgin. All around, on shelves, on tables, are books large and small, with armchairs, a sofa or two, a large fireplace and a dozen or more pictures of all sizes hung on the panelling and over the book-shelves. "You can paint in here, if you'd like," says Egremont quietly in his soft Sussex brogue.

The year before, Turner had been given open house at Farnley, with the great wide spaces of Wharfedale and the moors waiting at his pleasure. Now another rich man with a reputation for informality, hospitality and an unbridled zest for living had offered him the freedom to paint in one of the great rooms in all England on the edge of a breathtaking landscape. Apart yet at one with the house, secluded yet accessible, the Library was quiet yet never far away from a party. More, Egremont's hospitality reached out to artists in particular. He had the sense and the sensibility to see that a great art collection such as the one he had inherited needed continual re-weighting at its bottom with old master additions, as well as the evolving of lustrous new wings with a stream of works by living artists.

Thus artists were constantly in residence at Petworth. They were part of the fluid dynamic of the place, along with Egremont's own little fleet-footed creations, his flocks of illegitimate children and their put-upon mothers. Lord Blessington remarked in 1813:

Nothing will convince Lady Spenser that Lord Egremont has not forty-three Children, who all live in the House with him and their respective Mothers; [and] that the latter are usually kept in the background but when quarrels arise, which few days pass without, each mother takes part with her Progeny, bursts into the drawing room, fights with each other, Lord E., his children, and, I believe, the Company, and makes scenes worthy of Billingsgate or a Madhouse.[25]

So artists and their families could turn up at any time, make no difference to the temper of the household, and be welcomed, housed, fed and set to work. By the time of Turner's first visit to Petworth the house was hung with big Van Dycks and little Elsheimers, a Claude, countless Dutch paintings and a monster Reynolds set piece, *Macbeth and the Witches*. There were classical sculptures with broken limbs and bashed noses in niches and corridors, and in the North Gallery which Egremont had enlarged in 1794, and was to enlarge again thirty years later. Artists who were in and out of Petworth around 1809 included Turner's old friend the portrait painter Thomas Phillips, Richard Collins the miniature painter, Sir William Beechey RA and the sculptor Richard Westmacott.

This was a time of new social opportunity for Turner. He had already been given a second home at Farnley, and now there was another at Petworth had he wanted it. The chaos at Petworth, despite the presence of the laid-back Earl calm amidst the domestic storms, was in vivid contrast to the peace of Farnley and the happy Fawkes family. Had Turner said the word there is little doubt that he could have moved into Petworth from 1809 as often as he had wished. That he appears to have chosen Farnley suggests that although he had a deep seated wish to be part of it, to have all the fun yet none of the responsibility, there was a level of other people's family life that he simply could not take.

Meanwhile, the Council of the Royal Academy were beginning to wonder when Turner was going to start his lectures. They wrote to him gingerly in December 1808 asking whether he proposed to start the following month, but no reply has survived.[26] It was not until October 1809 that Turner wrote to say he would be ready to teach the following January once improvements to the seating and lighting of the lecture room at Somerset House had been completed.[27] This renewed confidence indicates that he had made more time in 1809 to read further around the subject and to continue to work on an extended series of large diagrams and perspective watercolours of buildings in London and elsewhere to illustrate his words. Turner was expected to give six lectures, each lasting about half to three-quarters of an hour to whomsoever might turn up. The primary intention of the lectures was to teach the Academy students, but anybody else could attend, provided they came with an admission ticket endorsed by a Royal Academician. Turner might have reasonably expected that his first audience would contain not only the students but most of his fellow Academicians and Associates, collectors, connoisseurs and critics, a smattering of whom would be there to report on the lectures for the press.

So it was a most important event in the winter season of the London art and literary world. Lecturers received a fee of £60 for the course of six, no mean sum, the equivalent of £500 a lecture in the 1990s, and the Academy got an influential audience from out of the drawing-rooms and coffee houses of London. While the size of the hall limited the audience to about three hundred, this was nevertheless a large proportion of the available informed audience of London.

Turner's lectures would be the first time that he had made any kind of public statement about art in his exhibiting career. A series of lectures on the dry, technical subject of Perspective by J. M. W. Turner RA, that unconventional, unpredictable artist, might conceivably produce fireworks, at least a new perspective on the subject. The Academy Professorial lecture audience were no strangers to fireworks and fury. In his series on Painting in 1798 James Barry had caused anger and hatred when he publicly condemned the Academy and its administration, and officers dead and alive, from the podium of its own lecture room. John Soane's lectures on Architecture in January 1810, a few weeks before Turner's were due to begin, caused yet more uproar, so it was a disappointment, mixed in some quarters perhaps with a temporary relief, when Turner asked for more time, another year to prepare.

The time that Turner might have been spending on the preparation of lectures he had in fact spent painting. In 1809 he had shown sixteen new works at the Turner Gallery and three at the Academy. Those shown at his own gallery included two grand paintings with exquisitely managed aerial perspectives. *London* is the view from above Greenwich Hospital looking west, and *Thomson's Aeolian Harp* is a classical landscape based on the view from Richmond Hill looking west up the river valley. These were classic statements, among the great performances of Turner's art, and immediately recognised to be so. "A masterly exemplification", wrote Robert Hunt of *Thomson's Aeolian Harp* in the *Examiner*.[28] To his signature on *London* Turner added the letters "PP", for "Professor of Perspective", as if to say, "Here you have it; this is how to do it."

Of the three paintings shown at the Academy in 1809, the two views of Tabley commissioned by Sir John Leicester held within them a subtle example of the perspective trickery and skill of which Turner had long been a master. The middle ground of both is dominated by Tabley's castellated water tower on an artificial island in the lake. Turner has shown how a small change of viewpoint, a step or two to the left or right, can make a distant object – here Tabley House itself – jump about the horizon as if on legs. This curious phenomenon of perspective, as well known to carriage travellers in the nineteenth century as to car drivers in the twentieth when observing a distant landmark from a winding road, had never before been demonstrated so clearly or so wittily in painting. Without uttering a word in public, the Professor of Perspective had already by the late spring of 1809 given ample evidence of means to solve perspectival problems to anybody who cared to look.

The series of notebooks surviving from this period reveal the cross-currents flowing about in Turner's mind during the preparation years. While writing extended notes about perspective and bits of art history in the red morocco leather notebook known now as the ''Perspective'' sketchbook,[29] he also composed long ruminative poetry and explicit erotic verse. This tiny notebook, less than pocket sized at 3½ by 4½ inches, is buzzing with Turner's own and other people's ideas, with partly formed proposals in muddled syntax discussing the differing expressive opportunities of poets and painters.

Despite his difficulties with the written word, he persevered, turning with some palpable relief from prose to verse, nearly three hundred lines of which are in this one small book alone. From the evidence of the occasional pencil sketches of boats and figures, Turner was sitting on a river bank as he wrote, with his fishing rod beside him:

> Below the Summer Hours they pass
> The water gliding clear as Glass
> The finny race escapes my line
> No float or slender thread entwine.[30]

There is ruminative verse touching upon the nature of labour, creativity and patriotism:

> Must toiling Man for ever meet disgrace
> And eat his hard earn'd bread with heated face
> And all his acts in dull Oblivion lay
> And not with honor pluck one little spray
> Of Fame's famed laurel, while in brass
> Some work their honors some in Glass
> Some paint some chisel out the stone
> And pray to Clio for melodious tones
> Some dare the restless billows to provoke
> And float secure to fame in British Oak ...[31]

... and so on. One of Turner's great problems with his verse is to know when, indeed how, to stop. It churns on in wave after relentless wave, sticking more or less to the chosen metre but slipping in and out of meaning, the author being quite unable by all appearances to find the brake.

All this intellectualising and social concern must needs have had relief, and this came through sex. In the first decade of the 1800s he made the one sheet of pornographic drawings that survives outside his sketchbooks.[32] The two drawings are coldly businesslike, with emphasis on practice rather than pleasure. This sheet should be seen in context with other female nude studies by Turner, some of which are clearly academic exercises, while others are much more intimate, even erotic, charming and evidently drawn in private. It is possible that Sarah Danby was the model for some of these.[33]

Sex had become a central diversion from Turner's work on perspective, and he expressed it also in verse. A poem which seems to have pleased him greatly settles at the end of the "Perspective" sketchbook, putting a soft human perspective onto his granite thoughts. The first draft of this six verse poem, *Molly*, is followed immediately by a fair copy:

> Be still my dear Molly be still
> No more urge that soft sigh to a will
> Which is anxious each wish to fulfill
> But I prithee Dear Molly – be still
>
> By thy lips quivering motion I ween
> To the center where love lies between
> A passport to bliss is thy will
> Yet I prithee dear Molly be still
>
> By thy Eyes when half closed in delight
> That so languishing turn from the light
> With kisses I'll hide them I will
> So I prithee dear Molly be still
>
> By thy bosom so throbbing with truth
> Its short heavings to me speaks reproof
> By the half blushing mark on each hill
> O Molly dear Molly be still
>
> For love between them takes his rest
> I am jealous of his downy nest
> My rival in his lair I'll kill
> So I prithee dear Molly lye still
>
> By the touch of thy lips sure loves band
> By the critical moment no maid can withstand
> Then a bird in the bush is worth two in the hand
> O Molly dear Molly. – I will.[34]

Who Molly was – a lover, a prostitute, a pseudonym for Sarah, or a woman of Turner's imagination – we have no way of telling. Loving women physically as he did, he was nevertheless equivocal, writing "Women is doubtful love" into one sketchbook of the period.[35] Sarah was, in 1809, living with Turner.[36] He had that year let 64 Harley Street to a dentist, Benjamin Young, and at the same time became a tenant in 44 Queen Anne Street, around the corner. This was part of a radical change in arrangements, for Turner appears to have sold the lease of a property in Norton Street by auction in August 1809 or 1810.[37]

By his own calculations, it appears that around 1810/11 Turner had about £12,000–£13,000 in hand, that is perhaps three-quarters of a million pounds in the late 1990s. He spent some of this money in April 1809 to hire a lawyer to prepare a set of complicated and detailed legal documents setting out clearly the terms of his ownership of the cottage and land at Lee Clump in Buckinghamshire that he had bought at auction over two years earlier.[38] This purchase had been no momentary whim. Why Turner should go to so much trouble over so isolated and modest a property is unclear, as are the reasons why he wanted it in the first place. Lee Clump is high on the Chiltern Ridge between Chesham and Great Missenden, difficult to get to or away from, and known then to local sheep and cattle drovers but to few others.

One explanation is that Turner bought the Lee Clump property in 1806 in a hopeful attempt to give Sarah and her daughters safe, healthy accommodation many miles away from London, well out of his way, so that he could continue with his professional and private activities unhindered by family. It was specified in the legal documents that the property was "free and clear" of Land Tax, so there are no Danby or Turner references in the relevant Land Tax records.[39] As John Danby's widow, Sarah was eligible throughout her life to allowances from the Royal Society of Musicians, provided she did not remarry or live with another man. Payments were made monthly, and while Sarah signed personally for some, the majority in the years 1810–12 were collected by deputies, including, on occasion, "William Turner".[40] Sarah stands out in this period as being almost alone as a claimant on the Society who does not sign monthly on her own behalf, suggesting that she was either ill, lazy or geographically distant. Alternatively she may have been nursing a baby, because it was possibly about this time that Sarah gave birth to her and Turner's second daughter, Georgiana. If Sarah did leave London, it cannot have been for long, for on an undated slip of paper, probably 1813–14, she gave her address as 10 Warwick Row.[41]

As Sarah prepared to move out of Harley Street, Hannah Danby, John Danby's twenty-three-year-old unmarried niece, seems to have moved in to act as Turner's housekeeper and custodian. She remained faithful to Turner for the rest of his life, cooking for him, letting in (or more often keeping out) visitors to the Gallery, and putting up with his errant comings and goings and his long absences.[42]

There were further cross-currents in Turner's activities during the years 1809–11. He took himself on walks around London to observe the scale and the substance of public buildings, and the manner in which they presented themselves to a roving pedestrian eye. His purpose was to demonstrate the way their aspects changed as a person moved about them on foot, and this led to his making more large-scale perspective studies of such buildings as Carlton House, the Monument and St George's Church, Bloomsbury to illustrate his coming lectures.

At the same time as he was looking carefully at London's new classical architecture, Turner was thinking also about architecture of his own – about constructing a house for himself and his father at Twickenham. The "Windmill and Lock" sketchbook[43] holds a mellifluous stream of linked ideas, its early pages having perspective notations for the Monument and St George's, its later ones a group of exquisite drawings and plans developing Turner's ideas for his own house. Notions of escape, which are suggested by the house sketches, the lists of building materials and prices, even the pages of accounts of money received and owing from patrons and of stock bought and sold, begin to fill yet more of his little red books.[44]

Yet other cross-currents were professional rather than personal. He had quarrelled with Charles Turner in 1808 over the latter's apparent delay in completing the prints in part III of the *Liber Studiorum*, missing opportunities to advertise them and nearly missing the opportunity to show them at Turner's Gallery before this closed for the summer in June 1808. Turner was strict with his engravers, and struck a tough deal. The engravers provided the means by which his images became more and more widespread, and although he needed the benefit of their technical skill and their workshop system, he was, he knew, unique, and they were not. The public following was for J. M. W. Turner's images, and not for any particular engraver. In a letter written in 1809 to the Oxford picture dealer James Wyatt, Turner runs ruminatively and a touch dismissively through the names of some of the London engravers:

> ... but concerning the Engraver it is a difficult thing to know who to choose, their prices are as different as their abilities, and therefore that point must remain with you. But if Mr Warren will undertake a large plate, surely his abilities may be said to [be] equal to the task, or Middiman, Lowry, Young, Byrne, or Milton [Mitan] &c.[45]

Charles Turner worked very closely with J. M. W. on the production of the first parts of the *Liber*. J. M. W.'s original expectation was that he himself would etch the outlines and pass the plate on to Charles Turner or another engraver to add the aquatint, mezzotint and further engraving as required.

In the event, as he might have known, J. M. W. did not have enough time to be so closely and practically involved in the production, so by default he found he had to delegate more and more to his engravers. Charles Turner engraved the first twenty plates, suffering as he did so the more or less continuous onslaught of his client's snappy remarks, and bitter master-servant attitude. On a proof impression of *Dunstanborough Castle* (1808) J. M. W. wrote to Charles: "Sir, You have done in aquatint all the Castle down to the rocks: Did I ever ask for such an indulgence?"[46]

A break between the two men came in 1810 when Charles Turner demanded an increase in his fee of from eight to ten guineas a plate.[47] At the same time Turner spotted a proof of *A Shipwreck* on sale in London with colouring which he claimed that he himself had not added. This brought forth the spluttering, even querulous note, written in the tones of a formal demand: "Mr Turner requests Mr C. Turner to explain through what cause the Print of the Shipwreck now in a shop in Fleet St late Macklin happens to be *coloured* when Mr C. Turner expressly agreed that none should be coloured but by J. M. W. Turner *only*."[48]

But as the clouds grew over Turner's relationship with his old friend Charles Turner, the sun came out brightly on another business relationship. While he was quickly displeased if people did not come up to his exacting standards, Turner was touchingly trusting at the beginning of a relationship. He had met the ambitious Oxford picture dealer and framer James Wyatt (1774–1853) most probably during one of the visits to Oxford in the early 1800s, when he was making his series of watercolour views in the city commissioned for the *Oxford Almanack*.

Wyatt wanted to commission another view of Oxford from Turner, which, like the *Almanack* series, would be engraved. He clearly knew exactly what kind of view he wanted; the only thing that had not been spelled out between him and Turner was size and price. The correspondence between Turner and Wyatt, though only one side of it survives, is one of the clearest expositions we have for the period between artist and commissioner, reflecting on the nuances of the relationship between the two men, and on the clear trust and understanding that the one professional had for the other. James Wyatt was no ordinary entrepreneur. He was the Curator of Pictures at Blenheim Palace, at the time when that title meant that he cleaned and repaired pictures as well as hung and listed them; and he had local political ambitions which he largely fulfilled when he became Mayor of Oxford in 1842–43.

Thanking Wyatt for the compliment of engaging him, Turner writes:

... probably you have made up your mind as to the expense of a drawing or Picture, therefore if you will mention – I then can tell you what size I can make it, for the subject is an excellent one. The sketch I have includes the entrance & part of University Coll ... with do. of All Souls, St Mary Church, All Saints, and looking up the High Street to Carfax Church, and of course may be considered a very full subject, and being chiefly buildings am inclined to think that 24 inches is rather small even for an engraving.[49]

Turner and Wyatt are clearly speaking the same language, both being brisk and kindred souls in business matters. In the correspondence that follows Turner asks very firmly to see proofs of the prospectus with which he expects Wyatt to advertise the proposed engraving, and to make it clear that the painting would not be as big as the frame Wyatt has in mind, but would instead be of Turner's standard size for this kind of thing, three feet by four, at 200 guineas – or 100 guineas for half size.[50] Turner gave his advice on engravers, and then more advice, very gently but firmly from his own hard-won experience, on how to handle the publicity, how to woo the customer and how to treat the engraver:

> ... you should by all means particularize how many *proofs* you intend to take off, and at what price, for the public like to have more than assurances: they now want particulars, and which leads me to hope that you will be very particular about mentioning Mr Middiman's name, for to insert it in the prospectus without being *sure* of his co-operation would marr your endeavour in the eye of the public: for the least deviation from a proposal renders all subscriptions void.[51]

A few days after Christmas 1809 Turner travelled to Oxford to do a detailed study for the painting, which by mid-March was finished.[52] During the course of the correspondence with Wyatt, Turner asks to be supplied with details of Oxford academic dress, and should the Bishop crossing the road be wearing a cap? And what kind of staffs do the Beadles carry, and do they wear caps?[53] The precision with which Turner approaches the task in hand encompasses both contractual as well as matters of local visual detail.[54] The businessman in him respects the hopes and intentions of the businessman Wyatt, and in further letters he ties up final details.[55]

Like Turner's *London* and the Tabley paintings of 1809, his *View of the High Street, Oxford* for Wyatt, exhibited in his own gallery in 1810, was yet another suggestive and confident example of his presenting to the public his manifest skill in perspective. It is a magnificent piece of work, in which the curve of the High Street adds spice to the already intricate perspective plan. Only Canaletto, or the seventeenth-century Dutch painters Peter Sandraedam or Gerrit Berckheyde, had the same confidence to create such satisfying pictorial records of architecture and its relationship with the lives that go on within it.

In one letter to Wyatt Turner reveals, in passing in a postscript, that he is "now so very busy".[56] April always was the busiest month of his year, when the opening of the Royal Academy exhibition and the exhibition in his own gallery were upon him. This year, additionally, he was finishing one of the most spectacular paintings he had ever made, and preparing it for transport. *Wreck of a Transport Ship* was bought, most probably by May 1810, by Charles Pelham of Brocklesby Park, Lincolnshire, whose father Lord Yarborough had six years earlier bought *Opening of the Vintage of Macon*. There is precious little literature on this work, primarily because it was not exhibited publicly until 1849. Hanging now in Lisbon, it remains, for the English-speaking world, perhaps the least known Turner of its period. Its spectators in the nineteenth century were comparatively few and from a limited circle; after some years at Brocklesby Park the painting went to the Yarborough mansion Appledurcombe in the Isle of Wight. There is a progression of fervour and hopelessness in Turner's sea disasters, starting with *Calais Pier* (1803) and continuing with *Shipwreck* (1805). *Wreck of a Transport Ship* holds up the ultimate in maritime terror of its spectators. "No ship or boat could live in such a sea," reflected an old Admiral on seeing the picture in Edinburgh in 1851.[57] In Turner's two previous maritime storm paintings, the horizon creeps gradually up the canvas – in *Calais Pier* it is moderately low; in *Shipwreck* it is just over halfway up, giving the spectator little air, though he does just about have the benefit of lurching on the crest of the rising right-hand wave. In the 1810 painting there is no such shred of comfort. The horizon is practically unidentifiable, though there may be a rock or spit of land visible in the background. The cataclysm that Turner has painted is illimitable, the spectator being in the cold boiling sea, about to be swamped from right and left. In size, the three shipwrecks are practically identical – at about 5 feet 8 inches by 8 feet each there is only a fraction of an inch between them. This too suggests that they were seen in Turner's mind at least as a series, one leading on to another, and although two were bought from the studio by aristocratic patrons, none had been commissioned.

Evidently, they were rooted in internal concerns. Butlin and Joll have suggested that *Shipwreck* was prompted by the re-publication in 1804 of William Falconer's poem "The Shipwreck", with illustrations by Nicholas Pocock.[58] Falconer was himself a sailor and wrote with the eye of one who had seen all that the sea could throw at a ship and its sailors:

> Again she plunges! hark! a second shock
> Tears her strong bottom on the marble rock;
> Down on the vale of Death, with dismal cries,
> The fated victims, shuddering, roll their eyes

In wild despair; while yet another stroke,
With deep convulsion, rends the solid oak:
Till like the mine, in whose infernal cell
The lurking demons of destruction dwell,
At length asunder torn, her frame divides,
And crashing spreads in ruin o'er the tides.

Verse of this kind had a particular appeal to Turner, not only through its terrifying imagery but also in the swelling rhythms of the iambic pentameter. This was the metre of Thomson's *Seasons*, and the metre that Turner himself struggled with in his own poetry:

Thou bids the sailor hoist the pliant sail
That struggling flies beneath the rising gale

. . .

When the furious North and E Winds prevail
And kindest thoughts to stay him aught avail
In harsher accents all the storm defies
Alike to him the danger and the prize ...[59]

The magnitude of *Wreck of a Transport Ship*, its ambitious scale and subject matter suggests too that it was on the stocks in Turner's studio for some time. Cataclysm was much in Turner's mind in early 1810, for in late April he hung his *Fall of an Avalanche in the Grisons* in his gallery for all to see. There is a passage in Thomson's *Winter* describing an avalanche in the Swiss canton of Grisons, and although Turner knew it well his painting was accompanied in the leaflet catalogue of the 1810 exhibition with eight lines of his own resonant verse. These were early lines from the rolling epic poem which Turner was later to refer to in print as his manuscript poem "Fallacies of Hope".[60] Perhaps all his verse had been tending towards this end, and although it rolled on through the years, "Fallacies of Hope" was never completed, still less edited into a coherent whole. Instead it flashed out of him in occasional fragmented public utterances, being published only in couplets in exhibition catalogues until the year before he died.

Turner's *Fall of an Avalanche* is a trenchant disavowal of hope of any kind, as are his eight published lines:

The downward sun a parting sadness gleams,
Portentous lurid thro' the gathering storm;
Thick drifting snow on snow,
Till the vast weight bursts thro' the rocky barrier;
Down at once, its pine clad forests,

And towering glaciers fall, the work of ages
Crashing through all! extinction follows,
And the toil, the hope of man – o'erwhelms.

There had been a terrible avalanche in the Grisons in December 1808, during which twenty-five people had been crushed in one cottage.[61] This may have prompted Turner to paint the subject, but nearer home, political and natural events were brewing that had an immediate bearing on every Briton. Since 1807 harvests all over the country had suffered heavily from disastrous weather. In 1807 itself much of the harvest in the north of England and Scotland was destroyed by a harsh September frost. The following year heavy thunderstorms in July and August damaged crops, and in 1809 heavy rains began throughout the country in July and carried on until October. From 1807 to 1810 the price of wheat rose from 75s 4d to 106s 5d a quarter, increasing the price of bread and fomenting discontent throughout the country.[62] This dismal state of affairs was underscored by the continuing Napoleonic Wars, the British army being bogged down in northern Spain, and forced to retreat in 1809 to Corunna where Sir John Moore was killed.

Hope was a scarce commodity in 1810. It was scarce in Windsor Castle, where George III was entering his second, prolonged phase of madness, and the possibility of a permanent Regency was rapidly becoming real. It was scarce out in the country, where spring that year was late and cold, and the hay and wheat crops came in poor, undernourished and damaged. Country people suffered again from the scourge of sheep rot, an infestation of worm in the sheep's liver, which led to the widespread destruction of flocks. Hope was scarce too in the discontented manufacturing towns, which depended on good supplies of bread and meat.

Over the roofs of London hung a perpetual cloud of poisonous smoke clearly indicated in Turner's painting *London*. The painter Benjamin Robert Haydon remembered how the first smell of the London smoke in 1808 had, perversely, delighted him:

So far from the smoke of London being offensive to me, it has always been to my imagination the sublime canopy that shrouds the City of the World. Drifted by the wind or hanging in gloomy grandeur over the vastness of our Babylon, the sight of it always filled my mind with feelings of energy such as no other spectacle could inspire.[63]

Beneath the canopy of smoke, London in 1810 was a city on the brink of insurrection. Only a few days before the Royal Academy exhibition opened at the end of April, there were riots in the streets in support of Sir Francis Burdett MP, who had courted arrest by publicly attacking the conduct of the House of Commons, and preaching reform. Troops took up positions in Piccadilly, and charged the mob there and in Sackville Street. They formed up in Green Park, and pinned the rioters down by positioning artillery in Soho Square to the east and Berkeley Square to the west. The Riot Act was read and after two days and nights of violence, window smashing and house burning, Burdett was carted off to the Tower.[64]

One of Burdett's close political associates was Walter Fawkes, and Turner's sympathies too were with Burdett. Both during and after his brief parliamentary career Fawkes committed himself with Burdett to parliamentary reform. He was named as a steward at a meeting of the Friends of Parliamentary Reform in March 1809,[65] at which Burdett spoke as a prelude to a passionate speech on the subject in the House of Commons the following June. So staunch was Fawkes's loyalty to Burdett and to reform that on the 1812 anniversary of Burdett's election Fawkes delivered his own speech on the subject at the haunt of radicals, the Crown and Anchor tavern in the Strand, and subsequently published it.

Fawkes's speech outlined the reformers' basic demands – a King "armed with every prerogative necessary to conduct the affairs of the Country, with energy and promptitude; but ... strictly limited by the laws", a House of Lords "to protect the Crown against the People, should faction ever prevail; to protect the People against the Crown, should timidity or subserviency ever sway the votes of their elected Representatives", and a House of Commons "composed of Members fairly, and really and honestly chosen by the People themselves, and thus with the People feelingly sympathising in the enactment of every law, the grant of every supply, the removal of every grievance, and the correction of every abuse".[66]

These lucid phrases, with their falling cadences and assertions through repetition, show Fawkes to have been a natural writer and orator. His handling in this speech of the three key points of reform prefigures the style of two great orators to come, John F. Kennedy and Martin Luther King. Fawkes's affection for Burdett extended to his displaying an over-lifesize bust of his friend by Sir Francis Chantrey in his drawing-room, with the inscription "Sacred to Public Principle and Private Friendship".[67]

Turner's oratory was of a different kind. Stumbling and indecisive though he may have been in his speech and his poetry, with his brush his eloquence was unbounded. *Fall of an Avalanche in the Grisons*, a distant and exotic subject, depicting an impossible enough event for Britain, is nevertheless a profound reflection on the physical effects on human endeavour of political and social forces run out of control. We might take the painting at its face value were it not for Turner's accompanying lines: "... Extinction follows, and the toil, the hope of man – o'erwhelms." He knew at least two recent paintings of avalanches, both by de Louther-bourg and both in the collections of patrons, Lord Egremont and Sir John

Leicester. Neither of these precursors, however, confronts the profound shock of two giant flying rocks so impersonally destroying a mountain cottage and splintering a fir-forest to matchwood. And more, the hemmed in, claustrophobic quality in the painting is quite new in Turner. "Not in his usual style, but [it] is not less excellent", wrote a puzzled correspondent to the *Sun* of this picture when exhibited in Turner's Gallery. The energetically gestural knife-work in the passages of falling snow against a grey storm is also unlike any in Turner's previous paintings, much more prominent indeed than the area of spray and spume applied with a palette knife in *The Fall of the Rhine at Schaffhausen* of 1806.

If in *Fall of an Avalanche* Turner is painting his fears, he is doing so as an advocate for the nation rather than for himself. His own life, now, was in the ascendant – he had plenty of money, he had in his father a willing, hero-worshipping assistant to do his bidding in the studio, he had status and a public following, he was designing a house of his own away from the smoke on the river bank, he had his own gallery in a fashionable part of London, and he was Professor of Perspective at the Royal Academy.

Between the closing of his Gallery for the summer on 9th June 1810 and his visit to Farnley that year, Turner travelled south to Rosehill Park, Brightling, Sussex to attend a new patron, a politician of an entirely different kidney to Fawkes, the Tory MP John Fuller. "Mad Jack" Fuller was the heir to a fortune amassed by forebears who had been plantation owners in Jamaica and ironfounders in Sussex. His interests, however, were scientific and cultural. He was a founder of the Royal Institution, and on his Sussex estates built follies and an observatory which he filled with astronomical instruments. Fuller had bought *Hastings – Fish Market* from Turner's Gallery that year, and commissioned the artist to paint the landscape around Rosehill in oil and watercolour. Being near at hand, Turner made notes on the same trip for a painting of another country house, Somer Hill, near Tonbridge, the home of Major W. F. Woodgate. Both houses and their landscapes became the subject of paintings, *Somer Hill*, never in the event bought by Woodgate, being exhibited at the Royal Academy in 1811.

Turner was now able to slip around the country from great house to great house with comparative ease. But Farnley Hall was his second home, and by August he was there with Walter Fawkes and his family. Farnley Hall was big, but so, in 1810, was the Fawkes family. Though the oldest children, Walter and Francis Hawkesworth, were fifteen and thirteen, Walter was away at school and "Hawkey" was over-run by sisters – Maria, twelve; Amelia, eleven; Frances Elizabeth, nine; Anne, eight; Harriet Esther, six; Charlotte, three; and younger brothers, Ayscough, five; and Richard, one. Their mother, Maria, was five years younger than their father, and, like him, came from a deep-rooted Yorkshire family, the

Grimstons of Neswick. The Fawkeses lived well and gave and entertained generously, to the very limit of their resources.

Young Walter went to school possibly at Iver, Buckinghamshire, while the younger children were taught at home by governesses and tutors.[68] A tax return for 1802 shows that Fawkes kept fourteen male servants, to which we may add at least the same number of female servants plus gardeners and stablemen, and staff at the London house in Grosvenor Place. In addition there were two four-wheeled and two two-wheeled carriages to maintain, with sixteen horses for riding, nine other horses and fifteen dogs to keep.[69]

All this was a considerable drain on Fawkes's resources, as was his penchant for keeping zebra, wild hogs and deer at Caley Hall across the valley. His support as a regular and generous patron of Turner was a further financial burden that was increasingly becoming too much for him. The fruits of Walter's natural kindness, his relaxed business sense and the heavy expenses he had incurred as an active politician, came to a head fourteen years later when he narrowly avoided bankruptcy.

However, during the 1810s Farnley Hall appeared to be a happy, active household, with shooting parties going off for the day on the moors, fishing parties to the Wharfe, jaunts into the country or to Otley and Leeds by carriage, expeditions to find birds' eggs and feathers for the family collection, and much gardening and potting of plants. There were dinner parties for local and visiting gentry, many of whom were caricatured by Hawkesworth in an album of watercolour portraits of visitors to Farnley and family staff. Turner was one of the caricature subjects, and took part in family events with enthusiasm, as he did with the Trimmer and Wells children. He drove a carriage rather recklessly and one day turned it over – leading to his earlier nickname in the London press being repeated in Yorkshire – "overturner". He showed the children how to paint in watercolour, until they annoyed him, and was no doubt aware that they peeped into the upstairs room with its easterly view to see how he strung up a kind of washing line with "papers tinted with pink and blue and yellow hanging on them to dry". Turner was always relaxed with children, perhaps because they put no social burden on him, and accepted his graceless manner and rough way of speaking. Some of the girls seemed to be afraid of him: "Go away you little baggages!" he said when they came across him working in the grounds. One girl was terrified when a sister teased her by saying that she might have to marry the ugly old man. But to a Fawkes daughter who asked Turner for his advice he gave it direct: "The only secret I have got is damned hard work."[70]

Of all the Fawkes children, Turner seems to have made a special bond with Hawkesworth. No doubt the armies of sisters forced Hawkesworth to be apart and seek other company, which the stocky, fascinating, dare-devil visiting friend and artist amply supplied. If this is the case, it was the beginning of a friendship that was to last, through meetings, correspondence and the annual Christmas present of a Farnley goose pie, to the day of Turner's death over forty years later.

Paintings by Turner had one by one come into Farnley during the course of Hawkesworth's upbringing. When he was four or five, the first Turner watercolours came; when he was nine or ten *Portrait of the Victory in Three Positions* dropped her anchor on the wall of the Farnley drawing-room; a couple of years later a small version of *The Sun rising through Vapour* arrived, and, perhaps at the time of Turner's 1810 visit, his great *London* came up to Farnley. Hawkesworth was not to know (yet) that his father could barely afford these luxuries.

In the presence of the Civil War relics at Farnley, Fawkes and Turner undoubtedly discussed reform, the Napoleonic War and Fawkes's publications, his speech-making and other political activities. Fawkes's *Chronology of Modern Europe* touched on Napoleon, and it was but a short imaginative step for men with classical interests and intuitive intelligence to see parallels between the long struggle of Britain and France, and the classical struggle of Rome and Carthage, with the great journey of Hannibal, his army and his elephants across the Alps as the heroic centrepiece of the story.

These thoughts were surely in Turner's mind as he looked out over Wharfedale, went walking, fishing and sketching. The weather in Wharfedale has sudden spasms of summer storm and thunder interspersed with sun. It was during one of these passing storms that Turner, looking out of the window, called Hawkesworth to him. Hawkesworth later told the story to Thornbury:

> All this time he was making notes of its form and colour on the back of a letter. I proposed some drawing block, but he said it did very well. He was absorbed – he was entranced. There was a storm rolling and sweeping and shafting out its lightning over the Yorkshire hills. Presently the storm passed, and he finished. "There," he said, "Hawkey; in two years you will see this again, and call it Hannibal Crossing the Alps."[71]

# SIX

# "The difficulty great..."

1811–1812

Turner climbed the rostrum in the Great Room of Somerset House, to give his first public lecture at eight o'clock on Monday 7th January 1811.[1] He had the memory of Sir Joshua Reynolds at the forefront of his mind. With some of his large perspective diagrams displayed around him, and more ready to be pinned up by a porter when he gave the nod, he will have felt prepared and at home; but he could never have been entirely at ease with his diction and with his abilities as a public speaker. He was no Walter Fawkes, whose plain spoken, honest oratory had swayed meetings of mill and iron workers in Yorkshire during the 1806 election campaign.

During their long conversations in the years of preparation for the lectures, Turner must have sought Walter Fawkes's advice about delivery. The older man had been speaking in public for years; the younger was characteristically tongue-tied, even when trying to put words onto paper, and had the coarse accent of the London streets. The first lecture, in which Turner introduced the subject of perspective and geometry, began with orotund phrases in praise of Sir Joshua, which smack of the style of Fawkes: "Sir Joshua left to future art a volume rich, full and inexhaustible; emblazoned by the powerful imagery of his own works and clasped with the strongest tie he could leave: his advice. But it is the lot of all to follow, and mine is a humble one."

That Turner had been thinking, talking and reading for a year or two about his delivery is made clear by long notes about phrasing and style written in the "Derbyshire" sketchbook. "In discourses that are to be spoken, regard must be had to the easiness of pronunciation. Example of Style Periodique – viz several sentences linked together the sense only given at the close. Sir Wm Temple."[2] He read about style and clarity of writing, his notes clearly demonstrating how valiantly he tried to get both his written and his spoken style into some kind of order. From Hugh Blair's *Lectures on Rhetoric and Belles Lettres* (1784) Turner noted:

> Perspicuity in writing is not to be considered as merely a sort of negative virtue, or freedom from defect. It has higher merit. It is a degree of positive Beauty. We are pleased with an author, we consider him as deserving praise, who frees us from all fatigue of researching for his meaning; who carries us through his subject without any embarrassment or confusion, where we see to the very bottom.[3]

With the help of his wide reading, and with the example of Walter Fawkes before him, Turner addressed his audience, which included the President of the Academy, Benjamin West, Academicians and students. Turner's father was certainly there, and perhaps Walter Fawkes himself. The lectures continued for six weeks, on six successive Monday evenings. Turner gently eased his students into the subject, the first lecture being an examination of the importance of perspective and geometry to the artist: why they had to work hard at it, and how it would give them the essential foundation for success in their chosen profession. The central four lectures Turner outlined as:

2. Vision. Subdivision of the elements and forms of perspective. Parallel perspective. The cube by the Old Masters.
3. Angular perspective. The circle, [?column]. The difficulties attending the circle. The impropriety of parallel explained.
4. Aerial perspective. Light, shade and colour.
5. Reflexes, reflections and colour.

The final lecture, "Backgrounds: Introduction of Architecture and Landscape", barely touched on perspective itself, but looked at the importance of what went on in a painting beyond the main foreground figure.[4]

Turner was only too aware of the complex nature of the subject he was trying to teach, aware too that it had been set about for centuries with complicated and contradictory rules which, depending on the attitude of the teacher, could be deployed either to enliven the subject or to suck the joy right out of it. He admitted that perspective could be an "arduous ... trite, complex [and] indefinite" subject, and that it was "trammelled with the turgid and too often repelling recurrence of mechanical rules".[5] Having been a student of perspective himself fifteen years earlier, Turner will have had his share of boredom and of the mystification of the subject by unsatisfactory teachers, to balance the extreme excitement of discovering its beauties and putting them into action for himself. Turner was with the Italian fifteen-century painter Uccello, who would exclaim to his wife with delight: "What a sweet thing perspective is!"

Turner concluded his final lecture with encouraging words to young students, in full understanding of the difficulties they faced. The patriotism which ran through him indelibly like the veins in marble, and which coloured every attitude he took, emerged also in this context:

> To you, therefore, young gentlemen, must the nation look for the further advancement of the profession. All that have toiled up the steep ascent have left in their advancement footsteps of value to succeeding assailants. You will mark them as positions or beacons in your course. To you, therefore, this institution offers its instructions and consigns their efforts, looking forward with the hope that ultimately the joint endeavours of concording abilities will, in pursuit of all that is meritorious, irrevocably fix the united standard of the arts in the British Empire.[6]

These words – getting them right – had preoccupied Turner for some time. There is an early draft of them in the "Windmill and Lock" sketchbook.[7] Turner's efforts to express clearly what he truly wanted to say demonstrates his concern to give the students as much encouragement as he possibly could, because he knew well that they all faced enormous difficulties ahead. The press, after the first lecture at least, was kind when reviewing Turner's performance. John Taylor, writing in the *Sun*, outlined his approach "which was rather introductory than technical", adding "the lecture was written throughout in a nervous and elegant style and was delivered with unaffected modesty."[8] Others were not so openly generous to the new lecturer, putting their fingers on Turner's weaknesses. John Landseer told Farington that Turner "read too fast",[9] while after the second lecture Charles Rossi said that Turner spoke "with much hesitation and difficulty".[10]

Academy student audiences were used to mumbling speakers – Reynolds seems to have been almost inaudible; Benjamin West's American accent, not to say his generally incapable diction, was exasperating, to the extent that George III – who loathed him anyway – laughed about his pronunciation of "Hackademy"; and John Soane was said by Farington's doctor to have been "the worst reader he had ever heard".[11] Some years later William Frith suggested Turner had a stammer,[12] and although he seems to have been hesitant in the way he delivered his words, repeating phrases, pausing and generally um-ing and err-ing, he does not appear to have become repetitively stuck. C. R. Leslie described his voice as "deep and musical".[13]

Turner was excessively uncomfortable in front of his audience. He would address the notes in front of him, or talk to the porter, rather than face the people who had come to listen. He muttered directions to the porter – "Next illustration please; no, not that one, *that* one ..." – breaking off as the man shuffled about amongst the rolls of drawings to find the one that Turner wanted.[14] The perspective drawings displayed as illustrations were entrancing, and the audiences quickly came to expect great visual pleasure. One student, Richard Redgrave, recalled gratefully:

> Many of these were truly beautiful, speaking intelligibly enough to the eye, if his language did not to the ear. As illustrations of aerial perspective and the perspective of colour, many of his rarest drawings were at these lectures placed before the students in all the glory of their first unfaded freshness. A rare treat to the eye they were.[15]

The lectures generally seem to have lasted for about half an hour, quite long enough for any audience to sit through such a stumbling performance before becoming restive, however well illustrated it may have been. The only blissfully happy member of the audience seems to have been the Academy Librarian, Thomas Stothard, and he was stone deaf. "Why do you go to all his lectures?" one Academician asked him. "Sir, there is so much to *see* at Turner's lectures – much that I delight in seeing, though I cannot hear him."[16]

Two independent drawings, by Thomas Cooley[17] and John Linnell, of Turner lecturing show him with downcast eyes, reading from his text. John Linnell's drawing, made during the second series of lectures in January 1812, also shows a profile of Turner's father who was sitting near Linnell in the audience.

Turner was now preoccupied with other activities, far beyond lecturing, which affected his business and reputation. His *Liber Studiorum* was reaching part seven; by 1st June 1811 thirty-six subjects had been published. Since his quarrel with Charles, J. M. W. Turner was publishing and selling the *Liber* plates himself from his own address, and trying with great difficulty to maintain a tight control over the project and its management. There is a pencilled note in a sketchbook of 1813/14 that shows the kind of detail which he had to attend to himself as a result of his own actions: "Sir W. Pilkington Bart. 1 Number of the Coast – 18s. Has no 1 and 3 of Liber Studiorum, the rest to be sent."[18] Turner's control over the *Liber Studiorum* was so complete that the business suffocated itself, and caused the financial failure of the project – five thousand unsold *Liber* prints were discovered in Turner's studio after his death.

Nevertheless, Turner's determination to have his works circulated widely remained. In the early summer of 1811 he was preparing to set off for the West Country under a new contract to John Murray and William and George Cooke to begin making an extended series of watercolours for publication as engravings. This unabated enthusiasm for publication was bolstered by a change in technique. The *Liber Studiorum* prints had been a mixture of etching and mezzotint, but the new series was to be made in the tougher medium of line engraving. *Liber* prints have a characteristic soft warmth; in a line engraving on the other hand the image is tighter, with a harder edge and a glint to it. Line engravings were much clearer, and yielded more impressions than etchings and mezzotints, because the plate lasted longer.

This self-imposed involvement with engravers and publishers, over and above his painting commitments, came at the same time as Turner chose to bring builders in to alter his gallery, and give it a new entrance in Queen Anne Street. He referred obliquely to the chaos in an undated letter to James Wyatt of May or June 1811: "... I must request you to let me call upon you, for really I am so surround[ed] with rubbish and paint that I have not at present a room free."[19] Until these alterations took place, admission to the Gallery still ran through 64 Harley Street, which Benjamin Young now occupied. This arrangement led to growing inconvenience for everybody, and to friction between Turner and the tenant.

Over at Twickenham, the land called "Sand pit Close" was coming to the end of its fallow period.[20] From evidence in other sketchbooks,[21] Turner was still developing ideas for the basic outline of the house in early 1812, so it is unlikely that construction began much before this. It was completed by July 1813 when rates were first charged. The first appearance of the address in Turner's professional record is in the 1813 Royal Academy exhibition catalogue where Turner gave it as "Solus Lodge, Twickenham". This has always been taken to be some kind of private joke, suggesting that he built the house because he wanted to be alone. That is as may be; but the fact remains that he was not alone there, he entertained quite liberally, and of course lived there with his father. He fitted heavy iron bars, some of which are still in place, to all the windows against burglars, as if he feared he might not be alone there enough.

Had he wanted to be alone, Turner would not have chosen Twickenham. Since the seventeenth century Twickenham had been the airy and accommodating small country town that the rich, famous and artistically inclined moved in upon. It had the gentle wooded hill forms and soft-flowing river of a para-classical landscape, and if they imagined hard enough and the weather was right residents could pretend they were living within a landscape created by Claude or Poussin. Curious and accomplished people had been residents there for decades: Sir Godfrey Kneller lived in Twickenham from about 1700 until his death in 1723; Lady Mary Wortley Montague had lived there; Horace Walpole built Strawberry

Hill overlooking the river; and Alexander Pope had built his villa there also. Louis-Philippe, later to be King of the French, rented High Shot House, Crown Lane – parallel to what is now Sandycombe Road – from 1800 to 1808, and in his second exile returned to live at Orleans House from 1815 to 1817. Nearby lived well-rooted indigenous aristocracy – the Duke of Northumberland at Syon House, Lord Burlington at Chiswick, the Earl of Jersey at Osterley, and the Prince Regent lived over the river at Kew. Turner chose to live in fashionable places, and Twickenham in the 1810s was the place to be.

Turner's house is set on slightly rising ground above the river, which curves around the site at about half a mile's distance. Even in the late 1990s, with the entire eastern prospect fully developed, it is clear that Turner could never have had a view of the Thames, so that cannot have been the reason he chose the site. By the evidence of Turner's own hand, in *England: Richmond Hill on the Prince Regent's Birthday*, the area to the north of the river was in 1819 heavily wooded. If the vaguely lit line to the right of the house in Havell's watercolour, later engraved, is meant to represent the River Thames with sailing boats upon it, it was pure invention.

Solus Lodge, as it seems briefly to have been called, does, however, look practically due east, directly across to Sir Joshua Reynolds's house, The Wick, on Richmond Hill, and towards the former home of James Thomson in Kew Road. From his large first-floor bedroom window Turner would see magnificent sunrises at any time of year coming up behind Sir Joshua, and his ground-floor studio will also have got the best of the morning light. The latin for the genitive case of "sun" is *solis*, a word Turner will have known even from his fractured classical knowledge. Although Turner refers to "Solus" in a letter of 1815,[22] it is nevertheless but a small typographical error from Solis to Solus. Our main evidence for Solus referring to Turner's presumed desire for solitude comes from the none-too-reliable Thornbury who wrote that the title was "bestowed, I suppose, in commemoration of its owner's desire for solitude."[23] So if Thornbury was not sure, nor need we be.

But whether Turner wished to commemorate the sun or solitude in the name of his new house, he very rapidly referred to it as Sandycombe, at least by 1814, the name it has today.[24] Sandycombe Lodge stands close to the edge of a lane, now considerably widened, pavemented, developed and adopted as Sandycombe Road. A step or two from the pavement is a wide front door, too wide, elegant and welcoming to be the entrance to any house designed for a recluse. The hall is short, neat with classical proportions, reminiscent of the architecture of John Soane who might have advised on the design.[25] It is articulated with simple incised lines which run like wrapping ribbon from the floor on one side, over the barrel vault and down to the floor on the other side. At the end of the hall is a corridor lying at right angles along the beam of the house: at one end is the dining-room, at the other what was perhaps the library or a music room. In the centre, the heart of the house, is Turner's studio, a clearly lit square room with a tall rectangular window which in 1813 looked down a roughly cultivated garden falling away to a small pond.

The house seems small, is small, but everything is neat and well made like the interior of a doll's house. This is particularly marked in the staircase up to the two bedrooms, which curves upwards within an internal well, lit from above by a clear glass oval skylight articulated with a golden florette.[26] Halfway up the stair is a round-headed niche. In its miniature state this is as classically simple a stair as one might find in a Soane house or at Pompeii, a light and refreshing means to make the journey upstairs.

Below, however, is the dark surprise of the house. Through an almost invisible door in the hall the stairway continues downstairs. This is a real cold stone cellar stair with no view of what is to come until one arrives outside the coal hole at the bottom with the scullery ahead. Where the upper rooms are high and light, the ceiling of the scullery presses downwards. The only natural light comes from a lunette window opposite. This is the same window which, seen from the garden, is set low down as if it were the entrance to a cavern. To the left of the scullery is the kitchen, equally low, equally gloomy.

The essential neatness of Turner's architecture expresses itself also in the details of the house. In the studio and dining-room are two clean-lined fireplace surrounds, one wood and one marble, the former at least having been conceived in a surviving sketchbook.[27] High up on the eastern (garden) elevation of the house are – or were, for they are now missing – a run of Grecian brick corbels proud of the surface of the stuccoed façade. These are echoed by decorative brickwork on the curved corners of the wings, and by blind pilasters flanking them. Within the hall there is a deep hidden cupboard, ideal for the neat storage of easels, paint and canvases. There is a kind of homely perfection in Sandycombe Lodge that suggests the hand of a happy, fulfilled amateur architect.

Soon after Turner acquired the land in Twickenham he painted two pictures which reflected the particular intensity of his feelings, and of his knowledge that soon he was himself to live in that river valley. One was *Thomson's Aeolian Harp* (exh. 1809), a grand canvas of the proportions of *Opening of the Vintage of Macon* showing the wide curve of the river as seen from Sir Joshua's back door on Richmond Hill, with dancing figures in the foreground. Knowing as he did when he painted the picture that he would soon be living within the scene – but out of sight, behind the central clump of trees – this is on one level a reflection of delighted anticipation. It is also a plea for the memory of Thomson, which Turner himself invoked in the thirty-two lines of his own verse which he published with the painting, a reprise of the landscapes Thomson conjures up in *The Seasons*.

The other picture painted in anticipation of Twickenham was *Pope's Villa at Twickenham* (exh. 1808). This cool landscape, which focuses on the dilapidated wreck of the villa in the background, was only one of Turner's responses to the destruction of this building. Over sixty years after Alexander Pope's death, his villa on the northern bank of the river still retained vibrant poetic echoes of his presence – his Grotto beneath the house, for example, was much visited by sight-seers, and the continuing good health of his weeping willow, supposedly the first in Britain, was of great moment to the literati.[28] The villa had passed through three hands since Pope's death in 1744, and had been much altered, until in 1807 it was bought by its fourth and final owner, Sophia Charlotte, Baroness Howe. Within the year, Baroness Howe had demolished the house and destroyed the garden, acts that caused wide resentment and fury.

The reticence of the title that Turner gave the painting, and the fact that the villa itself is distant in the picture but clearly being demolished, indicates how topical the painting was, and how well understood its meaning would be. But Turner had wider intentions. His imagery, with the rustic lovers, shepherds and sheep, fishermen and eel-pots in the foreground, and the allusion in the fallen tree-trunk to Pope's willow, suggests the cyclical nature of life, youth, maturity, age, decay and rebirth, continuing while man's creative endeavours die under the impact of fashion in the background.

This was Turner's response as a painter; and in enabling the painting to be engraved in 1811 with the yet more reticent title *Pope's Villa*, and the yet more visible scaffolding on the ruinous building, he made clear his response to a widely controversial act. John Pye's engraving marked a sea-change in the expression of Turner's attitudes. It was the first time in which his personal judgement on a place and an associated event had become engraved and thus more widely known. He was delighted with the result, saying to Pye: "This will do! you can see the lights; had I known that there was a man who could do that, I would have done it before." It was also the first engraving after Turner to be accompanied by written commentary on the image, giving further range to public understanding of his intentions. The text, which Turner himself approved in draft, was written by John Britton, the publisher of the print: "In contemplating the picture ... the mind is alternately soothed and distressed, delighted and provoked. The most pleasurable sensations are awakened by the taste and skill of the painter ..."[29]

Turner's response as a poet to the demolition of the villa was as cool as his painterly response. Despite the destruction of Pope's willow, Turner describes himself as fostering a cutting from it and optimistically nursing it to life for the future:

> ... to mark the spot with pride
> dip the long branches in the rippling tide
> And sister stream the tender plant to rear
> On Twickenham's shore Pope's memory yet to hear.[30]

Before Pope's Villa, designed by James Gibbs, had been enlarged in the 1760s, it was a four-storey central block flanked by lower three-storey side wings, with a semi-circular arch – Pope's Grotto – at the ground floor.[31] Turner's Sandycombe Lodge, which originally had similar, if lower-level features, is a neat modern variation on the original appearance of Pope's Villa. In Sandycombe Lodge Turner gave back to Twickenham an honest aftertaste of the lost flavour of Pope.

The prospect of Sandycombe will have given Turner some kind of relief from the pressures he was under in 1811 and 1812. With his greater visibility at the Royal Academy as a teacher, his business there increased. His hot-headedness of the previous decade had been entirely forgotten, and he was back again on the Academy Council. He was particularly close to Callcott, and at the meeting on 8th January 1811 the pair seconded each other's motions about turning the apartment of the recently dead Academy Secretary into more exhibition space, and proposing that as compensation the incoming Secretary should be paid a further £150 a year on top of his salary.

Over the years between Turner walking out of the Academy in 1804 and his first course of lectures as Professor in 1811, his perceived brusqueness in Academy matters had evolved into a nature that was no less combative than before, but he was combative now *on behalf of* the Academy, to protect its public reputation and to maintain the quality of its teaching. This was the beginning of the period, lasting to the end of his life, in which he saw himself as the keeper of the conscience of the Royal Academy, and the protector of its chattels. In 1823 this role was formalised in his being appointed Auditor of the Royal Academy, a post he held for twenty-two years.

With the well-being of the Academy uppermost in his mind, Turner proposed in February 1811 the motion preventing members removing from Somerset House paintings, sculptures or drawings belonging to the Academy. Hoppner's Diploma picture had long disappeared, removed probably by the artist. Turner also voted to sack his friend John Soane as Professor of Architecture, when Soane had criticised the work of another Academician, Robert Smirke Jr, in one of his professorial lectures. This led directly to the Council banning its own Professors from criticising "the opinions or productions" of any artist living in this country. This extra-ordinary authoritarian motion, which on the face of it proposed a gag on freedom of opinion of a magnitude that no artist or critic would normally tolerate, indicates just how insecure the Academy felt its position to be. The Academy was threatened from without by the growing influence of the British Institution which was now under the nominal Presidency of the Prince of Wales.

Turner, newly and publicly brought back into the Royal Academy circle as a lecturing Professor, had completed his evolution from a renegade to become one of the Academy's greatest assets. He was elected onto the committee to decide the hang of the 1811 exhibition, which the Council all knew would be a crucial one, for the Prince of Wales – by now Prince Regent – had agreed to grace the Private View and Dinner with his presence. And not only the Prince Regent had been invited, but also his two brothers, the Dukes of Clarence and Kent, and his sister Princess Charlotte, the rising generation displaying its pomp and power in the organisation that wished to reassert its claim to be the centre of the world of art.

Turner's own gallery was closed this year for its alterations, and so, coincidentally or not, he could hang his complete production of new paintings at the Academy, and devote himself to ensuring that the Academy looked its best on this vital day. Aware as he instinctively was of the importance of neatness, order and planning in presentation, Turner moved a hurried motion at the Council meeting two days before the Private View that the chairs in the Council Room be changed for the royal visit. The members of Council looked down at their well-worn chairs, and around the room at the other two dozen or so which had probably not been re-covered since they were new in Sir Joshua's day, and realised that this man was talking good sense. So they agreed to hire two dozen new ones "to be placed in the Council Room during the Exhibition, and that the old ones be removed".[32]

At the Academy Dinner the members and guests stood to hear the Prince Regent speak in what Farington described as a "manly and graceful manner".[33] The Prince praised the exhibition highly, saying that he had seen works "which would have done honour to any country; portraits which might vie with the pictures of Van Dyck; landscapes which Claude would have admired".[34] This speech will of course have been prepared in advance, and in the time-honoured tradition of official launches, the Prince Regent and his advisers had decided beforehand what the Prince's position was to be. This clearly was to assure the Academy of continued royal support, and to signal the Court's understanding of the international importance for Britain of a strong official body of artists who were both productive and knew themselves to be appreciated.

For Turner there was an additional, albeit only a momentary frisson. Somebody thought that somebody else had said that the Prince had been referring to Turner's *Mercury and Herse* when he said that here were paintings that Claude would have admired. Perhaps the Prince had nodded towards Turner's painting on the wall when he said this, or perhaps it was just a trick of the light. However it was, Turner seems to have got the idea that the Prince Regent wanted to buy *Mercury and Herse*, a picture which would undoubtedly have been admired by a host of old masters. The consequence of this episode was recorded by Farington:

> Earl Grey was understood to be willing to pay 500 guineas for the picture when the report was circulated that the Prince had bought it, which not being the case, Turner was embarrassed about it, and under these circumstances with his usual caution, will not name a price when asked by his acquaintance.[35]

So the picture remained unsold for more than a year, during which time it was exhibited again at Turner's Gallery in 1812. If this raising of his hopes that at last he might have a royal patron had encouraged and then disappointed Turner, the disappointment did have its benefits. The general gossip that the evanescent royal nod towards Turner had generated caused the press to look at *Mercury and Herse* very carefully, and to praise it to the skies because this seemed to be the thing to do. John Taylor had in 1811 been continually generous about Turner, sitting through all of his Perspective lectures and praising them fulsomely in the *Sun*. His further praise of *Mercury and Herse* gratified Turner so much that he transcribed the paragraph into his "Hastings" sketchbook:

> Highly as we thought of Mr Turner's abilities he has so far exceeded all that we or his most partial admirers could expect from his powers. We will not attempt to describe this admirable picture, but we can confidently recommend it to the attention of our readers as one of the most excellent efforts of the artist, in colouring, lightness, truth, elegance and all the qualities of natural beauty animated by genius, and rendered more interesting by a kind of classical charm which characterises the whole composition.[36]

This was good news, and it clearly gave Turner great pleasure. Cheered by good reviews, he was visibly hurt when the papers criticised his work. "No one felt more keenly the illiberal strictures of the newspapers," Trimmer remembered, "and I have seen him almost in tears, and hang himself, though still only valuing their opinions at their worth."[37] The "Hastings" notebook contains other things to cheer Turner, lines of figures, with notes of the large sums paid by various patrons for pictures in 1810 and 1811: Lord Pelham: £423.5.7; Lord Egremont: £428.11.3; Lord Lonsdale: £423.5.7. But on other pages there are suggestions that other parts of his life were less satisfactory. There is a barely legible recipe for some medicament, "Dis[solve] Blue Vit[riol] in Spring Water ...", and the note "The Herb Stramonium. Smoke 2 or 3 pipes every day. Swallow the saliva."[38] Stramonium is thornapple, a narcotic herb which was a popular recipe for asthma and bronchitis. It is, however, extremely dangerous, and the dosage Turner smoked (if he did so) would have brought on vivid hallucinations and prolonged disorientation. Blue Vitriol is an emetic which has nauseous side-effects and can lead to copper poisoning.

The "Hastings" sketchbook further contains scraps of poetry about writhing pythons, probably related to the conception of *Apollo and Python* (exh. 1811), Turner's metaphor for the artist hitting back at the critic:

> Coil after coil ... Where the rocky deep ...
> Until the monster weltered in his gore ...[39]

Other poetry in this sketchbook is of greater length and completeness, and most of it is gloomy and highly introspective. An ode-like poem of Shakespearean intent dwells on thoughts of despair, disappointment and the approach of death, even of suicide, feelings that could result from an overdose of stramonium:

> World I have known thee long & now the hour
> When I must part from thee is near at hand
> I bore thee much goodwill & many a time
> In thy fair promises repos'd more trust
> Than wiser heads & colder hearts w'd risk
> Some tokens of a life, not wholly passed
> In Selfish strivings or ignoble sloth
> Haply there shall be found when I am gone
> What may dispose thy candour to discover
> Some merit in my zeal & let my words
> Out live the Maker who bequeaths them to thee
> For well I know where our possessions End
> Thy praise begins and few there be who weave
> Wreaths for the Poet brow, till he is laid
> Low in his narrow dwelling with the worm.[40]

Although earlier verses had skirmished with death in a jesting spirit,[41] these lines are the earliest in which Turner seems seriously to consider his own mortality, and seriously also to consider putting an end to it all.

At about the time the lines were written there was a sudden and shocking death in the Fawkes family. Walter and Maria's eldest son, and his father's heir and namesake, drowned himself in the canal at Denham, near his school, in the early summer of 1811. The death shook Farnley and the neighbouring families in Wharfedale profoundly, and the event became the subject of newspaper speculation. One neighbour, Joseph Crompton, wrote to his son:

> The papers will have furnished you with what has happened to the Farnley family – they are very much to be pitied – poor young man – that at 16 years he should take the dreadful resolution of destroying himself and what must he have felt before he could bring himself to that state of mind. Various have been the conjectures in this part – but we hear his Parents support themselves wonderfully, considering all circumstances.[42]

Turner will have been aware of the suicide, given the publicity, and troubled by it, as any good friend would be. It may not in itself have been the cause of Turner's apparent depression, but it would certainly have affected his outlook.

In May 1811 he was preparing his extended tour of the coastline of the south-west peninsula of Britain to gather material for *Picturesque Views of the Southern Coast of England*, the title of the new publishing venture between Turner, John Murray and the Cooke brothers. This was to be a momentous journey for him. It had a purpose that was total, a specific commission from a publisher of a kind that he had not had since 1799 when as a young man he went up to Lancashire to make views for Thomas Whitaker. That, however, was for a publication which had a strictly limited, local and antiquarian relevance, the *History of Whalley*. Now, in a partnership, Turner was engaged on a project that was distinct and challenging, and would not only broadcast his work widely, but enable him to interpret and indeed define and direct the Englishman's vision of his coastal and littoral scenery.

The past twenty or thirty years had seen a great increase in the ability of English men and women to travel: by 1810, there were 20,000 miles of turnpike roads in Britain. These developments and the increase in sea travel from port to port meant that more and more people were becoming aware of the shape of their land, the way one region connected to another, the way hills folded into valleys, how towns spread outwards into the countryside from a crossroads or a river crossing, how the land fell down to the sea. A hill or mountain was no longer something to be contemplated with fear, but an obstacle that a traveller would pay a coachman to negotiate as an everyday event. Recent experience of inland and overseas wartime troop transport, the collective memory of road-builders and canal navigators digging lines over the landscape, the first sight of land after a long sea journey or naval campaign, all these contributed to a growing understanding of the roundness of the Earth and the scale of the nation within it.

Before he left London in mid-July Turner bought a copy of Nathanial Colman's *The British Itinerary*, a guidebook and timetable listing coach routes, distances and journey times, clear evidence in itself of the growth in the popularity of travel and the ubiquity of transport systems throughout Britain. Turner's travels over the previous two decades had given him an experience of landscape that he desired urgently to share with others. Awareness of the forms of landscape carried with it in Turner a sharp feeling for its history, for those who had passed this way before, who had affected its appearance, and who had fused it into Britain. As he prepared to travel to Devon, these feelings seem to have been at an apogee. Turner's copy of *The British Itinerary* was interleaved with blank sheets, and on these he began writing his epic poem of about seven hundred lines concerning Britain, its history, industries and landscape. This is the longest and most sustained piece of writing Turner ever did. He was well into the composition, perhaps had even finished it, before leaving London, for the lines of many of the pencil drawings made on adjacent blank leaves during the outward journey run on top of the spots where the ink has blotted.

A typical passage, which evokes movement, history and manufacture of civilisation, is:

> Hill after hill inccccuunt chentn the eye
> While each the intermediate space deny
> The utmost long call to attain
> When still a higher calls on toil again
> Then the famed Icknield street appears a line
> Roman the work and Roman the design
> Exposing hill or streams alike to them
> They seemed to scorn impediments for when
> A little circuit would have given the same
> But conquering difficulties cherished Roman fame.[43]

Concentrated as the writing must have been, the verses give as clear a verbal picture as we have from him of Turner's attitude to his landscape subject and to Britishness. They are the first Calibanic stirrings of Turner the historian. The Devonshire verses have been overshadowed in his output as a writer by "The Fallacies of Hope", of which only about one hundred lines were ever written, because Turner himself published snatches from the "Fallacies" as epigraphs for exhibited paintings. The

Devonshire verses, on the other hand, were never published in his lifetime, nor have they been given the compliment of a title. If there had ever been a plan to publish them as texts for the *Southern Coast* engravings this did not come to fruition.

Although they are sometimes waylaid by irrelevance, the verses have a relentless and driving enthusiasm and a strong sense of purpose.

> If heat is requisite more than our suns can give
> Ask but the vast continent where Hindoo live
> More than the mother country ten times told
> Plant but the ground with seed instead of Gold
> Urge all our barren tracts by Agriculture skill
> And Britain Britain British canvass fill
> Alone and unsupported prove her strength.
> By means her own to meet the direful length
> Of continental hatred called blockade
> When every power and every port is laid
> Under the proscriptive term themselves have made.[44]

The Britain that Turner tries to define in his verse is the same reawakening Britain with a patriotic sense of its history that Winston Churchill came nearly a century and a half later to touch in *A History of the English-Speaking Peoples*. Further, when Churchill spoke before the Battle of Britain of "broad and sunlit uplands", he was firing a nation in danger with images of a world at peace in renewed prosperity and hope. In using such a vivid landscape metaphor, Turner cannot have been far from Churchill's mind.

The nation was embroiled in an earlier but no less testing war when Turner wrote his "Devonshire" verses. In contrast with the state of affairs in 1940, however, the nation was not only at war with a foreign power, but also with itself. Luddism had reached its height, and in 1812 an Act was passed making machine-wrecking punishable by death. There were violent bread-riots and loom-wreckings in Nottingham, where, by the autumn of 1811 12,000 troops had been drafted. If he could not seriously have intended to fire a nation under arms with his words, Turner most certainly did hope to present it with a sense of nationhood and identity in his engraved landscape watercolours.

The watercolours he made from sketches on his return to London depict the sea in all conditions, from the flat calm in *Falmouth Harbour, Cornwall* to the dark blue storm of *The Mew Stone*. There are people at work – carters, fishermen, women drying clothes, boat breaking; and people at play – sailors and soldiers carousing, lovers, children running about. And there is plain evidence that Britain was very much under arms – naval ships are at anchor in Plymouth and Falmouth harbours, and forts are prominently visible on many hilltops. Turner also makes clear the structure of the land – rock fissures in *Tintagel Castle, Cornwall*; and fossils, or very like, in *Lulworth Cove, Dorset*.

Such rock forms make their appearance in the verse:

> Of Horizontal strata, deep with fissure gored
> And far beneath the watry billows cored
> In caverns ever wet with foam and spray
> Impervious to the blissful light of day
> Blocked up by fragments or by falling give
> a rocky Isle in which the sea maids live
> Bear their rough forms and brave the utmost rage
> Of storms that stain our British parish page ...[45]

From the way Turner approaches the writing of his "Devonshire" verses it seems that he set off with a full heart and high hopes, aware of the extent of his powers. However, he seems by 1811 to have begun to acknowledge that these powers might not always be available to him, nor yet be all his own. While, let us say, he was still planning his route, Turner wrote these first lines inside his copy of *The British Itinerary*:

> To that kind Providence that guides our step
> Fain would I offer all that my powers hold
> And hope to be successful in my weak attempt
> To please. The difficulty great but when naught
> Attempted nothing can be wrought
> Trials thankful for the mental power givn
> Whether innate or the gift of Heaven ...

He made thorough preparations for the journey. There are some notes in a sketchbook which show that he had read widely about the towns and villages he was to visit, and found out about their special features.[46] The key piece of preparation, however, was of a highly characteristic kind, to make sure he had all his contacts lined up. Charles Eastlake (1793–1865), a promising and enthusiastic eighteen-year-old student at the Academy Schools, wrote to his father in Plymouth asking him to be sure to introduce "the first landscape painter now in the world" to people who would be able to help him on his way, and to make sure he would have access to what he would need to see: "What he wants is to go on board some large ship, & I dare say George will be very happy to take him on board the Salvadore, and perhaps into the Dockyard &c."[47] There is no evidence from the surviving sketchbooks that Turner did in fact get aboard a ship in Plymouth Harbour, but doubtless he did, and that it all added to his store of knowledge of naval architecture and practice. There are, however, very many views of ships in harbour taken from high ground, and Turner's thrill at being in this particular landscape is palpable. In one sketchbook he notes, under a pencil sketch, "The Hoo [i.e. Plymouth Hoe] green brown and yet light and warm yet distant and clouds warm sky blue shadows grey Hooe greeny, red all delightful."[48] In this and the other sketchbooks of the trip, Turner produced pages of fine pencil studies of foiding landscape, harbour views and town and village scenes. The effort is prodigious. No corner seems to have been turned on the journey without his jotting down the view. The majority of these are no brief notations, but delicate evocations in which his pencil barely strokes the paper, of ships at anchor or villages falling down into the sea.

On this same trip Turner may have met the Plymouth painter Ambrose Johns (1776–1858), who was himself at the centre of the web of literary and artistic activity in Devon. Johns was to become a source of introductions and a companion on Turner's second tour of Devon in 1813, when he based himself in Plymouth, but on the first trip Turner had many miles to cover. From Salisbury, he went south to the sea at Christchurch, and then kept to the coast, with a few short inland detours from there all the way round Devon and Cornwall in a clockwise direction until he reached Minehead and Watchet some time in September.

On his way, Turner took the opportunity to call on his Devon relations, his Uncles John and Price, respectively in Barnstaple and Exeter, and his cousins by them. Turner's father had been to Barnstaple that February to visit the family, and considering the distance involved the elder Turner's visit will not have been just a social call, but one in which there was family business to transact.[49]

The Devon end of the Turner family was prospering, and scoring points off each other. Jonathan the baker wrote competitively in a letter of 1811 to John, the Master of the Barnstaple Poor House, that he had been in business for twelve years, had a house worth £700, had bought a flour loft for £160, and had "some money beside to carry on the trade so I leave you to judge whether I have done well or not and if I live and I be in business as long as you and brother Price I shall be cock of the walk."[50]

That such a letter had been written in 1811 suggests strongly that this was the time when the Turner family was looking collectively at its financial health and future security, and that the visits to Barnstaple and Exeter of both old and young William had some bearing on this. Nine years after Rebecca Turner's death, the family had still not yet settled her will.[51] Turner's friendship with members of his father's family were as distant emotionally as they were geographically. There are no further recorded instances of meetings between him and the Devon Turners, except when a nephew, Thomas Price Turner, a musician, called on Turner in 1834 at Queen Anne Street. He was received frostily, and not asked to call again.[52]

Those friends whom he chose, however, he nurtured fondly and was regularly in touch with. During the 1810s, there were two or three distinct circles which overlapped – Academy friends of his own generation, Francis Chantrey (1781–1841), Richard Westmacott (1775–1856), Thomas Phillips (1770–1845), Henry Thomson (1773–1843) and Henry Howard (1769–1847); watercolourists such as James Holworthy (1781–1841) and William Wells (1762–1836); and sympathetic amateurs Henry Scott Trimmer, Walter Fawkes and Samuel Rogers (1763–1855). William Wells was a leading light of the Old Watercolour Society, a man of great experience of teaching and exhibiting, and one with whom Turner could joke and talk in puns and riddles of a kind that they both understood, but which would be meaningless to an outsider. Writing of the rebuilding of his gallery, which had once been a school room that Wells had attended, Turner said:

> Shall I keep you a bit of the old wood for your remembrance of the young twigs which in such twinging strains taught you the art of wiping your eye with a tear purer far than the one which in revenge has just dropt into mine, for it rains and the Roof is not finished ... However, joking apart ...[53]

With Wells's elder daughter Clarissa, known in the family as Clara, Turner had something of a *tendre*. Clara (c. 1790–c. 1871) must have been about twenty when Turner was planning Sandycombe. She recalled in the 1850s to Thornbury that

> to me he was an elder brother. Many are the times I have gone out sketching with him. I remember his scrambling up a tree to obtain a better view, and there he made a coloured sketch, I handing up his colours as he wanted them. Of course, at that time I was quite a young girl. He was a firm affectionate friend to the end of his life; his feelings were seldom seen on the surface, but they were deep and enduring. No one would have imagined, under that rather rough and cold exterior, how very strong were the affections that lay hidden beneath.[54]

That passage may refer to about 1800, and the following perhaps to eight on ten years later:

> In after life of course our paths diverged and we saw less of each other, yet I feel sure that with both of us, there was not the smallest

diminution of real affection and true esteem – we each respected the other – and I am sure no two persons (man and wife excepted) ever knew each other to the heart's core better than we did – but enough, it is dangerous to open memory's floodgates.[55]

Turner was perhaps fifteen years older than Clara, by 1811 or 1812 a famous man, energetic, highly sexed, determined and with a romantic way of life. Although there has been speculation that the pair were in love to the point that Turner hoped they might marry, this is circumstantial and hangs on an inventive interpretation of a letter written by Turner in 1815.[56] And if Clara was star-struck by Turner, the state was temporary. Though each was clearly deeply fond of the other, and they were evidently confidants, Clara kept Turner, as her other men friends, at a distance. She found safety in numbers, and in the playful exercise of her singularly active mind. She possessed

> more constitutional liveliness & elasticity of mind than most people, & having long been accustomed to the unreserved society of pleasing & estimable men, of whose principles & good intentions she felt secure, she had been accustomed to treat her male friends as brothers.[57]

One of Clara's admirers observed to another, Robert Finch, that some might suggest that she would flirt with "you the next half hour, ... me the next, ... Turner the next, ... Wilson the next ..."[58] Turner was just one of Clara's many male admirers, and that was undoubtedly just how they both liked it to be. Turner had not, and never had, any intention of marrying. Indeed, he expressed his views on marriage quite forcibly when speaking of the engraver James Willmore: "I hate married men, they never make any sacrifice to the Arts, but are always thinking of their duty to their wives and families, or some rubbish of that sort."[59] The friendship with Turner was always platonic and unpressured by emotion most of the time, and as both Clara and Elliott independently observed, sisterly. As a result the friendship had no known crisis, and lasted for the whole of Turner's life. He wrote affectionately to her as late as 1844,[60] and left her £100 in the 1849 codicil to his will.

Soon after his return from the west in early October 1811, Turner and the Trimmer family got together again. This year was the last in which he kept the house in The Mall, Hammersmith; indeed he may already have reduced radically the time he spent there, for life on the river's edge at Hammersmith by now had become intolerable. The water company was continuing to raise money through Acts of Parliament to extend the Middlesex Water Works, and by 1811 or 1812 a 120-feet-high chimney had been built behind Turner's house. By now, the river would have become one big lighter basin, continually churned up by the removal of spoil, and the delivery of load upon load of bricks and iron. The noise and movement of men will have given Turner no peace there. With building work going on also at this time at Turner's Gallery there was no peace there either, so it is no surprise that Turner willingly escaped from London to Devon and Cornwall in the summer of 1811, and looked forward so much to moving to Sandycombe.

Turner, Trimmer, Henry Howard and the Trimmer boys went out on sketching trips regularly together. Thornbury reported how on one, to Penn in Buckinghamshire, Turner worked in a ditch on that sunny day to avoid showing the others how he painted.[61] This reads as if it may have been a tease, for Turner was characteristically generous with his advice to Trimmer:

> Turner was very communicative to my father, and would point out to him any defect in sketching. I think he fairly instructed my father in painting in his own method; which was to lay the dead colours as nearly as possible in the forms you wished, leaving as little as possible to finishing, using as a vehicle nothing but linseed oil, diluted as required in spirits of turpentine.[62]

One remark to Thornbury dates some of these family meetings precisely. It also shows that in this case the son who is talking must be the eldest, Henry Syer Trimmer (b. 1806). Thornbury says that "It was [at Hammersmith] that Mr Trimmer remembers walking, when a child, with his father and Turner at night under the blaze of the great comet."[63] This was the Caledonian Comet, which passed across the sky from August until October 1811.[64] The Trimmer sons remembered how Turner made them laugh, and "how pleasant and sociable he was. They recollect him mixing some sort of paste with his umbrella, and their mother, in fun, carrying off one of his sketches against his will, for he was by no means a member of the 'give away' family."[65] As the guest of a churchman, Turner did the proper thing while at Heston, and accompanied the family to church.

Turner was now returning to Royal Academy business with a vengeance. No detail was too small for him. At the 7th October meeting, the first after the summer recess, he moved that the chairs in the Council Room that had been hired the previous April for the royal visit be bought. There is no clue that this may have been in his mind when he moved the hiring of the chairs, but as he spoke the Council Members were no doubt sitting on them, and in no mood to send them back and return the Council Room to its old shabbiness. That it should have been Turner who moved the motion, suggests both that he was foremost in a tendency to modernise the general appearance of the Academy, and that he could sense general feeling and be bold enough to express it when necessary. He saw himself as a voice of senatorial calm, moderation and balance, and took upon himself responsibility for the Academy's present and future well-being. His peers also saw this potential, and rewarded him by voting him into the Chair for the 7th December General Assembly in Benjamin West's absence.

In this perception of Turner, dating from about 1811, lie the roots of the view of the man as the dogged, good-hearted but sometimes grumpy and unfathomable Brother of his profession. He was no more an orator at Academy meetings than he was as the Professor of Perspective. C. R. Leslie remembered that Turner would make long, confused and rambling speeches at General Assemblies, "and if interrupted or called to order for not confining himself to the subject in question, he would become angry and say 'Nay, nay, if you make an abeyance of it I will sit down.'"

Thornbury also discussed Turner's manner of delivery of speeches:

> There is no doubt that his speeches at the Academy councils were extremely difficult to follow, for he spoke in a deep and, latterly, in an indistinct voice. You saw the great man's mouth move, and imperfectly heard certain sounds proceed therefrom; but out of these you seldom caught more than "Mr President" and "namely", the two verbal forms to which the speaker had recourse when he had hopelessly entangled himself in the subtleties of his own rhetoric ... [Then] the bells of St Martin's would break in, "Dong, dong, ding, dong," and then came a lull through which you heard "Mr President ... namely ..."[66]

From about this time Turner became something of a pet to the Royal Academy, revered as the artist who had been bright and brave enough to survive as the butt of the criticism of an unkind public and shine through. He had a benign presence, and characteristically acted as balm during difficult Council meetings:

> Turner was ever anxious to allay anger and bitter controversy. Often I have heard him, in subdued tones, try to persuade the excited to moderation; he would do this by going behind the speaker, and by a touch or a word soothe an acrimonious tone by his gentleness.[67]

This potential for promoting calm and good sense led to his being elected as one of the four Visitors to the Academy Schools, with Augustus Wall Callcott, Thomas Phillips and Martin Archer Shee.[68] The Visitors were in effect the teachers at the Schools, and in voting two landscape painters into post this year, the Council gave the lie to the rumour – possibly put about mistakenly by Turner himself – that landscape painters were not eligible to be Visitors to the Academy.[69] Over the following twenty-six years, when he served on and off in the Life Academy, Turner became a greatly loved, if laconic presence in the Schools. "Humph!" or "What's that for?" he might say to a student, poking him in the side and pointing at his drawing, or pulling his thumb and fingernail down over the student's drawing, the more firmly to define the correct line of the figure. Richard and Samuel Redgrave recalled "Turner's conversation, his lectures, and his advice were at all times enigmatical . . . from want of verbal power. Rare advice it was, if you could unriddle it, but so mysteriously given or expressed that it was hard to comprehend."[70]

Turner went north to Farnley in mid-November, his first visit since young Walter's death. The visit was brief; he was back in London by 4th December. Turner's journey north must have been one of condolence. Walter's father had promptly announced the death in the *Gentleman's Magazine*,[71] but thereafter the young man's existence was never referred to. His manner of death was not spoken of either, to the extent that Forster's *Pedigree* lists him as having died in infancy, which, technically, he had.[72] Fawkes and Turner will also have talked, now, about the perilous state of the nation, and discussed the "Hannibal" subject that was to be Turner's main exhibit at the 1812 Academy, and talked also about the forthcoming anniversary of Francis Burdett's election as a radical Member of Parliament, and how Fawkes was to mark it.

Early in the new year of 1812, Turner repeated his series of Perspective lectures at the Academy. If his audience had hoped that miracles might have happened, they were disappointed, for his delivery had not improved. Rossi reported to Farington that the series was "much laughed at, as being ignorant and ill-written",[73] while Soane suggested that Turner was encroaching on the territory of other Professors, himself included, saying that the fourth lecture "seemed a lecture for the Professors of Painting and Architecture, the word Perspective hardly mentioned".[74]

Turner's refreshed activity is a positive sign that the depressions of the previous year had lifted, and that he was facing life with a new enthusiasm. The stacks of paintings in his studio were growing. He had finished his second Oxford view for Wyatt in time for John Pye to engrave it and for it to be exhibited at the Royal Academy in 1812, and he was making a group of scintillating oils and watercolours of Devon and Cornwall life and landscape as a direct result of his 1811 trip. There was a fine coherence about the two distinct groups of works in the 1812 Academy and his own reopened gallery. At the latter he showed six glowing Devonian and Cornish subjects, including the riverscapes *Hulks on the Tamar* and *Teignmouth* – both bought by Lord Egremont – and the pair of populous harbour scenes full of incidental detail and wit, *Saltash with the Water Ferry* and *St Mawes at the Pilchard Season*. Fresh off the easel, and fresh too out of his sketchbook and his mind, they were as topical a group of pictures as he ever showed together. We can picture the artist standing proudly in his gallery showing the paintings off to his friends and patrons, and talking at length about his travels the previous summer. At the Turner Gallery this year, too, was the unsold *Mercury and Herse*.

Across London at Somerset House, Turner exhibited his two new Oxford views and a reprise of a subject he had shown after his 1802 Alpine journey, *View of the Castle of St Michael, near Bonneville, Savoy*. Why he should have painted and exhibited this subject now is unclear. It is unlikely that he painted it for a quick sale; but more as a continental scene-setter or catalogue-companion for his main exhibit of 1812, *Snow Storm: Hannibal and his Army Crossing the Alps*.

Though apparently inspired by a storm in Wharfedale, the country Turner transports us to is the Alpine valley above Aosta. When *Hannibal* came to be hung at Somerset House in April 1812, it was at first placed high up over a door into the Great Room. This completely destroyed the effect of the abnormally low viewpoint that Turner had constructed in the picture, the main action of its figures taking place in the lower quarter, even the lower eighth. The viewer should be peeping nervously out at the turbulent scene from behind one of the shattered rocks in the foreground. When he saw what the hanging committee had done with it, Turner was furious. That year's committee, Farington, Smirke, Dance, Fuseli and the Academy Secretary, had given the best places in the room to large paintings by Fuseli himself and the President, and tried to fob Turner off by saying how good his *Hannibal* was, how it was "seen to great advantage" up there, and that the President agreed with them.[75]

Turner was having none of this soft soap. He told them straight, but using Callcott as his mouthpiece, that if it was not hung "under the line", from the picture-hanging rail set more or less at eye-level, he would take the picture away, presumably to show it to great effect in his own gallery. The committee did take *Hannibal* down, and tried it elsewhere, but they decided nevertheless that it would stay where it was, as that was where there was a gap for it.

Turner was in 1812 one of the few artists whose threats and opinions carried weight. He had a wide and influential constituency of artist friends and patrons, and had an alternative "court" of his own at Queen Anne Street. His own displeasure, which he would freely and unequivocally express privately or in public, and the displeasure of his friends was something to be feared. He could have stormed in and demanded immediate satisfaction, as he had stormed out of the Academy in 1804.

But he did not behave in this way. Instead, according to the bland diary report of Joseph Farington, Turner dropped in at the Academy the next day while the committee members and others including Henry Howard were having dinner. He sat with them for a while. They chatted about this and that, about gout and about health generally. Benjamin West said how healthy he was and that he had not spent £5 on medicines in the past fifty years. Both Turner and Smirke said that they could not drink wine of any kind without suffering from it. Both complained of "want of strength in the stomach".

They all seemed to be avoiding the big issue, until Turner asked Farington quietly what the committee had done about all his pictures, the two Oxford views included. Farington replied that they "had much difficulty about your *Hannibal Crossing the Alps*". Turner slipped upstairs and stayed for a while in the exhibition. He saw *Hannibal* hanging up over the door just where he did not want it to be. He came down again, smiling quietly, and joined the party. After a minute or two he caught Henry Howard's eye and beckoned him out of the room.

"I want my *Hannibal* below the line."

"But it's seen to better advantage over the door."

"No. Tell them to bring it down. If not, I'll take it away. I don't want to spoil the party, so I'll go. I don't want my disappointment to show. I'll be back at noon on Monday."[76]

When Howard relayed all this to the committee, Smirke and Dance said that Turner could do what he liked; the hang would stay as it was. But at noon on Monday, he firmly repeated his demand, and this time the committee wavered. Turner went away, and Farington suggested that as a compromise they put *Hannibal* at the head of the room where the Secretary's old office had been. But Turner did not give his final approval of this change until Callcott had reported back to him, and until he had seen it both in candlelight and by day. His final proviso was that other artists should be able to have their work hung near *Hannibal*.

This tells us a great deal about Turner's means of getting his way – how in his maturity he used assertion rather than aggression or swagger, how he worked through other, weaker personalities, using them as go-be-tweens, and how he used pressure of time as a bargaining tool, fully knowing that if he insisted and refrained from giving his approval for long enough time would run out for the hanging committee and he would be bound to get his way. There came to be a *frisson* of suspense when an important Turner was hung, with the risk that he might peremptorily remove it, deny the Academy the reflected glory of the public's apprecia-tion of it, and ostentatiously remove it and show it in Queen Anne Street.

*Hannibal* was a highly important painting, emotionally, artistically and politically for Turner this year. It was the result of perhaps ten years of brooding not only on the subject of Hannibal, but on the parallels between Hannibal and his Carthaginian army's struggle with the tyrant Rome, and with the long war between Britain and the tyrant France.[77] The storm that

Turner had seen in Wharfedale in 1810 was probably the culmination rather than the beginning of the gestation process for the painting. Hannibal's army had not only crossed the Alps – an extraordinary enough feat – but had besieged Saguntum in Spain, crossed the Pyrenees, run through southern France defeating the Gauls, and had defeated two Roman armies one after the other on Italian soil. Hannibal was a potent and aggressive force within Italy for at least ten years, the same length of time that Britain and France had been at war, and was a parallel hero and symbol of liberty for Turner with Wellington. By April 1812 the tide had turned and Wellington's armies were dominating the Peninsula, and beginning to push Napoleon out of Spain. The moment Turner takes in the painting *Hannibal* is the moment when, at the height of the Alps, the general, the tiny gesturing figure on the back of the elephant in the far distance, rallies his long-suffering troops and camp followers to yet greater endeavour, and urges them to follow him out of the storm.

For the catalogue of the Royal Academy exhibition Turner had submitted eleven lines of his poetry. It stood out clearly on the printed page below the entry for *Hannibal*. Turner wanted his painting to be as prominent on the wall as was its entry in the catalogue, because for the first time he had felt bold enough, as a poet, to publish his own lines and reveal their source. He did not go quite so far as to say that they were by himself, J. M. W. Turner, RA, PP, but he did reveal that they were from the "MS.P[oem] Fallacies of Hope".

The painting and the poem carry both hopes and dire warnings. The poet in Turner wrote:

> Craft, treachery and fraud – Salassian force,
> Hung on the fainting rear! Then Plunder seized
> The victor and the captive, – Saguntum's spoil,
> Alike became their prey; still the chief advanc'd,
> Look'd on the sun with hope; – low, broad, and wan;
> While the fierce archer of the downward year
> Stains Italy's blanch'd barrier with storms.
> In vain each pass, ensanguin'd deep with dead,
> Or rocky fragments, wide destruction roll'd.
> Still on Campania's fertile plains – he thought,
> But the loud breeze sob'd, "Capua's joys beware"!

In these words, Turner is cataloguing the difficulties faced by Hannibal and facing him still – attack from behind by the Salassi, natives of the passes above Aosta; winter storms (the "fierce archer of the downward year" is the constellation Sagittarius); and the future months that his armies would spend among the Italian luxuries at Capua. On another level, Turner's *Hannibal* had added power. Even as Turner was finishing the painting, Walter Fawkes was preparing a blockbuster of his own on the subject of liberty over a tyrant, the speech on Parliamentary Reform, which he was due to give at the Crown and Anchor tavern in the Strand in May.

Turner's threats to remove *Hannibal* must have been one big bluff. It was inconceivable that he would have taken his great statement on liberty, and the imperative need for the free man to stand up to the tyrant despite fearsome odds, away from the public Academy and from the sight of the mass of people to whom it was addressed. The key reason for this was that on 23rd May 1812, when at one end of the Strand Turner was showing *Snow Storm: Hannibal and his Army Crossing the Alps*, at the other Walter Fawkes was giving his long-awaited speech at the Crown and Anchor: "I have ever cherished a deeply-rooted conviction of the absolute necessity of some great and efficient change in our system, as the first step to any hope or prospect of improving our condition."[78]

Ironically, being shown low down in a smaller room, *Hannibal* became obscured by the crush of people wanting to see it, as C. R. Leslie found.[79] That the Academy had a great deal to lose from losing Turner is revealed in the quality of the press reports that were now circulating about him. *Hannibal* was widely fêted:

> as the effect of magic, which this Prospero of the graphic arts can call into action, and give to airy nothing a substantial form ... All that is terrible and grand is personified in the mysterious effect of the picture; and we cannot but admire the genius displayed in this extraordinary work.[80]

There was no buyer for *Hannibal*. Yet it had an extraordinary staying power for it remained in the mind's eye of Henry Crabb Robinson, the lawyer and diarist, who wrote in 1849 – thirty-seven years after the painting had appeared at the Academy:

> This day (5th May 1812) I saw at the Exhibition a picture by Turner, the impression of which still remains. It seemed to me the most marvellous landscape I had ever seen, – Hannibal crossing the Alps in a storm. I can never forget it.[81]

*Hannibal* was not engraved, and although it was seen over the years by diminishing groups of people at Queen Anne Street, it slipped back into the obscurity of the studio stacks until the 1850s.

Turner's casual remarks about his health at that tense dinner with the Academy hanging committee seem to have been prophetic. At the end of the year, he confided to Farington that he was feeling extremely ill. At the first Academy Council meeting of the autumn, Turner

> complained much of a nervous disorder, with much weakness of the stomach. Everything, he said, disagreed with him, – turned *acid*. He particularly mentioned an aching pain in the back of his neck. – He said he was going to Mr Fawkes' in Yorkshire for a month, and I told him air, moderate exercise, and changing his situation would do most for him.[82]

However it was caused, the aching pain in the back of his neck would have been exacerbated by his leaning over an easel or desk to make etchings and watercolours, or leaning too much into his canvases and standing still for too long. His constitutional biliousness, a tendency that had dogged him all his life, would have got worse when he became over-tired. What Turner was suffering from was Malta Fever, a form of brucellosis carried in goats' milk which causes sweating, pains and swelling in the joints. He wrote out on the first page of the red morocco pocket book that he was using in 1812 or 1813 a remedy for what he termed "Maltese Plague",[83] with the symptoms "Sickness, debility, shivering, heat, thirst, headache. Delirium, darkspots, ulcer". As an emetic Turner took a strong dose – ten grains – of Ipecacuanha and as a drastic purge five grains of the mercury compound Calomel and ten of the Mexican resin Jalap. He then noted that he should take a teaspoonful of Sal Mendeveri every two hours, drink plenty of lemonade, shave his head and apply vinegar and water with a sponge to his head and body.

Taking Farington's advice for fresh air and a change of scene, the shaven-headed Turner went to Farnley in November to recuperate. While there, undoubtedly at Fawkes's insistence, he wrote to the Academy Secretary asking if he might be allowed to postpone his next series of lectures for at least a year. Malta Fever got Turner down for months. With the remedy in the "Chemistry" sketchbook are some copious notes of other chemical recipes and compounds, most of which are painting recipes, but some may have been attempts to cure himself.[84] There was evidently a hypochondriachal streak in him, which for all his supreme physical and mental energy encouraged him to take remedies if he feared the onset of a new illness, and may have contributed to thoughts of suicide. His smoking of the herb Stramonium suggests he may have been taking serious if drastic steps to cure himself of breathing difficulties.

This same strain in his nature, quite apart from his needs as an artist, contributed to his restlessness, to his need for constant change, and to his urges to get away from London and out into the fresh air. It also helps to explain his departure in a rage from the Royal Academy in 1804, his enthusiastic re-engagement with the Academy around 1812, his constant chopping and changing of the architecture of his gallery in Harley Street, his impatience with his engravers, and his departure to Sandycombe Lodge, Twickenham. Once at Sandycombe, his restlessness prevented him from staying there and enjoying it for long, and indeed by 1815, two years after he had finished the laborious task of designing and building it, he was already contemplating selling up.

# SEVEN

## "... the first genius of the day..."

### 1813–1817

I f in body and attitude, Turner's restlessness kept physically pushing him on from places or situations at which he had barely arrived, it gave a corresponding boundlessness to his cerebral life, an omnivorous excitement and interest in all that was around him. His range of interest can be measured in the heights and depths that his work touches, from the muck and litter on a sea shore, to the piling up of classical architecture in grand evanescent ancient heaps; the crumbly texture of brickwork, the strength and palpability of smoke, his curiosity about the costumes of different people from different parts, his invention of vast historical pageants, his observations of the smallest details of the moment-by-moment progress of a passing cloud or a setting sun.

At the artists' dinner at the close of the Academy exhibition in late June 1813, Turner sat next to John Constable. There was only a year between these two painters, and they shared, too, an insatiable interest in warmth, damp, light, atmosphere and the integral effect of these realities on the momentary appearance of landscape. Turner had been lionised by the Academy from an early age; Constable, however, though no less eager than Turner had been to become one of the elect, would not be made an Associate of the Academy until 1819.

Constable's admiration for Turner was conditional and puzzled. He had an equivocal opinion of *Hannibal*, as expressed the year before to his fiancée Maria Bicknell: "It is so ambiguous as to be scarcely intelligible in many parts (and those the principal), yet, as a whole, it is novel and affecting."[1] Sitting beside Turner in 1813, however, Constable could flesh out his view. Turner impressed him greatly, and their conversation was fluid and touched on very many subjects: "I was a good deal entertained with Turner. I always expected to find him what I did – he is uncouth, but has a wonderful range of mind."[2]

Turner's one exhibit at the Academy this year was *Frosty Morning*. Constable had already had one discussion, albeit by letter, about this picture. His great friend and patron Archdeacon Fisher had only two weeks earlier written to Constable congratulating him on his own entry in the 1813 exhibition, *Landscape: Boys Fishing*. Fisher thought that only one painting was better, Turner's *Frosty Morning*: "But don't repine dear Constable at this decision of mine you are a great man like Buonaparte and are only to be beaten by a frost."[3]

*Frosty Morning* is a strange, wistful picture, a mass of contradictions, a masterpiece of artifice blended effortlessly with realism, a narrative without a story. It is traditionally said to be a scene in Yorkshire, the carriage approaching in the distance on the left being one in which Turner himself had travelled. Turner very likely did travel in the frost in Yorkshire when he was at Farnley in the late autumns of 1811 and 1812, but the landscape in the painting is too vague to play any specific part in a narrative, despite the report that he told Trimmer that he had sketched the scene *en route*. The possibility that *Frosty Morning* is a piece of artifice is strengthened by Trimmer's further report that the horses in the painting were both modelled by Turner's own "crop-eared bay", a great favourite of the painter, and that the little girl with the hare over her shoulders reminded Trimmer of the young girl resembling Turner "whom he occasionally saw at Queen Anne Street", and whom he "took to be a relation".[4] This was probably Evelina. The old man leaning on his gun in a melancholy way has not been satisfactorily identified; indeed there is not enough detail to suggest more than that he may have been modelled by another person as close at hand to the artist as his daughters, Turner's father.[5]

The painting evokes time and change – the moving carriage just touched by the rising sun; the frost melted and melting where the sun lights the bank, but not melting yet where the bank is in shadow. This carefully observed realism is counteracted by the artifice of the horizontal frieze of figures, static to a classic degree, across the central band of the picture, and offset in a regular cruciform shape by the vertical line of the winter tree and the ditch below. But what is happening? Has the old man just shot the hare? He is sufficiently relaxed with his gun to suggest that it is no longer loaded. Is the little girl feeling the last few moments of dying warmth from the hare's body as it lies over her shoulders? And what are the two farm labourers, one with a billhook, doing with so little evident movement so early in the morning in such hard ground with a disinterested audience of three? The empty wheelbarrow, the spade and the pickaxe tell us nothing, and the rising bank conceals the men's activities completely. Only the cow preparing to piss with its backside near centre, brings warmth and movement to this sad, threnodic painting. Are the labourers digging something up, cutting something down or even burying something, a suicide perhaps, at this lonely crossroads? Information in *Frosty Morning* masquerades as clues teasingly set out; and there are no answers.

That a second major painting representing winter should follow *Snow Storm: Hannibal and His Army Crossing the Alps* in Turner's œuvre may reflect nothing more than coincidence. But there may be some connection to the facts that over this winter of Turner's serious illness, at the end of a year – 1812 – in which rain had ruined the harvest across the country and produced the highest average annual price for wheat recorded during the Napoleonic Wars;[6] when the Prime Minister, Spencer Perceval had been murdered; when Luddites were smashing machinery in the manufacturing towns; when Walter Fawkes was foreseeing national catastrophe through present contitutional "abuses of the grossest description" in the months after the suicide of his eldest son;[7] when Turner was being verbally abused by Sir George Beaumont in drawing-rooms in London and the country; when he was feeling physically incapable of giving his lectures in January 1813 to an institution he revered and students he cherished; and when he had to face the world with a shaven head bathed with vinegar and wrapped in brown paper – all these universal and individual events and situations thoroughly dampening to the liveliness of the spirit, and barely graspable in their meaning, were enough to give a purpose and intent to so enigmatic and bleak a painting as *Frosty Morning*. That we may not be able to understand it fully is I suggest part of its point.

How tantalising in its extent and content the conversation between Turner and Constable must have been that evening in June 1813, with *Frosty Morning* on display nearby. Turner's intelligent and roaming conversational manner drew Constable's comment on his "wonderful range of mind". It also led Constable to describe him as "uncouth", a word which did not mean, as we now accept it, "unmannerly", but, in Dr Johnson's definition, "odd, strange, unusual". That Turner patently was.

Though it had many admirers, *Frosty Morning*, like *Hannibal*, did not sell from the Academy exhibition. Henry Scott Trimmer coveted it, and Turner seems to have talked of giving it to him;[8] but nothing came of the idea. He offered it for sale to Dawson Turner in 1818,[9] but to no avail, and the painting remained in the artist's studio until his death. Although Lord Egremont bought two Thames subjects from the Turner Gallery in 1813, Turner's careering run through the favour of wealthy collectors had now begun to lose momentum.

In 1811 and 1812, Turner's production of oil paintings had been energetic, enthusiastic and extensive. In 1813, by comparison, the rate dropped dramatically. His exhibited work in oil was fleshed out this year by older paintings, *The Deluge* of 1805 at the Academy, and a group of earlier works, whose precise mix is unknown, at the Turner Gallery. There are three likely reasons for this apparent decline in output, two of which are probably interdependent. The first is, quite simply, that Turner was too ill over the winter and spring of 1812 and 1813 to take on the heavy physical and intellectual task of making more than one large exhibition painting. The second is that he was still working up, in the far less physically demanding, even restorative, medium of watercolour, the Devonshire subjects from his 1811 tour to meet his obligations to the Cooke brothers. He was also, up to about 1815, continuing to make watercolour drawings in retrospect of subjects from his Scottish tour of 1801 and the Swiss tour of 1802, and some of these occupied him in 1813.

A third reason for the shrinkage in exhibited oil paintings this year was the result of the sudden bursting of the raging, aggressive and destructive attitude to Turner's work of Sir George Beaumont. This was extraordinarily debilitating and probably contributed to his illness. Turner and Beaumont were openly at war by 1809 when Turner had the "proud pleasure" of refusing to sell *Fishing upon the Blythe-Sand* to "his old enemy".[10] Turner continued to express his contempt towards Beaumont in his verses, and an elliptical symbolic fury in his painting *Apollo and Python*. Within the manuscripts of his perspective lectures are verses written about 1810 that refer directly to Beaumont:

> Boisterous in art, unfortunately rude,
> Noise for opinion and theory n'er understood; ...
> ... Dam up the current of your purse or try
> To prevent another catch a patron's eye,
> If chance discernment or occurance join,
> To point out rising work or smiling line
> By innuendo censure, each has some frail part.
> Thus rules dictators round all things in art.[11]

Callcott reported Beaumont's "continued cry against Turner's pictures" to Farington, and while Beaumont allowed that Turner "had merit ... it was of a wrong sort and therefore on account of the seducing skill displayed should be objected to."[12]

Beaumont kept up the pressure in the salons and drawing-rooms of London and the country, speaking out loudly against Turner, as if it were a political issue of national importance that was at stake. To Farington, who was one of Beaumont's autumn guests at Coleorton Hall in 1812, he set out his case against Turner:

[He] had done more harm in misleading the taste than any other artist. At his setting out he painted some pictures, "The Plagues in Egypt", which gave great promise of his becoming an artist of high eminence, but he had fallen into a manner that was neither true or consistent; his distances were sometimes properly finished, but when he came to the foreground it bore no proportion in finishing to the distance beyond it.

Beaumont went on to say that younger artists (citing Callcott) had become drawn into Turner's manner and that "Much harm ... has been done by endeavouring to make paintings in oil to appear like water colours, by which, in attempting to give lightness and clearness, the force of oil painting has been lost."[13]

By highlighting the damage that he believed Turner was doing to the younger generation, Beaumont attempted to gain sympathy for his view. He had considerable perverse success. Callcott complained bitterly to Farington in April 1813 that he had not sold a picture in the past three years, and was not exhibiting in 1813 because of Beaumont's widespread abuse of his work. Beaumont had cut Callcott dead at the private view of the 1812 Academy exhibition when the younger man tried to speak to him. Beaumont's reputation followed him, for many years later Hugh Munro wrote: "Sir G. Beaumont committed a much greater crime as a judge of art than preferring Claude to Turner, for he ruthlessly condemned the works of Turner without reference to any other painter."[14]

However firmly held his views may have been, Beaumont was behaving villainously by denying artists their livelihood. Turner, however, refused to be browbeaten, although he had wavered, and indeed had called on Callcott at home in Kensington – probably some time early in 1813 – and said that he would not exhibit that year "from the same cause that prevented Callcott, but he has since altered his mind and determined not to give way before Sir George's remarks."[15]

By the early summer of 1813 Sandycombe Lodge was completed, and Turner's indefatigable father, now aged sixty-eight, was making the regular walk up from Twickenham to look after the gallery in Queen Anne Street. He told Farington in May that "he had walked from Twickenham this morning, eleven miles; ... In two days the last week he said he had walked 50 miles."[16]

Moving into Sandycombe gave Turner the emotional lift that he so desperately needed. His illness seems by now to have passed, the expense of the building works had come to an end, and he needed no more to make all the frenetic little calculations about the control of building costs at Sandycombe that crop up in his notebooks. For the next year or so the only building works Turner took on were confined to paint on canvas – there is a knowing little still life of a pile of bricks in the bottom left-hand corner of *Dido Building Carthage* (exh. 1815). What he needed now was to relax at a summer party, and that is indeed what happened at Sandycombe one warm summer Saturday in late July 1813.

One of the organisers of the "little party we have in agitation for Saturday next"[17] was Turner's firm and lively friend Clara Wells. Turner was on the guest list from the start, and of course a squint at the house that the painter had so busily been planning and building in Twickenham for the past few years had to be part of the fun of the day. In a crowded four-oared boat, Turner and sixteen friends rowed up river from London to Richmond. Henry Elliott was of the party, and he left a refreshing account in a letter to another of Clara's admirers, Robert Finch:

> The expedition ... took place and afforded one of the most delightful days I have ever spent – everything went off well, & there was no drawback to our enjoyment. Our four-oared boat just held our party of 17 consisting of the Wells's, Herbsts, Miss Perks, Turner, Wilson, Thos, Chas and Jas Wheeler, Edward and I. The six last only rowed, Wilson all the way there & back, Edw & I provided one oar between us, & the Wheelers for the other two. We dined in a beautiful part of Ham Meadows upon half-made hay, under the shade of a group of elms near the river, & had coffee and tea at Turner's new house. Miss Perks took a guitar and Edward a flute & we had a great deal of music & singing ... we had good veal & fruit pies, beef, salad &c – but our table cloth being spread on the short grass in a lately mown field we reposed after the Roman fashion on triclinia composed of the aforesaid hay ... [18]

There was much country wooing going on that day, as four at least of the party were soon to pair off in marriage – Clara Wells married Thomas Wheeler, and Maria Perks married his brother Charles. Turner, fifteen or twenty years older than the others, could only watch the developing relationships from the sidelines and take part as best an older man may. He was good company when on form, and entertained his friends happily and generously, but without pretension. Sandycombe Lodge became something of a country retreat for Turner's artist friends Chantrey, Havell, Howard and others. Turner entertained William Mulready and other fellow Academicians there, and "once feasted" his engraver friend John Pye "with cheese and porter". Chantrey, according to Thornbury, gave Turner a "pretty little piece of sculpture" of St Paul Preaching at Iconium, after the Raphael cartoon, to hang over the dining-room fireplace.[19]

The informality of Sandycombe was, to Turner's friends, part of its charm. Trimmer remembered it as "an unpretending little place", perfectly in tune with the frugal nature of Turner's life. He and his father ate off earthenware rather than china, and used archaic two-pronged forks and knives with round spatulate ends. For all the discreet modernity of the architecture of Sandycombe, the two Turners lived in it like happy but hard up peasants. There was drink, but it was not splashed about; food, but it was of the simplest kind. Friends who turned up unannounced were welcome to share what he had, and cake and wine were brought out if he had it. "Old dad," he once said to his father when Trimmer and one of his sons were with them for lunch, "have you got any wine?" The old man produced a bottle of currant gin that he had made. Turner sniffed it, grimaced at its strength, and put it on one side, ticking his father off mildly as he did so. "Why, what have you been about!"[20]

Turner and his father were perfectly happy in each other's company, resourceful and self-sufficient. The older man found security in his son's success, for which he had himself worked so hard in the early years, and found pride in working directly for the painter. They were a well-bonded team, brought together in affection, were complementary, symbiotic, with shared memories and experiences of difficult early years. For Turner, his father's presence and reliability was a reciprocal security. He looked after the gallery, stretched and prepared canvases, tried to make something of the garden and cooked for his son. But the son worked the father hard. Even when the old man was over eighty, young William was sending peremptory letters to him instructing him to get pictures ready for despatch, or to send him on some extra clothes, or some more paint, or run errands about this and that; and with no evident pleases or thank yous.[21] Trimmer picked up this imbalance in the relationship very perceptively, recalling that "the old man latterly was his son's willing slave."[22]

Financially, father and son kept themselves on a tight rein. Old habits died hard. It was against old William's nature to spend excessive amounts of money on travel. Soon after the couple moved to Sandycombe the old man tired of walking the eleven miles, and as Trimmer recalls resented spending money on coming up to town daily to open the gallery. But before long he found a solution that amused him no end:

> Why, lookee here, I have found a way at last of coming up cheap from Twickenham to open my son's gallery. I found out the inn where the market-gardeners baited their horses; I made friends with one on 'em; and now, for a glass of gin a day, he brings me up in his cart on the top of the vegetables.[23]

Turner set off that summer 1813 for his second visit to Devon, leaving his father at Sandycombe to mind the house and to get on with the garden. On this Devon visit Turner used Plymouth as his base, for he wanted specifically to concentrate on the landscape of south-west Devon. His aim was to collect more information for the *Southern Coast* series, and to make watercolours for another engraving project that the Cookes had proposed, *The Rivers of Devon*. As with his Devon trip of 1811, Turner prepared the ground well before he left. The energy and integrity that he showed while in Devon in 1811 had made him many new friends and confirmed others, including Ambrose Johns, Charles and George Eastlake and their father, and John Collier the future MP for Plymouth. These, and more, laid on all the assistance and accommodation he could possibly need.

People showed him round the region, gave him introductions, put him up, and laid on boats and carriages for him as required. He was a highly influential tourist, well respected and widely known to be making a collection of images of the south-west which would be definitive, a crucial factor indeed in bringing travellers, trade and national recognition to Devon and Cornwall. One man who was of particular help and a companion for a large part of the 1813 trip was Cyrus Redding, a Devonian whom Turner had met in London in 1812. Redding was a journalist, and thus instinctively aware of the good that Turner could bring to the region. When, nearly a century later, Thomas Hardy published the lines in his poem *Weathers*:

> And they sit outside at "The Traveller's Rest",
> And maids come forth sprig muslin drest,
> And citizens dream of the south and west,
> And so do I,

the original catalyst of the citizens' dream had been Turner's *Southern Coast* series.

After Turner's death, Redding wrote a memoir of the artist which recalled their time together.[24] Throughout this account Turner's physique, his strength of mind and character and his simple durability are plainly emphasised. While sailing out in dirty weather to Burgh Island in Bigbury Bay, Turner exclaimed "That's fine! Fine!" at the sickening motion as their little boat pitched and tossed and the other passengers threw up or lay groaning. Caught at nightfall up the River Tamar, three or four miles from Tavistock, it was Turner who proposed staying just where they were, out under the stars, rather than retreat to the comfort of the town. On an occasion when their gig became stuck in a lane, he and Redding took the horse out of the traces and lifted the carriage bodily over the hedge.

There is a kind of hero-worshipping wonderment in Redding's

retrospective account, but it nevertheless has the ring of truth. This is sometimes at the expense of the writer himself, as when, standing together only three or four feet below a battery of twenty-four-pound cannon at Plymouth, the guns went off without warning above their heads. Redding was reduced to jelly; but Turner remained "unmoved at the sudden noise and involvement in the smoke as if nothing had happened."

On the long walks over the Devon countryside Turner set the pace, regularly choosing to walk rather than take a horse or carriage. He rose early, and at the end of a long day joined in companionably with picnics and tavern suppers. He tended not to chatter, normally remaining reserved in his conversation; but when they had had an exciting, successful day, and he was not under pressure as the celebrity artist of the party, he would open up. The evening they were stranded outside Tavistock, Turner and Redding slipped off together to an inn:

> Very good bread and cheese was produced, and the homebrewed suited Turner, who expatiated upon his success with a degree of excitement, which, with his usual dry, short mode of expressing his feelings, could hardly be supposed ... I found the artist could, when he pleased, make sound, pithy, though sometimes caustic remarks upon men and things with a fluency rarely heard from him. We talked much of the Academy, and he admitted that it was not all which it might be in regard to art.

Though he could sleep on a sixpence if required – "Turner leaned his elbow upon the table, and putting his feet upon a second chair, took a position sufficiently easy, and fell asleep" – the Devon visit had its interludes of good luck and luxury. Turner and his party, which in addition to Redding, Charles Eastlake and Ambrose Johns also seems from time to time to have included the painter James Demaria, happened to bump into Lord Boringdon who invited them to spend the night at Saltram, his country house near Plymouth. They had a happy musical evening, listening to songs sung by Madame Cantalini, and slept for once between linen sheets. As they went to bed Turner looked at the paintings by Angelica Kauffmann of scantily clad nymphs and shepherds that decorated Redding's bedroom. "Goodnight in your seraglio," he said, with a wink in his voice.

During the 1813 Devon visit Turner made sketches of a different kind to those he had made two years earlier. The 1811 studies were characteristically finely detailed and sharply observed, but this time his pencil was more relaxed, and ran speedily over the page. One reason for this change may be that being part of a party of friends, Turner did not want to sit and draw in detail, as it would have encouraged an audience. Charles Eastlake told Thornbury that "Turner made his sketches in pencil and by stealth,"[25] and Redding observed how "Turner's glance seemed to command in a moment all that was novel in scenery, however extensive, which he had never before encountered. He would only make a few outlines upon paper, scarcely intelligible to others." On another occasion, Redding found Turner with a pencil and small book near the summit of Burgh Island. "I observed, too, he was writing rather than drawing."

Drawing at speed, Turner may have looked as if he were writing, though he did from time to time make notes in his small spidery handwriting of the colour values he saw in the landscape. At other times he worked in oil on millboard from a small portable painting-box which Ambrose Johns had fitted up for him. "When Turner halted at a scene and seemed inclined to sketch it, Johns produced the inviting box, and the great artist, finding everything to hand, immediately began to work."[26] If he may sometimes have been secretive in the manner of his collecting information, he was certainly not so when it came to showing off the results to a convivial group of friends.

> There were eight or nine of the party, including some ladies. We repaired to the heights of Mount Edgecumbe at the appointed hour. Turner, with an ample supply of cold meats, shell-fish, and wines, was there before us. In that delightful spot we spent the best part of a beautiful summer's day. Never was there more social pleasure partaken by any party in that English Eden. Turner was exceedingly agreeable for one whose language was more epigrammatic and terse than complimentary upon most occasions. He had come two or three miles with the man who bore his store of good things, and had been at work before our arrival. He showed the ladies some of the sketches in oil, which he had brought with him, perhaps to verify them. The wine circulated freely, and the remembrance was not obliterated from Turner's mind long years afterwards.[27]

Here is Turner the good companion, the great man come from a great distance, to enjoy the local landscape and express it as only he could. He was generous, open-hearted, entertaining and amusing in an allusive kind of way, and perhaps amused too in his turn at the electrifying effect that his work seemed to have on those welcoming people who charmingly held him in such awe. Redding described him at this time as stout and bluff-looking:

> rough, reserved and austere in manner ... In personal appearance he somewhat resembled the master of a merchantman. But the gold lay beneath the rough soil. The unprepossessing exterior, the natural

reserve, the paucity of language, existed in combination with a powerful intellect, a reflective mind that lived within itself.

Where else in Britain but Plymouth, where reserved, reticent, bluff master mariners roamed the streets night and day, could such a man as Turner be so readily understood and accommodated, and so affectionately and pithily described.

The warmth of his welcome and his recollection of it drew him back to Devon the following summer, where he sketched around the River Tamar, making studies of the river valley at Gunnislake and Calstock.[28] His Devon friendships gave Turner the impetus also to send paintings to a local exhibition in Devon in 1815, the only time in his life that he allowed his paintings to be exhibited outside London before they were sold.

There was, however, more to it than just making convivial new friends. Devon was a very long way from London. Geographically, in dialect, in customs and manner and above all in landscape it was still an undiscovered country. Turner could relax there, safe from the backbiting of Academy rivals, and move about the county finding rare and exotic vistas of a kind unknown in London and the south-east of England. Redding remarked that Turner had said that "he had never seen so many natural beauties in so limited an extent of country as he saw in the vicinity of Plymouth. Some of the scenes hardly appeared to belong to this island. Mount Edgecumbe particularly delighted him; and he visited it three or four times."

This affinity drew an unguarded remark from Turner. When Redding listed names of artists whom Devon and Cornwall had produced, Turner said "You may add me to the list: I am a Devon man – Barnstaple." Of course Turner was empathising, as they sailed lazily down the St Germains River, recalling his father's Devon roots, and recalling too no doubt his father's Devon drawl and tales of a Devon childhood. He was not pretending he had been born anywhere but Maiden Lane, though Devonian patriot Redding leapt on the statement and presented it as important new information. Turner no more saw himself as Devon-born than John F. Kennedy believed himself to be German, when in 1963 he proclaimed: "Ich bin ein Berliner." But Turner did seem to have toyed with the idea of visiting Devon more regularly, according to the solicitor Henry Woollcombe who wrote in his diary that Turner was

an artist whose works I have so much admired; he is brought hither by the beautiful scenery of our neighbourhood, there is a chance of his occasionally residing amongst us. I certainly wish this may take place, as it is always desirable to attract talent around, where it is accompanied by respectability.[29]

Turner may have momentarily been wooed by the beauties of Devon and the amiability of its people to consider going to the south-west more regularly. But his true love was Yorkshire; Yorkshire saw Devon off. There are enough studies surviving to show that when Turner went out to paint in Wharfedale he regularly took company. There are groups of people picnicking, scrabbling about on the rocks, or waiting quietly on the hill with gun and a gundog. His many sketches and finished watercolours – the "Wharfedales" of which Andrew Wilton lists a total of forty-eight made between about 1816 and 1820 – are a clear reflection of the landscape and the enveloping light in all its moods and weathers.[30]

The series of interior views of Farnley in the 1810s are, however, curiously wooden, with little feeling for place. Despite the fact that his great friends were here, people make only a very fleeting and distant passage through these gouache watercolours. In one, a servant in full livery is just about to disappear from the hall into the dining-room; in another a groom latches a gate in the background; in a third a woman skitters up the library stairs out of the room and out of sight. The only glimpse Turner gives us of the family are the three ladies sitting at the very far end of the drawing-room sewing perhaps and playing the piano. This is in complete contrast to the sketches Turner came to make in the later 1820s of the households at East Cowes and Petworth, which are full of vibrant life, atmosphere and jolly good fellowship.

For all the grandeur of the Farnley interiors, there is a palpable sadness, even a hollowness, within. Perhaps this is just a reflection of the Regency tradition of room portraits, an uncommon enough subject for Turner, as gouache was an uncharacteristically dry medium for him. The wide empty depopulated central spaces, empty chairs, figures fleeing rooms and books left scattered on floors, suggest a sadness. These characteristics recur so regularly in the Farnley interiors that one begins to wonder if Turner may not be making a point. There had already been enough unhappiness at Farnley, set off by the suicide of young Walter in 1811, and by old Walter's financial problems which were beginning inexorably to deepen, to suggest that some areas of family life were either taboo, or only uneasily spoken of. And there were others – Walter Fawkes's wife, Maria, died in December 1813, and in August 1816 Walter's youngest brother Richard was fatally wounded in a shooting accident on the moors above Farnley.

The Farnley family had many artistic pursuits to keep them occupied in these difficult years. Walter and his brother Francis[31] had an engaging and infectious zeal for natural history of a kind that only the most enthusiastic and knowledgeable of amateurs show. This drew them to organise the family to collect specimens of birds killed on the estates and further afield, and to mount their feathers in a growing series of leather-bound folio volumes. Walter Fawkes himself wrote extensively about the animal kingdom as he saw it in texts published in four volumes in 1823 as *Synopsis of Natural History*. He and Francis corresponded with the great naturalist and wood engraver Thomas Bewick, asking advice and seeking the identification of specimens that puzzled them, and they encouraged friends to illustrate the volumes with them. If the *Synopsis* further demonstrates Fawkes's energy as a writer, the four volumes of the *Ornithological Collection*, which are filled with sheet after inscribed sheet of mounted feathers and watercolour illustrations, these reflect his passion for organisation, method and completeness.[32]

Turner was central among the friends drawn in to contribute watercolour drawings of birds to the *Ornithological Collection*. Twenty bird watercolours have been ascribed to Turner, though of these, to the eye of the present writer, six have slipped into the Turner canon on the strength of over-enthusiasm or over-reliance on an evidently spurious signature.[33] Other contributors to the albums included Samuel Howitt, Charles Collins, Samuel Northcote Sr and other friends and members of the Fawkes family.[34]

Another project that Fawkes encouraged, and which Turner realised for him over the course of about ten years from the mid-1810s, was the making of an album of watercolours and texts to celebrate the triumph of democracy in Britain from the rise of Oliver Cromwell to the Glorious Revolution of 1688. The album, entitled *Fairfaxiana*, was intended as a companion piece to the collection of Civil War relics that Fawkes had inherited and which he installed in the Oak Room in the original part of Farnley Hall. The relics came down from General Thomas Fairfax (1612–71), a hero of the Battles of Wakefield, Naseby and Oxford, and one-time MP for Yorkshire. It was the historical resonance that they held that was so special to Fawkes. To touch them was to feel the link between the Parliamentary struggles of the seventeenth century, and the current political struggles for reform that were taking so much of Fawkes's time, money and energy.

It may in fact be too tidy to say that the relics were "inherited". Fawkes had inherited Farnley from his father, who had in turn inherited from a distant cousin. On one of Turner's *Fairfaxiana* watercolours, *The Three Swords*, Fawkes wrote in 1821 that one particular document – and we might assume the rest of the collection – was "found at Farnley Hall ... addressed to the proprietor of that mansion, Thomas Fawkes Esq., AD 1626." It would be more realistic to suggest that the relics were so much lumber found, perhaps by Walter as a young man, knocking about Farnley when his father came into possession. For a young man with latent democratic sympathies to discover such material in the late 1780s when France was on the verge of revolution would be a life-defining experience. How natural it would be for him in later life, while giving so much of himself in contemporary radical politics, to exalt the Fairfax collection through display at home and through the work of his old, generous, sympathetic and trusted friend, J. M. W. Turner.

Turner made the frontispiece to *Fairfaxiana* in 1815.[35] Thereafter, on visit after visit, he made seventeen watercolours, vignettes and allegorical subjects within their own painted mounts all directed to the subject of the triumph of democracy in Britain. Many have extensive texts written with a brush in the minuscule hand that Turner could adopt or dispense with at will. There is a wry self-mocking humour at the medievalising tendency of the series, and some pictures contain further surprises, such as the frontal view of a seventeenth-century oak cabinet, with doors that open to reveal tiny painted swords, portraits, documents and Oliver Cromwell's hat. Turner's application to the task was intense. It was a labour of deep friendship, and made with the cheerful spirit of a fellow traveller. The painting of the *Fairfaxiana* pages continued until at least 1823, when the radical politician and writer John Cam Hobhouse stayed at Farnley, and was staggered to find "the most celebrated landscape painter of our time – I mean Turner, who was employed in making designs for a museum intended to contain relics of our civil wars and to be called Fairfaxiana."[36]

The delicacy and precision of the *Fairfaxiana* watercolours are an echo from Turner's manner in architectural subjects of the 1790s. While there had developed an increasing breadth of scale and handling in Turner's oil paintings over the intermediate years, he never abandoned the minute, calligraphic touch that would offset the effects of even the wildest storm. In the bottom right-hand corner of *Snow Storm: Hannibal and his Army Crossing the Alps* there is a detachment of tiny soldiers who seem to have been written rather than painted onto the canvas in reddish gold paint; while in *London* the shadows on the upper range of windows of the easterly block of Greenwich Hospital are likewise put on with little calligraphic flicks of the brush. This delicate, undemonstrative, house-trained manner of painting, undoubtedly in the case of *Fairfaxiana* done with the help of a strong magnifying glass, prefigured the vignettes that Turner was to make in great quantity from the late 1820s. And one of the first patrons, not to say impulses, for the vignettes was Walter Fawkes himself, who encouraged Turner to paint a set of five literary illustrations incorporating texts from Byron, Scott and Moore.[37]

From 1812 until well into the 1820s, Turner was in close contact with the Cooke brothers over the engraving and publication of the *Southern Coast* series. Engravings of watercolours which Turner had developed from his tours of the south-west were by 1812 and 1813 in production in the Cookes' studio. There is terse correspondence over this period between Turner and the Cookes,[38] touching on the correcting of proofs, the nature of the accompanying texts, and the marketing of the first group of engravings which suggest that all involved were becoming nervy as publication day approached. Turner somewhat naïvely asked William Cooke: "What difference could it make if the two [rival] numbers of the *Coast*, Daniel's [*A Voyage Round Great Britain*] and yours, came out on the same day?"[39]

For the engraving *St Michael's Mount*, Turner seems to have offered Cooke some lines of verse as a caption. This was found to be garbled and unusable, as William Combe, to whom Cooke had sent the copy for editing, pointed out:

> Mr Turner's account is the most extraordinary composition I have ever read. It is impossible for me to correct it, for in some parts I do not understand it. The punctuation is everywhere defective, and here I have done what I could ... I think the revise should be sent to Mr Turner, to request his attention to the whole, and particularly the part that I have marked as unintelligible. In my private opinion, it is scarcely an admissible article in its present state ...[40]

Promptly, Turner asked for the text back, and in doing so threw light on the sensitivity of his feelings for his written work, and his sudden retraction of it when it was criticised:

> as I shall not change [charge?] or will receive any remuneration whatever for them, they are consequently at my disposal, and ultimately subject only to my use – in vindication; never do I hope they will be called upon to appear, but if I ever offer'd that they will be looked upon with liberality and candour, and not considered in any way detrimental to the interests of the Proprietors of the Southern Coast work.[41]

At other times Turner communicated with his engraver through marginal notes on proofs. On a proof of *Teignmouth* (1815)[42] he wrote:

> The tone of the church requires a little more solidity about the upper part but take care of the blackness. One of the figures standing on the shore is too much a Falstaff, the other Master Slender. Make the sun, if you can more visible as to *disk* [sketch] at the uppermost side, and then the plate will *do*. The boats foremast has no bottom to it, burnish one in and make a shadow. Rather too positive.

The attitudes Turner expressed in these exchanges reflect his continued insistence on involvement at every level with the production of engravings of his work - the balance of light and dark, the appearance of figures as real people not as caricatures, the wording of captions, the manner of marketing. They are another side of the same character trait that also expressed itself in the joy of painting and drawing on a minute scale, and, as an architect, in designing for himself a neat and practical little house in Twickenham. If he could never have expected to keep complete control of the production process of engravings of his work, however devoutly he may have wished it to be so, he could have complete physical control over himself when he chose to focus down to the tiny scale of *Fairfaxiana* and the vignettes.

Turner rediscovered his public profile in 1814 when he stepped up to the rostrum in Somerset House on 3rd January to deliver the first of his new series of Perspective lectures. He promptly stepped down again, having announced that his audience might as well go home, because he had left all his notes in a portfolio in a hackney carriage. He used a novel and economical way of getting them back, perhaps to avoid their being held hostage against the prospect of a greater reward, by feigning a limited interest in their return. His advertisment in the *Morning Chronicle* concluded: "[The finder] shall receive two pounds reward, if brought before Thursday, afterwards only one pound will be given for them at the end of the week. No greater reward will be offered nor will this be advertised again."[43] The notes somehow found their way home, and the lectures began the following week.

Turner's loss of his lecture notes will not have surprised his friends. Thinking of other things, no doubt, he would put something down, and walk away without it. Clara Wells summed him up when she advised Robert Finch *not* to ask Turner to take some books for him to Italy: "... he would be quite sure to lose your books, as he invariably does, more than half his baggage in every tour he makes, being the most careless personage of my acquaintance."[44]

There was a pugnacity about Turner that emerged regularly when he felt challenged. In 1814 he took the intemperate decision to tweak the dragon's tail and enter a painting for the annual premium competition at the British Institution. The competition was intended as an encouragement for younger artists, not for established middle-aged men such as Turner, and the fact that he submitted his painting eleven days after the closing date did not go down well with the Institution's directors. But Turner's challenge to the British Institution had a serious purpose. In choosing to garble his subject and reference in the nonsensical title to his painting *Apullia in Search of Appullus vide Ovid* he was thumbing his nose at the classically-educated directors who ran the British Institution, men who included Sir George Beaumont and Richard Payne Knight, "no friends of his", in Michael Kitson's words.[45]

*Apullia ...* was very closely based on Claude's painting *Jacob with Laban and his Daughters* which Turner had seen at Petworth in 1809. So near indeed is the similarity that it drew the complaint in an anonymous letter to the *Examiner* that it was "not an original composition, being really a direct copy of Lord Egremont's Claude".[46] In a further tweak to the dragon's tail, Turner's subject was one that another of the Institution's directors, the Marquess of Stafford, owned in a version by Claude. Turner did not win the prize, which went to Thomas Hofland, but he did demonstrate in the clearest possible manner, and directly in the face of those connoisseurs who had abused him, that he, Turner, could paint exactly like Claude. He seems to have nursed this particular grievance for eleven years, ever since Beaumont cut him to the quick in 1803 by saying that the subject of his *Macon* "was borrowed from Claude but the colouring forgotten".[47] What also comes across in this encounter is the strength of Turner's *amour propre*, his sense of manhood, which, feeling crushed by unpleasantness and jealousies, would leap up and recklessly get its own back even at the expense of greater unpleasantness.

The spirit of Claude loomed large in both of Turner's exhibition pictures in 1814. At the Royal Academy, which opened shortly after the British Institution exhibition had closed, he showed one painting, *Dido and Aeneas*, a glistening, airy, wholly Turnerian work in which a dancing frieze of Dido's women are met by an advancing party of Aeneas's horsemen against a vision of Carthage. Being a leading figure on the Academy's Council, and a central opinion former within it, Turner knew directly of the current bitterness between the Academy and the Institution, and suffered for it. The former was resentful that the Institution mounted loan exhibitions of old master paintings during the same months as the Academy exhibited works by living artists. The world of patronage in London was still too small to enable the Academy to feel confident that its artists would sell their paintings while the Institution was busily encouraging the market in old masters and rivalling the Academy as an alternative patron for younger artists. With his *Dido and Aeneas* on show at the Royal Academy, Turner was bullishly saying "Buy your old masters here."

The same defiant mood seems to lie behind his superfluous announcement that the summer 1814 season was the last "but two" in which the Turner Gallery would be open. How general this announcement was is unclear – probably not general at all, for it has only been found in one handwritten note given to Turner's friend James Holworthy. It does show, however, that Turner was making forward plans for yet another bout of alterations for the gallery, the third, while taking out a Reversionary Lease on 44 Queen Anne Street.[48] Thus, he was investing soundly in himself and in his future. He was also beginning to regret that he had put himself out on a limb, geographically and financially, in building and living in Sandycombe Lodge. If a somewhat internalised letter to Henry Scott Trimmer of August 1815 is to be believed Turner was by then trying to

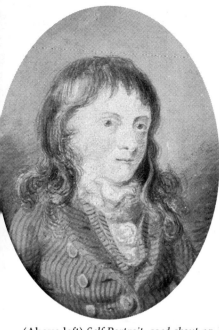

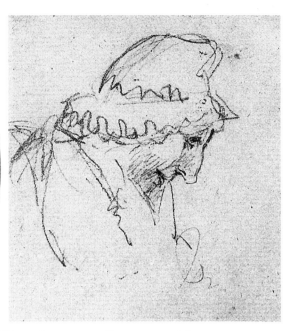

(Above left) *Self Portrait, aged about 15*. Watercolour, *c.* 1791. By courtesy of the National Portrait Gallery, London.

(Above right) *Study of a woman's head – possibly Turner's mother*. Pencil, mid 1790s. 'Marford Mill' sketchbook, TB xx. Turner Bequest, Tate Gallery, London.

(Below left) Henry Howard: *Sarah Trimmer*. Oil on canvas, 1798. By courtesy of the National Portrait Gallery, London.

(Below right) Charles Turner (attrib): *Portrait of William Turner*. Chalk, 1820s. Private collection.

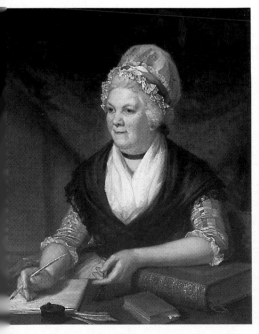

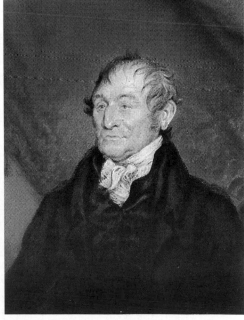

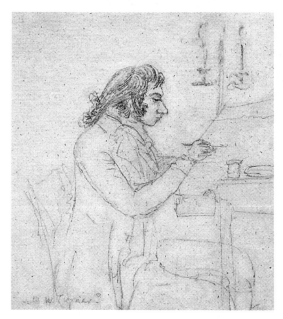 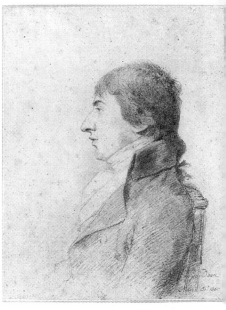

(Above left) Dr Thomas Monro (?): *J. M. W. Turner at a Drawing Table.* Pencil, *c.* 1795. © 1996 Indianapolis Museum of Art, Bequest of Kurt F. Pantzer.

(Above right) George Dance RA: *J. M. W. Turner ARA.* Pencil, 1800. Royal Academy of Arts, London.

(Below left) William Daniell after George Dance RA: *Thomas Girtin.* Engraving; drawn 1798, engraved 1814. Royal Academy of Arts, London.

(Below right) Charles Turner: *A Sweet Temper – Portrait of J. M. W. Turner.* Pencil, *c.* 1800. © British Museum, London.

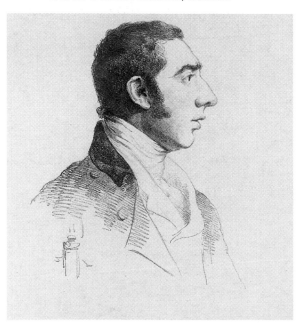 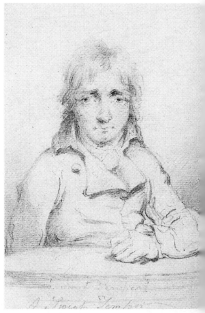

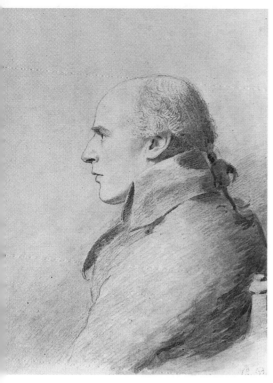

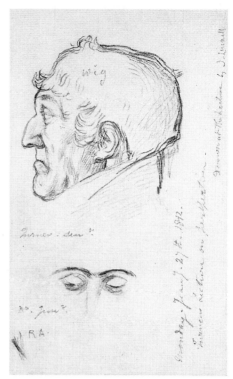

(Above left) George Dance RA: *Joseph Farington RA*. Pencil, 1793. Royal Academy of Arts, London.

(Above right) John Linnell: *Portrait study of Turner's father, with a sketch of Turner's eyes, made during a lecture*. Pencil, 1812. Tate Gallery, London.

(Below left) W. F. Wells: *Portrait of the artist's daughter, Clarissa*. Pencil, 1801. Private collection.

(Below right) John Linnell: *Portrait study of the Rev. E. T. Daniell* Contained in a Linnell sketchbook, 1976–1–31–6. © British Museum, London.

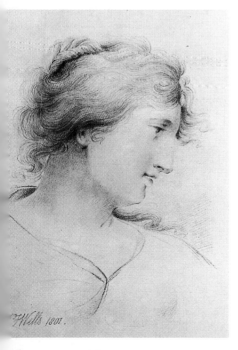

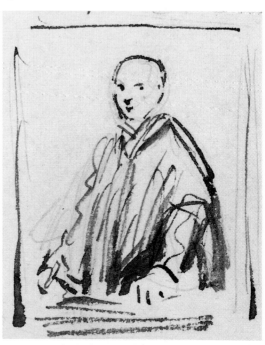

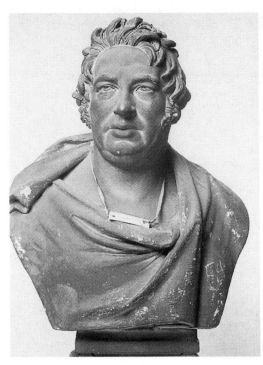

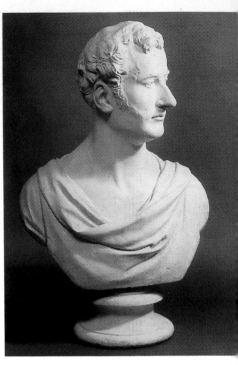

(Above left) Sir Francis Chantrey: *Bust of John Fuller MP*. Plaster, 1820. Ashmolean Museum, Oxford.

(Above right) Sir Francis Chantrey: *Bust of Sir Francis Burdett MP*. Plaster, 1810. Ashmolean Museum, Oxford.

(Below left) Thomas Phillips: *Portrait of George O'Brien Wyndham, 3rd Earl of Egremont*. Oil on canvas. Petworth House, Sussex. National Trust Photographic Library/A. C. Cooper.

(Below right) John Varley: *Walter Fawkes*. Pencil, *c*. 1820. Victoria and Albert Museum.

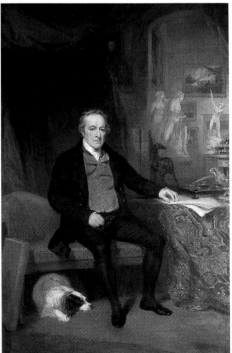

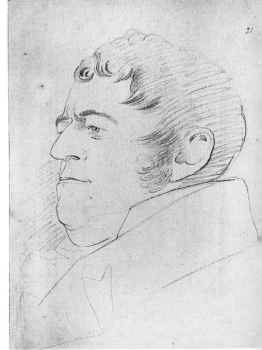

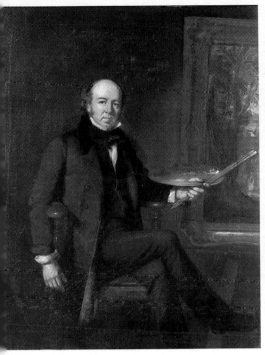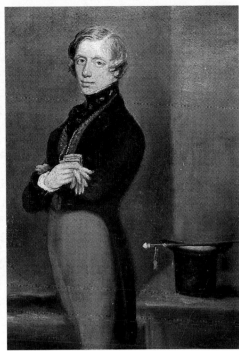

(Above left) William Wallace: *Rev. John Thomson of Duddingston.* Oil on canvas.
National Galleries of Scotland.

(Above right) Thomas Richmond: *Portrait of John Ruskin.* Oil on canvas, 1840–41.
The Ruskin Foundation.

(Below left) Rev. John Eagles: *Self Portrait.* Pen and ink. City of Bristol Museum and
Art Gallery.

(Below right) Artist unknown: *Portrait of Rev. James Skene.* Watercolour. National
Galleries of Scotland.

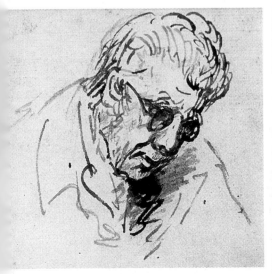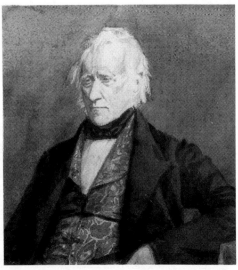

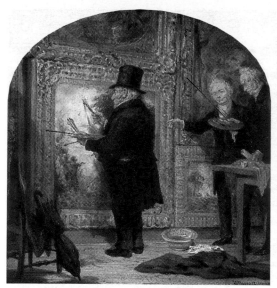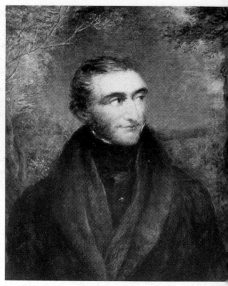

(Above left) S. W. Parrott: *Turner on Varnishing Day*. Oil on panel, late 1830s/1840s. Published by permission of the Ruskin Gallery, Guild of St George, Sheffield.

(Above right) John Linnell: *J. M. W. Turner*. Oil on canvas, 1838. By courtesy of the National Portrait Gallery, London.

(Below left) Charles Hutton Lear: *J. M. W. Turner*. Pencil, 1847. By courtesy of the National Portrait Gallery, London.

(Below right) Artist unknown: *Portrait of Dr David Price*. Watercolour, 1840s. Private collection.

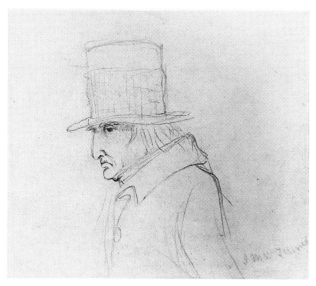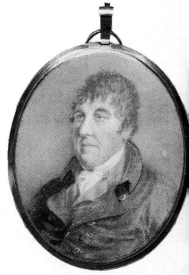

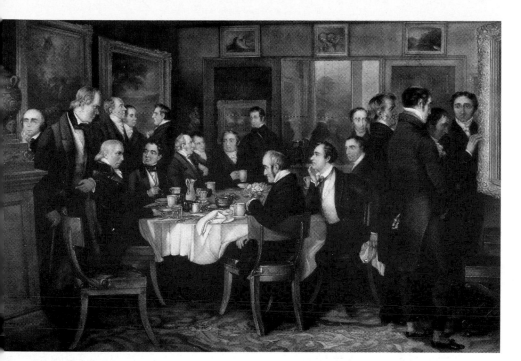

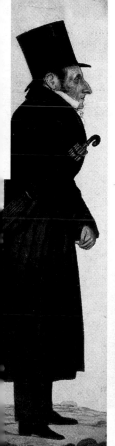

Charles Mottram, after John Doyle: *Samuel Rogers at his Breakfast Table at 22 St James's Place in 1815*. Engraving, *c*. 1823. Tate Gallery, London. Turner is standing second from the right, partly obscured, between Thomas Lawrence and Thomas Campbell. Rogers is seated centre. Others include P. B. Sheridan, Thomas Moore, William Wordsworth, Robert Southey, Lord Byron and Thomas Stothard.

(Left) Richard Dighton: *J. M. W. Turner*. Watercolour, 1827. Victoria and Albert Museum.

Silver Palette of the Society for the Promoting of Arts, Manufactures and Sciences, presented to Turner in 1793. Whereabouts unknown; reproduced from *The Connoisseur*, 1923.

Snuff box presented to Turner by King Louis-Philippe, 1838. © British Museum, London.

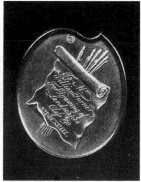

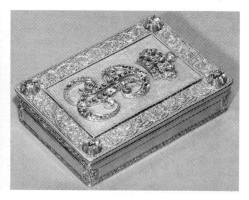

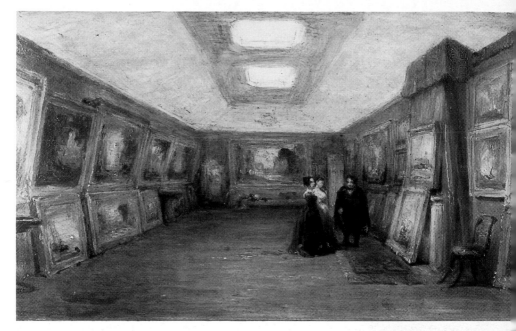

(Above) George Jones RA: *Interior of Turner's Gallery – The Artist Showing his Works.* Oil on millboard, late 1840s. Ashmolean Museum, Oxford.

(Right) Sandycombe Lodge, Twickenham. Photographed in 1995.

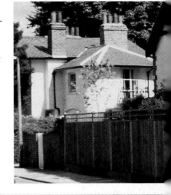

(Below left) 47 Queen Anne Street West, photographed in the 1880s. Photographer unknown. Westminster City Archives.

(Below right) John Archer: *6, Davis Place, Chelsea.* Watercolour, 1852. © British Museum, London.

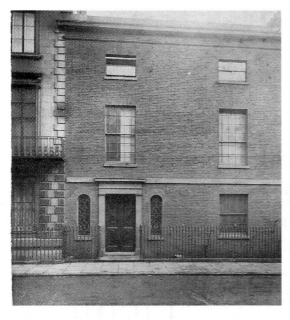

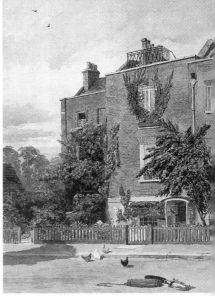

sell his Twickenham house; certainly he thought of it at this time as "an act of folly".[49] Renovation to the gallery was some kind of an attempt at retreat and retrenchment in London.

A child born at the beginning of the war with revolutionary France would have been twenty-two years old when he first experienced his nation at peace. But it was not much of a peace for the man at the loom or the woman in the fields. Britain in 1814 and 1815 was almost bankrupt and on the verge of revolution. Turner watched the decisive events in Europe, as most Englishmen did, through the papers and conversation. Some of his conversations, however, will have gained insights denied to ordinary Englishmen. They took place with his near neighbour in Twickenham, the exiled Louis-Philippe, pretender to the throne of France. Louis-Philippe, Duke of Orleans, had lived at Highshot House in Crown Lane, Twickenham for seven years from 1800, and returned to the town to live beside the river for four months when Napoleon escaped from Elba and returned to power in March 1815. His and Turner's first meeting may have been as early as 1806 or 1807 when the latter was looking for building land in Twickenham, and found a site only two hundred yards from Highshot House.

Louis-Philippe, who became the Citizen King of the French after the July Revolution of 1830, was a modest, approachable man who made many friends in London and Twickenham. One of his soldiers wrote of him after he became King:

> If, by chance, you meet in the streets of Paris a tall and erect man who seems both martial and gentle ... dressed in a simple overcoat with an umbrella tucked under his arm, and is greeted by everyone with a respectful informality to which he responds with a pleasant and confident smile, approach this man and offer him your hand, he will shake it: he's the King.[50]

There is no documentary trace of he and Turner having met in Twickenham, but they were already good friends in the 1830s, and Twickenham is the only reasonable place they had in common.

At the 1815 Academy exhibition Turner showed *Dido Building Carthage*, a great classical composition incorporating people working in unison, buildings, light and water. It is a composition of a type that had been in Turner's mind, and expressed again and again in his sketchbooks, since 1805 or 1806. His Carthage is constructed out of elements of classical architecture recollected in tranquillity from memories of Claude, of Aosta and of the architecture of Chambers and Hardwick. The subject is renewed optimism, with a rising sun, and the construction of a maritime civilisation in a vivid model for a heroic post-war Europe. Turner's source was Virgil's

*Aeneid*, which, in Dryden's translation, describes a busy, peaceful, co-operative nation building for the future not only with stone and marble, but also with law and democracy.

The vision of the building of Carthage that Turner paints was described by Virgil, who speaks of Aeneas watching the scene, invisible in a cloud. As invisible, indeed, as is Turner:

> The toiling Tyrians on each other call
> To ply their labour: some extend the wall;
> Some build the citadel; the brawny throng
> Or dig, or push unwieldy stones along.
> Some for their dwellings choose a spot of ground,
> Which, first ordain'd, with ditches they surround.
> Some laws ordain; and some attend the choice
> Of holy senates, and elect by voice.
> Here some design a mole, while others there
> Lay deep foundations for a theatre;
> From marble quarries mighty columns hew,
> For ornaments of scenes, and future view.
> Such is their toil, and such their busy pains,
> As exercise the bees in flow'ry plains ...[51]

Far from being a melancholy work musing on the rise and fall of empires, Turner's *Dido Building Carthage* is a challenge to new thinking, a picture of hope in a shattered world, sufficient to inspire an aspiring king. Reconstruction was in the air in 1815, in England and in France, so from whatever angle we may take it, *Dido Building Carthage* was a timely and calculated piece of work. Its effect, however, was compromised because before it could be exhibited Napoleon had escaped from Elba in March 1815 and was at large. It was the third great canvas, *Hannibal* and *Dido and Aeneas* being the first two, in what was to become a lifelong series of paintings reflecting on the history of Carthage. To Turner, Carthage was the paradigm of a noble civilisation built in hope and determination, but which was bound to decay through greed, human weakness and folly. In thinking in these terms over the previous ten or twelve years, Turner was the supreme realist; and in painting thus he was laying an eloquent trail of images down the decades, ruminating through collective human experience on the rise and fall of empires.

*Crossing the Brook*, Turner's second 1815 Royal Academy exhibit, was equally timely. In the foreground two girls and their dog cross a small, shallow stream; in the background the stream has grown into, or flowed into, the River Tamar with Calstock Bridge beyond, and Dartmoor rolling away into the distance. But in the middle distance, arching down to the river, are aqueducts and giant waterwheels of the type then in use at china clay mines.[52] From the primitive peace and innocence of girls crossing the brook, the eye leads to the churning wheels of a modern country that is winning peace and has crossed the Rubicon from a rural to an industrial economy. The inspiration of Claude is the common factor in both *Crossing the Brook* and *Dido Building Carthage*, and that an Englishman should complement the French to so great a degree by paying such a generous tribute to Claude can only have attracted Louis-Philippe to Turner the more.

William Turner the elder celebrated his seventieth birthday on 27th June 1815, the week after Waterloo. His son, working at Queen Anne Street in the morning, travelled down to Twickenham to celebrate in the afternoon.[53] Such fine cutting of his time was forced on Turner by pressure of work induced both by his own driven nature and his instinctive need for work to draw a screen between himself and his domestic responsibilities. He had a son's normal concern for his father, particularly as he reached seventy, and seems to have been worried about the amount of physical work that the old man was taking on at Sandycombe.[54]

But Turner may not have been too effective at relieving pressure on his father, because at times of stress he would demand action from him in the most peremptory of terms.[55] Turner had the artist's certainty that his work was of paramount importance, and that the juggernaut must grind on regardless. In sending two canvases, *Jason* and *Fishing upon the Blythe-Sand*, down to Devon for the first exhibition of the Plymouth Institution in 1815 he was seeing to the promotion of his own reputation in a friendly country, just as eagerly as he was helping out a friend by raising the standard of this provincial exhibition. And in welcoming a visit by the Italian sculptor Antonio Canova to his studio in November 1815, he was knowingly admitting a man who might carry reports of his genius back to Rome in advance of Turner's own proposed visit. And how right he was: *"Grand génie!"* Canova exclaimed,[56] and set about laying the foundations for a firm official welcome to Turner in Rome in 1819: *"Furono acclamati in accad. di onore ... il Sig. Touner Paesista di Londra."*[57]

Turner took on more responsibilities at the Academy when he was elected Visitor to the newly established School of Painting in December 1815, and yet more when he dug himself in to the management of the Artists General Benevolent Institution, an independent self-help group pledged to support artists and their families in hard times. He was, in sum, exceedingly happy in his work. He was doing precisely what he wanted to do; it had paid him richly from the beginning; it had given him worldly status and recognition; and it enabled him to travel at will. Turner was a workman who used his hands and fingers as easily as he used his brushes. He might mix his paint with a stick or with his hands, which, thus, can never have been clean; he scratched at his paint or pencilled surfaces with his finger nail, and sometimes left fingerprints when he did so. When, at the end of his life, a young man claiming to be a painter came to see him, Turner said "Show me your hands!" They were clean. "Turn the fellow out, he's no artist."[58]

Turner wanted to take the earliest opportunity to see Europe after the Battle of Waterloo.[59] He had hoped to go in the summer of 1816, but as time went by the prospect receded. He was instead committed to the north of England to make drawings once again for Thomas Whitaker, this time for a projected *History of Richmondshire*. By September he had left it too late and was stuck in Yorkshire in torrential rain, in the wettest, coldest, bitterest summer in memory. A volcano, Mount Tambora, had exploded in Indonesia in 1815, causing havoc to weather patterns around the globe. "Rain, Rain, Rain, day after day. Italy deluged, Switzerland a wash-pot. Neufchatel, Bienne and Morat Lakes all in *one*. All chance of getting over the Simplon or any of the passes *now* vanished like the morning mist . . ."[60]

The commitment to Whitaker and northern England was sealed for Turner by the offer of the massive fee of 3,000 guineas through the publishers Longman for 120 drawings,[61] and with the certainty before he left of payment on delivery, business took precedence over a speculative journey to Europe. On the way north he stayed at Farnley, and was accompanied for part of the way into "Richmondshire" by Fawkes and his new wife, named Maria like the first, whom Walter had married in January. They all returned to Farnley in the middle of August for the grouse shoot, where Richard Fawkes was fatally injured. During the few days that Richard lay dying, Turner slipped away north again to make more drawings,[62] before returning to Farnley on 27th August and then off into Richmondshire once more in the rain. He came back to London, via Farnley, in late September.

The pattern of summer tours allowed Turner to spend the autumn, winter and spring working up watercolour subjects and painting his set piece exhibits for the Academy. In the three years 1815 to 1817 the oil paintings all had a staunch undertow of political allusion. Although they were received with great praise by sympathetic critics and artists, it was with partial understanding. The painter Thomas Uwins RA wrote of the 1815 exhibits by "that greatest of all living geniuses, Turner, whose works this year are said to surpass all his former outdoings."[63] In May 1816 the critic of the *Sun* described his pair of *Jupiter Panellenius* paintings as "like two new guineas fresh from the mint; yellow, shining, gorgeous and sterling."[64] And of *The Decline of the Carthaginian Empire* in 1817: "Mr Turner has only one [exhibit], but that one is a lion . . . excelling in the higher qualities of art, mind and poetical conception, even Claude himself."[65]

Steady over three years, these critical comments were welcome enough. The "enemy" on the other hand, Sir George Beaumont, put a counter view, as unwavering in its bitter line as Turner's supporters were warm in theirs. Beaumont could not find much right in *Dido Building Carthage*, despite its being "so much cried up by artists and newspapers", and went back to the Academy a second time in early June 1815 "to satisfy himself that he was not mistaken in the judgement he had formed upon it."[66] Farington reported that Beaumont

> felt convinced that he was right in his opinion, and that the picture is painted in a false taste, not true to nature; the colouring discordant, out of harmony, resembling those French painters who attempted imitations of Claude, but substituted for his purity and just harmony violent mannered oppositions of Brown and hot colours to cold tints, blues and greys: that several parts of Turner's picture were pleasingly treated but as a whole it was of the above character.[67]

Beaumont had become stuck in a cycle of partisan fury that reflected the taste of a limited circle whose influence was already waning. "These are my sentiments," he said, "and I have as good a right and it is as proper that I should express them as I have to give my opinion of a *poetical* or any other production."[68]

As Chairman of the Artists' General Benevolent Institution, as a Professor at the Royal Academy and as himself, Turner held a highly influential position in the world of art in the first years of European peace. The men who had advocated war with France, the generation of Pitt the Younger and Sir George Beaumont, was waning, and power now belonged to those of the age of the Duke of Wellington, Sir Marc Isambard Brunel and J. M. W. Turner. As the landed power base decayed, so their institutions felt the wind of change. One such was the British Institution, which was throatily mocked by two succeeding anonymous pamphlets, circulated in 1815 and 1816. These *Catalogues Raisonnés* as they were called, attacked the conceit of the connoisseurs of the British Institution whose "only standards are old pictures", and specifically rallied to the defence of Turner, though he was unnamed:

> When men will stoop to condemn high talents with the virulence which ought to be reserved for criminal actions, when men of undoubted judgement and ability will ... use all their influence to oppress, when they will unblushingly proclaim their determination to deprive the first genius of the day of encouragement, and set up inferior works, to put him down, they must expect to have their actions narrowly scrutinised and the purity of their motives suspected.[69]

The author or authors of the *Catalogues* were never discovered. R. R. Reinagle, Smirke, Thompson and Callcott were some of the suspects,[70] and speculation about who was behind them fuelled paranoia. Beaumont was deeply wounded: "He appeared to be quite broken up in constitution, his countenance fallen, his spirits gone. He seemed to be fast declining towards dissolution."[71] The chief suspect, however, was Walter Fawkes, who everybody around the Academy knew to be a very close friend of Turner, and no friend of the British Institution. Turner and Fawkes had sat next to one another for years at the annual dinner marking the exhibition openings,[72] and in his direct northern way Fawkes did not hold his tongue when talking about the politics of art. Furthermore, he had the eloquence to compose the elegant essays in the *Catalogues*. Farington reported Thompson as saying that the *Catalogue Raisonée*

> ... perfectly agreed with much that [Fawkes] had said of the British Institution exhibition of the works of the Flemish and Dutch masters, and he had been for a week together at this exhibition when it was first opened, and loudly expressed sentiments agreeably to those in the Catalogue, and his friendly feeling for Turner is well known.[73]

The influence of Beaumont as a mouthpiece against Turner was stifled by the *Catalogue Raisonnée*. Nothing more was heard from him on the subject. William Hazlitt, a critic whose forthright views were always tempered with admiration, wrote in 1815, in one of his final passages on the artist, words that were unwittingly highly prophetic:

> The artist delights to go back to the first chaos of the world, or to that state of things when the waters are separated from the dry land, and the light from darkness, but as yet no living thing nor tree bearing fruit was seen upon the face of the earth. All is without forms and void. Someone said of his landscapes that they were pictures of nothing, and very like.[74]

Having failed to reach Europe in 1816, Turner made every effort to prepare for a productive visit the following year. He planned his route, which would take him to Ostend, Bruges, Ghent, Brussels and on to Waterloo. His notebook[75] has brief notes, taken before he left from Charles Campbell's *Traveller's Complete Guide through Belgium and Holland* (1817), to remind him of what to look for. There are further notes reminding himself to take "Books, Pouch, Fever medicine, Bark, Pencils, Colour," and some useful phrases to commit to memory such as "Vier is myn simmer – Where is my Chamber." The tour would take him down the Rhine to Mainz and back again to Rotterdam.

The trip to Waterloo had been taken by R. R. Reinagle in November 1815. Then, he had seen "the cinders of the thousands of bodies that were burnt on the spot", and bloodstains still vivid on walls and buildings.[76] By 1817, the journey was already "a kind of pilgrimage", as Charles Campbell had described it. If Campbell described good routes around the country, we might reasonably expect Reinagle, in conversation with Turner at the Academy, to have given a more graphic account. On 10th August, full of expectation, Turner left London for Margate, and embarkation to Ostend.

# EIGHT

## Into Europe: I

### 1817–1819

Having been confined within the shores of Britain for fifteen years, Turner made two long and energetic European tours in quick succession. As was the case in 1802, new peace in Europe gave British travellers the opportunity to leap onto packet boats and head across the Channel. The route Turner took to Waterloo in 1817 – from Ostend, via Bruges, Ghent and Brussels – exactly matches the plan he had written out in advance in the "Itinerary Rhine Tour" sketchbook.[1]

He was at Waterloo, the village and the unpretending nearby farm-steads, fields and crossroads where the future of Europe had been decided, for one day only, Saturday 16th August. Although he had the same enquiring attitude to the events of the battle as he had had for the events of Trafalgar, Waterloo was not a place to linger. He might have hired a guide and questioned the locals about what had happened and where, just as he had questioned the Trafalgar veterans at Sheerness in 1805; but the events of 22nd June 1815, minute by minute, were so well known in Britain that Turner will have read it all up in advance.

Two years after the battle the bodies had been cleared away, but nevertheless the place was redolent of slaughter. From a high point near the battlefield, Turner drew a view of La Haye Sainte, marking the pencil sketch with annotations – "Line of Army E[nglish]"; "Picton killed here"; "4000 killed here"; "orchard"; "1500 killed here" and "Causeway down which Bonaparte advanced". On another sketch he wrote "Hollow where the great Carnage took place of the Cuirassiers by the Guards."[2] Details of this kind suggest that Turner had it in mind before he left England to make a painting of the battlefield. There was talk of a prize for a painting to commemorate the battle and its outcome in Britain,[3] but at this time, as he stood looking down at the battlefield, he had not fully resolved how he would approach the subject.

From Waterloo, Turner took a stage coach via Liège and Aix la Chapelle to Cologne, where the most dramatic part of his journey began. This was to be Turner's first sight of the Rhine gorge. His preliminary notes told him what to look out for, such as:

Mentz [i.e. Mainz] to Bingen 21 miles between which there are 40 towns with several castles ... 3 miles below Baccharah a Platz and a castle on a rock in the middle of the R[hine] ... A small distance below Vessel a dangerous Whirlpool a mile below where the banks are very close ... A league below towards Cologne Rowland's Keitz Castle – v romantic with Umkel or Unkel.[4]

Turner walked the first thirty-five or forty miles from Cologne to Remagen and then went by boat up as far as Mainz and back to Cologne.[5] Those eleven days in August 1817, spent between massive precipices falling down to the river, beneath castles soaring skywards, and on a river that runs quietly and with a calm sobriety – a gentle paradox, this, which teases the physical energy of the landscape – those few days gave Turner a new source of inspiration and subject matter. Refreshed by later visits, it was to last his lifetime.

Leaving Cologne, Turner returned to Liège by coach the way he had come, and travelled north-east to Antwerp. He was there for two days, and undoubtedly carried out his plan to see Rubens's paintings in the city. He went north to Dutch towns, including Rotterdam and Amsterdam, where his "Itinerary" sketchbook particularly reminded him to see Rembrandt's *Night Watch* and *The Anatomy Lesson*. One of his final ports of call before leaving for England was Dordrecht, where he watched and sketched the life of the waterside on a calm, clear late summer day.[6] One study of the harbour at Dordrecht is inscribed "Dead calm. Water lighter in the Nort."[7] Another, of a sight that deeply impressed Turner, and one which he could never have seen in England, is inscribed: "Float of timber 1000 feet long at least lashed in two places and guided by the cross piece of timber which hauls either part of the float or buoy in two lines – and drawn by 3 horses down the canal."[8]

After the visual drama of the Rhine gorge, the slow pace of the life and flat landscape of coastal Holland came as an extreme contrast. A cabbage boat caught Turner's eye,[9] as did the sight of men ploughing with four horses[10] and dozens of other incidental details. Turner was blessed by prolonged fine weather that August and September of 1817, and by a reflective mood which echoed the calm that he found in the harbour. In the same "Dort" sketchbook is an early idea for one of the three large paintings that Turner made for the 1818 Royal Academy exhibition, the work with a title as long and slow as its subject, *Dort, or Dordrecht, the Dort Packet-Boat from Rotterdam becalmed.*

Probably through his own carelessness, if we take Clara Wells's observation at face value, Turner lost his knapsack, his "walett", on his travels. As he travelled on foot this will almost certainly have been his sole article of luggage, and the contents that he lost, listed in his sketchbook, reveals how light he now travelled. In one hand he held his umbrella, and on his shoulder was the knapsack containing a sketchbook, pencils, his paints, his Campbell's guide to Belgium, shirts, a night shirt, stockings, a waistcoat, seven cravats, a razor and a spare ferrule for his umbrella. The seven cravats suggest he was anxious to keep his neck warm – a sensible precaution, given his susceptibility to illness.[11]

Turner came back to England from Rotterdam to Harwich, and almost immediately travelled north. He had work to do in County Durham, to make studies for a painting of Raby Castle, commissioned from William Vane, the third Earl of Darlington, and to make drawings for a proposed *History of Durham* by the antiquary Robert Surtees. The two projects interlinked, for Raby Castle, as well as Hylton and Gibside, was among the proposed subjects for Surtees. Another host on this north-eastern tour was Lord Strathmore, who picked Turner up from Raby and took him north to Durham and Newcastle.[12]

A great deal hung on the Raby commission. Vane was an enthusiastic, even obsessive, sportsman. He kept a stable of successful racehorses, and is said to have hunted six days a week.[13] Before succeeding to his earldom in 1792 he sat as a Whig MP for Totnes and later for Winchelsea, and was well-connected in political and social circles in London and the north of England. The connection that brought him and Turner together may have been their mutual friends Neweby Lowson and Walter Fawkes. Darlington had expressed to Henry Lascelles his "great intimacy with Mr Fawkes's family" in 1806 when he turned down Lascelles's request for his support in that year's parliamentary election.[14]

Turner's visit to Raby coincided – inevitably – with a meet. In the "Raby" sketchbook there are drawings of huntsmen and hounds interspersed with detailed drawings of Raby Castle itself. That Turner could move so effortlessly from expressing the clatter and breathy vivacity of conglomerating hounds and horses on an autumn morning, to sparkling drawings of a great house, demonstrates how integrated and organised was his mind and how controlled his energies. Notes on one of the panoramic studies of the castle and its landscape show his eye for tree types, and the importance to him of getting the planting of the grounds right – "Sycamore – Ash – Fir – Ash and holly" he wrote on the drawing.[15]

We do not know how far the Earl suggested the subject matter of his painting to Turner, but he might have specially asked for a fox hunt to be prominent, for one most certainly was when the picture was exhibited at the Royal Academy the following May.

X-rays of *Raby Castle* reveal mounted horsemen in the right foreground, with the dead fox being held aloft by a huntsman at left centre. This was the only fox hunt Turner had exhibited, and it seems to have upset an influential portion of his loyal public. The *Literary Chronicle* lambasted *Raby Castle* as Turner's

> ... detestable fox hunting picture, which we consider a disgrace to his great talents. If there is one man in existence whose works possess the quality [of poetry] in a higher degree than another, it is Turner; but we should be sorry to carry our admiration of his genius so far as to tolerate his failures or applaud his errors.[16]

As the painting is known now, the fox hunt is restricted to a relatively discreet gallop across the wide sweep of the middleground, and there is no doubt that after the Academy exhibition Turner painted out the offending hunt himself, and added what we now see. If it were not through pressure from his patron, his reasons for replacing the original detail with a lower key version more in the manner of the early-eighteenth-century painter John Wootton, remain a mystery.

*Raby Castle* is the most overtly Rubensian of all Turner's oil landscapes. The fact that it was painted soon after his visit to Antwerp can be no coincidence. Turner had set country houses within wide landscapes in earlier oils – *Pope's Villa*; *Petworth ... Dewy Morning*; *Somer Hill* – but in all these the house had been rooted in the background, at the far end of the painting. *Raby Castle*, however, picked out by a strike of sunlight, has far greater distances beyond it than the acres before; the Castle sits in the landscape like a jewel on a beautiful breast. It is comparable more to Turner's *London*, then with Fawkes at Farnley, than it is to any other of Turner's house portraits.

While he was in County Durham, and in the following weeks when he moved south to Farnley, Turner worked energetically on a series of watercolours of scenes up and down the Rhine. From outline pencil drawings expressing prosaic landscape fact, Turner made fifty-one watercolours which were acquired in their entirety by Walter Fawkes. Though Fawkes's good humour and generosity may have kept him well armed against some of his difficulties, it tended to blind him to others. For ten years or more he had been refusing to look his financial problems squarely in the eye. The root of these must have been excessive expenditure during the election campaign of 1806, continual political expenses, together with the cost of running Farnley and the Grosvenor Place house. Fawkes began regularly to mortgage property on his estates, and to accept loans from individuals. He did not listen to his accountant, in whose view Fawkes spent far too much money on inessentials, such as books, prints and paintings.[17] When Fawkes bought paintings from Turner he was spending money he could not afford.

Although Turner was fortunate in Fawkes's support and friendship, Fawkes was equally so in having Turner's constancy. When quiet remarks passed, as they must have done, between the two men about finance – the cost of running the house and remaining estates, of educating Fawkes's sons, of publishing political opinions of the greatest importance and urgency for the nation – Turner was the incarnation of practical help and generosity. Some time around 1818 he made part, if not all, of the loan of £3,000 that appears as an outstanding debt to Turner in Fawkes's accounts for 1824. This was generous, but not that generous. Fawkes's 1824 accounts show that Turner's £3,000 loan carried an annual rate of interest of £150. In the "Liber Notes (2)" sketchbook of 1818 or 1819 is a memorandum which includes the reference: "Mr Fawkes: Bond £1,200; Note £780."[18]

Turner's own financial situation was as secure as any could be in the early post-war years. He did not keep his money in the commercial banks, but instead invested through his stockbroker, William Marsh, in government and other stocks at the Bank of England. The "Finance" sketchbook gives Turner's own extended lists of figures of his income, investments and interest payments over the period c. 1809–14, and throws light on his attention to detail in handling his money.[19] Watching his close friend ignoring advice and slipping from a position of great wealth and status inexorably through misplaced generosity towards ruin will have terrified him. Though Turner had been naturally cautious about money from his youth, having earned every penny he owned, Fawkes's situation confirmed and hardened his attitude. Most stories of Turner's alleged meanness, as opposed to his tough business deals, emerge from the years after his experience with Fawkes, as do his own forebodings about personal ruin. Watching Walter Fawkes, Turner could see how vast sums of money could evaporate; his own wonderful flashes of generosity were always tempered with caution, as was his attitude to money. "Don't wish for money," he said to an "intimate friend", "you will not be happier, and you know you can have any money off me you want."[20]

The £500 that "it is said"[21] Fawkes paid for the fifty-one Rhine watercolours and the further 500 guineas that Farington recorded, from gossip he had heard,[22] that Fawkes had also paid for the *Dort*, may well have remained unpaid, and the paintings actually comprise a proportion of the debt. The evidence of the payments for these paintings is so vague, that under the circumstances that Fawkes and Turner found themselves to be in, they can probably be discounted. We may also be able to clear up the mystery of the ownership of Turner's *London*. It was with Fawkes by 1811, and then mysteriously "exchanged".[23] This may mean that *London* was quietly returned as a collateral for the debt.

For Turner the years 1818 and early 1819 were transitional; they were years in which he absorbed his new experience of Europe and prepared for its consequences. It had a parallel marker in what family life he had by the marriage on 31st October 1817 at St James's Church Piccadilly of his elder daughter Evelina to a self-opinionated young diplomat, Joseph Dupuis. The marriage took place with Turner's "consent and approbation".[24] Turner had no cause to refuse to allow his daughter to marry an honourable man with prospects; there is no evidence that he had shown any responsibility for her in the past. Dupuis was waiting to leave England "to fill a Consular situation abroad", and nearly a year after the pair married they went off together to Ashanti, in the Gold Coast, where Dupuis was to be Consul.[25]

The 1817 Rhine journey was to be the first of seventeen or eighteen journeys in Europe. While his focus began now increasingly to include Europe, Turner was able in the light of foreign travel to reflect more keenly on the social history of Britain, on what it meant to be British and on the meaning of his own life. After the 1817 tour, he undertook a curious apprenticeship for his long awaited journey to Italy. An acquaintance, the architect and topographical draughtsman James Hakewill (1778–1843), proposed to John Murray that he publish a book of landscape engravings to tempt the post-Waterloo tourist market. This was to be called *A Picturesque Tour of Italy*. Turner was drawn in, at first as one of a number of artists, then as the sole artist, to make watercolours for engraving based on Hakewill's own run-of-the-mill sketches of Italian views.[26]

The eighteen watercolours Turner made for engraving for Hakewill were evocations of what he hoped to see, and how he saw it already, both in his mind's eye and through the work of brother artists. A commission of much the same kind as Hakewill's, though for one image only, came at about the same time for the frontispiece to *Picturesque Views of the Antiquities of Pola, in Istria* by another architect and draughtsman, Thomas Allason (1790–1852). Although Turner had not been to Pola, now Pula on the Croatian coast south of Trieste, he knew Aosta, a remarkably similar Roman city set, like Pola, on the fringes of Roman Italy.

As Turner's 1802 sketches of Aosta show, he had already seen for himself the way a Roman provincial city was set out, how its remains were pillaged for building materials by inhabitants over the intervening centuries, and how its street plan dictated the layout of the new city. Like Pola, Aosta had an amphitheatre, temples and a great triumphal arch, and like Pola, too, its carved stones, inscriptions and so on were scattered about, as if they were leaf mould redistributed by ants. Turner's depiction of Pola's buildings, though imaginary in their juxtaposition, was based on first-hand knowledge, experience, and mature recall. The Hakewill and Allason commissions were practice, neat but brilliant little sparring punches in the air before Turner could take on the real thing in earnest, with plenty of time to set about it. One romantic watercolour jousting exercise of this kind, *Landscape: Composition of Tivoli*, had a public outing in the 1818 Academy exhibition.

At the same exhibition, Turner displayed three muscular reactions to the reality of post-Waterloo European landscape: *Raby Castle, Dort* and *The Field of Waterloo*. These three large oils express three very present European questions: *Raby* in its original form showed an England at peace, but with blood on her hands; the future of Europe and its independent nationhoods as it waits for the wind to get up is expressed in *Dort*; and the burnt and bloodsoaked fields that the new Europe now had to plough is tragically evoked in *Waterloo*. All three paintings have their roots in the seventeenth-century European painting that Turner had seen in Holland and Flanders the previous year – Rubens, Cuyp and, in *Waterloo*, a specific amalgam of Rubens and Rembrandt's *Night Watch*.[27] And all three aspire to be read as European art.

Real estate was high in Turner's mind at this time. The parliamentary acts that led to enclosures, the creation of fields throughout rural England, and hedges, walls and ditches to mark them out, had the effect of causing land here and there to be redistributed as compensation for acres lost elsewhere. Turner made a net gain in 1818 when he was given about an eighth of an acre sited two and a half miles west of Sandycombe on common land down by the River Crane.[28] This award came partially at least out of the blue; but Turner's response showed foresight and fore-thought. He immediately bought three similarly awarded plots adjoining his own to the south, giving him almost an acre of contiguous land.

This determined action marks the first practical step Turner took towards his dream of building a set of almshouses for "decayed male artists". He first voiced this formally in the will he drew up in 1829. The realities implicit here are an awareness of his own mortality, and his deep and practical concern for members of his profession less fortunate than he. His work with the Artists' General Benevolent Fund, and his long-running commitment to the Royal Academy made the idea of founding almshouses for artists a logical extension of his interests. Although it was not in itself particularly special – charity almshouses were being founded up and down the country every year – in the light of Fawkes's troubles it was purposeful philanthropy intended to assuage financial suffering among artists. Turner laid down no conditions of the quality of the work that his "decayed artists" had produced over their lifetimes, but appeared to be very strict on other matters – the artists had to be landscape painters, male, legitimate, and born in England of English parents.

His own children would never have qualified had they become painters, and not only because they were both girls. This insistence on nationality, gender and legitimacy has been interpreted as a piece of jingoism and hypocrisy on Turner's part; but we must remember the unwavering strength of Turner's well-intentioned and staunch patriotism, and the fact that he knew that his wishes had to be carried out after his death by others under the public gaze in a climate of strong social disapproval of promiscuity and illegitimacy. It is irrelevant that Turner was himself sexually active and interested. He may not have been particularly open about his proclivities, but on the other hand he did not take any active steps to conceal them by destroying his sex drawings. Others did most of that for him. He did, however, have the greatest concern for the well-being of his brother artists, and by being seen to nod towards the reality of social conventions as they were, Turner took steps to ensure that the great majority of English artists at least would be eligible for his charity.

At much the same time there were changes to Turner's property holding in Harley Street and Queen Anne Street. The lease on his former house 64 Harley Street was reassigned by the Portland Estate Trustees to the dentist Benjamin Young "as occupier" at the expiry of ten years after Turner had sublet it to Young. The property at the end of the back yard of number 64, however, that fronting onto Queen Anne Street with some land beyond, had been leased to Turner and others since 1809 as "44 Queen Anne Street". He now prepared to enter into a legal agreement with the Portland Estates Trustees which would oblige him to demolish the property and rebuild it "before Michaelmas 1821 in a workmanlike manner". In doing so he took the opportunity to build a second gallery afresh within his new boundaries. But as if he, Mr Young and the Portland Trustees were playing a game of musical chairs around this small corner of London, Turner also took the leases of numbers 65 and 66 Harley Street. Whether by accident, design or desire Turner now had Mr Young the dentist surrounded.[29] He probably started making plans for the new gallery before he left for Italy in the summer of 1819, and arranged for the foundations to be laid while he was away. The property was listed in the Marylebone rate returns as "empty and in building" at Christmas 1819.

Before going to Italy, Turner had yet another job to complete. Such was his esteem for the work of Sir Walter Scott that he agreed to be one of a group of artists contracted to make illustrations for engraving and publication in *The Provincial Antiquities of Scotland*, a compilation of writings on the history and archaeology of Scotland assembled by Scott. This brought to seven the number of different publications or serials in which he was currently actively engaged by making watercolours, either by contract, friendly agreement or his own desire. It was by any standards a heavy workload. Scott and his publisher made no bones of the fact that they were bringing Turner into the project because they knew that his name would purchase them a good opinion, and far greater sales. Turner knew this too, and pressed for the highest possible fee, 25 guineas for drawings made on the spot, and 20 if made from sketches. This was more than twice the amount offered to the other artists, who included Edward Blore, John Thomson, J. C. Schetky, Hugh William Williams and A. W. Callcott.[30] Blore at least accepted this situation, as he wrote to Scott: "We cannot too highly appreciate the advantages which his [Turner's] name is likely to confer on our work."[31]

Because of the expense of a publishing project such as this, risks were spread among the author, artists and engravers involved, by each becoming a shareholder. What detailed haggling there may have been with Turner in advance of signing the contract took place either in lost correspondence or face to face in London. Scott wrote bitterly to a friend: "Turner's palm is as itchy as his fingers are ingenious and he will, take my word for it, do nothing without cash, and anything for it. He is the only man of genius I ever knew who is sordid in these matters."[32] This is less than fair; Scott wrote for money too. This was the kind of gossipy remark that gave Turner a bad reputation in the publishing market, and has coloured the general perception of him for 150 years or more. Turner was in business, had a living to make and a high reputation, and five or six hundred miles to travel to carry out this particular work.

Although the letter above was written some months after Turner's 1818 visit to Scotland, the suggestion that Scott felt that he was employing a primadonna preceded Turner to the dining-rooms of Edinburgh. He was invited for breakfast with the painter John Christian Schetky and his family, but for reasons unknown – the mood of the moment, the effects of a long tiring journey – the famous artist came across as distant, reserved, even cold in his manner, and his hosts abruptly cancelled a dinner they had planned in Turner's honour. Schetky's sister wrote: "We intended to have a joyous evening on his arrival, but finding him such a *stick*, we did not think the pleasure of showing him to our friends would be adequate to the trouble and expense."[33] Things having got off on the wrong foot, Turner continued to behave badly, and reportedly let down a party of lads who had expected to spend a rollicking evening with him. The putative host, the portrait painter William Nicholson, complained that: "after preparing a feast and having ten fine fellows to make merry with him, Turner never made an appearance."[34]

With some of his fellow artists on the *Provincial Antiquities* project, Turner made sketching trips out into the landscape around Edinburgh. He stayed at the manse with the Rev. John Thomson, Pastor of Duddingston, a village at the foot of Arthur's Seat. Thomson was a talented amateur painter, warmly appreciative of his famous friend and colleague. Stories of how secretive Turner was of his sketches on these trips, as on others with fellow artists, are familiar enough. The gist of one which attached itself to this particular episode is that Turner would not let the others see his sketches when his friends showed off theirs; and that he chased after the pastor's wife when she found one of his sketchbooks on the hall table and ran off with it.[35] The point of Turner's reluctance to show his preliminary work was because it was just that; initial ideas, bland and unremarkable in themselves, on which he would later work magic in the quiet of his own studio. It was the results of the magic that he would exhibit to anybody with great pride and delight; the preceding raw material on the other hand was his own business entirely, and would probably be intensely disappointing to the casual viewer. In the quiet of his studio Turner would transform sketchbook drawings from workaday pencil studies to great narrative watercolours, by introducing weather effects, human figures and a moral allusion.[36] The difficulty that some of Turner's amateur friends had was that they continued to expect him to perform like a magician – indeed there are many instances when Turner's great talents were described as magic powers.

On the way home from Scotland, Turner called at one of the few places where he was not expected to perform, Farnley Hall. But so relaxed was he within those four walls that on this particular visit he did in fact perform as an artist, in front of an audience, on demand. Perhaps Walter and Hawkesworth had been talking over breakfast about the scale of things, the size of a great man o' war in particular: "I want you to make me a drawing of the ordinary dimensions that will give some idea of the size of a man o' war," Fawkes asked his friend. Turner laughed, took Hawkey aside, and said "Come along we will see what we can do for Papa."[37] (Although this story has always been read as if Hawkesworth were a child, he was in fact twenty-one by now.)

Upstairs in Turner's painting room, over the course of the morning, Hawkesworth witnessed the gradual evolution of *A First Rate Taking in Stores*, in which the giant ship, standing high in the water, with her masts far beyond the top of the picture, takes on provisions from two small lighters. The young man sat entranced by Turner's side as he worked, and later described how Turner began by saturating the paper with wet paint, then tearing, scratching, scrubbing at it in a kind of frenzy until all he had created was a chaotic mass of colour. But, "gradually and as if by magic the lovely ship, with all its exquisite minutia, came into being and by luncheon time the drawing was taken down in triumph." The magic was in the painter's hands and fingers, and in his gentle and persuasive use of the brushes, which Hawkesworth does not mention but which were surely there, and in his instinctive knowledge of the architecture of shipping.

There is a subtle parallel in the compositions of the *Dort* and the *First Rate* watercolour, which may have been auto-suggestion. Turner's glowing exhibit at the 1818 Royal Academy, *Dort, or Dordrecht, the Dort Packet-Boat from Rotterdam becalmed*, had just come to Farnley. Hawkesworth, in a jocular manner throwing his weight around as the new heir, had insisted that his father buy the painting, threatening to cut off the entail to the Farnley properties if he refused. Walter protested, in his first known acknowledgement of his financial situation, that he had already spent more money on pictures than he was justified in doing.[38] So *Dort*, paid for or not, came to Farnley to hang over the drawing-room fireplace where Turner showed it in his painting of the interior of that room. Presumably at about this time, Turner began a companion watercolour to the *First Rate*, an image of a violent shipwreck. This colour study, known as *Wreck of an East Indiaman*, is inscribed "Begun for Dear Fawkes of Farnley", as clear and piquant a measure as any of Turner's loyalty to Fawkes at this difficult time in his life.[39]

In these transitional years, a further change in Turner's life came when in January 1819 he scrapped his *Liber Studiorum* venture. This had been sustaining him intellectually for more than a decade, but certainly not financially or socially, for it lost him money and friends among the network of London engravers and print publishers. It also affected his reputation among collectors, for the *Liber* parts came to be issued sporadically and late, and many subscribers did not get the quality of proofs they had paid for. The original purpose of the *Liber*, as dreamt up at Knockholt, had been achieved, but not as expected. Though the *Liber* had firmly sealed the identity and ownership of Turner's compositions, and acted as a security measure, his subsequent work for engravers demonstrated to him how the process could be turned on its head for everybody's benefit. Now, in his work for the Cookes, Walter Scott and others, the preliminary watercolour image was a means to an end; the engraving, with its wide circulation, was the final product.

More changes concerned Turner's attitude to his teaching commitments. He made radical amendments to his Perspective lectures in the 1818 and 1819 series, writing new texts, changing the running order and drawing new diagrams to show his audience. There had been criticism of the Academy in the press, and Turner may have been reacting to this through these changes. As a senior Councillor of the Academy he shared a collective responsibility for its public image and its effectiveness as a teaching institution. Notes on some of the lecture sheets suggest that Turner was also stung by the students' lazy reluctance to grapple with perspective problems, so in the time-honoured professorial tradition he felt justified in criticising them roundly.[40]

Turner had a pronounced sense of duty towards his work, his students, his engravers and to the Academy. Looked at with a wider perspective, this sense of duty, one of his noblest qualities, was directed at the public, whom he rarely, if ever, let down. It may be fairly weighed in Turner's defence against his apparent lack of interest in his own two children. Even when he was feeling as sick as a dog Turner would plough on with his work until he was satisfied, and would react quickly to events. Writing to W. B. Cooke in February 1819 Turner asks to be sent his cover design for *Views in Sussex* for reworking:

> Just send me the vignette Helmet for an Hour or so I think I can further improve it at least Allen will be released from a little more of the coat of mail. I have got a most confounded cold and swelled throat by *paddling* ... *last night*; send *it* if possible before the Evening because there will be a General Assembly tonight which I mean to attend.[41]

Before Turner went to Italy in 1819 two old friends honoured him with two separate exhibitions of his paintings in their London houses. In March, Sir John Leicester showed his Turners off at his gallery in Hill Street, while the following month Walter Fawkes opened his house in Grosvenor Place for the public to see his collection of one hundred or more Turner water-colours, and further paintings by other contemporary watercolourists. Fawkes's exhibition had been long in the planning, with Turner's own involvement, for Fawkes produced a printed catalogue with a cover designed by Turner. This showed a classical plinth surmounted by a watercolourist's palette, brushes, paint, ink and sketchbook, and inscribed with the names of nineteen watercolour painters, professional and ama-teur, one for each year of the century. Turner's name, "Turner RA PP," heads the list.

The exhibition at Grosvenor Place pleased Turner no end. He was ineffably proud of his achievement, and properly so:

> [He] generally came [to the exhibition] alone, and while he leaned on the centre table in the great room, or slowly worked his rough way through the mass, he attracted every eye in the brilliant crowd, and seemed to me like a victorious Roman general, the principal figure in his own triumph.[42]

While Fawkes's exhibition was taking place, the largest painting Turner had made was then on show at Somerset House – *England: Richmond Hill, on the Prince Regent's Birthday*. This canvas, eleven feet long, was a celebration of nationhood, and of the unity of the nation under the crown. Turner had been thinking about the subject for at least two years, for, as Jean Golt has pointed out, it is based on an actual event, the birthday celebration given for the Prince by Lady Cardigan at Cardigan

House, Richmond on 12th August 1817.[43] Here at the party was the future of England after the Napoleonic Wars – a few men in uniform, some children and many women. They all seem to stand around as if waiting for something to happen, perhaps the arrival of the Prince himself who, with the royal party "after dinner promenaded in the delightful walks".[44]

If this is so, then we are standing in the position of the Prince, for something exciting has just caught the attention of the central figure of a young girl who looks directly at the viewer, and sends her excitement out in ripples to the other party-goers. If this is Turner's intention, it is a characteristically dramatic narrative engagement. Turner had not yet had any royal patronage, and it may be that this was his pitch for such recognition.[45] If this was one impulse for the artist, it was an over-elaborate, even obvious gesture dangerously liable to misfire. More likely, knowing as he did that he would be leaving England soon enough for Italy and who knows what rival inspiration and influence, *England: Richmond Hill* was Turner's adieu, for the time being, to a long and nourishing relationship with his native landscape, in which the view from Richmond Hill had been an ever recurring theme. How touching that out of sight in the plumb centre of this great panorama of England should be Sandy-combe, and that the viewer, standing in the shoes of the Prince Regent, is looking directly towards Turner's own country house, and at his own place in the landscape of Britain.

# NINE

# Into Europe: II

## 1819–1820

Turner left for Italy in August 1819 with the high excitement of a man who knew that he was going to have a good time. He was urged on his way by friends, was sent off by friends, and had friends waiting for him on arrival in Rome, the most sociable foreign outpost for artistic Britons. As Britain's – this meant the world's – greatest landscape painter, his were the pair of eyes eagerly expected to transform responses to Italian light and landscape. Two weeks before Turner was due to leave, Farington received a letter from Sir Thomas Lawrence:

> Turner should come to Rome. His Genius would here be supplied with new Materials, and entirely congenial with it ... He has an Elegance and often a Greatness of Invention, that wants a Scene like this for its free expansion; whilst the subtle harmony of this Atmosphere that wraps everything in its own Milky sweetness ... can only be rendered according to my beliefs, by the beauty of his Tones.[1]

Lawrence mused to another correspondent, Samuel Lysons, the Antiquary Professor at the Royal Academy that

> The only person who could do [Tivoli] justice, would be Turner, who ... approaches, in the *highest* BEAUTIES of his noble works, nearer to the fine lines of composition, to the effects, and exquisite combinations of colour, in the country through which I have passed, ... than even Claude himself.[2]

These were eloquent and affectionate testimonials from the man who, within months, would be the next President of the Royal Academy, writing to members of the passing generation. But Turner had long decided to make the journey, and mentally at least was already on his way. His intention was not to make directly for Rome, but to see as much of Italy as he possibly could *en route*. Before leaving London, Turner had hours of detailed conversations about routes and sights with James Hakewill, perhaps while the two men were working together on the *Picturesque Tour of Italy*. Like others before him, Hakewill wrote long travel notes and tips into Turner's notebook:

> Como ... Take two boatmen and pay them 3 francs ea. p. day. The men will point out what is worth seeing ... At Milan – go to the Albergo Reale in the Street, tre Re (sounded tra ra) ... A few doors higher up lives a Printseller who talks English well, and will be civil, buying of him the maps &c which you may want. Perhaps he will remember my name.[3]

Turner committed many particularly important Italian views to memory by drawing dozens of tiny thumbnail sketches, no bigger than a postage stamp, from engravings.[4] He also made his own written notes of things to see and do, and these are even more detailed than Hakewill's, running to twenty-two closely written pages. The bulk of Turner's notes are taken from a popular four volume guidebook of the period, the Rev. J. C. Eustace's *Tour Through Italy*.[5] Eustace cannot, however, have been Turner's sole source of information, for writing of Paestum he makes a note, *inter alia*, of "where prostitutes sleep at night".[6]

Taking perhaps £40 or £60 with him, and some Louis d'Ors to change, Turner left £10 each with Hannah and his father.[7] He left London on 31st July, and embarked from Dover the following morning. Turner had never attempted to write a diary before – or if he did, it is lost – but as this journey began, he jotted down in minuscule handwriting his impressions of the first day and left a record of some scraps of the conversations in the diligence. "Left Dover at 10, arr. Calais at 3 in a boat from the packet boat. beset as usual. Began to rain next morning on the setting out of the diligence."[8] His fellow travellers seem to have been one Russian, two Frenchmen and five Englishmen, and they chattered idly about international affairs: "Russe great par Example the Emperor Alexander tooit part tout the French tres bon zens but the English everything at last was bad, Pitt the cause of all, the Kings death and fall and Robespierre their tool. Raind the whole way to Paris." Just north of Paris the diary account stops, with the words: "Beaumont sur Oise good," meaning, presumably, the landscape; and then Turner picks up his pencil again and begins to draw.

There are some small studies of Paris and its surroundings, but as the journey begins in earnest and he bowls down the same road that he took to

Lyons in 1802, his sense of excitement increases like a heartbeat. At Chalon this time he must have taken a lift on one of many of the boats that plied up and down the Sâone to Lyons, for many sketches are drawn from the middle of the river. He passed through Tournus, the unwitting inspiration for his oil painting *Opening of the Vintage of Macon*, and sees Macon itself which he drew from many angles. "Beautiful afternoon," he wrote on one sketch.[9]

On this journey Turner crossed into Italy by the Mont St Cenis pass, where he began to make rapid-fire landscape sketches, sometimes three to a page, flipping the notebook pages over as he goes, and sometimes, when running out of space, sliding the right-hand page up to continue the sketch at the end of the sheet below. This had been his practice since his earliest travels. He went down into Turin and then to Milan where the studies reflect his passion for architecture. There are pages of townscapes from afar and from within, details of buildings and studies of Turin and Milan Cathedrals. This natural affinity with architectural form speaks straight from the heart of his upbringing as if he were still an excited young architect. Nor does he forget that he is Professor of Perspective at the Royal Academy. In attending so closely to architectural subjects, he is using the very short time he has at each stopping place to amass material for future lectures and for paintings yet to come.[10]

But once he reaches Venice it appears from the tenor of the sketches, and from the way that the pace of the sketchbooks slacken, that Venice was a principal goal for him. There are dozens of intricate drawings of a variety of views; Venice at work as well as Venice on display. One of the first Venetian drawings is a detailed study of a gondola, followed by sketches of how they work and what they do. Though he was the acknowledged master of boats and ships of every kind in British waters, Turner had never seen such water transport except in other men's paintings. There is a precision and an expansiveness in the drawings in the two Venice sketchbooks that shows Turner taking his time, and assuring himself that he would return again and again.[11]

The shock of this first encounter with Venice is palpable in the watercolours of the city. He makes colour notes in his sketchbooks – "Blue – Mass of Light – White – Sky purple – water green – and dark blue"[12] – and the watery nature of the light has the effect in the watercolours themselves of softening Turner's colour, making his forms mistier and evoking a strong sense of the particular time of day by the way shadows fall or colour hangs in the sky. For the first time in his watercolour painting, Turner begins to experiment with hieroglyphic forms, strange superficially abstract shapes in the foreground or middleground which may be gondolas or harbour paraphernalia seen through haze.

His itinerary took him south-west across the Po valley to Bologna, where he made detailed studies of the city, in particular the extraordinary towers, then back to the Adriatic coast to Rimini, Fano and Ancona. There is such a thrilling and evident expenditure of pent-up energy on this journey; Turner has so much to see, so much to catch up on. He had been well ahead of the game when he made his opportunist journey to the Alps in 1802, but now, seventeen years later, he had slipped behind. Too busy at home with the English landscape and the great professional demands it was making on him, he had been passed on the inner track by other artists who had rediscovered Italy, and particularly Rome, before him. Lawrence had got there, so had young Charles Eastlake. Thomas Phillips, Henry Howard, the sculptor John Gibson had all beaten Turner to Rome; and the Danes and the Germans had been there for years. Turner's detour to Bologna and his return to the Adriatic coast indicates how eager he was to see Italy from all its angles, and not just the obvious sights. He was one of the few Englishmen of the period immediately after Waterloo to consider a journey to Ancona to be worthwhile. When he reached this town he found it peppered with Roman remains, as Eustace had told him it would be, and sweeping dramatically down from the hills to an elbow-shaped harbour at the sea. Though relatively remote to an Englishman, Ancona was a town every bit as exciting visually as Bologna or Turin.[13]

At Loretto, fourteen miles out of Ancona in the Umbrian hills, Turner noted he saw "the first bit of Claude".[14] He had been over two months on the road since leaving England, and that it had taken him so long to notice a "Claudean" view in the French and Italian landscape suggests that Claude had, if only temporarily, been replaced at the front of his mind. Instead his interests were becoming increasingly architectural, factual, and, lately seduced by Venice, he was beginning to see landscape through a palpable atmospheric screen.

Climbing over the intervening hills towards Rome, Turner sketched places en route – Foligno, Terni, Narni – in the quick and effective pencil shorthand that he had developed over years of travelling. But on arriving in Rome, as when arriving in Venice, Turner was drawn up short. Once again there is a sudden change of tempo in the sketchbooks, from light expressions of landscape to closely studied pencil or pen and ink drawings of architectural form, decoration and colour. Turner's central purpose on this journey was to study the art and example of Raphael. Studies of Raphael's Loggia, for example, are glossed with extensive written notes indicating that it was specific details that Turner wanted to make quite sure he remembered accurately and took home with him: "... the Band dark green with yellow arabesque. God divides darkness from Light over the door. Figures both Lake and the Sun and Moon opposite a light gr each of them in [illeg.] with an angel in red lake upon a blue ground."[15]

Other painstaking studies of the view of Rome from the loggia in the

Vatican, and compositional ideas placing Raphael himself within the Vatican, reveal something of the course of Turner's thought, and suggest that already he had a major painting in mind.[16] In addition, there are examples of the critic in Turner exercising himself, in notes on paintings and sculpture in the Corsini and Farnese Palaces.[17] Coming face to face with the supreme architectural achievements of the western world, Turner looked at them with a detached professional eye. The range of his critical opinion was impressive, but as so often his grasp of expressive English seems to have let him down while he was in full flood:

> St Peters. The part by Bernini good in the arrangement of the columns but being very large they carry the idea of greatness away from the facade of the building which being but one order, tho the atten ... has in the fascias of the pannal a capital, to carry an entablature without support, and the Dome colossal has [sic] it certainly is by measure rather ...[18]

Turner's application to the work he had come to Rome to carry out was resolute, and his production relentless. The same sketchbook, "Vatican Fragments", that contains his comments on St Peter's, also has many hundreds of small pencil drawings of carvings, pedestals, capitals, inscriptions, figures and so on. Anything and everything architectural and decorative caught his eye, and he sucked up the traces as a whale sucks up plankton. He climbed up the hills of Rome to draw the city from high ground, and went out into the countryside around to make watercolours of the landscape in which Rome was set.

Some time in mid-October, Turner met Thomas Lawrence and Charles Eastlake and his other friends, and was drawn into the social life of the English set in Rome. Chantrey and Jackson arrived on 13th October. Canova's introduction of Turner to the Academy of St Luke, which deeply flattered him, led inevitably to further soirées, one, on 15th November, including Canova, Lawrence, Chantrey, Jackson and Turner.[19] On one occasion, Turner was reported to have been put in the position of having to lend his umbrella to the Princess of Denmark when they and a fashionable soldier called Camac were together on a windy day on the Capitol. The wind blew the umbrella inside out, which annoyed Turner greatly.[20] As this was an expensive umbrella, with a two-feet-long dagger hidden in the handle to guard against felons, Turner's annoyance was understandable; but how he, the Princess and the colonel could find themselves shoulder to shoulder on the Capitol is anybody's guess. It does, however, reflect the social level that Turner naturally slipped into in Rome.

Another popular and well-connected host with whom Turner and others dined was the chemist Sir Humphry Davy (1778–1829), who was then in Rome with his wife. Davy had also come to Italy to look closely at Raphael, specifically to find ways to preserve the frescoes, as well as to carry out experiments in vulcanism during one of Vesuvius's eruptive periods. Turner and Davy had much in common. Both had reached the peak of their profession and were widely fêted. Both were amateur poets, both informed and eager fishermen, both omnivorously interested in the natural world. Among Davy's writings are perceptive observations of landscape form, and a poem dedicated to Canova, in which he describes the sculptor as "Master of Art yet Nature's simplest child."[21] Both Davy and Turner were visionaries, Davy creating in his words images of the most extraordinary power. In one vision, which he writes of having had in the Colosseum on 4th November 1819, he sees himself flying through the solar system to Saturn, experiencing brilliant colours and forms and meeting strange beings.[22]

Turner also met the architect Thomas Leverton Donaldson, a recent silver medallist at the Royal Academy, who was one of his former pupils.[23] Donaldson seems to have been Turner's travelling companion when he went yet further south towards Naples at the end of October, to see Vesuvius erupting. This was just one of the planned highlights of the Italian visit, as was time to draw and paint in Naples and the surrounding area, visits to Pompeii and Herculaneum just being excavated at the foot of Vesuvius, and a further journey possibly by boat around the Lattari peninsula to Sorrento, Amalfi, Salerno and Paestum. As Turner had followed his written itinerary to Rome almost to the letter, so he followed it faithfully south as far as Paestum.

Vesuvius is dull from the Naples side. It is not one sleek conical mountain as some tourist images suggested, but two connubial humps. Since the eruption of 79 AD when the top was blown off, Vesuvius has been partially surrounded by Monte Somma, the remains of its upper cone. As the traveller skirts around the seaward side, the two masses move with each other as a stiff neck moves in a starched collar. It is only from Sorrento that Monte Somma is obscured and Vesuvius becomes the typical volcanic conical shape. Significantly, though there are many sketchbook drawings of Sorrento,[24] there are none of Vesuvius from Sorrento. He was not especially interested in the mountain; it was the bay as a whole that thrilled him, with the islands of Ischia and Capri lying offshore like dismasted capital ships. Unlike the wide spaces of the Roman campagna, where the Tiber flows in curls, the landscape of the Bay of Naples is enclosed and fully integrated with Vesuvius as one, but only one, visual focus.

Naples itself, seen as Turner recorded it from the wide harbour and from the heights above at Capo di Monte, was – is still – a light-filled, expansive city. To reach this vantage point, however, Turner had to walk up dark narrow streets, long man-made caverns formed by hard, high stone churches and fine houses. These look inward onto warmly lit courtyards or end with the sudden appearance of stone balustraded staircases running up and down hill, surprising spaces which open up and disorientate the traveller and just as suddenly close down again. Naples was then as now a frightening place where figures lurked in doorways and corners, and the nervous traveller was distinctly in danger. It was to protect himself in precisely this kind of circumstance that Turner brought his umbrella with the dagger in its handle.[25]

Turner's drawings and sketches of Naples all reflect the light side of the city, the views from the heights or of the harbour basin. Though he undoubtedly saw it, he makes no record of the darker side of the city. Larger sketchbook drawings,[26] some of which were drawn from a boat, were the basis of watercolours worked up in the evenings. The change that we are now seeing in Turner's watercolour technique is away from the tonal approach that characterises many of his pre-1819 paintings of English subjects, towards a vivid exploration of colour. The marine light of Venice and of Naples is the key to this, and it also suggests a reason why he did not look into the darkness of the town for subjects.

While in the neighbourhood of Naples Turner was entranced by the Bay of Baiae, to the west of the city. There must be two dozen pencil studies of the Bay from all angles,[27] some of which he worked up in watercolour. The particular attraction of this place for Turner was the symbiosis between the landscape, its long history, and its place in the mythology of both Greece and Rome. In his pair of paintings of the building of Carthage and its decline Turner had used his imagination and his knowledge of the ancient world to create a vivid evocation, laced with modern parallels. Here, however, in the Bay of Baiae, he was at the very spot where the Greeks had first established a colony in Italy, where the Cumaean Sibyl had lived, and where Apollo had offered the Sibyl eternal youth in exchange for her love. Woven into one strand in this place was landscape, history and myth as told by Virgil in the *Aeneid*. Four years later the strand came to form the subject of Turner's oil painting *The Bay of Baiae with Apollo and the Sibyl*.

The search for a holistic integration of place, history, legend and morality was one of the central purposes of Turner's tour to Italy, and the tap root of his mature art. One particularly moving moment on this part of the journey came when he visited Virgil's tomb outside Naples. Against one pencil study he wrote a small but heartfelt eulogy for the poet: "This are [sic] the remains of Tomb which contains the cinders of him who sang the pastorals of the country."[28] Turner's written note on the temple at Paestum, which follows Eustace's text very closely, unites place, fact and fiction, and expresses the painter's interests succinctly: "... built for the

Dorians from Doria a city of Phenicia first called Posetan or Postan which signifies Neptune's first temple."[29]

The seductiveness of Neapolitan light, landscape and history extended for Turner also to its people. This had been a characteristic since the 1790s, be the people Midlanders, Scots or Swiss. The men and women we see in the Neapolitan pencil studies are the same people whose figures and expressions were also immortalised in the traditional Neapolitan art of tableau making, the creation of small groups of wax or plaster figures painted to within an inch of real life. The figures appear as religious groups, in secular tableaux and singly.[30] On making his drawing of a group of peasant men and women dancing to the tambourine, Turner writes one of the longest descriptions that he had ever given of a scene. His application to making such a written record underlines the importance to him and his art of seeing and describing local life at its roots wherever in the world he may be:

> Girl dancing to the Tabor or Tamborine. One plays and two dance face to face. If two women – a lewd dance and great gesticulations. When the man dances with the women a great coyness on his part till she can catch him idle and toss him up and out of time by his trip. Then the laugh is against him by the crowd. Boy with Ring and Ball holds out cards or the ... Ball. Man selling acqua vita by a handcart. Boy drawing it painted red and green and ornamented with ?paper. Boys with dogs meet and Hawking Butchers with Tongues and ...[31]

While giving his time to such urgent explorations of real life, Turner made considerable effort when invited to meet the great and the good in Naples. Feeling underdressed during his visit to the city, and bidden for dinner with the British Ambassador, he spent some time searching in the markets for a white waistcoat.[32] Nonetheless his aims and methods baffled his hosts. John Soane's son wrote to his father: "Turner was in the neighbourhood of Naples, making rough pencil sketches to the astonishment of the fashionables, who wonder of what use these rough draughts can be – simple souls!"[33] In the same letter Soane goes on to gossip about Turner's way with money, bolstering the received view of his apparent meanness: "On the journey, having occasion for a *nap* [a gold Napoleon] he produced one which had been concealed in a purse that he had within an inner pocket. A king could not have been ushered into the world with more ceremony." If this tells us anything about Turner, it does not reflect meanness, but instead his prudence as an experienced traveller. To carry gold coins ostentatiously in Naples in the early nineteenth century was to ask immediately for trouble. It still is.

Turner was back in Rome by the middle of November, and by the end of the month he left the city to begin his long journey home.[34] His route via Perugia, Cortona and Arezzo took him to Florence, where he made studies in the Uffizi, and to the hills around to draw the city from the classic viewpoints of Fiesole and San Miniato al Monte.[35] By mid-January he was on his way over the Alps at Mont Cenis, partly by coach, and partly on foot when the coach turned over in heavy snow at the top of the pass. He had been warned to wait for a thaw in Turin, but insisted on pressing on, and with other travellers paid a coachman enough to make it worth his while to continue in the bad weather. While he waited for the coach to set off, he naturally pulled out his sketchbook and drew, as he inscribed: "Men shovelling away snow from the carriage. Women and children begging. The [?] very pink – the light and the ... rather warm. Trees all covered in snow. The trees in the distance and wood getting darker."[36] Nothing, but nothing, kept Turner away from his gentle and perceptive examination of the particular conditions of light, colour and human activity that he happened to come across.

The coach crash on the mountain gave him a full fund of anecdotes with which no doubt he regaled his friends at dinner for some time to come, and he made a watercolour of the incident as a present for Walter Fawkes. Typically, this shows the moment just before the calamity; Turner squeezed every drop of drama from the situation.[37] Six years later he was still talking about it, in a letter to James Holworthy:

> We were capsized on the top. Very lucky it was so; and the carriage door so completely frozen that we were obliged to get out at the window – the guide and the Cantonier began to fight, and the driver was in the process verbal put into prison, so doing while we had to march or rather flounder up to our knees nothing less in snow all the way down to Lancesbyburgh [Lanslebourg] by the King of Road-maker's Road, not the Colossus of Roads, Mr MacAdam, but Bonaparte, filled up by snow and only known by the precipitous zig-zag.[38]

Turner was a brave and doughty traveller, and a good companion for anybody who was willing to take the difficulties of travelling with the pleasures, the rough with the smooth, to leave him alone when he needed solitude, to talk when he wanted to talk. As Turner sat with his eyes closed on the final leg of the journey, the glories and opportunities of his Italian visit gestated vividly in his mind's eye.

Soon after he got home Turner sent at least a dozen sketchbooks away to be bound in plain card boards with leather spines.[39] He had taken them to Italy as floppy, unbacked notebooks, for the sake of lightness and ease of transport. We know this from the instructions to the binder left in one book,[40] and because some pencil drawings run into the gutters where they have been tightened by binding. All the sketchbooks have identical bindings. And there is still more evidence that after the long, productive journey to Italy Turner made an innovation in his life, a tidying up of his studio in order to take special care of things that were particularly precious to him. He set about numbering, titling and making spine labels for many of the two hundred or more sketchbooks he had used so far.

Turner's numbering sequence is incomplete, indicating both that some sketchbooks are missing, and that some of the paper labels, glued in many cases onto the spines, have come off. But the lowest surviving numbers – 2, 3, 5, 6, 9, 12 to 17 – all congregate around sketchbooks used on the 1819–20 Italian trip, and simple logic would point to the conclusion that these books were the nearest to hand and perhaps the newest when the numbering was begun. This is clear evidence of his determination in these early weeks of the new decade to keep his affairs in good order, to organise his thoughts, and to make sure that when he needed information he could find it.

He had been away from London for six months to the day. He sat next to Farington at an Academy Club dinner on 2nd February, the evening after his return. Either Turner chose not to talk much, or Farington was not listening; but all Farington could find to record in his diary was: "Turner returned from Italy yesterday: had been absent 6 months to a day. Tivoli – Nemi – Albano – Terni – fine."[41]

# TEN

# "The author of gamboge light"

## 1820–1828

R unning back from Italy there was one thing central in Turner's mind. It may explain the urgency that drove him home, despite the warnings of very dangerous conditions in the Alps at Mont Cenis. It may also explain his apparent reticence to Farington, and his talk of Tivoli, Nemi, Albano and Terni, rather than of Rome, the Vatican and Naples. All the former are classical sites which had been greatly revered by connoisseurs and travellers for a century or more, and their mention was bound to excite Farington. But although Turner had visited them, none were to play any significant part in his painting over the next few years, so his talk of them looks like cunning camouflage.

Turner's preoccupation, which he was prudent not to discuss in detail, was now with the problem of the integration of high colour with architectural form and space. He had never seen architecture anything like that which he walked around, savoured and drew in Rome. Nor had he seen light quite as clear as the light he saw there. The 1819 and 1820 visit to Italy changed his life, and changed his art.

Turner had only about eight or ten weeks to paint his contribution to the 1820 Academy exhibition. Studies made in Rome show that he had worked out the general bones of his Academy exhibit while he was there,[1] and had thought deeply about the message he wanted to convey. The painting was to unite atmosphere and architecture, past and present, art and history, biography and autobiography. It would interfere with time by placing the figure of Raphael in front of Bernini's Colonnade, not built until the seventeenth century; and with rules of perspective by playing jokes on the classical Vitruvian method of drawing architectural form. Turner gave it the extensive title *Rome, from the Vatican. Raffaelle, accompanied by La Fornarina, preparing his Pictures for the Decoration of the Loggia*, and he must have worked on the painting night and day on returning to London.

Long, wordy titles had become characteristic of him. The writer and teacher in him found it impossible to desist from *explaining*; so his sentences grew longer, and syntax flabbier. In the case of *Rome, from the Vatican*, Raphael stands with his favourite model among emblems of his work as an artist – the religious painter, the portrait painter, the great decorative designer, the architect, the sculptor (in 1820, the 300th anniversary of his death, Raphael was thought to have been a sculptor too). Raphael was the definitive universal genius, and a beautiful young man as well. Though Turner aspired to some of these things, and may well have been showing his public that he too had such accomplishments, he was also demonstrating what extraordinary social and political power the artist has, how the artist's genius could transform everyday life when effectively harnessed. As the Pope in Rome has nurtured artistic genius, so too if they would only put a bit of enthusiasm behind it could the King and Parliament in England.

There was much in *Rome, from the Vatican* for the general visitor to the 1820 Academy exhibition alert to Raphael's tercentenary: the translucent blue sky, lots of it, with high clouds; the crab-like claw of Bernini's Colonnade keeping the city at bay; a procession in the sun; and the refreshingly playful perspective games in the arches of the Pope's apartments on the left – one floor is seen as if viewed from the left, another from the right, another from below, from above and so on. The particularly breathtaking achievement in the painting, however, is the perspectival arrangement of the arches on the right. If approaching the painting at an oblique angle from the left, the viewer has the sensation of actually walking within the space of the painting, which seems physically to advance until he or she reaches the end of the arcade. It is an incredibly sophisticated and skilful piece of painting, a trick of the Professor's which Raphael himself seems to be looking at in admiration.

We must also put ourselves in the position of ordinary Academy visitors in 1819 and 1820. In 1819 they had enjoyed *England: Richmond Hill*, the largest Turner there had ever been, with flighty Watteauesque figures, ideal evanescent trees, and a horizon so extended as to be unreal. The following year what should they see but a painting of identical dimensions with a comparable title, set in real architectural space that actually worked. Immediately following a real England made ideal, came an ideal Rome made real.

This was the product of Turner the public artist. In his private capacity he worked up six Italian scenes in watercolour for Walter Fawkes, some Rhine subjects for Sir John Swinburne, and finished his Scottish watercolours for *Provincial Antiquities*. Fawkes gave him another exhibition at Grosvenor Place, this time open only to friends and invited visitors.[2]

Swinburne's commission probably came as a result of seeing Turner's watercolours in Fawkes's house, and it may be that despite the fact that Fawkes had now fallen very ill,[3] he was in a friendly and informal way acting as the artist's agent.

Though none of Turner's male friendships were quite as close as that with Walter Fawkes, he kept his other long-standing friendships going assiduously and with affection. William Wells offered refuge to Turner at his house on Mitcham Common while the messiest part of the rebuilding of 47 (renumbered from 44) Queen Anne Street was going on, as did the watercolour painter James Holworthy. He held out a hand to Turner, giving him a temporary home at his house in New Road, Marylebone, in December 1820 while he himself was away. In return Turner was expected to be the head of the Holworthy household for a few days. Turner sent news and an interim domestic report to his host:

> The garrison is well in the New Road only besieged Morning and Night ... by General Miss Croker who has not forgotten the sweets of that delicious wine you gave at Nine at night, which appear the favorite hour of attack ... hasten home Dear General or your weak Aid de Camp may be forced to capitulate.[4]

Turner and Holworthy had known each other since the early years of the century at least. As an original member of the Old Water-Colour Society, Holworthy was part of the same social circle as Wells, so the threads of friendship were intricate. Holworthy was an active print collector, and had probably been among the subscribers to Turner's *A Shipwreck* engraving in 1805. The nature of their friendship had evolved to such a degree that it was to Holworthy that Turner wrote some of his most intimate surviving letters.

Turner was forever dropping in on his friends, moving from household to household. He may not have been a particularly tidy or attractive guest – sons of Henry Scott Trimmer, with the sharp cruelty of the young, described Turner as "an ugly, slovenly old man, with rather a pig-like face; in fact somewhat of 'a guy'". Mitcham, Heston, New Road, as well as Grosvenor Place and Farnley, these were some of the places Turner went for company and conversation when he was not at Queen Anne Street or Sandycombe. In the meantime, presumably, his father was at one or other of their houses, and Hannah Danby was left to mind the builder's rubble at Queen Anne Street.

For his part, Turner upped and supped when and where he needed to do so. He returned hospitality from time to time, but had he wished to, he could have done more. Another life-long friend, the painter and former soldier George Jones acted after his death as Turner's apologist in this matter, recalling how, despite Turner and their mutual friend Francis Chantrey being "fond of amusement, cheerful living and hilarity," Turner

> would have followed the [hospitable] example of his friend, if his domestic circumstances had enabled him to do so, for he often expressed to me his regret at his inability to spend a portion of his gains in receiving his friends; but certainly his early life, his ignorance of good domestic arrangements and long habit of living with his aged father, and after his parents' death his own solitary mode of life, prevented him from indulging the kindly feelings of the heart.[5]

The real truth of the matter is probably that Turner was a much better guest that he was a host; happier holding forth at another's hearth, than keeping conversation going at his own.

Turner did not go away for his customary summer tour in 1820. It might have been the rebuilding at Queen Anne Street that kept him in London, or some kind of accident that he seems to have had after he got back from Italy.[6] He was also having neighbour trouble, and this may also have kept him at home. The dentist Benjamin Young seems to have reneged on the rental arrangement for 64 Harley Street, forcing Turner to apply to Clerkenwell Sessions to serve at least two affidavits on him.[7] The main hidden benefit of not leaving London in the summer was that he could study at leisure Géricault's masterpiece *The Raft of the Medusa* which was exhibited at the Egyptian Hall, Piccadilly, from June for six months.

The building work on Turner's house and gallery amounted to a complete reorientation, giving the property a new frontage on Queen Anne Street. Turner designed the whole thing, down to details for heating the gallery, and took care to abide by the demands of the Portland Estates Trustees that the front wall be built with "newly picked Stocks neatly pointed, it is not to be stuckoed".[8] The reorientation gave Turner a north facing aspect to his first-floor studio, something he had never had before, with two generously high studio windows.

He was of course paying for all this, and kept a close eye on expenditure, making notes in a current sketchbook of £5 for paint, £20 for Carpenter's extra work, £7 2s 6d for a stone floor for the kitchen, and "£14 to Jones for Water Closet".[9] This latter emendation to his house was a creditable technological leap for Turner. There was no such thing at Sandycombe, and even forty years after Joseph Bramah had first patented the water closet, they were still considered to be "newfangled".[10] Yet the building works depressed him, and it is no wonder he fled to Mitcham or the New Road to escape. He wrote to Wells:

... it rains and the Roof is not finished. Day after day have I threatened you not with a letter, but your Mutton, but some demon eclypt Mason, Bricklayer, Carpenter &c. &c. &c. ... has kept me in constant oscillation from Twickenham to London, from London to Twit, that I have found the art of going about doing nothing – "so out of nothing, nothing can come."[11]

Another event to keep Turner in or near London was the death of his uncle, J. M. W. Marshall, in Sunningwell in June 1820. Joseph Marshall had owned property in Wapping and Barkingside which he had inherited from his father. As Joseph had no surviving children of his own, this property was divided between his nephews, Henry Harpur, and his late sister Mary's son, J. M. W. Turner. While Turner's relations with his Devonshire uncles and cousins were poor or frosty, those with his Marshall uncle seem to have had a warmth that had continued from the Brentford days.

The Marshall property in Wapping was a group of houses, 7, 8, 9 and 10 New Gravel Lane, Shadwell, one hundred yards from the river, near Wapping Wall. In the parish of Dagenham he owned four acres of marsh land at Barkingside north of Redbridge. These properties were divided by the drawing of lots between Harpur and Turner, the former winning the houses numbered 9 and 10, and the latter 7 and 8 and the Barkingside land. Despite the addition of the land, Turner's lot was valued by his friend Thomas Allason at £1,123, as opposed to £1,165 for Harpur's share. They reached agreement by Harpur paying Turner £42 as a balancing sum. The indenture between them[12] was drawn up with the greatest care, and inheriting the property in June gave Turner one more reason to stay in London that summer. When they came to him, the Wapping houses were in bad repair. There are clues during the course of the decade of rental payments and, in 1827, of changes of tenant and of substantial repairs being carried out when Turner converted the houses into a tavern, The Ship and Bladebone.[13]

Marshall's widow Mary received an annuity from the will, which Turner appears to have administered. He visited his aunt soon after her husband's death, making sketches of Oxford and Sunningwell in the "Folkestone" sketchbook on the way.[14] Turner ensured that she got the money safely, once in 1822 even using his publisher, W. B. Cooke, as the messenger to bear it to Sunningwell with a receipt to sign. His affection for his aunt was such that he reminded Cooke to take a pound of black tea to her, and a pound of green tea to her friend Mrs Lovegrove. These easy gifts seem to have been a common courtesy between them, for by 1827 the contact was still going on, Mrs Lovegrove promising to send Turner a turkey and a saddle of mutton.[15]

Yet more family matters pressed on Turner that summer, all adding to the need for him to stay in London. Evelina and her husband came home from West Africa in July. Joseph Dupuis, sent off to Africa with good prospects and the command of His Majesty to ease political difficulties in the Gold Coast, so upset his British counterparts that he was recalled after only fifteen months.[16] There is no record of Evelina and her father meeting on her return, but Turner must have been aware that his elder daughter was *en route* for England in the summer, and at the very least liable to call.

All these interferences took up a great part of his time. He had no major commissions in 1821, nor did he send anything to the Academy that year. He had the "art of going about doing nothing", as he had described it to Wells, thrust upon him. There are indications that Turner enjoyed the cut and thrust of litigation or the threat of it, so he may have passively encouraged confrontations with tenants rather than working to ease them. When chasing Benjamin Young through the courts he went in person to Clerkenwell Session House twice at least, the second time urging Holworthy to join him.[17] He was careful, even pedantic, with paperwork, telling Cooke precisely how he wanted a receipt for Mrs Marshall's money worded, and making somebody (the recipient?) copy out the receipt he himself had given for rentals paid for the Wapping properties.[18]

Exasperating though it may have been to anybody at the wrong end of it, it was this innate attention to detail that made Turner such a very good officer of the Royal Academy. Applying his own personal measure of financial caution, he was already keeping a tight account of Academy expenses in 1819, four years before his election as Auditor,[19] and with this knowledge was aware that the Academy could well afford to pay increased pensions to widows of deceased Associates and Members.[20] Turner's motion proposing the increase was passed.

His weeks in Rome had reinvigorated his understanding of classicism, by replacing the learned imagination of his Carthage paintings and the Hakewill watercolours with experience. Turner was one of a growing community of writers, painters and architects, including Henry Gally Knight, Hugh "Grecian" Williams, Charles Eastlake, Thomas L. Donaldson and the architect C. R. Cockerell, who had all travelled widely in Greece and Italy during the previous decade, and who all contributed to the increasing momentum in Britain of neo-classicism in art and architecture. Cockerell, whom Turner also knew through the Holworthy circle and through Thomas Allason, invited him to see drawings he had made during his seven-year tour of Asia Minor, Greece, Italy and Sicily. This invitation led to a pledge between the two men to work together, and to a friendship which blossomed in the coming decade.

The arrangement was that Turner make fifteen watercolours from Cockerell's drawings of the Temple of Jupiter Panellenius at Aegina in

Greece, for eventual engraving and publication in a book on the temple by Cockerell. There can have been no formal contract, no deadline or agreement of fees at the start, for the plan meandered on for four or five years, eventually petering out in 1825 with only one work by Turner completed.[21] But there were compensations. Turner and Cockerell found themselves to be kindred spirits, and they talked extensively. Talk was the chief creative bond between them, for Cockerell had a very busy architectural practice, and this took precedence over the writing and publication of the book on the Temple of Jupiter. Cockerell wrote in his diary of an early meeting in November 1821: "Turner came to look at my drawings. Did not find him so methodical or stiff as he had seemed before. Liked the subjects. Stayed from 10 til 9. It was a vast pleasure to me to look over my views with a man who felt them as he did."[22]

Over four years later, progress on the Jupiter project had been slow. In fact nothing had happened; the pair were still discussing what size the drawings should be.[23] Then in February 1825, Cockerell "... visited Turner found he had done little or nothing ... stood more than two hours with him talking of Vanbrugh, Hawksmoor, & other he as usual standing with his hat on." Two weeks later, Cockerell "... arranged Aegena Papers in book called on Turner found his drawing advanced felt much pleased with its effect ..."[24]

There is no suggestion that either man felt under any pressure to complete the project, but both evidently enjoyed the intellect and knowledge freely expressed of the other. The same easy sociability also comes in Turner's friendships with his immediate Academy circle. David Wilkie invited him to dinner with some senior painters and sculptors, Chantrey, Westmacott, Henry Howard and others in December 1821. This was the first time that Wilkie had received Turner at his house, evidence in itself that whatever early professional *froideur* there might have been between them had long since disappeared. Wilkie found Turner "a good humoured fellow, neither slack in wit himself, nor loth to be the cause of wit in others."[25]

As the work at Queen Anne Street was under way, Turner was clearly thinking about the next stage in his life, how his house might be furnished, and how, as a wealthy and successful artist, he would present himself to the world. The inventory drawn up after his death lists plenty of good mahogany furniture – in the studio a "Large Mahogany Oval Table on pillar and Claw", in the parlour "Mahogany Cheffonier with Drawer" and "Pair of large Sienna scagliola marble pedestals".[26] These and a quantity of other pieces are all expensive contemporary objects which Turner may either have bought or even commissioned for his rebuilt house in the early 1820s when he at least had the intention to impress friends and potential patrons and make his own statements about personal style.[27] The care and the eye for quality with which he tried to choose his clothes and his sketchbooks he now applied to his choice of furnishings.

The entrance hall of 47 Queen Anne Street, lit from a skylight or perhaps from small windows on either side of the front door, was alive with the slow tick-tick from the 8-day mahogany clock. Around the walls, as the inventory indicates, were four plaster casts from the Parthenon frieze, some good shield-back hall chairs and one or two marble-topped hall tables. Ahead, the staircase, with its carpet and shining brass rods, ran up to the studio and gallery. Visitors were first ushered into the parlour on the right of the hall by Hannah Danby, smiling, handsome, thirty-something, appearing up the cellar steps from the kitchen followed by a tail-less cat.

The parlour ceiling was low, but the room, well lit from the window, was brightened by yellow morine curtains. We might suppose that, extending Turner's growing predilection for yellow, the curtains matched yellow walls. The furniture, heavy, shiny brown mahogany, glowed on the Turkey carpet. There were two chiffoniers, one with a pinkish scagliola top, some leather covered chairs, bookcases, pedestals with sculpture casts on them, china and plaster figures and some glum pictures from the past century. On a sideboard stood a plaster skull, and near it, or in a drawer, Turner kept his double-barrelled pistol. This did not seem to be the house of a painter; a worthy citizen, certainly, a collector with a fondness for the classical, possibly, but surely not an artist. So formal and sober indeed was his parlour, that Turner appears to have been placing himself in the same bracket of solidity and taste as his merchant patrons. There was no hint of eccentricity, and no sign, apparently, of Turner's paintings.

The dining-room was of much the same character – a good brass stove and fender, a glowing gilt cornice over the window, a mantelpiece mirror, mahogany dining table and perhaps some bits of Turner's forty-piece Wedgwood Willow Pattern dinner service. Although the intention to entertain his friends must have been one of the many driving forces behind Turner's rebuilding and furnishing of his house, his parties were probably rare. At some point, possibly as early as the 1820s, Hannah began to develop the malignant skin condition that disfigured her face in her later years, and this, with Turner's own recurrent illnesses, may be a partial explanation. Referring to Turner's dining table, Samuel Rogers remarked: "It was wonderful ... but how much more wonderful it would be to see any of his friends around it."[28]

Upstairs, the gallery ran deep into the property from the top of the landing, with a storage area off at right angles at the far end. The studio door, next to the gallery door, would be shut or quickly pushed to as the visitor approached, sent upstairs, on some signal, by Hannah. One early visitor, the Rev. William Kingsley, saw the gallery when it was new and remembered the colour of the walls as

Indian red, neither pale nor dark. It was the best lighted gallery I have ever seen, and the effect got by the simplest means; a herring net was spread from end to end just above the walls, and sheets of tissue paper spread on the net, the roof itself being like that of a greenhouse. By this the light was diffused close to the pictures.[29]

Though the visitor would not see Turner unless he chose to come out of the studio, Turner could watch his visitor's every move from the small peephole in the dividing wall. If he saw anybody touching his pictures, or making discreet copies, he would rush out like a terrier and send them off at once.

By the early 1820s Turner had achieved almost every prize open to a painter of his generation – full membership of the Royal Academy, riches, fame, a new studio and gallery in one of the most fashionable parts of London, and foreign travel whenever he wanted it. He had the freedom to refuse a commission if he chose, and to paint pictures for friends for nothing if he wished. The one prize that still eluded him, however, was acceptance by the head of the British establishment. Although it had nodded in his direction, the royal family had not yet shown any serious interest in buying or commissioning his work.

A year after the old king, George III, had died mad at Windsor in January 1820, his eldest son was crowned George IV. This merely confirmed the status quo. George IV had already exercised all the power of the monarch since Parliament had declared him Prince Regent in 1811. One early decision of the reign was to arrange a state visit to Scotland, to display the king's person in Edinburgh and to confirm the Union formally and symbolically. Turner travelled to Edinburgh by sea in August 1822 to witness the occasion.

Two incentives at least drew him to Edinburgh in 1822. One was to witness the state visit, while the other was to protect his investment in Scott's *Provincial Antiquities*. The publication was not selling in the quantities the shareholders had hoped. "The truth is," one shareholder, the engraver William Lizars, wrote to another, Edward Blore, in 1820 after the first number had been published, "I fear the Work is too great and too expensive ... to meet the purse of the public."[30] As it came out in parts, the shareholders had the option to vary individual numbers to meet public taste. Sir Walter Scott, thinking aloud in a letter to Blore in 1819, had proposed that more illustrations be made for the series in the form of vignettes of coats of arms or ornaments. As a result of this proposal, Turner determined to prepare a group of illustrations of the royal progress through Edinburgh for the book. The other incentive that drew Turner to Edinburgh was a piece of characteristic entrepreneurship. As an eyewitness at the ceremonies, which Scott was stage-managing, Turner would be able to gather ideas for a series of grand paintings which would carry great weight when exhibited in London, and project his name into the heart of royal Britain. Dozens of artists had variations of this same idea. Such a historic royal event was bound to reap enormous commercial benefits to any artist able to work fast and produce images for sale on mugs and bowls, broadsheets or engravings.

The King landed from *The Royal George* at Leith Harbour on 15th August, to fanfares and salvoes from anchored ships, the Castle and Salisbury Crags. C. R. Cockerell, another eye-witness, recorded the scene: "Saw the whole from Calton Hill. Like a scene in a play. Much pleasure in the people who called it *awful*. No noise or clamour but a collected satisfaction."[31] The quay at Leith was thronged not only with Scottish subjects, but also with artists lining up with their sketchbooks to make notes. Two, William Collins and David Wilkie, were quite staggered to see that Turner had appeared, as Wilkie recorded later: "Collins saw the landing to great advantage; and, to our surprise who should start up upon the occasion to see the same occurrence, but J. M. W. Turner, Esq., R.A.P.P.!!! who is now with us we know not how."[32]

Turner was serious competition. He did not let his intentions be known to anybody, except perhaps to Cockerell who got him permission to observe the banquet that the Provost gave for the King.[33] There are, however, inside the cover of one sketchbook,[34] a series of nineteen thumbnail sketches of compositions of events on the royal progress through Edinburgh which suggest that something ambitious was in Turner's mind all along. The sketches are as delicate as gossamer, rubbed and faint, concealing almost as much as they reveal. But as Gerald Finlay has suggested, they represent quite clearly the first ideas for a long cycle of paintings that may have been Turner's bid for extended royal patronage at the beginning of the new reign.[35]

The subjects include "The King in the Royal Barge", "Receiving the Keys of Holyrood Palace" and "The King at St Giles's Cathedral", all images which, if developed into large scale oil paintings, might even rival such cycles of royal triumphs as those by Mantegna or Rubens. When he returned home, Turner took four oil paintings to various stages of completion – *George IV at St Giles's, Edinburgh* is one of the furthest forward – but that is all that was heard of the project. Events outside his control put an end to the idea – perhaps he made a political miscalculation; perhaps he failed to convince engravers that there was a commercial future for the project, which would have depended for its success on continuing warm relations between England and Scotland. Writing to J. C. Schetky in 1823 about the loan of Schetky's drawing of the Royal Barge, he seemed to suggest that the latter at least was the case: "... there is an end to that commission owing to the difficulty attending engraving the subject."[36]

There may also have been a third incentive that took Turner to Scotland when he did. Edinburgh in the early 1820s was the home of a network of scientists, engineers and philosophers, a second generation of practical intellectuals born out of the Scottish Enlightenment of the eighteenth century. He had made many friends while in Scotland in 1818, and some of these were contributors to *The Edinburgh Encyclopaedia*, which was then being compiled under the editorship of the physicist David Brewster. Contributors whom Turner knew, both in Edinburgh and London, included Charles Babbage, Thomas Chalmers, John Herschel, John Lockhart, James Skene, Robert Stevenson and the Rev. John Thomson of Duddingston. There is a report, quoted by Gerald Finlay, that Turner met Chalmers and Lockhart, in the company of Walter Scott and others, at Oman's Hotel in Edinburgh on 7th August 1822,[37] and Cockerell records two dinners "of much merriment".[38]

The list of contributors to *The Edinburgh Encyclopaedia* is a heavyweight one. Brewster himself was a brilliant and highly ambitious physicist, whose writings on optics and the properties of light were rapidly superseding the old theories of Sir Isaac Newton. He was a Fellow of the Royal Society and a Member of the Royal Institution, and had further professional links with learned societies throughout Europe and in America. Brewster had invented the Kaleidoscope around 1814, and published a *Treatise* on the instrument in 1819.

Turner was fully aware of the importance of Brewster's work, and, according to marginal notes, made passing reference to the Kaleidoscope in his lectures from 1818 onwards.[39] Thornbury suggests that Turner and Brewster met in John Thomson's circle of friends, perhaps in 1818 or 1822, though Brewster himself asserted that he and Turner did not meet until 1834.[40] Whatever the case, Turner had certainly read Brewster's writings, and found confirmation in them of his own discovery that the three primary colours, the active constituents of white light, were red, blue and yellow. Thornbury describes how Turner and the artist friends of John Thomson

> ... would constantly battle ... upon the subject of light, trying to gain from Brewster and other *savants* information thereon; ... To such a height, indeed, did [Turner] carry the verbal contests that the subject, it is said, finally was prohibited; and then he became more earnest to discover what combination of colour would produce light.[41]

Four hundred miles from London, Turner had found a close knit group of people whose interests ran to the very heart of his own. The most active link between Turner and Brewster's theories was the amateur painter

James Skene. As well as being one of the shareholders of *Provincial Antiquities*, Skene was also Walter Scott's partner in the stage-management of King George IV's visit to Edinburgh. He and Turner were at the Castle together drawing the scene at the moment when the King raised his hat on the Half Moon Battery in acknowledgement of the cheering crowds and saluting cannons. They will also have talked together at some length about colour theory, for Skene was even then drafting his long article on Painting for Brewster's *Edinburgh Encyclopaedia*. Skene had a modern thinker's grasp of the difficulties and the implications of landscape painting in the new century. As published in 1830, he writes:

> Painting can but approximate to all the niceties, combinations, and intricacies, of direct and reflected light, involving the contrasted obscurities of ... objects [in nature] or parts of objects, least exposed to it, and modified by the almost imperceptible gradation of intensity as it recedes from the eye. When we add to this, the infinite interchange of tints, affecting every object in nature, which may be said altogether to elude common observation, and not to be easily detected in all their niceties by those most familiar with the study, we shall be less disposed to underrate the merits and difficulties of landscape painting.

Here, the capturing of "the infinite interchange of tints, affecting every object in nature" is a summation of Turner's achievement up to the 1820s, and could almost be an abstract of a conversation between the two men. Skene continues:

> One of the greatest landscape painters of the present age, Mr Turner, seems to have grappled so vigorously with this important desideratum in the art, that much may be expected from his system of study and acute observation. So far as he has gone, eminent success has attended his footsteps; and, aided by the discoveries daily making in the mysteries of light, his scrutinising genius seems to tremble on the verge of some new discovery in colour, which may prove of the first importance to art. ... Turner has struck out a new route, by the singular mixture of prismatic colours, with which he represents sky and water; the idea is singularly acute and philosophical, if we consider the optical properties of the changing surface of water.[42]

"System of study", "scrutinising genius": with these well-chosen words Skene wrote the first considered review of Turner's scientific intentions as a painter of the nature of light, and in doing so prefigured John Ruskin. The 1820s were the hinge of Turner's life. During these ten years he changed from being a painter of tone and of "the infinite interchange of tints", to a painter of colour. Pure, lucid colour had been hovering about him in unfinished watercolours and colour exercises since the earliest years of his career – two potent examples from about 1800 are *Fonthill Abbey at Sunset* and *St Mary's and the Radcliffe Camera from Oriel Lane, Oxford*.[43] In the latter, Turner left unaltered an area of pure yellow and pink suffusing the end of the building to the left. We do not know why he abandoned this picture. But in leaving it where it was, with its bright light shining in sober grey and blue surroundings, Turner left an alarm clock ticking. The alarm was set to go off in twenty-five years time.

After years of trying to encourage the royal family's interest in his painting, Turner won his prize towards the end of 1822.[44] The King may have been made aware of Turner's proposal to paint a cycle of pictures commemorating the royal visit to Scotland, but commanded that he be invited to paint not that cycle, but instead a vast picture of the Battle of Trafalgar. Sir Thomas Lawrence, by now President of the Royal Academy, was best placed to advise the King to commission Turner.[45] To mark the start of the reign of George IV, the three principal rooms in St James's Palace were to be hung with paintings of great victories over the French. Among them were de Loutherbourg's *Lord Howe's Victory, First of June 1794* and George Jones's pair of paintings of the Battles of Waterloo and Vittoria.

Turner's *Battle of Trafalgar* of 1822–24 was his second version of the subject. The first showed the moment that Nelson was shot; the second, however, collapses time by showing all at once the battle at its height and the first few moments of victory as the news spreads out across the water to British sailors on rafts and lifeboats. The viewpoint is low, at water level, so the ship and its backdrop of clouds tower over the viewer. As in *Hannibal*, we are sharing the lot of the common man – sailors, dead, dying, or cheering victory. There is a reference to Géricault's *Raft of the Medusa* in the dead foreground figure and the raft beyond, and this sets the tone. The enormous painting, at 8 feet 6 inches by 12 feet long Turner's largest, took him nearly two years to prepare and paint, occupying his energies to a degree. When asked after his son, the elder William Turner told Trimmer he was "painting a picture of the Battle of Trafalgar".[46] This is the only record of Turner's father ever referring to a specific picture, suggesting its measure of importance to father and son, and indeed its imposing long-term presence in the studio.

Undoubtedly because *Trafalgar* devoured so much of his time, Turner had nothing new to show at the Royal Academy in 1824 when he was finishing it for delivery. Its blazing reds and oranges dominated the King's Levée Room in St James's Palace where it was hung in late May,[47] and before the month was out it was beginning to attract serious criticism as

Turner finished it in situ.[48] Sailors, and there were many of those walking in and out of St James's, gave the artist gratuitous advice about rigging and the set of sails and so on. So Turner would alter the rigging this way to suit one critic, and that way to suit another, all with great good humour.[49] The attitude of one particular critic of the painting made Turner snap. He and Turner argued until the man said: "I have been at sea the greater part of my life, Sir, you don't know who you are talking to, and I'll be damned if you know what you are talking about."[50] The critic turned out to be the Duke of Clarence, later William IV, the Sailor King.

The painting remained in St James's Palace until 1829 when, probably as part of a general reorganisation of the pictures in the Palace, the King gave it to the Royal Naval Hospital in Greenwich. It is now at the National Maritime Museum. In Greenwich Hospital, among an audience of generally lower ranking old salts, Turner's *Trafalgar* continued to receive criticism. "It's a d— deal like a brickfield. We ought to have had a Huggins," said one.[51]

Turner's work in the mid-1820s took him from the extreme of the scale of *Trafalgar* down to the intimacy of watercolour. Such a dramatic crashing down of his focus had long been a characteristic and would continue all his life. While painting theatre scenery in the 1790s he was also making small landscape watercolours; and while painting the larger canvases of the 1810s he would make time to work in the tiny scale of the *Fairfaxiana*. For ten or more years Turner had been working on his cycle of watercolour views of England, Wales and Scotland, and he would continue to do so until the late 1830s. They were commissioned for different, often rival, publishers, but their common factor was that they were all to be engraved for public sale. For a thirty-year stretch of his mature life, Turner's production as an artist was veined through and through by the collecting of material on his travels, storing it, refining, mellowing it in his memory, and then painting more than two hundred and fifty finished watercolours, his "Picturesque Views" of places from one end of the kingdom to the other. At the same time, year in, year out, he painted his exhibition oils. Though the oil paintings have carried Turner's name across the world, his watercolour cycles lie at the heart of his work and have carried his imagery into every home.

The series that engaged him in the mid-1820s included *Picturesque Views of the Southern Coast of England* (1814–26) and *The Rivers of England* (1822–26) for the Cooke brothers, *Picturesque Views of England and Wales* (1824–38) for Charles Heath, and, for Thomas Lupton, *The Ports of England* (1825–28). The key to these series of landscapes is memory. None of the watercolours was painted on the spot, but this was almost always Turner's practise as a watercolourist. They were made instead at his painting table in Queen Anne Street, under the London north light that filtered through the panes, some from pencil studies drawn as much as twenty years earlier. Reminded by his sketchbook studies, Turner would add topographical details from memory, exaggerating or diminishing as he chose, placing figures, carts, boats, animals or whatever it might be to create an internal narrative, and effects of weather for mood. Turner's weather effects, too, came from memory; over so many years of travelling he had seen them all. His 1811 sketches of Sidmouth, for example, in the "Devonshire" sketchbook[52] gave him details of the lie of the land about that small coastal town, and he turned back to a thirty-year-old sketch of Louth in Lincolnshire to remind himself of how that town was arranged.[53] Turner's need for quick access to the information he had gathered over the years gives us a clear indication of one of his motives in organising and numbering his collection of sketchbooks when he returned home from Italy.

The watercolours are laced with visual puns, rhymes and allusions, signs and messages, trains of throught more likely to evolve in the quiet of the studio than out in the open air. In one vivid example out of hundreds, the forms of the deer's antlers in *Arundel Castle on the River Arun* (c. 1824) rhyme with the crenellated castle in the middle distance, while the curling line of the distant river is continued by the mist rising up the river valley. Other allusions are historical and political: the engraving of *Wycliffe, near Rokeby* (c. 1816) has the subtitle "The Birthplace of John Wycliffe (The Morning Star of Liberty) near Rokeby, Yorkshire," while in *Battle Abbey, the Spot where Harold Fell* (engraved 1819) a hound chases a hare (a pun on Harold Harefoot) across the foreground. As the hare speeds to its death, the trees behind mark his passage, being, from right to left, in full leaf, then straggly, then dead.[54] In some images Turner evokes a nostalgic response by introducing soldiery, despite the fact that since 1815 the army was much less in evidence than it had been during the Napoleonic Wars.

The driving force of the watercolours, taken as a whole, is the story they tell. They are in microcosm a social history of Britain, shot through with tales of human behaviour, local history, customs and folk lore. Their strength as images to stand for Britain can be measured from the fact that the bulk was painted after Turner's two visits to Europe in 1817 and 1819–20. Despite the seductive light of his experience of the warm south, Turner found deep veins of inspiration and purpose waiting quietly at home in his numbered sketchbooks and in his memory.

The pressures on Turner now were intense. Other workshop and economic systems depended on his producing paintings at a required rate. He was subject to the agreements he had made with the engravers, who had commercial pressures of their own to cope with, and by entering into contracts with these men Turner had begun to surrender complete control of his life. He was, however, a supreme professional. Charles Heath found greater satisfaction in working with Turner than with any other artist. "When once he pledged his word as to time and quality, he might be implicitly relied on."[55] There is a touching insight into how Turner's time seemed no longer to be his own, even a quiet Sunday afternoon at Sandycombe:

> It was his habit, Mr Munro told me, to visit Turner on Sunday afternoons when the painter was often at leisure. In the course of a pleasant chat ... their social privacy was invaded by the irruption of Cooke, who, with all the air of a bullying tailor come to look after a poor sweating journeyman, wanted to know if those drawings of his were never to be finished. When the door presently closed behind him, the big salt tears came into Turner's eyes, and he murmured something about "no holiday ever for me."[56]

There may of course be some hidden prejudice in this account. Turner was perfectly capable of turning on the emotion on demand, and his friend Hugh Munro, a passionate collector and amateur artist, had every incentive to raise Turner at Cooke's expense.

Turner had an uncomfortably choppy relationship with William Cooke. Following the example of Walter Fawkes in 1819 and 1820, the Cooke brothers exhibited a group of Turner's watercolours, along with works of other artists, at their shop in Soho Square in 1823 and 1824. They had already invested heavily in Turner by buying the right to engrave his watercolours, but despite all this, Turner consistently believed he was undervalued or undercompensated for the work he did for the Cookes. This led to hard words, both in public and in correspondence. Thornbury told how the ill feeling flared up during a Conversazione in the Freemason's Hall about the return of some drawings to which both men laid claim: "Turner's red face became white with the depth of his rage, while Cooke grew hot and red, and high words even to the extreme of 'rogue', to the terror of those who unfortunately witnessed the verbal contest."[57]

When Turner and the Cookes had worked together on *The Southern Coast* in the 1810s Turner was continually rushing to meet deadlines and to help in the smooth running of the commission.[58] During their business partnerships in the 1820s Turner was likewise, from the tone of correspondence, an amenable man to work with,[59] though maddening to somebody quick to anger. Turner would send mysterious little notes to Cooke, thus: "Sir, Today is the 12 of June making four months since the 12 of February 1821;"[60] and exactly a month later: "Sir, Today is the twelfth of July being the fifth *Month* since Feby."[61] Cooke annotated this letter with the words: "A note to remind me of *publishing*."

These pedantic reminders from Turner to Cooke of his duties suggest that Turner continued to see this as a master-servant relationship, as he had with Charles Turner on the *Liber*, rather than one of equals in a creative process. It is the same kind of attitude that made Turner pack Cooke off in 1822 across the muddy fields of Oxfordshire to deliver a bag of cash and two pounds of tea to two elderly women. That these women evidently held Turner in some kind of awe may well have further irked Cooke as he wrote out a receipt for them to sign to the precise wording specified by Turner. Then, as was their custom, the good women loaded Cooke down with country fare to take to Turner. "And here's a pie for your trouble, Mister Cooke."

Cooke's angers were symptoms of the frustrations that were a permanent undertow to the publisher-engraver's trade. They invested large sums in engaging the artist, buying or hiring his work to engrave, paying the engraver to cut the plate, suffering the interferences, criticisms and alterations of the artist, and after all that, attempting to recoup their money with profits by selling the prints. A single plate might take two years to engrave: "Few have lived more solitary or more laborious lives," wrote Charles Radclyffe, the son of one of Turner's engravers:

> Bending double all through a bright, sunny day, in an attic or closework-room, over a large plate, with a powerful magnifying glass in constant use; carefully picking and cutting out bits of metal from the plate, and giving the painfully formed lines the ultimate form of some of Turner's most brilliant conceptions; working for twelve or fourteen hours daily, taking exercise rarely, in early morning or late at night; "proving" a plate, only to find days of labour have been mistaken, and have to be effaced and done over again ... such is too commonly the life of an engraver.[62]

Nevertheless, the market in early 1825 was buoyant, as Charles Heath revealed when he first embarked with Turner on the *England and Wales* series. He paid 30 guineas each for the watercolours, and was confident of selling them on for 50 guineas apiece. He had spread the cost of making the engravings by sub-contracting, benefiting from the economic climate. He wrote to Dawson Turner: "The Art of Engraving never flourished as it now does – there is so much doing that every engraver's full."[63] The row that Turner and Cooke had in the Freemason's Hall is probably the sound of two men finally snapping. Their formerly strong professional relationship, which by 1826 had resulted in the publication of over fifty engravings after Turner, seems to have broken over the issue of Turner's demand for twenty-five sets of proof prints of *Southern Coast* engravings printed on India paper, and his apparent threat to publish a rival set of coastal views. Cooke wrote furiously to Turner late in 1826, and again on 1st January 1827.[64] Cooke's letters prompted a reply from the painter of which only this fragment remains: "There is something in the manner of your note received yesterday Evening so extraordinary and differing so materially from the conversation of Wednesday last that I must request you to reconsider the following ..."[65]

Both parties seemed equally staggered by the nature of the other's misunderstanding of the real situation, which had been transformed and endangered by the financial crash of December 1825. Only Cooke's long letter of 1st January 1827, setting out the situation as he saw it, survives, in which the engraver accuses the painter of demanding more than the contracted fee for each drawing, and of trying to charge a loan fee for a work which Cooke understood Turner had presented to him.

The falling out with Cooke was a temperamental exception to the even pace of Turner's social and business life in the 1820s. He made new friends in this period, among them Hugh Munro, who had inherited large estates at Novar in Inverness, and confirmed relations with others such as George Jones and James Holworthy. George Jones (1786–1869) became one of Turner's greatest friends. They had shared roots in London, Jones being the son of a distinguished mezzotint engraver, John Jones. Although like Turner he set out to follow a career as an artist, his intentions were waylaid by the Napoleonic Wars, and in 1808 he joined the army. He survived the Peninsular War, and being demobbed at the rank of Captain, successfully picked up the threads of his career as a painter. He had been a loyal soldier, with a tall bearing and a noble Wellingtonian profile, and slipped easily into the role of a loyal Academician. Loyalty to the Academy was the great quality that he and Turner shared. That, and their good humour and love of order, kept them together for life.

Turner brought to the Royal Academy in the 1820s renewed vigour and new ideas. He continued to be appointed to official posts, being made Inspector of the Cast Collection in 1820, renewed in 1829 and 1838. As Visitor to the Academy Schools he seems to have introduced the practice of standing nude models beside antique casts. This technique, which Turner and his friends had seen at the Venetian Academy in Rome, gave students the opportunity to see living flesh and sculptural form side by side, and to distinguish between them in their drawings.[66] Turner also made the model stand against a white sheet to create reflections over the body, and, as Charles Eastlake warmly reported to Government Commissioners some years after Turner's death, Turner "infuse[d] new life into the practice of the students".[67]

It was the smallest step from the Royal Academy's door on one side of the portico of Somerset House to the rooms of the Royal Society on the other. This was the home of the distinguished body of scientists who, under their Royal Charter, had met since 1660 "for the Promotion of Natural Knowledge". Many of Turner's Academician friends – Chantrey,

Lawrence, Phillips, Soane – were also Fellows of the Royal Society, and very good for their business it was too. Francis Chantrey made busts of many Fellows, including Sir Henry Englefield, Sir William Blizard and William Woolaston. Phillips painted the portrait of the Society's long-serving President, Sir Joseph Banks, and Lawrence painted Sir Humphry Davy and Thomas Young.

Royal Society papers enquired into the physical and natural sciences, and took their audiences to the extremes of current scientific discovery and philosophy. This was in severe contrast to the practice at the Royal Academy, whose lectures were cyclic in nature, returning to the same themes annually, sometimes repetitively, to teach generation after generation of students. The brotherly proximity of the two organisations had made it possible for artists and scientists to meet in easy association at one side or other of the portico since Somerset House had been open to them in 1781. Royal Society papers gave artists breadth of mind and experience, as well as a fertile source of patronage. Thomas Hearne and Henry Edridge had, for example, attended regularly in the 1790s with their patron Sir Henry Englefield, and Joseph Farington attended with Robert Smirke and George or Nathaniel Dance to hear a paper on the properties of urinary concretions.[68] It was through conversations with Fellows of the Royal Society that Francis Chantrey's passion for geology was sustained.

The Royal Society was the place where Turner could with ease continue his friendship with Sir Humphry Davy, meet Charles Babbage and talk to Michael Faraday about light and colour, and the nature of the chemical constitution of pigments.[69] So too was the Athenaeum Club, of which he was a founder member in 1824. The Athenaeum evolved directly out of the membership of the societies that met at Somerset House, to create a place of informal friendly gathering and talk in the pattern of the military clubs that had sprung up in London since 1815.[70] The Athenaeum and the Somerset House societies were in this period open only to men. When the physicist Mary Somerville prepared her paper on "The magnetising power of the more refrangible solar rays", it had to be read, on 2nd February 1826, by her husband Dr William Somerville FRS in the author's absence. Turner knew William and Mary Somerville well, and met them at picnics and friendly gatherings regularly.[71]

Turner continued to be a regular theatre and opera-goer, to the extent that the theatre provided subjects for him.[72] There are many reports of Turner's attendance at soirées and Conversazioni in London in the 1820s. His "red face and white waistcoat" are remarked upon by Haydon in March 1825 at a soirée at Soane's house in Lincoln's Inn Fields. This was a stylish occasion at which Soane's newly acquired Egyptian sarcophagus was shown off to the London world of art and antiquities. Turner was a guest at two Fawkes weddings at St George's, Hanover Square, the wedding of Walter Fawkes's fourth daughter Anne in 1822, and of Hawkesworth in 1825. Anne's wedding to the Yorkshire landowner Godfrey Wentworth is recorded in Maria Fawkes's diary: "Anne and Godfrey married. A very long day. Had a large party to dinner. All tipsey."[73]

Turner entered into the swing of parties of this kind, and would have got as "tipsey" as the next guest. He warmed to people he met, as long as they took him at face value, and particularly if they were female and pretty. The phrase "Remember me to the ladies" crops up regularly in Turner's letters of thanks. He would talk about his work, never to excess, but very revealingly to the ladies. Leaning over to Mary Lloyd, a friend of Samuel Rogers's sister, he said: "People talk a lot about *sunsets*, but when you are all fast asleep, I am watching the effects of *sunrise* far more beautiful; and then you can see the *light* does not fail."[74] Mary Lloyd must have known Turner over ten or twenty years, because writing of him as an older man she distinctly remembered

> his small bent figure, his jewish cast of feature, and his kind, shy manner. His small "grey glittering eyes" were so like my idea of the Ancient Mariner's that I listened attentively to all he said. But he spoke little, as if painting were his only language. His voice was deep and husky, and full of feeling; his sentences broken but letting out flashes of wit and humour, almost involuntarily.[75]

Reported conversations of this kind are not always as reliable as Mary Lloyd's. We cannot be sure that we are hearing the exact words, still less the right voice. Turner's letters reveal something more. If we cannot hear the timbre of his voice we can catch the practical concern and patent affection for the particular friend. James Holworthy and his wife were about to move into a new house in Derbyshire by the autumn of 1826, and having had plenty of experience of this kind of thing himself, Turner expresses what amounts to a duty of care:

> ... mind you get the plaister'd walls tolerably dry before you domicile a camera. These things are not minded so much as formerly, and particularly in London, but when the *walls* weep there is some hazard. ... Bricks and mortar are said to be very beneficial in some cases, but in no case but of happiness may you ever be placed is the wish of your well wisher, and most truly yours, J. M. W. Turner.[76]

By the time of Hawkesworth Fawkes's marriage, Walter had moved out of Farnley Hall and handed it over to his son. Walter himself was now living permanently at 45 Grosvenor Place, but his health was rapidly declining. There was no possibility, now, of his solving his financial problems which had reached their crisis in 1824. In that year his expenditure was audited at £11,355, and his expendable income at £6,055. This situation had accumulated year on year, until in 1824 his annual burden of mortgage interest and insurance payments alone had reached £7,000. This included the interest on Turner's loan of £3,000, and on a further loan of £8,000 from his neighbour Joshua Crompton to pay his daughter Anne's dowry on her marriage to Godfrey Wentworth. With terminal exasperation, Fawkes's accountant wrote:

> ... whatever may be determined ... should not be postponed as on former occasions, when I have urged the necessity of retrenchment as much as I can possibly do now. Some of the booksellers seem to be in the habit of sending books without orders, a practice which should be put a stop to. And indeed the whole host of booksellers printsellers artists and tradesmen in all articles not of necessity, who yearly draw such large sums from Mr Fawkes, should be entirely avoided, except in dealings for ready money.[77]

The total capital sum Fawkes owed in 1824 was £69,734 – in late 1990s terms this is the equivalent of about two and a half or three million pounds sterling. That Turner seems to have made no attempt to get his loan back, certainly not during Fawkes's lifetime, nor from his estate after his death, shows him to have been extraordinarily generous to his friend's plight. These events reveal too that the regular gift to Turner of a Farnley goose pie and a brace of pheasant and a hare, sent to London each year until the year of Turner's death, was not only a Yuletide kindness, but also a small token of the discharge by Hawkesworth of his family's duty of gratitude to the old man. Walter Fawkes was sent to bed by his doctors in June 1825, and was convinced then that "he never more should get out of it".[78] Turner was one of the very few people whom he wanted to see, and during the early months of 1825 they dined together twelve times.[79] On the eve of Turner's departure for Holland, 27th August, they dined together for the last time. The two men were never to meet again.

While Turner was still abroad a disastrous slide in the value of the pound began, and in September banks across the country began to fail, including Fawkes's bank in Wakefield. Other smaller unfounded worries grew large for Fawkes. He had heard reports of a powder explosion on 20th September near Ostend and worried that Turner might have been nearby. He seems to have written to old William Turner, stirring up worries in him, too.[80] The slide in Fawkes's health continued in parallel with his declining financial fortunes, and, on 25th October, he died. His body was taken to Otley for burial on 8th November. Although Turner remained closely in touch with Hawkesworth Fawkes, and the two men met in London from time to time, Turner would never return to Farnley Hall. Its light had gone out for him.

In the spring following Fawkes's death, Turner exhibited *Cologne, the Arrival of a Packet Boat, Evening*. This is a reprise of the 1818 painting *Dort, or Dordrecht, the Dort Packet-Boat from Rotterdam becalmed*, which Walter Fawkes himself so greatly loved and owned at his death – same composition, same size, same kind of title, same time of day, same dying fall, almost the same picture. And in the foreground of *Cologne* curious iron riparian paraphernalia, wrought iron equipment for digging, fishing or lifting; tenacious, obstinate, practical, honest forks.

Fawkes's death removed one of the great certainties from Turner's life. He had lost more than a patron, but also a confidant and a refuge, both emotionally and geographically, and as time went by these gaps had to be filled. The corollary for the creative artist who needs space and solitude to pursue a task to completion, is that he also needs good company to crash into. Some of this he found at Sir John Soane's house, in Lincoln's Inn Fields.

This was then, and remains, the most extraordinary domestic interior of its period in Britain. The visitor enters a fairly ordinary town house front door, but gradually the house seems to close down upon him, funnelling him into smaller and yet smaller spaces, towards a breakfast room with mirrors, obscured windows and a suspended domed ceiling. At the heart of the house is a corridor running laterally right and left, stuffed with marble busts and antique fragments of every kind and body part, mounted on every conceivable surface, and up the walls until no square foot of surface area is left uninvaded. The house is as crammed with detail as is any one of Turner's Roman sketchbooks. One of the few oil painting commissions that Turner undertook during the mid-1820s was to paint *The Forum Romanum, for Mr Soane's Museum*. This was the third large picture Turner had made from ideas developed in Rome in 1819 and 1820, and is a painting of fragments quite as much as Mr Soane's is a museum of them. The picture is littered with fallen capitals, groups of singing monks, distant towers and so on, the whole flown over by an oppressive arch. It is high toned, startlingly yellow, with an extensive fan of blue sky in contrast. Soane and Turner must have had conversations about archaeological accuracy while the painting was in progress, for a day or two before it left for exhibition at the Academy in May 1826 Turner wrote to Soane to say he had "altered the inscription upon the Arch of Titus and it is said to be now quite right."[81] They may also have spoken about colour, for Soane painted his first-floor drawing-room yellow, echoing the colour that Turner was coming extensively to use in his paintings, and possibly echoing too the colour of Turner's own parlour.

The agreement between the two men was an informal one: this was clearly not a commission in the accepted sense of the word. Turner made it quite clear in his letter that Soane could refuse the picture if he did not like it, and this is what Soane proceeded to do, on the grounds that "the picture does not suit the place or the place the picture." "I like candour," Turner replied.[82]

Turner was roundly attacked in the press for the perceived excess of yellow in *Forum Romanum*, and in *Cologne, the Arrival of a Packet Boat, Evening* of the same year. In the 1810s it had been white that had upset the connoisseurs, now it was yellow. "In all we find the same intolerable yellow hue pervading everything," wrote a critic in the *British Press*, "whether boats or buildings, water or watermen, houses or horses, all is yellow, yellow, nothing but yellow, violently contrasted with blue."[83]

Turner dismissed the criticism of his use of yellow with something of a laugh, in great contrast to the sensitivity he had shown to criticism in the 1810s. "... I must not say yellow," he wrote to Holworthy, "for I have taken it *all* to my keeping this year, so they say, and so I meant it should be; but come and see for yourself."[84] And again to Holworthy: "Callcott is to be married to an acquaintance of mine when in Italy, a very agreeable Blue Stocking; so I must wear the yellow stockings."[85]

The regularity of Turner's life now made it possible for him to plan ahead, to know when the pressure would be on him to complete a group of works or to make a journey, and when he could unbutton in company. He was a professional artist and administrator, but he was also a professional friend. Turner had particular requirements for the right refuge and friend with whom he would stay for days, often weeks, on end. The refuge had to be away from London, from all sight and sound of his professional duties; it had to have challenging land and landscape around it to drive him out to draw and paint; and he had to have a room of his own with good light. The friends with whom he stayed, and just as important their local friends, had to be amusing, informal, intellectually stimulating and well-supplied with soft-skinned and smiling ladies. And if there was a good stretch of fishing water nearby, so much the better.

Hugh Munro of Novar was one possibility to replace Fawkes and Farnley, but Inverness was much too far away and would have to wait for a special trip. James Holworthy urged him to come up to Derbyshire a number of times, and Turner always hoped that perhaps one day he might, but he always made his excuses and found himself unable to go.[86] Despite his affection for Holworthy, Turner just did not want to go and stay with a modest family and their modest friends in a modest stone house in Derbyshire. Holworthy could come and see him in London. He had better options, two in particular, both south of London, nearer the sun.

One was Petworth, which Turner remembered well from nearly twenty years back. He had not exhausted the potential of the wide Sussex landscape, nor had he done anything to exhaust the hospitality of the amiable Lord Egremont. The other option was East Cowes Castle, the home of his friend and colleague the architect John Nash, who was also a good friend of Egremont. The views across the Solent and the mouth of the River Medina from the castle that Nash had built for himself were unparalleled. The marine light and the sight of constant traffic of boats of all sizes zipping across the water was, as Turner knew, breathtaking. Turner's first responsibility was to his art and its advancement. Quite deliberately and professionally he chose for the friends he would stay with those who would provide the circumstances he needed to progress yet more as a painter. He was beyond requiring such friends to be patrons – that now came naturally. Instead, as in a royal progress, he required and was granted their hearths, sunlight and landscape. In the summer of 1827 he stayed both with John Nash at East Cowes and with Egremont at Petworth.

At East Cowes Turner drew in his sketchbooks dozens of chalk and pen and ink studies of boats under sail, of the dancing light and views of the neo-gothic castle itself. There are drawings too of family and friends, resting and talking in the walks and arbours, playing the piano in the Music Room and parading their immaculate but extraordinary coiffures which he may have drawn to take home to amuse his father.

The great event of that summer at East Cowes was the Regatta. From the immediacy of his paintings of the Regatta it is likely that Turner extended his occasional practice of painting out of doors to painting in oil on canvas from the decks of a small boat or warship. He seems not to have anticipated such a possibility, as he had to send home to his father for a roll of canvas and some paint. He also asked his father to send him some nattier clothes. Clearly he was having a good time, and must have felt under-dressed: "I wrote a day or two ago to say that I shall want some more light Trouzers – and so I do of White Waistcoats. I ought to have 4, but I have but 2, and only 1 Kerseymere [woollen trousers]."[87]

White waistcoats, light trousers, kerseymeres – costume in which Turner could transform himself into a stylish guest amidst a happy house-party. In Nash's castle, as the sun went down over a sparkling sea and candles were lit, were the ingredients for evenings of fantasy and entertainment, gatherings of the kind that Watteau had painted a century earlier. One of the three exhibition paintings that Turner made after the visit to the Isle of Wight was a Watteauesque concoction of a musical and literary evening in the woods with East Cowes Castle in the background. The tower gleams mysteriously in the moonlight, with *Boccaccio Relating the Tale of the Birdcage*, as the title has it, his floppy velvet hat on his head and his lute lying on the ground at his feet. Dozens and dozens of little figures, almost all of them apparently women, listen attentively in the clearing and in crowds winding up through the trees to Boccaccio reading a naughty story.

This is less a painterly evocation of one evening at home with the John Nashes as an evocation of all those summer weeks at East Cowes, which were followed by more at Petworth in the early autumn with Lord Egremont. Artists, writers, politicians, and men and women of an entertaining character came and went erratically to Petworth, singly or in flocks, arriving and taking off again like starlings. This is precisely how Egremont liked it. After the diplomat Charles Fulke Greville visited Petworth in 1832 he wrote: "Lord Egremont hates ceremony, and can't bear to be personally meddled with; he likes people to come and go as it suits them, and say nothing about it, never to take leave of him."[88] Although the house "wants modern comforts, and the servants are rustic and uncouth," as Fulke Greville put it, Egremont took his hospitality seriously. Balls for the county and dinners for the tenants were regular events, as were performances by local military bands in the Gallery or a quartet in the dining-room. Five hundred people attended a ball in honour of the King's accession in 1822, with supper in the Tennis Court which was carpeted and hung with red cloth. In 1830, to celebrate the coming of the new decade, the Earl entertained two thousand women and children to dinner in the Riding House.[89]

C. R. Leslie, Thomas Stothard, Samuel Rogers the banker poet, Thomas Phillips, John Nash, Francis Chantrey and Turner were all mutual friends, and all friends of the munificent Earl. Egremont now had fifteen oil paintings by Turner, many of them having come with the following wind of critical comment in the London papers. All, now, hung in or near the North Gallery where an extension had that year been completed. Turner could, as none other, walk round Petworth in 1827 and see how greatly he personally had contributed to the ambience of the house, even though he had not set foot there for nearly twenty years.

But walking round the Gallery, looking at his pictures, we can sense that Turner had mixed feelings. There would have been pride, certainly, that paintings of his should hang under the same roof as Reynolds, Van Dyck, Claude and Poussin, but the pride that says "And so they should!" In Egremont's Gallery, Turner was looking at himself and at his own past as if in a mirror. He had travelled many miles since making these paintings, he had grown and changed, and had begun to see the world in a new light. The most recent of his pictures at Petworth was *Teignmouth*, which he had exhibited seventeen years before. Proud though he may have been of these old canvases, this was not what he was doing now. Confronted by his past, Turner had severe responsibilities to express at Petworth both his present and his future.

Petworth was a warm and convivial place to be on an October evening. Guests chatter before dinner; the vicar holds forth, warming his backside at the fire as he does so; two men slope off for a game of billiards; two more snore after dinner by the dying embers of the fire. Turner saw all these things as he sat quietly talking with the others, and, having his paper and paints with him, he sketched them there and then. That he was able to do so, that it was not considered *mal vu*, throws yet more light on the informal and uninhibited way of life at the 3rd Earl's Petworth. Uninhibited it certainly was, for though Turner came on his own, as the surviving Housekeeping Accounts show,[90] he found warmth and comfort in the pleasures of the flesh while he was there, and expressed it in gouache and watercolour.

It may have been on the October 1827 visit to Petworth that Egremont dropped to Turner the suggestion that he paint a group of long, narrow paintings to be set in wall panelling below the sombre sixteenth- and seventeenth-century portraits that gazed down at the guests as they dined in the Carved Room. The portraits were very fine, but Henry VIII, the Duke of Somerset and Egremont's late estranged wife Elizabeth were not the gayest of dinner party guests in the 1820s. The Earl had created the Carved Room thirty years before by knocking two smaller rooms together, and it was now the place where his grandest dinner parties were held. In his new red and yellow manner, "the author of gamboge light" as a critic had called Turner in 1826,[91] could happily lift the tone of the room, and give it colour that would sparkle in the candlelight and sing when the sun shone.

Turner had completed at least two of the paintings by the following summer, for Thomas Creevey referred to a pair installed in the panels in a letter of August 1828.[92] By the end of the decade he had made five or six full size oil studies, and his four finished paintings filled the spaces allocated to him in the Carved Room. If he had ever been troubled by the thought that his current manner of painting was not properly represented at Petworth, these new pictures put such thoughts at rest. The two views of Petworth Park and two more of Chichester Canal and the Chain Pier at Brighton created a dashing line of incandescent light running below the portraits like a row of Argand lamps. It was in a spirit of homage to the sun that Turner chose the colours he did for these paintings, whose format mirrored the extended horizon visible from the windows on the Petworth west front. The afternoon and evening sun shone directly on them – damaging them, incidentally, as the years went by.[93]

The two subjects taken from beyond Petworth, *Chichester Canal* and *Brighton from the Sea*, represent particular interests of Lord Egremont, who had financial stakes in both the Chichester Canal and the Brighton Chain Pier. The canal, intended to be the final link in a navigable waterway from London to the south coast, opened in 1822. The Earl had sunk enormous sums of money into it and other stretches of waterway towards London, but this final link came too late. The canal was a financial disaster, and at great expense to himself, Egremont pulled out of the Chichester Canal Company in 1826.

One wonders why Egremont would want to be reminded of this ignominious withdrawal by commissioning Turner to paint a canal subject. The reason may not be too far away. Among the list of shareholders for the Chichester Canal was one "William Turner".[94] If this was indeed J. M. W. Turner, he will have been encouraged to invest by Lord Egremont. So there is no wonder that he would want to paint the Chichester Canal for the Petworth dining-room to remind Egremont of his folly, for Turner will have lost money too. If it was not, that reason departs.

During the winter of 1827 and 1828 Turner appears to have had a further attack of breathing problems, or a bad cough, and perhaps had some concern about the state of his heart. He was given a prescription, which survives, for glycerine, scilla and ammonium acetate, common treatments for lung or cardiac disorders.[95] When he was not travelling, Turner was now living wholly in central London, where in the winter the air was thick with smogs and pollution from countless factories and domestic fires. Having spent the past summer entirely in the clear air of the south of England, it is hardly surprising that he should suffer from the ill effects of London in the winter.

Rather to his surprise, Turner began to lose weight from about the end of 1826, and into 1827. The caricaturist Richard Dighton drew a profile of a slim-waisted Turner which is at odds with the image of the well-rounded fellow whom Hawkesworth Fawkes painted into the Farnley album earlier in the decade. Turner noticed this change in himself in a letter to Holworthy: "But with myself I am as thin as a hurdle or the direction post, though not so tall that will show me the way to Hathersage."[96]

At a distance of nearly two hundred years it would be rash to draw any firm conclusions, but Turner's loss of weight and the generally pinched look that Dighton gives him suggests that he had been suffering. The past two winters had been exceptionally cold, and in another letter to Holworthy, Turner speaks of the cold and of the day when his father would no longer be alive:

What may become of me I know not what, particularly if a lady keeps my bed warm, and last winter was quite enough to make singles think of doubles. Poor daddy never felt cold so much. I begin to think of being truely alone in the world, but I believe the bitterness is past. But he is very much shaken and I am not the better for wear.[97]

Turner's red face had been pointed out by independent witnesses in the late 1820s, and it may be linked to a heart condition of some kind. He may also have been frightened of catching syphilis, if a particular reading of the letter quoted above is correct. The remark has usually been taken to mean that Turner was thinking of getting married, but he was no marrier, and his anxious tone, in the contexts of ailments, invites a rather more animal explanation.

Turner's concern for his father's health was growing to the extent that he sold Sandycombe Lodge in 1826, and moved the old man back to Queen Anne Street. The house and garden had become too much for William now, and he was in no state to help run two establishments. Sandycombe was becoming less and less useful to Turner as the 1820s progressed, and with the work at Queen Anne Street completed, and new furniture and furnishings installed, the Twickenham house was superfluous. With further properties in Wapping and Barkingside, and the freehold at Lee Clump, he already had enough in that department of his life.

Where Twickenham had fascinated him in the 1810s for its classical and literary associations, Wapping gave Turner opportunities of a different kind. Only 200 yards from the front door of the Ship and Bladebone Inn was the site of the northern entrance of the first pedestrian tunnel ever to be dug beneath a river anywhere in the world. It was a massive engineering undertaking masterminded by Sir Marc Isambard Brunel, who had devised an elaborate honeycomb shield, about twenty-five feet high by forty feet wide, to house the tunnellers. Men dug within its cells, and the whole structure supported the roof of each section being dug, and crept forward inch by inch as tunnelling progressed. The shield was fitted into place at the bottom of a seventy-feet deep shaft on the Rotherhithe bank on 2nd December 1825, and tunnelling began a few days later. Marc's son, Isambard Kingdom Brunel, oversaw the work on site. By late May 1827 the tunnel was about halfway across, 547 feet 7 inches having been completed.[98]

The physical and economic reverberations of the tunnelling work in Rotherhithe, and the anticipation of the tunnel's arrival in Wapping, spread through the parishes like a high tide. No inn anywhere near such industry could fail to make a profit if it were properly managed. Turner realised this only too clearly, and even while he was within the landscapes of Petworth in October 1827 he conducted urgent business by letter with his solicitor to ensure that a change of tenant at the Ship and Bladebone progressed smoothly, and a new joint lease was properly drawn up.

That Turner should be anxious to see this happen may not be so surprising given the inexorable approach of the tunnel; but that he, the client, should tell the solicitor precisely how to word the lease reveals the same exasperatingly legalistic mind, fearful of being done down, which had surfaced before in 1809 and 1821. Turner's instructions to George Cobb ran as follows:

> ... *then* you may proceed – to draw up the Copy – as follow[s] thus 14 Years Lease at £60 per year clear of all and everything – Church R[ate] &c&c&c to pay the insurance 600 each in joint names ... to

repair substan[ti]ally and a given sum to be Paid out for each House now and a further sum in future to prevent the Houses being left at the termination of the 14 Years End and to paint at a given time – and clear the Lawn [?] which belongs to them.[99]

In the event, Brunel's tunnelling activity came to an abrupt halt in January 1828 when the river flooded in for the second time, and work was suspended for what turned out to be seven years.

During the winter of 1827 and 1828 Turner was working on his four paintings for the coming Academy exhibition. Two poetic evocations of the East Cowes Regatta had been commissioned by John Nash, another was the Boccaccio fantasy already discussed, and the fourth, the largest of the group, was *Dido Directing the Equipment of the Fleet – The Morning of the Carthaginian Empire*. This was the first time Turner had returned, on canvas, to Carthage since 1817 when he exhibited *The Decline of the Carthaginian Empire*. The moment he chose for the new painting is Dido's generous welcoming of Aeneas's men and his storm-damaged fleet. The Carthaginian queen puts at Aeneas's disposal all of the repair facilities of her dockyard. Or, in the words of Dryden, translating Virgil:

> Your men shall be receiv'd, your fleet repair'd,
> And sail, with ships of convoy for your guard:
> Or, would you stay, and join your friendly pow'rs
> To raise and to defend the Tyrian tow'rs,
>   My wealth, my city, and myself are yours.[100]

The painting was a wreck when the Turner Bequest first came to the National Gallery, and it is in no condition for display. But what is clear from an early photograph is that it is practically a reworking, with added lines of riverside classical buildings, of *East Cowes Castle – The Regatta Starting for the Moorings*. Both paintings show a waterway running towards the sun, the one being the entrance to the harbour at Carthage, the other the mouth of the River Medina; both are lined with boats and boatmen awaiting the start of a big event – the one Aeneas's decision to stay or go, the other the Cowes Regatta of the past summer. But what gives the *Dido* the narrative juice that the *Regatta* lacks is the great tree which cuts the calm of the painting and which is the sign of the dilemma of Aeneas.

Both paintings were exhibited in the 1828 Academy exhibition, and taken together they demonstrate how closely Turner could draw fact and fantasy together until they intertwine. This is an observation we can extend to Turner's life. He took himself off to Carthage seven times at least in his exhibited paintings alone, and to other parts of the Greek and Roman mythical world a dozen times and more. There were sound rational reasons for him to paint ancient subjects, and through them to comment on contemporary life. The clear elision of these two paintings marks a crossing point both in Turner's art and his life.

Before the 1828 exhibition there is in Turner a presumption towards the rational. He plans, he prepares, he manoeuvres in the world of Academy politics, he builds for the future. When he travels, he plots his route in advance, discusses options and takes advice. He takes adverse criticism hard, and writes down word for word one journalist's unexpected praise. He struts proudly about his exhibitions, showing himself off. He dresses nattily. He gives public lectures. His pictures are well made objects. His range of colours is based on the browns, greens and blues which from the seventeenth century were seen to be worthy reflections of nature.

The eight or nine years between his first and second Italian visits was the period of change of an artist in the classic tradition of the eighteenth century slowly becoming a giant of the nineteenth. The change ebbs and flows, but once the wind has caught his canvas and has made it billow, Turner's life irrevocably enters its second hemisphere.

His colours move to red, blue, white and yellow. He begins to be able to dismiss criticism, or at least to turn a deaf ear, and advises others to do the same. Many other former certainties seem now to be turned on their heads – his paintings cease to be made so well, they blister, flake or crack owing to his experimentation with untried and insecure pigments and media. Claims that Turner is mad now become an accepted part of society lore. He slips in and out of the Academy on Varnishing Days, working hard on his paintings, but tending to speak to no one. He becomes shabbier in appearance. He adopts disguise, both in his name and, allegedly, his dress – he calls himself "Mr Booth", or even "Admiral Booth", and pretends to a professional photographer that he is a Master in Chancery, and is photographed as such. He lives at two London addresses where he is cared for by two single women, one of whom at least seems not to have been aware of the other's existence. He loses good friends to death, and begins to ponder his own mortality. He makes his first will; and then changes it; and changes it again.

At the beginning of the year in which he exhibited *Dido Directing the Equipment of the Fleet* and *East Cowes Castle*, Turner gave his last public lecture as Professor of Perspective at the Royal Academy. One member of the audience was the young Henry Cole, thirty years later to become the founder of the Victoria and Albert Museum. He wrote in his diary:

Mon 14th Jan: ... Attended Mr Turner's lecture on Perspective at the Royal Academy, he is almost perfection in mumbling and unintelligibility.

Mon 28th Jan: Turner's 4th lecture at the Royal Academy. No attendance by me.[101]

# ELEVEN

# Italy: "Terra Pittura"

## 1828–1829

Turner crossed to the Continent from England during the first week of August 1828, heading for Rome. Here is his own whistle-stop description of his journey south from Paris, as written to George Jones:

> Two months nearly in getting to this Terra Pittura, *and at work*; but the length of time is my own fault. I must see the South of France, which almost knocked me up, the heat was so intense, particularly at Nismes and Avignon; and until I got a plunge into the sea at Marseilles, I felt so weak that nothing but the change of scene kept me onwards to my distant point. Genoa, and all the sea-coast from Nice to Spezzia is remarkably rugged and fine; so is Massa.[1]

Pulled by two conflicting enticements, to see southern France and to rush to Rome, Turner did both, and made himself ill in the process. He had promised Charles Eastlake that he would be in Rome by 1st September, but he could not leave "the loadstone London" as he put it,[2] until he had finished some watercolours for the *England and Wales* series, and other commitments to engravers. He was torn between his professional responsibilities and his reluctance to disappoint friends, and his health took the rub. His further anxieties were that he should get to work as soon as possible, and not be hindered by the lack of the right materials. Writing from Paris, he asked Eastlake to buy him a canvas "8 feet 2½ inch by 4 feet 11¼ inch" – the dimensions are as precise as that – two of them if possible, so that he could set to work straight away on "my first brush in Rome" a large painting for Lord Egremont to hang at Petworth as a companion to the Claude *Jacob and Laban*. We cannot be sure that Egremont ever asked for such a painting, but nevertheless, knowing the great debt he would always owe to the Earl, Turner intended to paint the picture "con amore".[3]

The roads in France in the late 1820s were dreadful, poorly made and ill-maintained, and the country, even twelve or thirteen years after the end of the Napoleonic Wars, in a depressed and ruinous state. In 1828 he could not have bowled along at the rate he did in 1802. Mary Callcott had very recently travelled the same road as Turner and wrote home from Lyons:

> We do not find travelling in France half so well as in Italy – The Inns less comfortable the roads bitten & dreadfully rough being all made ... with such shingle as lies on the sea beach & quite as ill bound together, & on the whole the people less civil ... You would be sorry to see the ruined state of the churches & castles & country seats here remaining from the wretched times of the revolution.[4]

Turner's arrival in Rome was warmly awaited by the English artists there. It had been the same the last time. "Turner will be here in a few days and will perhaps occupy a spare study I have got," Eastlake wrote to Thomas Uwins, "at any rate he will paint a large picture, perhaps two. I talk too confidently even within range of the magician's circle, but within it 'none dare walk but he'."[5]

He came bearing mail from England, from friend to friend, and, delivering Maria Callcott's letter to the diplomat Auguste Kestner, Turner appeared "so modest that he shall not know the value of his own person."[6] Delayed in his arrival in Rome as he was, Turner hit the ground running: Eastlake had the canvas ready and waiting for his "first brush in Rome". From the day of his arrival, Turner was talkative and good-humoured, despite the fact that the girl next door "plays the piano wretchedly close to his bedroom so that he is not very comfortable."[7]

The best of Turner's talk survives in letters home:

> I have confined myself to the painting department at Corso [...] and having finished *one* [*Medea*] am about the second [*Regulus*], and getting on with Lord E's [*Palestrina*], which began the very first touch in Rome; but as the folk here talked that I would show them *not*, I finished a small three feet [by] four to stop their gabbling [*View of Orvieto*]; so now to business ...[8]

Remarks of this kind reveal the presence of a highly sociable, even patient man, as Turner characteristically became in the company of other artists, whether at home or abroad. If we take Turner's words at face value, the picture which he painted "to stop their gabbling" was a quick, sample piece containing all the elements that went to make a characteristic "Turner" that would already be familiar through engravings to local

Italian artists. It would have the central vista formed by a V-shaped foreground form, an ideal tree to one side, human activity to the other, a middleground bridge and distant focal point, all wrapped up in an effulgent light of evening (or morning). "There you are. Now let me get on with what I came here to do," we might hear him say as he picks up his brushes again and resumes work on *Palestrina* for Lord Egremont.

Looking afresh at the Roman paintings of 1828 there are completed canvases and unfinished threads that indicate his clear intention to break new ground. In three canvases completed in Claude's own city, and three or four others that were begun there but never finished, Turner stirred up the Franco-Italian master and re-energised him. Claude's paintings had been entering British collections now for more than a century, and we might expect the blindness of familiarity to surround them as they hung, taken for granted, by the new generation in aristocratic galleries and drawing-rooms. In *Palestrina* Turner turns the heat up on Claude. The composition has Claude's harmonics, but his cool greens and blues are accompanied by yellows, reds and pinks of Turner's own conception. Proposed for Egremont, this picture would have brought to Petworth a Claude reborn from the heat of the Campagna in the colours of the fire and steam of the Machine Age.

The heat is up also in *Regulus*, although the painting as we know it today was considerably reworked by Turner in 1837: "The painting was a mass of red and yellow of all varieties. Every object was in its fiery state ... [From the sun] were drawn – ruled – lines to mark the rays; these lines were rather strongly marked, I suppose to guide his eye."[9] This is a very clear indication of the original state of the picture, harder and fiercer than it is now. In *Regulus* Claude screams, as indeed did Regulus when he was led out into blazing Carthaginian sunlight after days in a darkened room where his eyelids were cut off. Thus, the sun blinded him.

Turner exhibited these two paintings, and his *Vision of Medea* and *Orvieto*, in rooms he had rented in the Palazzo Trulli. He framed them with lengths of thick rope because *Medea* at least was probably unfinished, and he did not want to go to the expense of having frames made for paintings he would soon ship to England.[10] That his name was as much a draw in Rome as in London is revealed by Eastlake's recollection that

more than a thousand persons went to see his works when exhibited, so you may imagine how astonished, enraged or delighted the different schools of artists were, at seeing things with methods so new, so daring, and excellencies so unequivocal. The angry critics have, I believe, talked most, and it is possible that you may hear of *general* severity of judgement, but many did justice and many more were fain to admire what they confessed they dared not imitate.[11]

The most vehement critics heaped insults on Turner's head, and became personal. A contemporary engraving shows a nude woman leaning on the Dome of St Paul's, breaking wind through a trumpet in the direction of St Peter's. "Turner! Turner! Turner!" blows the trumpet, while a defecating dog in the foreground barks: "Anch io son pittore." ["I'm a painter too."][12]

Other paintings made on this visit to Rome reflect the desire in Turner to move his art along. There are three large nudes, each unfinished, each on a scale that is unlike anthing else in his oil paintings. He had already skirmished with the nude in his work – for example in two *Venus and Adonis* subjects of around 1805, reflecting the manners of Titian and Veronese – but the fact that the 1828 canvases are unfinished suggests that he eventually tired of the idea. Their presence, however, indicates not only his eagerness to look at old masters again, but that the covey of British sculptors in Rome also had some impact on his art.

Sculpture was on Turner's mind as he had driven south to Rome, particularly when passing the marble quarries at Carrara. He wrote to Jones:

> Tell that fat fellow Chantrey that I did think of him, *then* (but not the first or the last time) of the thousands he had made out of those marble crags which only afforded me a sour bottle of wine and a sketch; but he deserves everything which is good, though he did give me a fit of the spleen at Carrara.[13]

The making of sculpture in Rome in the 1820s was a buoyant industry which British artists exploited liberally. Marble was easily available, labour cheap, and as wealthy English families rebuilt or extended their country houses in the post-war years, there was a ready market for sculpture at home. Canova and Thorwaldsen both had impressive sculpture studios in the city, and had trained some of the settled British artists. Rome was practically heaven, as John Gibson explained to Thomas L. Donaldson:

> ... I feel very happy here surrounded by all that I can desire as to the advantages of my art. Since your departure I have increased my establishment and have four good studios in the via Fontanella Babuino and a flower garden in the mids[t] of them and a fountain perpetually playing the music of which I hear whilst I am forming my nymphs & loves in marble and when tired I lay down my chissel walk among my roses & orange trees – it is here I conceive all my classical subjects. Fortune smiles on this spot for everything which I have done in clay for this last ten years has given satisfaction and have been ordered in marble by some of our principal nobility. I am advancing a group in marble of three figures the subject is young Hylas surprised by the Nymphs ...[14]

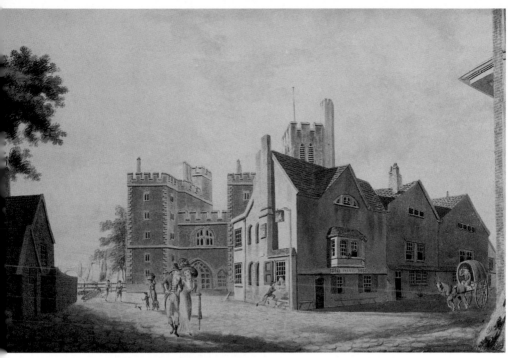

*The Archbishop's Palace, Lambeth.* Watercolour, exh. 1790. © 1996 Indianapolis Museum of Art, Gift in memory of Dr and Mrs Hugo O. Pantzer by their children.

*St Erasmus and Bishop Islip's Chapels.* Watercolour, exh. 1796. © British Museum, London.

*St Mary's and the Radcliffe Camera from Oriel Lane.* Watercolour, *c.* 1800. Turner Bequest, Tate Gallery, London.

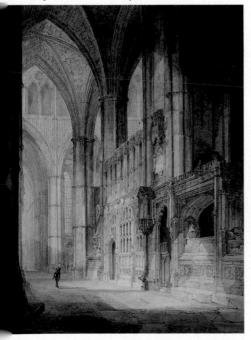

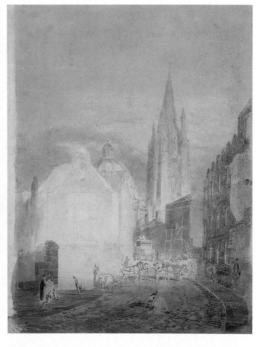

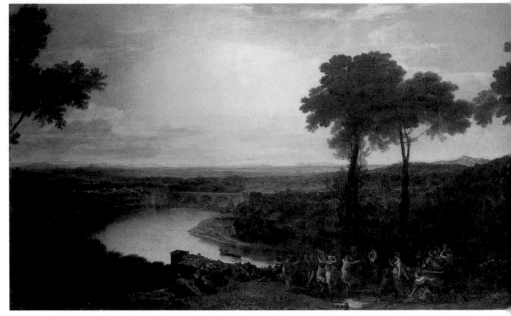

*Festival upon the Opening of the Vintage of Macon.* Oil on canvas, exh. 1803. Sheffield Arts and Museums.

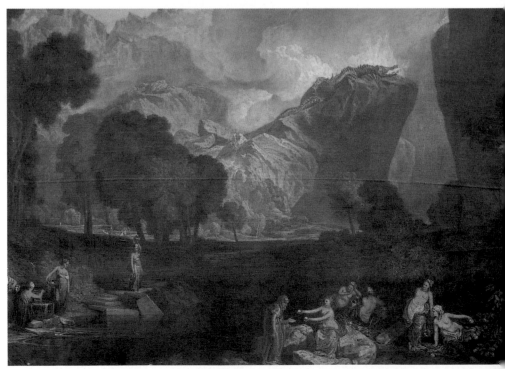

*The Goddess of Discord choosing the Apple of Contention in the Garden of the Hesperides.* Oil on canvas, exh. 1806. Turner Bequest, Tate Gallery, London.

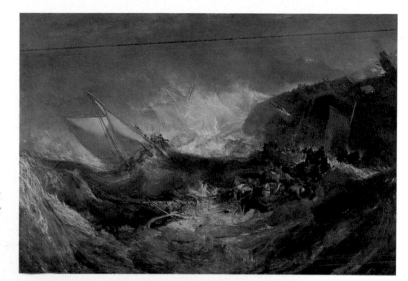

*Wreck of a Transport Ship.* Oil on canvas, c. 1810. Calouste Gulbenkian Foundation, Lisbon.

*Snow Storm: Hannibal and his Army Crossing the Alps.* Oil on canvas, exh. 1812. Turner Bequest, Tate Gallery, London.

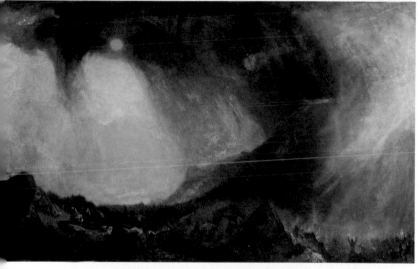

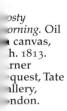

*Frosty Morning.* Oil on canvas, exh. 1813. Turner Bequest, Tate Gallery, London.

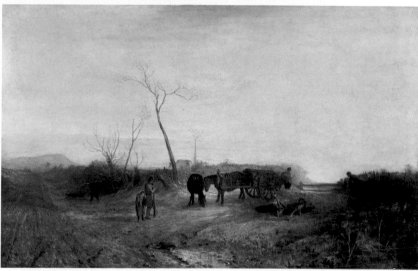

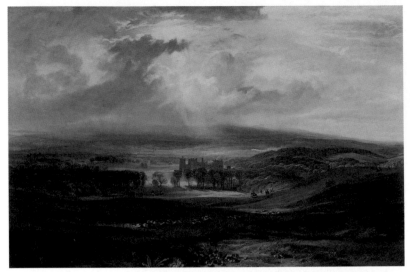

*Raby Castle, the Seat of the Earl of Darlington.* Oil on canvas, exh. 1818. The Walters Art Gallery, Baltimore.

*Dort, or Dordrecht: the Dort Packet-Boat from Rotterdam becalmed.* Oil on canvas, exh. 1818. Yale Center for British Art, New Haven, Paul Mellon Collection.

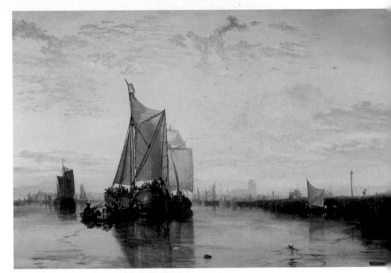

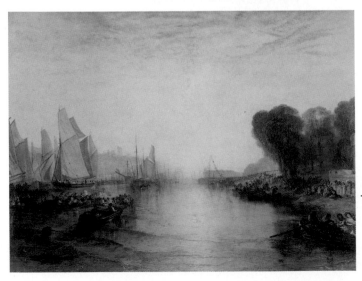

*East Cowes Castle, the Seat of J. Nash Esq.: the Regatta starting for their Moorings.* Oil on canvas, exh. 1828. Victoria and Albert Museum.

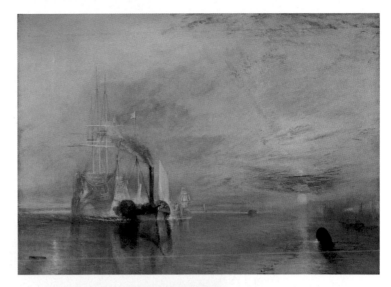

The Fighting 'Téméraire', tugged to her Last Berth to be broken up. Oil on canvas, exh. 1839. National Gallery, London.

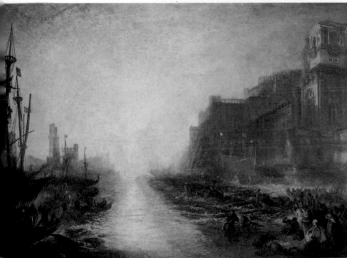

Regulus. Oil on canvas, exh. 1828; reworked 1837. Turner Bequest, Tate Gallery, London.

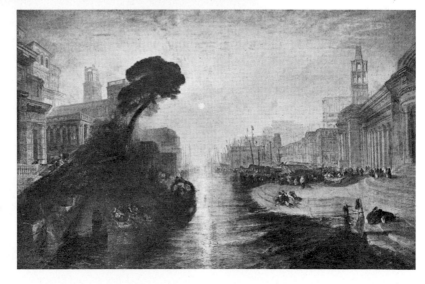

Dido directing the equipment of the fleet, or the Morning of the Carthaginian Empire. Oil on canvas, exh. 1828. Turner Bequest, Tate Gallery, London. From a pre-1917 photograph.

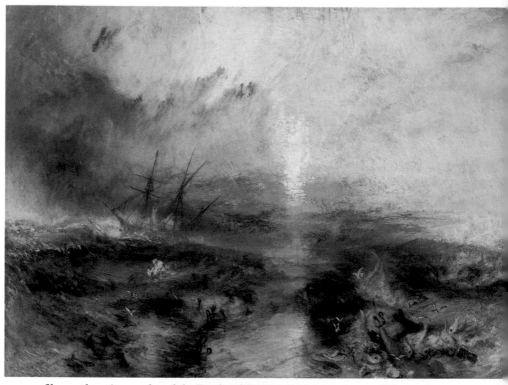

*Slavers throwing overboard the Dead and Dying – Typhon coming on.* Oil on canvas, exh. 1840. Henry Lillie Pierce Fund, Courtesy Boston Museum of Fine Arts.

*Ulysses deriding Polyphemus – Homer's Odyssey.* Oil on canvas, exh. 1829. National Gallery, London.

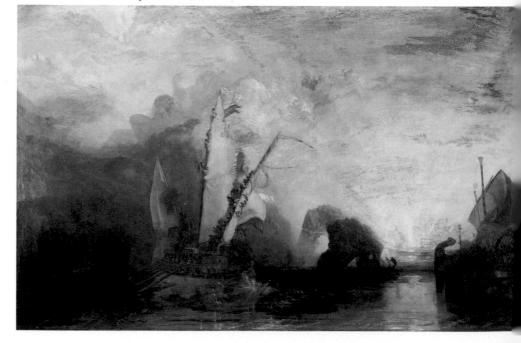

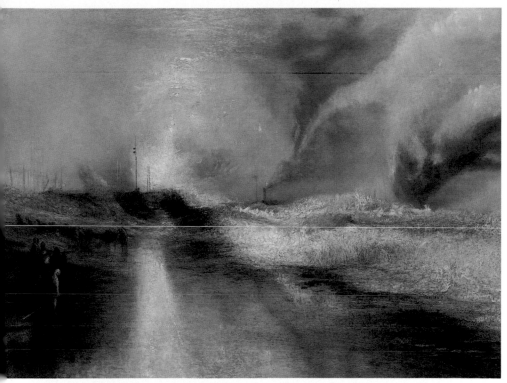

*Rockets and Blue Lights (Close at Hand) to warn Steam-Boats of Shoal-Water.* Oil on canvas, exh. 1840. Sterling and Francine Clark Art Institute, Williamstown, Mass.

*Rain, Steam, and Speed – the Great Western Railway.* Oil on canvas, exh. 1844. National Gallery, London.

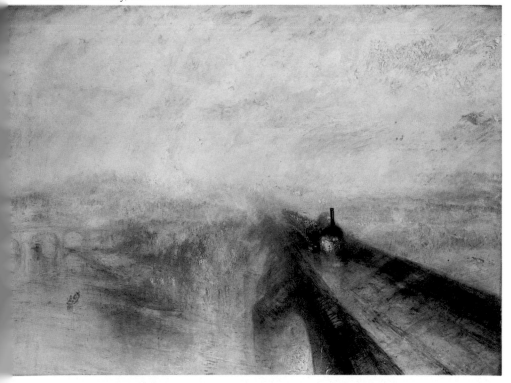

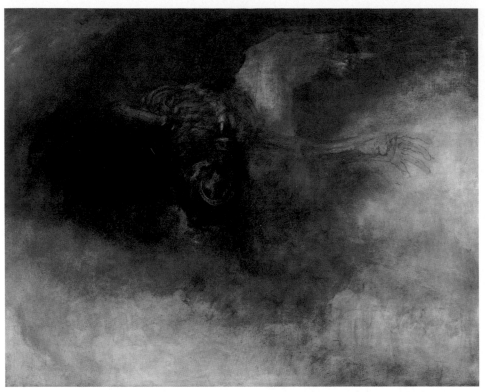

*'Death on a Pale Horse'.* Oil on canvas, ?1832. Turner Bequest, Tate Gallery, London.

*Burning of the Houses of Lords and Commons, October 6th 1834.* [First version] Oil on canvas, 1835. Philadelphia Museum of Art: The John H. McFadden Collection.

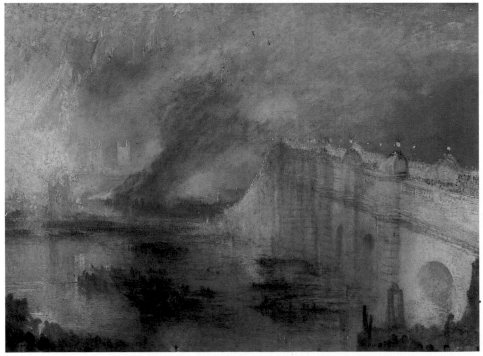

Turner reported a flavour of this back to Chantrey, who had not been to Rome for nearly ten years. Turner's letter has the smack of a commissioned report on the latest news, so that Chantrey would be aware of what was going on. Percipiently, in his time away from his easel, Turner cast his eye over studios large and small:

> Sculpture, of course, first, for it carries away all the patronage, so it is said, in Rome; but all seems to share in the goodwill of the patrons of the day. Gott's studio is full. Wyatt and Rennie, Ewing, Buxton, all employed. Gibson has two groups in hand, "Venus and Cupid", and the "Rape of Hylas". I doubt very much if it will be in time (taking the long voyage into the scale) for the Exhibition, though it is for England. Its style is something like "The Psyche", being two stand-ing figures of nymphs leaning, enamoured, over the youthful Hylas, with his pitcher. The Venus is a sitting figure, with the Cupid in attendance; if it had wings like a dove, to flee away and be at rest, the rest would not be the worse for the change. Thorwaldsen is closely engaged on the late Pope's (Pius VII) monument. Portraits of the superior animal, man, is to be found in all. In some of the inferior – viz. greyhounds and poodles, cats and monkeys etc etc.[15]

Despite the fact that it generally took two or three weeks for a letter to travel from Rome to London, from the evidence of the surviving letters Turner felt himself to be no further from Somerset House and the buzz of the London art world than he might have been in Twickenham. He congratulates Charles Turner on his long awaited election, by a whisker, to Associate Engraver at the Academy, but then spoils the warm tone of the letter by going on to lecture Charles about how he should show respect to the Academicians who supported him, and seems to remind him in a veiled hint that he should not be too money grubbing in future.[16] Here is a classic instance of the pot calling the kettle black – the remark probably refers to the row that J. M. W. and Charles Turner had had about eighteen years earlier over the latter's attempts to raise his prices for the *Liber Studiorum* prints J. M. W. had the memory of an elephant, a selective ability to bear grudges or to lay them to rest with a flourish. "You see I am acting again the Papa with you," he adds as a postscript, "but it is the last time of asking."

Occupied though he was with his large paintings, Turner also travelled in the country about Rome. He had passed through Orvieto on the way south, and while in Rome went "to Subiaco & is dissatisfied but did not see San Benedetto & it rained."[17] He received work from home, proofs of prints to correct for *England and Wales*. As the mail coaches bumped backwards and forwards across Italy and France they seemed always to have something on board for Turner. He had taken on business for Lord

Egremont, who wrote to him to say how much he was looking forward to having "the Torso".[18] This is likely to have been the piece of antique sculpture that was later restored for Egremont, and indicates a further dimension and purpose to Turner's interest in sculpture in Rome.

The expatriate colony of British artists in Rome welcomed to their table visitors who were ready to offer the latest news from home. Gibson assured Donaldson: "... We still keep up and meet at the leprosy table and now there is no necessity for the law which you once made. We are much more sedate. I suppose it is the effect of old age coming on. Of the old set at the table Eastlake Wyatt and myself."[19]

Turner was not allowed to leave for home until he had done his final round of parties. "He made himself very social and seemed to enjoy himself," C. R. Leslie heard.[20] His "last two or three days in Rome were in a whirl," Turner recalled, "remember me to all my friends, not forgetting the ladies."[21] He had fully intended to return to Rome within a year, and left money at banks in the city, and seems also to have reserved his rooms for the next visit.[22]

There were whirls of other kinds on the journey north through Italy in January, the bitter snowy weather. "Now for my journey *home* ..." Turner began with a deep breath in a vivid letter to Eastlake:

Do not think any poor devil had such another, ... for the snow began to fall at Foligno, tho' more of ice than snow, that the coach from its weight slide about in all directions, that walking was much preferable, but my innumerable tails would not do that service so I soon got wet through and through, till at Sarre-valli the diligence zizd into a ditch and required 6 oxen, sent three miles back for, to drag it out; this cost 4 Hours, that we were 10 Hours beyond our time at Macerata, consequently half starved and frozen we at last got to Bologna, where I wrote to you. But there our troubles began instead of diminishing – the Milan diligence was unable to pass Placentia. We therefore hired a voitura, the horses were knocked up the first post, sigr turned us over to another lighter carriage which put my coat in full requisition night and day, for we never could keep warm or make our day's distance good, the places we put up at proved bad till Firenzola being even the worst for the down diligence people had devoured everything eatable (Beds none) ... crossed Mont Cenis on a sledge – bivouaced in the snow with fires lighted for 3 Hours on Mont Tarate while the diligence was righted and dug out, for a Bank of Snow saved it from upsetting – and in the same night we were again turned out to walk up to our knees in new fallen drift to get assistance to dig a channel thro' it for the coach, so that from Foligno to within 20 miles of Paris I never saw the road but snow![23]

He loved it all, the bumps, the crush in the carriages, the thrill of danger, the upsets, the material for his sketchbooks. When Eastlake said of Turner "he is used to rough it,"[24] he was more right than he knew. Turner loved difficult travelling because he had travelled with difficulty all his life, and it *was* his life. He could only capture reverberating landscapes by travelling to see them. Telling about his journeys in words came as naturally to him as drawing the sights *en route*, and his friends just had to hear the ancient mariner out.

Such good spirits in the face of real danger made Turner an excellent travelling companion. This is one reason why his friends would travel with him, and still remain his friends. A young Englishman, travelling home on this 1829 journey, shared the carriage, and wrote about the indefatigable man he met:

> I have fortunately met with a good-tempered, funny, little elderly gentleman, who will probably be my travelling companion through-out the journey. He is continually popping his head out of the window to sketch whatever strikes his fancy, and became quite angry because the conductor would not wait for him whilst he took a sunrise view of Macerata. "Damn the fellow!" says he, "he has no feeling." He speaks but a few words of Italian, about as much of French, which two languages he jumbles together most amusingly. His good temper, however, carries him through all his troubles. I am sure you would love him for his indefatigability in his favorite pursuit. From his conversation he is evidently *near kin to*, if not *absolutely*, an artist. Probably you may know something of him. The name on his trunk is J. W. or J. M. W. Turner![25]

Turner was home in time for the Academy Council meeting on 10th February. It was important that he should be there because this was the meeting at which Eastlake was to stand as RA, and he needed Turner's support. Constable was the favourite, and Francis Danby ARA a serious contender for the one vacancy caused by the death of Edward Bird. In the event, Constable romped home with twelve votes, to Eastlake's two. Danby, bitterly disappointed by his own six votes, suspected that Constable had been elected through intrigue, "for the Academy I have much cause to be ashamed as it lowers their value when it is so evident that they have elected Constable for his money."[26] Turner himself was gnomic in his comment on the result, writing to Eastlake: "Constable 12; Danby 6; Clint 5; Briggs 2; Eastlake 2; Landseer 1. Draw your own conclusions from this petty treason ..."[27]

There was another reason for Turner to risk life and limb in an Alpine snowdrift. He had one more picture to paint for the 1829 Academy exhibition, and it was going to be a good one. The paintings he had made in Rome, finished and unfinished, were all on the high seas, or so he thought, due to arrive in London in time for the coming exhibition. The painting he still had to do, and for which he had made a small oil study in Rome, was of Ulysses and his men escaping from the giant Polyphemus on their way home to Greece. Turner had two months left to start and finish the painting. As he had in 1820, he wanted his Rome experience of 1828 to hit London hard with four or five canvases of blazing colour.

But as the weeks went by it became clearer and clearer that the consignment from Rome would not reach London in time. Where was it?

!!! Hope that my pictures are half way home and insured for 500 and you have the invoice [he wrote to Eastlake on 16th February]. Pray tell me how they are directed, who consigned to in London, they and the Torso [for Egremont], for I begin to be figgety about them. I know you will have directed right, but I should like to know How, for my last two or three days in Rome were in a whirl; and you at last packed me up.[28]

He did not know this, but although *Regulus* and *Orvieto* were on their way, his *Vision of Medea* was still sitting in its packing case in Rome, and by the end of March had not left for England.[29]

Having given up all hope of their arriving in time, Turner threw himself into his Ulysses subject. He stayed at home, he would not go out, even turning down an invitation from Clara Wheeler: "Dear Clara I must not allow myself the pleasure of being with you on Saturday to dinner. / Time Time Time / so more haste the worst speed."[30] He signs the letter not with his name, but with a swift drawing of a harassed palette, face-like, coughing out its brushes as a jar of varnish spills onto the floor.

*Ulysses Deriding Polyphemus*, completed just in time and exhibited in May 1829, is a blaze of dawning colour, as Ulysses and his men taunt the enraged giant from the sea off Mount Etna. They taunt him with shouts, gestures and the provocative display at the masthead of a banner depicting the Trojan Horse. *Ulysses Deriding Polyphemus* follows in its bare bones the composition of the sketch, but its colour is Italian light recollected and enchanted in the tranquillity of Turner's studio in smoky springtime London. Turner had a tendency to return to themes and compositions that affected him, and in *Ulysses Deriding Polyphemus* the echo comes from his *Garden of the Hesperides* of 1806, where the dragon lies dominating the garden from an enormous rock, just as Polyphemus lies on Mount Etna.

But *Ulysses* differs from the *Hesperides* in its veils of shimmering colour, evolved from the gold and jewelled tones of Italian Renaissance painting, its baroque gold-encrusted ships, the ribbed scallop effect of the dawning rays, and the glowing light from the fires of the grumbling volcano, Mount Etna. And well may it grumble as Ulysses escapes scot-free from having devastated the harmless Polyphemus. There is more. In *Hesperides* Turner is chained to the making of a picture that would settle happily in the eighteenth-century Poussinesque tradition. With *Ulysses* he has a new cast of mind and a new palette, in which all the colours of the spectrum find a place. Mythology goes hand-in-hand with scientific reality, as nereids play about the bow-wave of Ulysses's ship, preceded by flying fish that Turner will have seen in the Mediterranean. Turner has also painted the natural phosphorescence sometimes present in exotic waters, while the sunrise is enhanced by the horses of Aurora, the goddess of the dawn.

As Ulysses and his companions sail due east to Greece, they keep the northern compass point on their port bow. It can be no coincidence that Turner has floated a pale violet tone in the northern sky, the same colour that, in 1826, his friend Mary Somerville showed had the power to magnetise a needle, to make it point to the north.[31]

# TWELVE

## "My jaundiced eye"

---

### 1829–1836

In the early 1830s, Turner became a regular visitor to Margate. Before the railways came and made Brighton the handiest resort for Londoners, Margate, less than eight hours away from the capital by steam packet, was the neatest, cleanest, brightest, most invigorating and entertaining seaside town of them all.

The number of visitors arriving annually by steamer had tripled between 1815 and 1827 to seventy-eight thousand. They were attracted by the entertainments. The architecture and the society of the town, and also by the claim that the sea water and air could cure all ills. Margate was an old haunt for Turner, he had been there as a boy, and had returned many times to draw the harbour and marine paraphernalia. He knew the inland landscape of the Isle of Thanet, and the best views out over the sea. He knew the elegant Georgian squares, terraces, the theatres, music and society. He knew the bathing machines in the bay, where men and women would bathe naked to cure all manner of ailments by slipping modestly into the sea under the cover of wide canvas awnings.

There were two new landing places for steamers in Margate when Turner began to visit the town regularly. One, the Pier (in fact a harbour wall) designed by John Rennie to receive the new steam packet service in 1815, is a stubby claw of stone curving out to the west, with the Droit House at the landward end and the lighthouse at the other. The second, opened in 1824 and in use until it blew down in 1978, was originally a fifty yard long wooden structure pointing more or less due north, straight out to sea. The Stone Pier created an area of still water and a harbour which dried up at low tide, but the second structure, Jarvis's Landing Place, allowed steamers to land and turn round with the least hindrance of the tides and rocks because it reached out into deep water. The new pier grew from the root of the old, and together, like a pair of waving rose shoots, they marked the town's prosperity and confidence.[1]

The place where the two piers met was the place of the greatest marine and human activity in Margate. Readers of *The Steamboat Companion* of 1830 were told of its

> most enlivening scene ... The spectators assembled to witness the departure of the steam packet at eight [a.m.]; the porters wheeling their high-piled loads of trunks, baskets and band-boxes ... the repeated "good byes, God bless you!" as the vessel moves from the Pier, and the waving of handkerchiefs, so long as the fair wavers are visible – in short the *tout-ensemble* is animating and delightful in the highest degree.[2]

Visitors were encouraged to walk about the streets and squares nearby. There was a fort on the rocky promontory above the piers, a brewery within a hundred yards, barracks nearby, inns, hotels, a Billiard Room, the Customs House and lodging houses in Bankside and Cold Harbour. It was precisely this activity and the strong seas visible from the high ground that attracted Turner to it, and which drew him to find accommodation there. He took a room in a lodging house in Cold Harbour run by Mrs John Booth, a room with a grandstand view looking out north-west over the piers, the people and the sea.

Mrs Booth's lodging house was to become a second home to Turner. There were three reasons why this should be. First, the position of the house was perfect for him; second, Mr and Mrs Booth were evidently very welcoming to the quiet gentleman who made no trouble, who paid the rent in advance, and who would come out of season when Mrs Booth might otherwise find difficulty in letting his room to anybody else; and third, Turner was very soon going to need a new mother.

William Turner the elder had for thirty years been Turner's father, mother and willing slave. He was also the strongest influence on Turner in keeping him well dressed, and away from declining into an elderly shabbiness. As a barber he had a professional interest in making his most important remaining client look the part of an Academician, and by being on hand to send more white waistcoats to Cowes, so he did. William Turner was always there when his son called, always on hand to help, although it is clear that even in his eighties the older man kept a life of his own when he could. "The old gentleman was very well, but was out of town," Clara Wheeler found when she called at Queen Anne Street to seek news of him to send to Turner in Rome.[3]

In the intervening months William Turner's health deteriorated, and on 21st September 1829 he died at Queen Anne Street aged eighty-five. It may have been as a result of his father's condition that Turner changed his plan to return to Rome in 1829, and went to northern France instead. During the last few months of his father's life, Turner directed his thoughts to his own mortality and prepared a will. This had reached vellum by the day his father was buried in the church where he had been married, and on the day after the funeral, 30th September, Turner signed the will, naming Francis Chantrey, William Wells and Charles Turner as executors. He had been thinking about his will for a very long time, considering how best to distribute his large fortune, and how he might permanently secure his reputation as the greatest landscape painter of all.

It is unlikely that the instructions he put forward in the 1829 will were his and his alone; it must have been a point of discussion between him and his artist friends in Rome. Indeed, sensible men there like Eastlake, and others at home like Lawrence, Chantrey and Jones, all men of charitable spirit, could advise him on practicalities if not on policy. A story told by C. R. Leslie shows that Chantrey for one was bullish about his forthcoming task as an executor. "I have appointed you one of my executors," Turner told him. "Will you promise to see me rolled up in *Dido Building Carthage*?" "Yes," said Chantrey at this preposterous idea, "and I promise you also that as soon as you are buried I will see you taken up and unrolled!"[4]

Apart from some small – very small – family bequests, the main thrust of the will was to create provision for the almshouses for artists on his land in Twickenham, and a gallery for his own paintings. For two paintings, however, he had a particular destination, despite his threat to be buried in one of them: *Dido Building Carthage* and *The Decline of the Carthaginian Empire* were to go to the National Gallery – then in Pall Mall – where they were to "be placed by the side of Claude's 'Seaport' and 'Mill', that is to hang on the same line same height from the ground and to continue in perpetuity to hang."

With such thoughts of death and commemoration expressed as tidily as he could Turner embarked into the 1830s. Death, however, trailed its coat before him as the old decade turned into the new, and he found himself following funerals. A fortnight after William Turner had been buried in St Paul's Church, Covent Garden, a fellow Academician, George Dawe RA, died. Then at the change of the year Harriet Wells, Clara's sister, died. "Poor Harriet, dear Harriet, gentle patient amiability," he wrote to Clara on 3rd January. "Earthly assurances of heaven's bliss possesst, must pour their comforts and mingle in your distress a balm peculiarly its own – not known, not felt, not merited by all."[5] And, unexpectedly, the President of the Academy, Sir Thomas Lawrence, also died and was buried on 21st January in full pomp at St Paul's Cathedral in the presence of the Prime Minister and hundreds of mourners. Turner was one of the pall-bearers.

These were a melancholy few weeks, deeply affecting for so emotional a man. He opened up his heart to George Jones, now in Rome, in a letter of late February:

> I delayed answering yours ... to give you some account ... of the last sad ceremonies paid yesterday to departed talent gone to that bourne from whence no traveller returns. Alas! only two short months Sir Thomas followed the coffin of Dawe to the same place. We were then his pall-bearers. Who will do the like for me, or when, God only knows how soon. My poor father's death proved a heavy blow upon me, and has been followed by others of the same dark kind.[6]

Although he may sometimes have felt otherwise, there was never a time when Turner was alone in the world. But although his artist friends gave him intellectual companionship and conversation, he also needed uncomplaining, perpetual, dog-like devotion. His father had been both mother and father to him for thirty years; and for the next twenty the motherly role would increasingly come to be filled by Mrs John Booth of Cold Harbour, Margate.

Turner also needed an institutional mother, and he had such a one in the Royal Academy. He loved, cherished and worked for the Academy, and was a personal adviser in artistic matters to students and Academicians alike. He had become the conscience of the Academy and the personification of its traditions, but he was never its President. He was in a position to stand for the post when Lawrence died, and having coincidentally resigned the chairmanship of the AGBI in 1829, had no conflicting interests. Why did he not put his name forward? Others were jockeying for position – Martin Archer Shee, the personable, watchful Irishman; Sir William Beechey, the old friend of the late King George III and Queen Charlotte, though at seventy-seven far too decrepit for the job; David Wilkie, shy, awkward and no public speaker; and Thomas Phillips and Augustus Wall Callcott. There is no way of telling if Turner did discuss the idea that he might stand: Chantrey would have given him advice, so might Phillips or Callcott. If quiet conversations had been held Turner would have been subtly reminded that he had never been comfortable in front of an audience, students had avoided his Perspective lectures in droves, and his dress sense since his father died was practically nil.

These would have been side issues, excuses. The central reason concerned *realpolitik*. George IV was very ill in February 1830. He could not live much longer and would be succeeded by his brother the Duke of Clarence. The Academy depended heavily on royal and aristocratic patronage, and on maintaining the esteem of the King, their landlord. If the Royal Academy and the Palace were to be at loggerheads, as they had been in the 1790s, the Academy would suffer heavily. It was already suffering from the taunts of Haydon who, in 1829, had observed "people of rank and fashion" trying hard to avoid the necessity of passing an opinion on *Ulysses Deriding Polyphemus*. He saw them give "keen looks at each other, compliments of escape when pressed to praise, delicate shrugs, and sliding into other subjects."[7]

At this time of impending change, the Academy needed as its President a man whose own painting was elegant but uncontroversial, and who was a natural courtier. Turner failed the test on both these counts. Many misunderstood his art, some even thought it mad; and he was no courtier. In the event Shee won by a handsome margin. There is perhaps a sense of relief in a letter to George Jones that Turner himself was out of it all: "I wish I had you by the button-hole ... I could then tell more freely what has occurred since your departure of combinations and concatentions somewhat of the old kind, and to my jaundiced eye not a whit more pure."[8]

Though never to be its President, Turner was becoming the undisputed Grand Old Man of the Academy. His great public moments in the galleries at Somerset House took place during the "Varnishing Days", the five days between hanging and the opening of the exhibition when members had the opportunity and privilege of putting finishing touches to their paintings in the light of their surroundings. Varnishing was not all they did; some paintings were worked up from practically nothing. There were Varnishing Days also before the winter exhibitions at the British Institution in Pall Mall, and it was there that one of the most graphic Varnishing Day stories of the 1830s took place. In 1837 Turner reworked *Regulus* at the British Institution, transforming a bright red and yellow painting into seering white. "He was absorbed in his work," John Gilbert recalled,

> did not look about him, but kept on scumbling a lot of white into his picture – nearly all over it ... He had a large palette, nothing in it but a huge lump of flake-white; he had two or three biggish hog tools to work with, and with these he was driving the white into all the hollows, and every part of the surface. This was the only work he did, and it was the finishing stroke.[9]

As Turner worked, he invariably gathered an audience of admiring colleagues for his Master Classes. S. W. Parrott evoked this to perfection in his small oil study of the diminutive top-hatted Turner, palette and an arsenal of brushes in hand, scumbling a painting while others look on in admiration. The painting glows, and round about is Turner's paraphernalia: his brolly, a spotted neckerchief, a bowl of varnish. There are other paintings and drawings of Turner busily at work on Varnishing Day, and many more stories, right, wrong, contradictory and embellished. In one, for example, a fellow artist recalled that he saw Turner spit all over a picture, and rub a brown powder, probably snuff, all over it. At the 1827 exhibition a black paper silhouette of a dog was found stuck onto the parapet in *Mortlake Terrace*. Some said that Edwin Landseer had done it as a joke while Turner was out at lunch; whatever the case, Turner seems to have taken a liking to the dog and incorporated it into the picture. That, however, is the story that persisted until the 1980s when it was pointed out that Turner did stick paper shapes onto his canvases from time to time, and, from Turner's unperturbed reaction, this may have been one such.[10]

During the five days, Turner was always on hand to give advice to colleagues, though this advice may have been gnomic, or silent, conveyed by gesture. Unlike his terminated series of lectures, this was a form of teaching which Turner could do without stress, and enjoy. He arrived at the Academy very early, "at 4 a.m., never later than 6," according to Thornbury, and was the last to leave: "He might be standing all day long before his pictures and, though he worked so long, he appeared to be doing little or nothing. His touches were almost imperceptible; yet his pictures were seen, in the end, to have advanced wonderfully."[11]

This is in contradiction to the *Regulus* story, but with Turner contradictions become the norm. When Frederick Lee exhibited a picture of a farmhouse on fire, a bevy of Academicians gathered round giving the young man advice. Landseer dabbed at it with his brush, and as Turner approached Lee said "Ah, here is Mr Turner, but he never has anything to say." "Put more fire in your house," said Turner and passed on.[12]

When somebody suggested that the practice of Varnishing Day might be abolished, Turner was pulled up short: "Then you will do away with the only social meeting we have, the only occasion on which we all come together in an easy unrestrained manner. When we have no varnishing days, we shall not know one another."[13]

In the 1830s Turner used the jewel-like colouring he had introduced in *Ulysses Deriding Polyphemus* in a new series of crowded figure compositions. The precedent that these have in Turner's art is with the series of low-life paintings made around 1807–10 and with the Watteauesque subjects of the 1820s. Like the low-life groups these too were prompted by Turner acting on the suggestions or challenges of others, and getting caught up in the excitement of a new-found genre. They all too clearly demonstrate Turner's continual eagerness, his childlike wish to try something new, to compete and to win. His Rembrandtesque *Shadrach, Meshach and Abednego in the Fiery Furnace* grew out of a challenge which Turner himself prompted with George Jones. "What are you painting for the exhibition?" he asked Jones. "The delivery of Shadrack, Meshach and Abednego from the fiery furnace," Jones replied. "A good subject! I will paint it also. What size do you propose?" And so they both went away and did it, same size, on identical mahogany panels, and both were shown at the 1832 Academy exhibition.[14] With this and other paintings such as *Pilate Washing his Hands* (exh. 1830), Turner took Rembrandtism to an extreme and so transformed it with glittering encrusted detail that one critic called him "a Rembrandt born in India".[15]

Turner could pick up his brushes and play anybody's tune – Rembrandt, Watteau, the Dutchmen Ruisdael, Van Goyen and Cuyp, Claude and Poussin, Canaletto – the list goes on. No other great master had demonstrated this chameleon tendency with such seriousness even to the slightest degree. Only Turner so regularly throughout his career plays tricks with such panache and consistency while remaining indisputably himself. Genius accepted, it also reveals an insatiable curiosity and desire to learn, to see through other eyes, to pay homage to his heroes, and to show with good humour that he is quite as good as they. Turner's innate arrogance, insufferable and threatening when he was in his twenties, became, by the time he was approaching sixty, part of his charm.

His sense of humour when playing these games was infectious. Jones saw the point and joined in, so did Stanfield and Etty. Who could propose titles such as *Van Goyen, looking out for a Subject* or *Bridge of Sighs, Ducal Palace and Custom House, Venice: Canaletti Painting* without also giving a boyish smile. "Canaletti" [sic] can only be a bit of fun. Both of these paintings were exhibited in 1833 during the span of a few years when Turner painted his most moving and affecting paintings in his *own* current manner – *Childe Harold's Pilgrimage – Italy* (1832); *Staffa, Fingal's Cave* (1832); the two versions of *The Burning of the Houses of Lords and Commons* and *Keelmen Heaving in Coals* (all 1835). As Shakespeare could use comedy for the dramatic effect of underscoring his tragedies, so Turner would share a joke with his audience even if few of them actually got it. *Canaletti Painting* was the source of some amusement between Turner and Jones during the Varnishing Days of 1833. The pair had a ding-dong battle with the tones of their two neighbouring pictures, *Canaletti Painting* and Jones's *Ghent*, which Jones won by adding an excess of white into his sky, thus making Turner's sky look too blue. "The ensuing day [Turner] saw what I had done, laughed heartily, slapped my back and said I might enjoy my victory." But when Turner priced *Canaletti Painting* – a relatively small picture – at 200 guineas, he told Jones: "Well, if they must have scraps instead of important pictures, they must pay for them."[16]

Turner progressed in his art as does an embroiderer or seamstress, pressing forward but also going backwards under a stitch to bring the thread round again to the head of the line. The year he exhibited *Staffa* he also showed *Van Tromp's Shallop* and *Helvoetsluys*, two subjects painted in the manner of his seventeenth-century Dutch hero Jan van Goyen. These, apart from evident differences in tone and paint handling, he might cheerfully have painted twenty or twenty-five years earlier.

The shift in Turner's attitudes that had focused itself in the 1828 and 1829 Academy exhibitions were followed inexorably in changes in the attitude that Turner's public had to him. His first patrons and advisers, and his first enemies, were now dead – Sir John Leicester, Beaumont, Fawkes, Farington, Payne Knight and "Mad Jack" Fuller, all dead by 1834. The affection and the venom that they had variously felt for Turner was now rotting away in scattered country churchyards. Only Egremont remained, the great exception that proved the rule. This generation of inheritors was gradually being replaced in Turner's life by self-made men, entrepreneurs and factory owners who had harnessed the scientific discoveries of the Industrial Revolution with commercial reins. Men who bought Turner's work in the 1830s, or who began to consider it, were the coach-builder W. B. Windus, the whaling entrepreneur Elhanan Bicknell, the Manchester cotton spinner Henry McConnel, the son of a Leeds clothier John Sheepshanks, and the brewer William Whitbread. Although still a boy, John Ruskin, whose father John James Ruskin was a wine and sherry importer, was already regaling his parents with Turner and his works.

Having none of the aristocratic background of some of the first generation of Turner patrons, these men neither carried the aesthetic blinkers nor the family baggage of their predecessors. When the maid or manservant opened their bedroom shutters in the mornings, they were more likely to look out towards the smoking haze of a London, Manchester or Leeds skyline than across rolling landscaped acres. They tended to take Turner's yellow at face value and not to yearn for the palette of Claude. The living link between the old and the new in Turner's life was Egremont. He did look out over rolling acres, but he had a modern outlook on agricultural improvement, trade and social patterns.

In these years also, Turner began to rely on the services of a dealer. Thomas Griffith of Norwood had come sideways into Turner's life by 1829, when he acquired at least a dozen of his *England and Wales* watercolours from the exhibition organised by Charles Heath in the Egyptian Hall, Piccadilly.[17] Griffith was an avid collector who sold on to others. He impressed artists greatly, turning up regularly at the City of London Artists' and Amateurs' Conversazione, becoming a "wholesale purchaser of the *best works* of modern art," showing the widest knowledge of the field, and behaving, at least to John Sell Cotman, "like a prince".[18] Artists responded to Griffith's support by presenting him in 1840 with an inscribed piece of plate in recognition of his services to them.[19]

Turner suffered Griffith's involvement in his life, but by the 1840s they were good friends. His reliance on Griffith came about for a number of reasons. First of all, he had no choice; his paintings were in the market and would be sold or exchanged like any other commodity whether he liked it or not. Turner also knew that he was getting older, and tacitly welcomed somebody being as interested as he in keeping the prices of his works buoyant. It was as much as he could do to control the sale of paintings from his studio. When he did get involved in the market he wasted his time, upset himself, and although he may not have realised it, sometimes got the worst of the deal.

Over the years contracts with engravers and others which he had entered into became complicated as various parties sold up or went bankrupt and Turner's rights fled off to a third or fourth party. He was strenuous, even pedantic, in trying to assert his rights, on one occasion in 1833 going as far as a formal hearing in the Mansion House, in front of the Lord Mayor of London, to prevent the Fleet Street bookseller and publisher Charles Tilt from making small-scale copies of engravings after his watercolours for *Provincial Antiquities of Scotland*. He paid for a series of newspaper advertisements announcing that Tilt's prints "had NOT been engraved from his Drawings or touched by Mr Turner".[20] Interest in the case was such that the hearing was reported in *The Times*, whose readers heard how the giant Turner was laughed at ignominiously in open court.[21]

Whereas earlier in the century Turner visited his patrons – Fawkes excepted – as the hired artist, now he came to their dinner tables as an intellectual heavyweight, another self-made man and an acknowledged equal. Mary Lloyd recalled that Turner "was seen to best advantage with the poet Samuel Rogers and his sister, also with Mrs Carrick Moore and her family and at Sir Charles Eastlake's."[22] Dining at Hanover Terrace with Samuel and Sarah Rogers he will have discussed the proposal that he, with other artists, illustrate the new edition of Rogers's *Italy* that the poet was contemplating. Another time at the Rogers's table Turner was a fellow guest with the mathematician Charles Babbage, who, on one occasion, took Turner's umbrella home with him by mistake, and was shocked to find the dagger in its handle.[23] William and Mary Somerville were also of Rogers's circle in the 1830s, as were the scientists Sir John Herschel and Michael Faraday, the poets Thomas Moore and Thomas Campbell, the surgeon James Carrick Moore, and the writer and wit Rev. Sydney Smith. These social circles naturally interlocked. The Somervilles lived at that time in Hanover Square, a few hundred yards from the home of the publisher John Murray at one end of Albemarle Street, and of the Royal Institution at the other. Murray entertained Charles Eastlake, the traveller and writer Elizabeth Rigby (Eastlake's future wife) and many others, including Turner. Faraday, the guiding spirit behind the Royal Institution, allowed Carrick Moore's daughter, Harriet, a friend and hostess to Turner, to paint a pair of detailed watercolours of him at work in his laboratory.

Thus science, art and literature were entwined in these few hundred square yards. There were other hosts – Lord and Lady Holland at Holland House, Kensington, and Thomas Pettigrew, the surgeon and antiquary of Savile Street, off Burlington Gardens:

> At Pettigrew's no need of dice or cards
> Or any acts that human kind debase.
> There men of science, artists, wits and bards
> In social union dignify the place.[24]

The geographical area was so small, and entertainment within the intellectual circle so generous and welcoming that we approach the conclusion from the many sightings of him that Turner was as much a part of it as anybody else, if sometimes more withdrawn than others. That he had installed new furniture in his rebuilt house and gallery at Queen Anne Street early in the 1820s suggests that he had the intention of giving parties at home to return hospitality, even if he may never fully have got round to it. But now with his father dead it is to be expected that he preferred to eat out as much as possible in company.

When Samuel Rogers brought some daguerreotypes back from Paris, probably in the late 1820s, he showed them to his artist friends:

> They considered the discovery would injure Turner particularly. When he came they said "Our profession is gone." On looking at [the daguerreotypes] he answered "We shall only go about the country with a box like a tinker, instead of a portfolio under our arm!"[25]

With his positive outlook on life and scientific progress, Turner reveals himself to be challenged rather than discouraged by photography. This extended itself to meatier discussions with Faraday, whom Turner also met on boating parties with the lithographer Charles Hullmandel. Then and later they discussed the chemical constituents of pigments, and talked about the effects of light in the sky.[26]

Thus, the benign Turner was well known in the salons, drawing-rooms and boating parties of intellectual London. But the tempestuous side to him, which he had deployed so effectively as a young man, could still flash out furiously when roused. He was a regular guest of General Edmund Phipps (1760–1837), a distinguished soldier who had been MP for Scarborough for nearly thirty years. Phipps had been a collector all his life, and although he owned no Turners, his house in Mount Street, Mayfair, was hung with Dutch old masters and paintings by Wilkie, C. R. Leslie, Landseer, Callcott and others. David Roberts wrote a vivid account of Phipps's gatherings:

I have often met Turner at dear old General Phipps ... It was a little cosy house, a Bachelor's house, a soldier's house. The Old General's little dinner parties were of the best always ... A young man felt honoured and happy in being included, for those you met, all who were great or connected with Art; here I have dined with Wilkie, Chantrey, Landseer, the President of the Academy and last not least Seguier the Keeper, director and instructor of all who loved or took an interest in art ... It was at one of these parties an extraordinary scene took place, at least to me it was. Constable, Turner & Munro of Novar were of the party, Constable a conceited egotistical person, whatever Leslie may have written to the contrary, was loud in describing to all the severe duties he had undergone in the hanging of the [1831 Academy] exhibition. According to his own account nothing could exceed his disinterestedness or his anxiety to discharge that Sacred Duty. Most unfortunately for him a picture of Turner's had been displaced after the arrangement of the room in which it was placed ... Turner opened on him like a ferret; it was evident to all present Turner detested him; all present were puzzled what to do or say to stop this, Constable wriggled, twisted & made it appear or wished to make it appear that in his removal of the picture [Caligula's Palace and Bridge] he was only studying the best light or arrangement for Turner. The latter coming back invariably to the charge, yes, but why put your own there? I must say that Constable looked to me and I believe to every one else, like a detected criminal, and I must add Turner slew him without remorse. But as he had brought it upon himself few if any pitied him.[27]

Turner got his revenge the following year when, on Varnishing Day, he painted a red buoy on the grey sea of his *Helvoetsluys* which hung beside Constable's *Waterloo Bridge*. "Turner has been here and fired a gun," Constable observed wryly.

Turner travelled extensively each summer from 1829 to 1836. In August 1829 he went to Paris, and then down the Seine to its mouth at Honfleur, along the Normandy coast and into Brittany to collect material for a series of *Rivers of Europe* engravings, and for a projected set of engravings (which came to nothing) on the Channel ports. His tours were gradually becoming a national institution, on which he could be followed vicariously by readers in the short series of books entitled *Turner's Annual Tour*, first published in 1833, illustrated with engravings of his watercolours. In the summer of 1830 he avoided France, whose capital was in turmoil during the revolution that brought Louis-Philippe to the throne. Instead, he stayed in England, travelling to the Midlands to collect more imagery for *England and Wales*.

The most affecting studies in the sketchbooks in use on this trip are pencil drawings of Coventry, Birmingham and Dudley, three towns which he observes from a distance, from their rutted, wet and ramshackle edges. They are tiny drawings, but panoramic and painfully redolent of the muck and squalor of the new industrial landscapes. The watercolours that ultimately he made have none of the tragic quality of the sketches, but in *Dudley, Worcestershire* he considers the nature of the social and economic change, driven by industry, overcoming the old religious and feudal foundations represented by the church and ruined castle and priory on the hill.

Despite the fact that he always had very soon to move on, the sketch-books he made on the 1830 Midlands tour show his single-mindedness in selecting a viewpoint for the image that, through widely circulated engravings, would *ipso facto* stand as a representative for that place for years to come. Take Warwick for example. The ordering of the pages in the "Kenilworth" Sketchbook[28] suggests that Turner approached Warwick from Kenilworth, where he had drawn the Castle from many angles, and travelled along the cart road through Hill Wootton, now off the B4115. From here there is a magnificent view of the tall pinnacled tower of St Mary's Church rising above the floodplain of the River Avon, and this may be the subject of two watercolour studies, and of a mezzotint in the series "The Little Liber", which Turner himself engraved.[29]

Having arrived in Warwick, Turner went straight for what he wanted to see. He sketched Warwick Castle from the Avon Bridge, and then, walking past the gothic church straddling the town's entrance at Eastgate which he did not draw, he went to Warwick Priory where he drew the panoramic view of the Castle and St Mary's tower. Then he walked back to the Avon Bridge, looked again at St Mary's and St Nicholas's Churches, and finally turned east, walking along the river until he could catch the view of the Castle and St Mary's from the meadow, now St Nicholas's Park. In this walk, which anyone can do today by using the town's public parks, Turner saw the most dramatic views, but missed equally characteristic sights such as the High Street, Eastgate, Westgate or Northgate. This suggests that having already seen Warwick in 1794 he knew exactly what he wanted this time for *England and Wales*, and was not going to waste time looking for other subjects. The view of Warwick he eventually worked up in water-colour was of the Castle from the bridge, the same subject that he had made following the 1794 visit. The one difference is that then he drew from the bank, looking through and up at the bridge, and this time he was standing on the bridge itself thirty feet above the river. In 1794 the bridge was being completed; in 1830, though long built, Turner put a flashback reference in the watercolour, by showing men at work building the parapet.

Turner's summer tour of 1831 was an extended tour of Scotland, which took him further north than he had ever been. He was invited by the publisher Robert Cadell and Sir Walter Scott to make illustrations for a new edition of Scott's *Poetical Works*, to come to Abbotsford and to visit with his hosts as many of the places that Scott had made famous by his poems: "Every valley has its battle, and every stream its song."[30] One of Scott's subjects was Fingal's Cave, and writing from London Turner expressed his determination to see the sight: "I shall not like to turn back without Staffa Mull and all. A steam boat is now established to the Western Isles so I have heard lately ..."[31] Scott was in very poor health, and only had a year to live, but with the help of Cadell and his servant he travelled around Abbotsford showing Turner the best views and discussing their significance with him. Turner listened closely to Scott talking about the history of each place they visited and reciting ballads and poetry. According to Cadell's accounts of the expeditions, the party's working days were of an extraordinary length. Sunday 7th August seems to have been typical: breakfast at Abbotsford at nine; departure to Newark Castle at 10.20, with stops for sketches at Philiphaugh and Selkirk on the way; arrival at Bowhill just before midday, then by foot along Yarrow Water to Newark Castle; back by gig to Abbotsford eating a picnic lunch on the way because they had no time to stop; arrive at Abbotsford just after half past three, a quick change and off to Chiefswood on the Abbotsford estate, where they were expected for dinner with the Lockharts. When they arrived, Turner suggested he go down to sketch in the Rhymer's Glen, but this was overruled "on account of Mrs Lockhart's roast beef". After much wine and roast beef, Turner slipped off to the Rhymer's Glen, but was spotted and followed by Scott's daughters. Turner and the daughters disappeared for too long, and caused anxiety in the party, but when they finally came back, Turner was drunk, tired and wet having slipped on the rocks in the river. They drove home and arrived at Abbotsford after ten. Turner "berated Cadell for having left him in the Glen in the company of the women", and staggered off to bed. Even his great stamina had been exhausted.[32]

There were five days of this kind of intense social and artistic activity at Abbotsford. Turner never let up, and went on with Cadell to Jedburgh, Kelso, Berwick and Norham, where he doffed his cap at the Castle. "What the devil are you about now?" Cadell asked him. "Oh, I made a drawing or painting of Norham several years since. It took; and from that day to this I have had as much to do as my hands could execute."[33] Then up to Edinburgh – more sketches and watercolours – and dinner with Robert Scott Lauder and John Thompson of Duddingston.

From Edinburgh, Turner travelled north to Oban and on to Tobermory on the Isle of Mull where he caught the steamer, the *Maid of Morven*, which took him around the island to Fingal's Cave. He himself recalled the excitement of the journey in bad weather:

... a strong wind and head sea prevented us making Staffa until too late to go on to Iona. After scrambling over the rocks on the lee side of the island, some got into Fingal's Cave, others would not. It is not very pleasant or safe when the wave rolls right in. One hour was given to meet on the rock we landed on. When on board, the Captain declared it doubtful about Iona. Such a rainy and bad-looking night coming on, a vote was proposed to the passengers: "Iona at all hazards or back to Tobermory." Majority against proceeding. To allay the displeased, the Captain promised to steam thrice round the island on the last trip. The sun getting towards the horizon, burst through the rain-cloud, angry, and for wind; and so it proved, for we were driven for shelter into Loch Ulver, and did not get back to Tobermory before midnight.[34]

Turner was one of the brave souls that leapt off the steam ship's pilot boat and spent a cold, wet hour in the cave. His drawings there are vigorous, but the greatest product of the voyage, indeed of the 1831 Scottish trip as a whole, is *Staffa, Fingal's Cave*, painted in Queen Anne Street over the autumn and winter months. It has become a classic image of man achieving a tenuous control of the forces of nature, his grip on the future symbolised not only by the tiny steam ship, but also by the exuberant arc of smoke that leaves the funnel as a black smear, but becomes white and purified as it rises up to join the clouds.

As Turner was painting *Staffa*, Britain was on the edge of revolution. At the end of October, a few weeks after he had come back to London, the House of Lords blocked the passage of the Reform Bill for the second time. Bristol became a flash point, though it might have been any one of England's cities, and riots broke out. For two days Bristol was in the hands of the mob. Prisons, the Customs House, the Bishop's Palace and other symbols of government authority were destroyed in this bloody demonstration of fury against the repeated refusal of the Lords to assent to the will of the Commons, and do away with "rotten" and "pocket" boroughs.

The issue was not settled until the third reading of the Bill in May 1832, by which time Turner had conceived, developed and exhibited his three feet by four painting *The Prince of Orange, William III, Embarked from Holland, Landed at Torbay, November 4th 1688, after a Stormy Passage*. The title was followed in the Academy catalogue with a brief reminder about a "History of England" that Turner had read recently. This painting, and *Staffa* and some others, was being planned and painted as meetings and demonstrations, plainly audible if not visible from Turner's studio, were being held all over London. Given his own history of commenting on current affairs through allusion and historical parallel in oil and water-colour, this work is remarkably prescient and optimistic. In the spring of 1832, the struggle that Walter Fawkes had given his life and fortune to was on the verge of success or failure. Using the historical parallel of the Glorious (and bloodless) Revolution which brought William and Mary to the throne of Britain in 1688, Turner demonstrated that the will of the people had had its way before, and speculated that, despite a "Stormy Passage", it might do so once again.

At the same time, as a devilish sub-plot to the agitation for reform, Britain had a greater enemy, cholera. Of the twin threats to the British system, cholera was the less understood and thus the more dangerous and frightening. It insinuated itself everywhere, creating fear at all levels of society, and, uniquely, it connected rich to poor. Victims were thrown out of hospitals, families fought in graveyards, and a beautiful woman, preparing for a ball, might be taken ill, miss the party and be a blue-faced corpse by the time the ball was over. Charles Fulke Greville wrote at length about the effects of the disease:

> Some servants of people well known have died, and that frightens all other servants out of their wits, and they frighten their masters ... As long as they read daily returns of a parcel of deaths here and there ... they do not mind, but when they hear that Lady such a one's nurse or Sir somebody's footman is dead, they fancy they see the disease actually at their own door.[35]

Turner caught the national anxieties about the disease, which had spread from the north of England and Scotland in 1831. Writing to Cadell to tell him about his progress with his Scott illustrations, he asked for medical advice:

> In regard to the Cholera I will thank you to send me the paper which your medical-men printed as to the treatment &c. or if any thing has been discovered during the progress of the disease in Scotland and [in] your opinion is shown (contagious or Epidemic) from known cases. Here the dispute runs high and no treatment made known or Cholera Hospitals Established.[36]

In one of the sketchbooks he had just used in Scotland Turner made a note, as hundreds of other people were also doing, of a remedy for the disease: "25 drops of Cajeput oil in a glass of Hot Water, if not relieved in 5 min take 50 more. Sir M. Turpey [?] remedy for the Cholera."[37]

In these frightening few months, Turner absorbed himself in his work. There was no set quota of paintings to be met for the Royal Academy; he could send as many or as few as he wanted. That he produced six oils for the exhibition, one of them, *Childe Harold's Pilgrimage – Italy*, an eight-footer, when he was also under great pressure to meet Cadell's deadline, suggests that he spent more time than usual this winter and spring indoors, out of the way of the disease. In his letter to Cadell of 25th February he reveals that he is finishing twelve watercolours and vignettes for Scott, but "I fear I cannot hold out the prospect of doing the remaining six *Books* until my Pictures for the Exhibition are sent in to Somerset House (April 10th) tho I hope you will not call me very idle since January."[38]

There are some curious consistencies in the paintings Turner made over this difficult winter. Three are historicising subjects looking back at seventeenth-century Holland – *The Prince of Orange, Van Tromp's Shallop* and *Helvoetsluys* – each one painted in homage to the golden age of Dutch painting, the school that had inspired Turner from his youth. A. G. H. Bachrach has suggested that Turner painted one Dutch subject after another in 1832 to remind his compatriots "of a time when they had markedly benefitted from a Dutch initiative".[39] This may be so; but there is more. Turner was perfectly aware that he might easily have died of the cholera at any time in the first few months of 1832. To leave behind him three fine paintings in the Dutch manner would be to go out as he came in.

Another group of three paintings, one of which was certainly painted over this winter, is about the expulsion of intangible evil. In *Shadrach, Meshach and Abednego* (exh. 1832) the power of an enormous statue is overcome in the face of the worship of God; expulsion of an equally vivid kind is expressed in *Christ Driving the Traders from the Temple*. The third painting, almost certainly also made during this period is Turner's most enigmatic canvas, one which he never exhibited or titled, and which is unlike anything else he had ever done in oil. It is an image of a decomposing body slumped over the back of a ghostly horse, which has quite reasonably come to be known as *Death on a Pale Horse*. The image is loosely painted, with paint thinned with turpentine, and thinned yet further in the areas of the horse's head and parts of the corpse. Made at great speed, and evidently not touched again once the first brushing of paint had dried, it is a passionate reaction to the overwhelming power of death. It has been suggested that it was painted in the aftermath of the death of Turner's father in 1829,[40] but Turner's reactions to events were rarely direct, and characteristically allusive and teasing. Knowing his fears about cholera it may be that this painting is his response to the curse of the disease that swept Britain in 1831 and 1832. The coronet on the head of the corpse – if that is a correct reading – may indicate the point that cholera was no respecter of rank.

These three paintings, and *Pilate Washing his Hands* of 1830 suggest that Turner may have been expressing the inklings of religious feeling. He painted these subjects because he chose to do so, not because he was commissioned (*pace* the George Jones anecdote). The deaths of friends had made him touch, in surviving correspondence, on personal, quasi-religious matters, though he naturally shied away from explaining himself further. With the words "earthly assurance of heaven's bliss possest" he had comforted Clara over the death of her sister. This was not an entirely new area of thought for him – in 1811 Turner wrote of "... that kind Providence that guides our step ... whether innate or the gift of Heaven." We know that he accompanied the Trimmers to church when he stayed with them, and, through watercolour studies, that he did the same on Sundays at Petworth. There are many early drawings of church services, for example in the "Wilson" sketchbook of 1796/97.[41]

One short but intense personal friendship that Turner experienced in the mid-1830s may have had the effect of focusing his apparently latent religious instincts. He met the clergyman and artist the Rev. Edward Daniell when Daniell became preacher at St Mark's Chapel, North Audley Street, Mayfair. Edward Daniell (1804–43) had been brought up in Norfolk, the son of Sir Thomas Daniell Bt, an owner of sugar plantations and a one-time Attorney General of Dominica. As a young man he had been torn between becoming an artist and entering the professions. He was taught etching by Joseph Stannard and became an accomplished watercolour painter, and a collector. He knew Elizabeth Rigby, met John Linnell, and after leaving Oxford in 1829 travelled for eighteen months drawing and painting on the Continent. He visited Rome and Naples in 1830 where he met Thomas Uwins, who wrote:

> What a shoal of amateur artists we have got here! ... there is a Daniel too come to Judgement! a second Daniel! Verily – I have gotten more substantial criticism from this young man than anyone since Havell was my messmate ... If gentlemen all take to painting for themselves what is to become of us poor professional brushmen?[42]

When Daniell returned to England, he determined to settle to a profession, took orders and was ordained in 1832. Three years later he moved to London from Norwich to become preacher at St Mark's Chapel.

His natural milieu was with artists, and in his parish he found the circle of artists of whom Turner was the doyen. He took a house in Green Street, Grosvenor Square, where he held dinner parties and other gatherings for his artist friends. In his diaries Linnell lists Roberts, Mulready, Dyce, Phillip, Stanfield, Eastlake, Landseer and most particularly Turner as regular guests. New though he was to London artistic society, Daniell's sensibility, charm, connections and private fortune drew him immediately into the heart of the art life of London, and it to him.[43]

Evidently Turner and Daniell took to each other fast. Roberts recalled that he often met Turner at

the delightful little parties given by the Revd. E. Daniell [who] was ... an intense lover of Turner. Turner was equally a lover of Daniell; indeed I have every reason to know that, had he not been cut off prematurely from the friendship that existed, Daniell would have prevented all that confusion which unhappily terminated Turner's career. Turner told me more than once he would never again form such a friendship as with my friend ... He adored Turner, when I and others doubted, and taught me to see & to distinguish his beauties over that of others. He was to Turner what Ruskin may have become afterwards, only that the old man had really a fond & personal regard for this young clergyman, which I doubt he ever evinced for the other.[44]

Daniell told Roberts: "Extensive as my acquaintance is amongst artists, I never remember any of them ever coming to hear me hold forth, but Turner did, ... and I never felt more proud than when the great painter passed up the aisle with his old umbrella to take his seat."[45] There is only one remark about Daniell attributed to Turner. Asked his opinion of Daniell's work, Turner said: "Very clever, sir, very clever."[46] No traces of Daniell's sermons survive, but to have attracted Turner they would have to be intelligent, expressed in sparkling language, replete throughout with vivid religious imagery and laced with classical allusion. From his background and education as a Classics scholar at Balliol there is little doubt that Daniell would have been able to supply this, and also to be able to give the spiritual comfort that Turner required to help him fill the holes left by the deaths of his father and friends, and to ease the fears of a naturally reflective man approaching old age.

After Sophia Booth's husband died in 1833, Turner's regular visits to Margate increased. The unhealthy atmosphere in London in the mid-1830s drove him out of the city in the spring and summer, and directed him both to the Kent coast, and to the Channel Islands and the Continent. His health was intermittently poor; there is a strong recipe which includes laudanum in the "Guernsey" sketchbook of around 1830, labelled "within an hour after the attack". This is repeated in a similar recipe in another sketchbook of around 1837–38, indicating that whatever Turner was suffering from was chronic and recurrent.[47]

In the summers of 1832 and 1833 Turner crossed the Channel. While he was collecting material in Paris in 1832 for illustrations to Scott's *Life of*

*Napoleon*, he met Delacroix, and made only a "mediocre impression", as the Frenchman recorded more than twenty years later. "He had the look of an English farmer, black clothes, gross enough, big shoes and hard cold demeanour." Delacroix did, however, assert that Turner and Constable were "real reformers. They have come out of the rut of the old land-scapists."[48]

Turner's main task on this northern French journey was to travel along the River Seine and to the Normandy ports to make studies for a *Rivers of France* series to be engraved in partnership with Charles Heath. As he had at East Cowes and Petworth in 1827 he took with him sheets of blue sugar paper which he tore up into small rectangles about 5 by 7 inches. On these he painted in pen and ink and gouache a series of vivacious town and riverscapes, with all his perspicacious observations of the activities and people that he happened upon. These *Rivers of France* views are not so highly wrought or composed as were the English subjects that Turner made for engraving, nor are they as interwoven with historical or folkloric allusion: a reason for this is that Turner had not been steeped in French history for a lifetime. Instead they are documentary reportage, made for the new publishing market that Heath had entered, the market of travel books, the "Annuals" and collections of prose and poetry for the general reader.

In 1833 he made a longer journey into Europe, to Austria and through the Brenner Pass to Verona and Venice. He had been elected a member of the committee established to consider the rehousing of the National Gallery and the Royal Academy in a shared new building under construction in Trafalgar Square, and on this and a later journey Turner acquainted himself with the collections of picture galleries *en route* and with their approaches to hanging and lighting.[49]

On this second visit to Venice Turner sought out effects of night and darkness, in complete contrast to the sparkling light that entranced him when he first saw the city in 1819. He shows, in watercolours made on brown paper, a brooding city, lit by sudden flares from rockets or pools of light coming from doorways or windows. There are dramatic watercolours of the cavernous interiors of theatres, dark narrow alleys, and shadowy figures. Having no streets, only waterways, the physique of Venice was at odds with the physique of every other city Turner knew. It was a world turned upside down. Further, Venice was a city whose power as the hinge of the trading routes between east and west had been finally destroyed by Napoleon. The many night scenes that Turner painted on this visit make it patently clear that in Venice he turned his own world upside down, reversing his general practice of rising early to catch the sunrise, and instead stayed up late to experience the dark, and the very evident nocturnal pleasures.

Two anonymous tributes to Turner were published in 1833, indicating the buoyancy of the esteem with which he was widely held. The *Literary Gazette* published a long poem, dedicated to "J. M. W. Turner RA &c &c." It is a light, jingling piece, signed J. A. B., surveying with great admiration and many adjectives the wide range of Turner's achievement. The second tribute has great insight, and as a piece of thoughtful art criticism stands in progression between James Skene's article in the *Edinburgh Encyclopaedia* and the mature writing of John Ruskin:

> To scorn tamely following in the beaten tracks of others is a restless curiosity, but endeavour to discover new combination of objects or refined ideas, are powerful characteristics of a great genius, whatever may be his pursuit. Thus the most eminent painters have always been the greatest experimentalists; ... Turner, after having well grounded his talent, emerged as a meteor in colouring.[50]

\* \* \*

As a painter in oils, Turner now pleased himself. He worked to commission only rarely, and sold what he chose to paint from the Academy walls or from his studio. As a watercolourist, however, the pattern was different. He was in great demand from publishers and public as a creator of images of distant landscapes to be engraved for the enjoyment of a new breed of traveller. These were men and women with business or pleasure on their minds who wanted images to dream over in their armchairs, or to take with them on their journeys, or as souvenirs on their return. The market for landscape imagery had evolved from the restricted subscription issues of *A Shipwreck* or the *Liber* editions, into mass production. His clients included the publishers of periodicals with names such as *The Bijou*, *The Keepsake* and *The Amulet*. These, and *Turner's Annual Tours* carried his work into drawing-rooms and parlours in London and out across the English counties. The same market forces drove publishers to engage Turner as their lead artist, more often their sole artist, to follow the success of Rogers's *Italy* with a new edition of his *Poems* (1832), and the works of Byron (1832–43), Sir Walter Scott (1834–41) Thomas Campbell (1837) and Thomas Moore (1839).

The vignettes that Turner painted to illustrate these authors brought his manner down to as small a scale of imagery as any man could reasonably hope to achieve and still retain effective eyesight. Turner's touch in these little masterpieces is breathtaking, in pictorial detail, physical form and narrative atmosphere.[51] But springing back up from the vignettes he painted also over these same years in a broader manner, laying sweeps of watery colour over wetted sheets of paper, as preparatory bases for watercolour views. Finberg came to call those which remained unfinished "Colour Beginnings". Turner's practice was to work on a number of sheets at a time. He would have around him three or four painting boards with paper on one side and a handle on the other, and these he would douse one by one into a bucket of water and paint upon at speed while they were still wet:

> ... making *marblings* and gradations throughout the work. His completing process was remarkably rapid, for he indicated his masses and incidents, took out half-lights and dragged, hatched and stippled until the design was finished. This swiftness ... enabled Turner to preserve the purity and luminosity of his work, and to paint at a prodigiously rapid rate.[52]

By this manner Turner could create extraordinary effects. When he told Ruskin "I never lose an accident,"[53] he meant, as Ruskin deduced, that he used chance to "help, and sometimes provoke, a success". And when in the same context Turner advised one of Fawkes's friends or relations to dip an indifferent watercolour into a jug of water, he was not being unkindly dismissive, but giving the best advice he knew.[54]

Through a combination of accident and incompetence, a fire broke out in the cellars of the House of Commons early in the evening of 16th October 1834. It spread rapidly, got quickly out of hand and within hours had reduced most of the Palace of Westminster to rubble and ashes. Huge crowds gathered to watch the spectacle which lasted long into the night and illuminated the London skyline for miles around. Turner was among the crowds, and while the Palace was blazing made notes both from the bank and from a boat. He spent the whole night near Westminster, first on the Surrey bank, and, as the blaze died down at dawn, he went into Old Palace Yard to watch the feeble attempts to tackle it. In the crush of people it is unlikely that he would have been able to do anything more than make the barest pencil notes and commit the scene to vivid memory. His vivid watercolour studies of the destruction were painted very soon after he had returned home to the quiet of his Queen Anne Street studio. As he painted, his neighbours woke up to the fact that both Houses of Parliament had been destroyed, and what had been the seat of Britain's political power would have to be rebuilt from the foundations.

Turner did not rush immediately to begin making an oil painting of the fire. Over the autumn and winter of 1834–35 he was probably working on a companion painting for Henry McConnel, who in 1834 had commissioned Turner's *Venice*. The companion picture was, by contrast, of a thriving but unspecified northern English port, one of the departure points of British exports. *Keelmen Heaving in Coals by Night*, a reprise of his *Rivers of England* subject *Shields, on the River Tyne*, stands for industrial ascendency through hard anonymous labour, while Turner's *Venice* showed an exotic city in self-indulgent decline.

These few weeks gave Turner an extended opportunity to consider the burning of the Houses of Parliament, what it might mean, and how he might handle this gift of an image. In a previous winter, through rising national panic and his own lonely hard labour, he had had ample time to consider the symbolism of cholera. When a painter is alone in the quiet of the studio, face to face with a canvas for hours on end, he has plenty of time to think if he is of a mind to do so; plenty of time for ratiocination. More than the work of any other artist of his period, Turner's paintings had considered meaning, a profound language of signs which reached way beyond literal representations.[55]

When he did feel ready to commit the subject of the destruction of the Houses of Parliament to canvas, Turner took an extraordinary decision. He roughed out the merest beginnings of a composition on canvas, had it framed and delivered in early January to the British Institution in Pall Mall. He had remained aloof from the British Institution since he had exhibited *Apullia* with intentional insolence in 1814. Twenty-one years later his feelings had ripened. The Institution remained the creature of the aristocracy; its Directors represented the same body of peers and bishops who had delayed the passage of the Reform Bill for so long, and who until 1834 had kept their grip on the "rotten" and "pocket" boroughs. That Turner should choose to return to the British Institution with *The Burning of the Houses of Lords and Commons* was his way of sending the stark message to the heart of the British establishment that the old order was finished.

On one of the Varnishing Days at the British Institution, Turner got up very early and was at Pall Mall in front of his roughed out canvas at dawn. This is how the painter E. V. Rippingille described Turner's day:

Etty was working by his side and every now and then a word and a quiet laugh emanated and passed between the two great painters. Little Etty stepped back every now and then to look at the effect of his picture, lolling his head on one side and half closing his eyes, and sometimes speaking to some one near him, after the approved manner of painters: but not so Turner; for the three hours I was there – and I understood it had been the same since he began in the morning – he never ceased to work, or even once looked or turned from the wall on which his picture hung. All lookers-on were amused by the figure Turner exhibited in himself, and the process he was pursuing with his picture. A small box of colours, a very few small brushes, and a vial or two, were at his feet, very inconveniently placed; but his short figure, stooping, enabled him to reach what he wanted very readily ... In one part of the mysterious proceedings Turner, who worked almost entirely with his palette knife, was observed to be rolling and spreading a lump of half transparent stuff over his picture, the size of a finger in length and thickness. As Callcott was looking on I ventured to say to him, "What is that he is plastering his picture with?" to which inquiry it was replied, "I should be sorry to be the man to ask him." ... Presently the work was finished: Turner gathered his tools together, put them into and shut the box, and then, with his face still turned to the wall, and at the same distance from it, went sidling off, without speaking a word to anybody, and when he came to the staircase in the centre of the room, hurried down as fast as he could. All looked with a half-wondering smile, and Maclise, who stood near, remarked, "There, that's masterly, he does not stop to look at his work; he *knows* it is done and he is off."[56]

Before an audience of his peers, Turner created with his brushes and fingers a picture of a dreadful fire. In a mysterious, priest-like, silent ceremonial he conjured from nowhere a picture of nemesis. This was the most direct, least coded message that Turner had yet painted. Yet nonetheless there was metaphor wrapped within the clear-eyed image of a real event: it is "Gentlemen, this is what did happen; but it is also what *might* have happened." Walter Fawkes had used the same fiery metaphor when he addressed the radical meeting in the Crown and Anchor in May 1812. Quoting Edmund Burke, he said:

> Early Reformations are made when the blood is in a cool state – late Reformations are made in a state of inflammation. – In this state, the People see nothing respectable in Government – they see its abuses, but they see nothing else – they fall into the temper of a populace, indignant at the conduct of a house of ill fame – they never think of correcting, they go to work the shortest way – they abate the nuisance, but they pull down the house.[57]

And then, for good measure, Turner painted the subject a second time to show at the Royal Academy in the spring.

# THIRTEEN

# Gathering Mortality

## 1836–1842

At some time during the late summer of 1836, the Rev. John Eagles (1783–1855), the fifty-three-year-old Curate of the parish of Winford near Bristol, took up his pen to write a long critical essay. Eagles was a regular contributor to *Blackwood's Edinburgh Magazine*, a staunchly Tory monthly, for which he reviewed exhibitions in London and gave his opinion on the way of the art world. Although they had no by-line, Eagles's words were warmly awaited by his readers. One obituarist wrote later of the "singular sweetness and tone of composition" of his *Blackwood's* articles. Eagles had been contributing to the papers for more than thirty years, first to *Felix Farley's Bristol Journal* and since 1831 to *Blackwood's*. As an amateur artist, with strong views on colour, composition and subject matter, he also gave advice in *Blackwood's* under a pseudonym "The Sketcher". Under another pseudonym, "Themaninthe-moon", he wrote in *Felix Farley*, condemning in 1830 the proposal to build a suspension bridge over the Avon at Clifton "to invade the territories of King Oberon, and drive the merry monarch and his court from glade and glen."[1]

Eagles had great faith in fairies. He would whistle them up while riding through Leigh Woods, across the river from Clifton, and would swear he had seen, deep in the woods, an amphitheatre

> when the fairies held jubilee there, when the moon was but a lamp suspended over it, dimmed by the radiance that emanated from those illumined beings, and the stars in the heavens were but as spectators receding tier behind tier.[2]

He also had considerable sympathy for Polyphemus, the oversize but amiable shepherd of Mount Etna, and imagined his brothers lurking among the "many cavernous places" of Leigh Woods,

> for that vagabond Ulysses destroyed not the whole brotherhood when, as the old song says, he ungratefully treated his monster host in return for his kind promise of making him his last mouthful:
> "He ate his mutton, drank his wine,
> And then he poked his eye out."[3]

The lines Eagles quotes are from a song by Tom Dibdin, in the pantomime *Melodrame Mad! or, The Siege of Troy* which had been on many people's lips in London since it was first performed in 1819. Turner also knew it well, and, ribbing a friend over dinner, once swore that Dibdin's song rather than Homer had been the true source of his *Ulysses*.[4]

The over-imaginative and prolix Eagles looked in great depth in his unsigned article for the October 1836 issue of *Blackwood's* at three exhibitions in London, comparing and contrasting what he found. He had cumbersome prejudices to cope with:

> The nobler [old masters at the British Institution] create for themselves an enthusiasm, a passion ... But is it not extraordinary that our [modern] artists [at Somerset House] are the last to receive such an impression? It must be a very striking fact to the eyes of the most careless observer, that the aim of modern art is in direct opposition to the old. *Toto caelo* they differ ... The old masters delighted in shade and depth, and above all in an unpretending modesty, without which there is no dignity – modern artists delight in glare and glitter, foil and tinsel, in staring bare-faced defiance of shade and repose, as if quietness were a crime, and as if there were no greatness but in protrusion.

Eagles's prejudices were too much for him, because he soon became violent, using terms which Sir George Beaumont would have applauded:

> Our enmity to this false English School of Art shall never cease; we have taken out "Letters of marque" to "sink, burn and destroy" – and we will wage perpetual warfare with extravagant absurdities, though they be sanctioned with the whim of genius, academical authority of the present encouragement of foolish admirers.[5]

Eagles found enemy to engage not only at Somerset House, but also at the Society of Painters in Watercolour at their Suffolk Street exhibition rooms. There he discovered more work by the "white painters" whom Beaumont had castigated twenty years earlier. With his aversion to high, light colouring, Eagles rapped James Baker Pyne, whose *Richmond, Yorkshire* was

> from the white school . . . If nature always wore this aspect we should seldom stir out, and be tempted even within doors to shut the window shutters to keep out the daylight. Mr Pyne is a very clever man, and we are sorry to find him "following the leader" in this faulty course.

Eagles and his conservative readership objected also to the rough handling of paint, the manner that he saw at Somerset House in Constable's *Cenotaph to the Memory of Sir Joshua Reynolds . . . in the Grounds of Coleorton Hall.* These attitudes, clearly set out by an intelligent but critically blinded man, are the essence of the antagonisms faced by Turner in the 1830s. When Eagles regretted that Pyne was "following the leader", that leader was unquestionably Turner, whom he sniped at as one of the unnamed artists "who must be at the Rhone or Rhine for views, fortunate if they can outface the sun flaring in the middle of the picture."

Eagles was well into his stride – the ninth printed page of his article – when he began to write about Turner's *Juliet and her Nurse.* One young man, sitting quietly in a drawing-room in Herne Hill, reacted with fury when he came to these words:

> This is indeed a strange jumble – "confusion worse confounded". It is neither sunlight, moonlight, nor starlight, nor firelight . . . Amidst so many absurdities we scarcely stop to ask why Juliet and her nurse should be at Venice. For the scene is a composition as far from models of different parts of Venice, thrown higgledy-piggledy together, streaked blue and pink, and thrown into a flour tub. Poor Juliet has been steeped in treacle to make her look sweet, and we feel apprehensive lest the mealy architecture should stick to her petticoat, and flour it.[6]

John Ruskin had also seen *Juliet and her Nurse* at the Royal Academy exhibition. He was seventeen years old, and had within him the enthusiasm of a schoolboy and the serious determination of a scholar. His father's business took him on travels throughout Britain; and young John Ruskin had travelled widely with his parents, developing an early understanding of landscape form and structure, and an embryonic knowledge of the social and physical structure of England. Like others of his age and generation, he wrote diaries and notes of his travels, and sketched the landscape, no doubt eagerly picking up tips as he did so from none other than the pseudonymous "Sketcher" in "Maga", as *Blackwood's Magazine* was affectionately called. The extent of Ruskin's own eagerness to see and to express was unique. He had published papers on geology at the age of fifteen, and corresponded with eminent scientists and scholars four times his age. This was the level of precocity, but at a different time and with different focuses, that Turner himself had shown in his youth. The one crucial difference in their talents, however, was that whereas at an early age both Turner and Ruskin had travelled widely, Ruskin could express himself in words, but Turner at that stage could not.

Ruskin's first words on Turner were written "in a state of great anger" in response to Eagles's review of *Juliet and her Nurse*. Whereas Eagles had written from notes taken in front of the painting in the Academy, Ruskin wrote his passage on 1st October 1836, after the Academy exhibition had closed, and after the painting had entered the collection of Hugh Munro of Novar. Ruskin, therefore, was writing a recollection of a painting he had not seen since the early summer, but which had matured in his memory over the intervening months. Though deeply felt, Ruskin's words are pure invention laced with emotion, and are strained through memories of his own visit to Venice the year before. They reveal an imperfect memory of the painting he was defending:

> Many-coloured mists are floating above the distant city, but such mists as you might imagine to be aetherial spirits, souls of the mighty dead breathed out of the tombs of Italy into the blue of her bright heaven, and wandering in vague and infinite glory around the earth they have loved. Instinct with the beauty of uncertain light, they move and mingle among the pale stars, and rise up into the brightness of the illimitable heaven, whose soft, sad blue eye gazes down into the deep altar of the sea for ever, – that sea whose motionless and silent transparency is beaming with phosphor light, that emanates out of its sapphire serenity like bright dreams breathed into the spirit of deep sleep. And the spires of the glorious city rise indistinctly bright into those living mists like pyramids of pale fire from some vast altar; and amid the glory of the dream, there is as it were the voice of a multitude entering the eye – arising from the stillness of the city like the summer wind passing over the leaves of the forest, when a murmur is heard amidst their multitude. This, oh Maga, is the picture of which your critic has pronounced to be like "models of different parts of Venice, streaked blue and pink, and thrown into a flour tub."[7]

This is wonderful English prose, but as art criticism, now, it is boloney. *Juliet and her Nurse*, in an Argentinan collection, is, with *Wreck of a Transport Ship* in Lisbon, one of the two Turners least known to the English-speaking world. Ruskin's "appreciation" has made it remoter still. At the urging of his wise father, Ruskin sent the passage to Turner, rather than to *Blackwood's* for publication. Turner read it and replied, thanking the author whom he knew only to be "J. R. Esq", for his zeal, kindness and trouble', and revealed an apparent unconcern: "I never move in these matters. They are of no import save mischief."[8] Turner sent the manuscript to Munro, and although Eagles continued his attacks in *Blackwood's*, Turner heard no more of John Ruskin for four years.

The one quality that Ruskin's words do capture is the mood of slow elevation in *Juliet and her Nurse* – the high viewpoint, the Campanile of St Mark's rising above the horizon line, the crowds way below, the rocket reaching its apogee in the distance. The painting creates a palpable sensation of flying, particularly as the spectator's viewpoint is somewhere in midair off the edge of the balcony. Turner had raised himself and his viewers above *terra firma* in a significant number of paintings of this period – the two versions of *The Burning of the Houses of Lords and Commons* (1835), *Rome from the Aventine* (1836), and many watercolours including the vignette illustrations to Milton of 1835.

Sensations of free floating through the air were on Turner's paper and canvas, and, prompted by reports of a celebrated balloon flight, were also in his dreams. He wrote to Robert Hollond MP, whom he must have met at a dinner or soirée, to tell him of a dream he had had. Letters of this kind do not come out of the blue; a conversation about flight will have preceded it: "Your excursion so occupied my mind that I dreamt of it, and I do hope that you will hold to your intention of making the drawing, with all the forms and colours of your recollection."[9]

Hollond was one of the brave aeronauts who took off from Vauxhall Gardens on 7th November 1836 to fly towards Germany. They crossed the Channel at Dover, and eighteen hours later landed at Weilberg, north-east of Frankfurt. The leader of the expedition, Thomas Monck Mason, described the view from the balloon in much the kind of way, one would suppose, that Hollond described it, while Turner urged him to make a watercolour drawing of the subject:

> Behind us, the whole line of the English coast, its white cliffs melting into obscurity, appeared sparkling with the scattered lights, which every moment augmented ... On either side below us the interminable ocean spread its complicated tissue of waves without interruption or curtailment ... on the opposite side a dense barrier of clouds rising from the ocean like a solid wall fantastically surmounted, throughout its whole length, with a gigantic representation of parapets and turrets, batteries and bastions, and other features of mural fortifications, appeared as if to bar our further progress.[10]

We know of no direct desire in Turner to take a balloon flight, but the experience of others excited him greatly, and by an osmotic process the experience of flying transmitted itself to his painting. It was precisely this breadth of interest in Turner, this consuming desire to treat painting as his balloon and to float with it into other areas of enlightenment, that drew Ruskin to him and repelled Eagles. When Eagles went out to look for fairies in Leigh Woods, young Ruskin was discussing the structure of the earth with eminent scientists. "Mr Darwin ... and I got on together and talked all the evening," he wrote to his father.[11]

Being in advance of, or at any rate very different to the conservative taste of his time as represented by John Eagles, Turner's work appealed in the late 1830s to those self-made industrialists whom we have discussed, and also to scientists. Understanding or reflecting upon Turner was to them as enjoyable a challenge as was understanding the structure of the earth or the movements of the planets. These people did not speak the language of connoisseurs, and were probably irritated by it. Certainly, their views on the proposed Clifton Suspension Bridge, for example, would have differed profoundly from those of John Eagles.

Mary Somerville became a frequent visitor to Turner's studio. She was "always welcomed", she wrote. "No one could imagine that so much poetical feeling existed in so rough an exterior."[12] Mary Somerville had trained as a painter at Alexander Nasmyth's Academy for Ladies in Edinburgh, and on her marriage and removal to London took further lessons from John Glover. She visited Rome, where in 1817 she met Thorwaldsen, Canova and many of the resident English artists. She found John Gibson to be "the most guileless and amiable of men," and he became a "dear and valued friend."[13] When Mary Somerville looked at sunsets over Lake Albano, she saw them through Turner's eyes: "The sunsets were glorious, and I, fascinated by the gorgeous colouring, attempted to paint what Turner alone could have done justice."[14]

The studio traffic was busy both ways. The naturalist Richard Owen received "several visits from Turner" at his rooms in the College of Surgeons,"[15] and some time in the later 1830s, Turner was invited to dine with the zoologist and lawyer William Broderip in the company of Owen and the journalist Theodore Hook. Clearly the dinner was a success, and Turner invited the party back a few days later to see his pictures at Queen Anne Street. Owen recalled that this was a bright August day, and that having rung the bell the friends had to wait some time before "an elderly person opened the door a few inches, and asked them suspiciously what they wanted."[16] This was Hannah Danby. They replied they wanted to see Mr Turner, at which the door was immediately shut in their faces. They waited on the step until Hannah came back to show them into a pitch-dark room, where they were left for "a prolonged interval" until they were told to go upstairs.

There they saw Turner at work on a production line of paintings, standing in front of several easels ranged beside a circular swivel table. Turner's paints were on the table, which he swung to and fro to reach the colour he required. Then, loading his brush, he worked on one canvas after another until his brush was empty. This time-saving, scientific method of painting had evolved from years of studio practice and adaptation, and may help to explain Turner's extraordinary rate of production. Owen went on to say that when showing the party round the gallery, Turner explained the reasons for their initial plunge into darkness. He said that the bright light outside would have spoilt their eyes for the proper appreciation of his pictures, and that to see them to advantage they had to stand patiently in the dark for a while.

As he twizzled his efficient painting table round one way and another, from red to yellow to blue and back again, and welcomed scientists into his studio, we are witnessing another critical moment in Turner's life. It is a critical moment too in the history of art and science, because it can be taken as an expression of the point where the two disciplines began to separate. When the fissures started to open, Turner articulated the matter through his work and found himself on the side that the world would least expect him to be. Through the developing chaos of his colour he appealed to scientists' uncertainty, rather than to the comfort of admirers of painting. This may be his greatest achievement, but it is also Turner's tragedy. It led to his being patronised through the words of some of his artist colleagues, and to his being found unclassifiable by some of the scientists.

Turner was quite seriously ill during the winter of 1836 and 1837. The national threat of cholera had abated, but Turner was now struck down by "the baneful effects of the *Influenza* hanging upon me yet daily (for it alternates) and hourly." He felt a "lassitude" and a "sinking down", yet "compelled to work the same is not to be expressed but must be borne by me if possible 3 weeks longer without any help."[17]

The pressures on him this spring were greater than ever, for the coming Academy exhibition would be the first to be held in the new and much-heralded accommodation for the Royal Academy and the National Gallery in Trafalgar Square. Naturally the Academy wished to make a good show, for the King was to perform the opening ceremony. Turner was on the Hanging Committee, and as early as January he had been letting his anxiety about the exhibition show. He wrote to an old Yorkshire friend, Edward Swinburne: "Sorry I am the Pictures for the New Academy's (first show) calls for all exertion possible, of each member and myself being on the Council. I shall have more than usual turmoil and no hope of giving much satisfaction."[18]

Despite his suffering and self-doubt, a condition that he would never have owned to thirty years earlier, Turner carried out his duty to the Academy both as an official and as an exhibitor. This season, showing *Apollo and Daphne* and *The Parting of Hero and Leander* with two other large paintings, he was showered with praise by most journals, with the sole and inevitable exception of the unsigned *Blackwood's* articles. Of *Apollo and Daphne* the *Spectator* wrote that it was "a wonder of art; a splendid picture of nature, with a less share than usual of [Turner's] glaring defects." The *Literary Gazette* added that the picture was "one of those gorgeous effects of prismatic colours in all their original and distinct vividness, which under any other management than Mr Turner would be offensive; but which he renders absolutely magical."[19] Once again, the critics' cloud of disbelief is dispelled by invoking the supernatural, Turner the Magician. There seemed, indeed, to be only one living human being with whom Turner could possibly be compared, and that was the man widely tipped as being in league with the devil, the violinist Nicolò Paganini. Writing to John Linnell in 1838, Samuel Palmer was inclined to think that *Apollo and Daphne* "is like what Paganini's violin playing is said to have been; something to which no one ever did or will do the like."[20]

That such colours should come out of this unprepossessing little man, whether magician or devil, was beyond the belief of many of his acquaintance. Robert Cadell had found him in 1831 as "a little dissenting clergyman like person – no more appearance of art about him than a ganger."[21] Francis Moon the printseller noticed Turner's "coarse, stout person, heavy look, and homely manners contrasting strangely with the marvellous beauty and grace of the ... creations of his pencil."[22] The "homely manners" may have been Moon's discreet way of describing the behaviour that had caught David Wilkie's sister's eye in 1821: 'My sister has upon the occasion conceived the most rooted aversion to that Artist whom so many admire, from his habit of tasting everything and leaving a great deal on his plate."[23]

Of the dozens of unfinished oils on canvas found in Turner's studio after his death, many came from the 1830s. This was the period in which he did what he liked, resigned to the frustration and excitement of being way ahead of his time. The scale of some of the unfinished paintings, and the lengths to which Turner had taken them before abandoning them, indicates how hard won were those paintings he did complete. *Harbour with Town and Fortress*[24] has the ring of a "Carthaginian" harbour scene with dozens of figures, palmed into a recollection of a northern European harbour. A week's more work and it would have been finished, so one wonders why so advanced a canvas was put aside. Another, now known as *Rocky Bay with Figures*[25] may be a further subject in the story of Ulysses, perhaps Ulysses and his companions cast up on Circe's island, though this does not adequately explain the flotilla of ships.

A third canvas has been known as *Fire at Sea*, but Cecilia Powell has proposed a new title, *The Female Convict Ship: Women and Children Abandoned in a Gale*.[26] Powell's vivid contention is that the painting is Turner's angry response to press reports of the wreck of the *Amphitrite*, a ship transporting women convicts and their children to a penal colony in Australia,[27] which went aground off Boulogne Harbour in a violent storm in 1833. The entire manifest could have been rescued, so near were they to the harbour, but the captain (who perished) refused all offers of help because he knew that once ashore in France, his "passengers" would never be recaptured. So everybody drowned. Although this interpretation does not explain the flames and fiery debris falling from the sky, in the circumstances that powerful expression of the artist's anger is not troubling. Turner's response to the shocking fate of the *Amphitrite* is entirely in character, and in its unfinished state we can consider it as a precursor of *Slavers* of 1840. Unlike many of Turner's earlier paintings that parallel contemporary events, *The Female Convict Ship* is neither an allegory nor is it allusive. It is direct in its message, referring both to a particular isolated incident and to ingrained attitudes, and screams like a tortured cat. It proceeds from the shipwreck subjects of the 1810s, and gives more than a nod to Géricault's *Raft of the Medusa*.

In printmaking, the medium which took his name and imagery into countless parlours throughout the land, Turner looked with high professional interest on new avenues of engraving technology. The modern medium of electrotype attracted him, as it allowed greater print runs even than steel engraving, because the plate itself could be copied. He spoke too with engravers about enlarging the plate size, and worked closely with James Willmore (1800–63) and William Miller (1796–1882) on the making of engravings from *Ancient Italy* and *Modern Italy* (exh. 1838; engravings published 1842) which were as large as 24 by 18 inches. These developments kept him closely in touch with advances in printmaking and publishing through subscription clubs known as "art unions". The integrity and technical ability with which Turner proceeded as a maker of images for reproduction is directly comparable to Dickens's pioneering intentions with his weekly magazine *Household Words*.

It is always easier to begin something than to finish it. Waning strength, intermittent illness, took their toll on Turner's production as a painter, as well as on Turner himself. These are the years of the trend that may quite simply be a gathering mortality which led Turner to begin more canvases than he could ever have expected to finish and exhibit. Some of them tend towards the condition of pure painting, symphonic colour arrangements on canvas in which formal subject gives way to exposition of light.

*The Evening Star*[28] is one such – a calm horizon over the sea, a pinkish sunset partially obscured by cloud, a boy checking his catch as he walks home with his dog, and a curious piece of seashore paraphernalia, perhaps the support for a leading-light. There was once a small boat drawn up on the beach to the right of centre effecting the geometry, but Turner painted it out. The one constant within the painting is the reflection of the eponymous star, itself a tiny dab of paint that one has to work one's way carefully up from the reflection to find. The title is not Turner's; it was given when the painting was first catalogued. The message of the painting lies in its exquisitely tonal colour and calm geometry: the horizontal offset by the diagonal of the seashore and the opposing diagonal created by the paced verticals of the wooden structure, the reflection and the boy. The reflection is dead centre.

The King died on 20th June 1837. When his niece ascended the throne, trailing after her an evolving set of steely social proprieties, three eminent artists, Callcott, Westmacott and the miniature painter William Newton, were knighted within weeks. Both Chantrey and Wilkie had been knighted in the final years of the reign of William IV, but no honour then or now settled upon Turner. British royalty appeared to be blind to him, but compensation came to Turner from the honour and esteem of his friends. Amongst the most touching expressions came from his namesake Dawson Turner when writing to present to him a set of his wife's portrait etchings:

> I am most happy to place [a set in your hands]. I should be insensible indeed, did I not feel how much honor the name I bear derives from my bearing it in common with you; & I should have a very low estimate of my own feeling for art, were I not morally certain that the time must come, will soon come, when your works will be ranked above those of any painter in your line, who have ever yet appeared upon the face of the earth.[29]

Turner returned to northern France this summer to make studies for illustrations to a new edition of Scott's *Life of Napoleon*, returning to London in early September. From 12th to 15th October he was at Petworth, as a fellow guest of Lord Egremont with Samuel and Sarah Rogers.[30] Egremont was now very ill, and was calling his friends down to see him for the last time. He had suffered from severe inflammation of the windpipe in the late 1820s, and had been ill on and off ever since.[31] Egremont had called George Jones down, but for some reason Jones did not come until Turner himself had written from Petworth insisting he make the journey, which he did, on the instant. "I did not hesitate, but went – fortunately I did so for in three weeks the kind and hospitable nobleman ceased to be."[32] Against the date 11th November 1837 in the Petworth Housekeeping Account Book is the heavily underlined entry

"The Earl of Egremont Died ¼ past 11 at night." Beside it in the margin is a black hand with a pointing finger drawn in ink.

Turner returned to Petworth once more and once more only for the Earl's funeral, "deeply affected", as Thomas Phillips put it, and attended in a borrowed mourning cloak.[33] He walked with fellow artists and Egremont's staff in front of the coffin, while a long line of family, friends and school children of the town followed in a tail behind.[34] This was the end of life at Petworth as Turner knew it; the Earl's heir, his eldest son George Wyndham, inherited the house and the estates, and began to clear up. Within months, the architect Charles Barry was invited down to draw up plans to improve and alter the house, and as the artist painters moved out, painter decorators moved in to whitewash the place.[35] George Wyndham gave orders that the Earl's private papers be burnt and this was all too successfully done, taking with them to the flames most of the documentary evidence of the extraordinary easy-going ménage which suited Turner down to the ground. The Liberty Hall of Sussex closed down.

Turner caught a bad cold at the funeral – either there or at the Academy Life Class which was cold and damp – and spent the best part of December at home under doctor's orders trying to recover. He was not too ill to paint or write, and in two letters written a few weeks after the funeral he mused on the loss of his friend. His affection for Egremont was widely known amongst his other friends, for both John Maw and Dawson Turner sent condolences, Maw with an invitation to Turner to spend Christmas with him and his family at Guildford, and Dawson Turner with a gift of a barrel of Yarmouth herrings.[36] Condolences of this kind – and there may have been more – will have focused Turner's thoughts for Egremont, helped him to mourn, and may have led him to pick up his brush and paint his feelings.

A debate broke out in the late 1980s about the painting traditionally known as *Interior at Petworth*. One point of view, supported by X-ray evidence, suggested that this is a reworked canvas of a musical party first painted at East Cowes Castle in 1827, and developed inconclusively a year or two later into a subject tentatively entitled *Study for the Sack of a Great House*. The other, however, believed it to be one of a pair of paintings reflecting specifically on Egremont's death, and titled it *The Apotheosis of Lord Egremont*.[37] In late November and December 1837 Turner was busy not only with Academy business, both teaching and Council responsibilities, but he was also ill, and he had his 1838 British Institution and Academy contributions to consider and to paint. Two of these were seven footers, and two were four foot canvases; one of the large paintings, *Fishing Boats with Hucksters Bargaining for Fish*, was due for the British Institution in January. There were other ways of mourning Egremont – painting good exhibition pictures, for example, and delivering on time. If *Interior at*

*Petworth* is a memorial to Egremont it need not have been posthumous, or even particularly specific. Turner's thought processes were, as we have seen time and again, characteristically elliptical. Egremont was an old and sick man when he died, and Turner must have known that any visit to Petworth might be his last. That the painting is a sombre reflective elegy for a person, a place or an idea seems to the present writer to be beyond doubt; but it could be as well for Walter Fawkes and Farnley as for Egremont and Petworth, and one may hazard that it is for both.

Turner resigned as Professor of Perspective at the Royal Academy at the Council meeting of 28th December 1837. His own private thoughts about his coming announcement will not have eased his feelings of sadness in the last weeks of the year. Although the Council received the news "with great regret", the regret was mixed with relief, for Turner had not given a lecture for nearly ten years, and there were times when the President had had to make excuses for the Professor, most embarrassingly after official criticism of Turner's performance in the Government inquiry into the Academy in 1836. His departure may have been the cue for the *Athenaeum*, a literary review usually so staunch in support, to perform Turner's funeral rites. Reviewing his 1838 Academy contribution generally, it said:

> Mr Turner is in all his force this year, as usual – showering upon his canvas splendid masses of architecture, far distant backgrounds; and figures whereby the commandment assuredly is not broken – and presenting all these objects through such a medium of yellow, and scarlet, and orange, and azure-blue, as only lives in his own fancy and the toleration of his admirers, who have followed his genius till they have passed, unknowingly, the bounds between magnificence and tawdriness. ... It is grievous to us to think of his talent, so mighty and so poetical, running riot into such frenzies; the more grievous as we fear it is now past recall.[38]

Turner's paintings of the middle to late 1830s weave in and out of reality. The two versions of the furious blaze at the Houses of Parliament create as convincing an account of the actual event as any news item seen in the twentieth century on film or television. The cataclysmic *Snowstorm, Avalanche and Inundation ... Val d'Aosta* (exh. 1837) on the other hand is no less terrible, but although painted soon after Turner's visit to the Val d'Aosta with Munro in 1836, this is not an event he could possibly have witnessed this summer. He moves with ease, too, from the ancient to the modern worlds, exhibiting in 1838 and 1839 two pairs of paintings contrasting ancient and modern Italy and ancient and modern Rome.

Creating related or contrasting subjects was for Turner a long-standing practice, which might emerge either in a pair of pendant works exhibited together, such as *Modern Italy – the Pifferari* and *Ancient Italy – Ovid Banished from Rome* (both 1838), or his long-running programme of paintings with a Carthaginian theme in which there is characteristically a contemporary subtext. In another of the paintings exhibited in 1838 the complementary subjects appear, unusually, in the same canvas. This is *Phryne going to the Public Baths as Venus – Demosthenes taunted by Aeschines*. The story of Phryne was an obscure theme from ancient history, one that had not appeared on any canvas exhibited at the Royal Academy for over forty years.

That Turner dusted it down in 1838 of all years is highly significant. As in any good drama there is in *Phryne* a plot and a linked sub-plot. On the right we have the eponymous courtesan, whose beauty had brought her great riches. She became the model for both the sculptor Praxiteles and the painter Apelles, and offered to rebuild Thebes after its destruction by Alexander the Great. She is being taken in a great popular parade, preceded by a statue of Cupid, as a personification of Venus and as the beautiful young wished-for saviour of the nation, to bathe naked in the public baths. On the left of this roaring, happy crowd are two old Greek politicians, Demosthenes and Aeschines, taking no notice of the parade but arguing furiously with apparent good humour. Demosthenes is accusing Aeschines of being the son of a courtesan, while Aeschines taunts Demosthenes, who had once been pressed to be King of Greece, by rattling a small crown at him.

This painting hung, with its allusions to youth, beauty, popular acclaim and kingship, in its one and only exhibition in Turner's lifetime on the walls of the Royal Academy in Trafalgar Square in May and June 1838. As it did so, a great public event, a year in the planning, took place only a few hundred yards away. This was the coronation of Queen Victoria, the beautiful young sovereign of the nation, whose procession passed by Trafalgar Square on its way to and from Westminster Abbey on 28th June 1838. Did Turner choose the obscure subject of Phryne to be his major exhibit in 1838 by coincidence, or was it his considered comment on the fickleness of popular acclaim and the pointless arguments of politicians? From what we know of Turner's deep knowledge of the classical world, his own democratic tendencies, his internalised, ironic humour, and the fact that the British royal family had done no good to *him*, we might suggest that Turner's timing was perfect and his allusions subtle. Far too subtle, for no contemporary source yet found drew any attention to the parallels. One friendly king did, however, honour Turner in coronation year. Louis-Philippe, King of the French, Turner's old friend from their Twickenham days, came to London for the celebrations, and, summoning him, gave the painter a gold snuff box with LP picked out in diamonds on the lid.

That summer, after all the junketing, Turner slipped off to Margate to stay with Mrs Booth. No doubt he left Blackfriars or Greenwich in good spirits. The ballad, "The Margate Voyage" captures the thrill of departure in the steamboat *Adelaide*:

> Off we went with our tall chimney smoking,
> Five hundred, all squeezing and choking;
> Some their heads o'er the vessel's side poking,
>     Which made their gay spirits much tamer.
> But John Bull, though ever so cross, sir,
> Is never at meals at a loss, sir;
> So they soon began beef-steaks to toss, sir;
>     Down their throats in the Adelaide steamer.[39]

These journeys gave Turner the opportunity to watch the sea and sky from a small, precarious viewpoint within its vastness. In the crush of fellow passengers he will not have been able to do more than make quick customary pencil sketches in his notebooks, and absorb the light and movement of the waves and clouds in the extraordinary visual memory that had made his *England and Wales* watercolours such an effective and potent document:

> Most of the time he hung over the stern, watching the effects of the sun and the boiling of the foam. About two o'clock he would open his wallet of cold meat in the cabin, and, nearing himself to one with whom he was in the habit of chatting, would beg a clean plate and a hot potato, and did not refuse one glass of wine, but would never accept two. It need hardly be added that he was no favorite with the waiters.[40]

Turner was now released from the burden of making finished watercolours for *Picturesque Views of England and Wales*, as the ultimate owners of the enterprise, Longman's, cancelled the series in 1838. It was not a release Turner had in any way sought; *England and Wales* and the other print series were the drum he had been beating for Britain for twenty years.

The summer of 1838 became one of those in the second half of the 1830s in which Turner painted some of his most bleakly reflective seascapes, both in watercolour and in oil. In many there may be only the slightest hint of human reference in the placing of a pier or breakwater or of a wallowing ship in trouble. There were many moods in Margate, but two oil paintings, taken from practically the same spot on the beach just to the east of Mrs Booth's house, characterise the extremes of weather that drew Turner to Margate in particular. In one, *Waves Breaking on a Lee Shore*, Turner has been standing facing the wind, which is blowing towards the shore, bringing the waves more powerfully upon it. The ship (if it is a ship) with its prow raised in the centre of the painting, is in grave danger of being driven onto the Fulsam Rocks beyond Jarvis's Landing Place. In the distance to the right, black clouds are rolling in with the wind, and on the left the sun is going down beyond Margate Pier. It will be a filthy night. This painting was never exhibited; it is one of nearly fifty oils of the sea, many with little or no reference to place, that were found in Turner's studio after his death, plain evidence of the enormous physical energy he continued to invest, aged sixty-four or sixty-five, in capturing the power of the sea.

In complete contrast to *Waves Breaking on a Lee Shore*, Turner painted *The New Moon*, a Margate beachscape with a woman trying to control three squabbling children and two dogs on a limpid evening at low tide. Again, Fort Point is visible to the left, with the jetty and Margate Pier beyond. The new moon is high in the sky and a few other people paddle in the shallows as the sun goes down. Though the sea may be calm, Turner reveals the ever present danger of Fulsam Rocks by painting the choppy water as it runs over the wide area of shoal. *The New Moon* was exhibited in 1840 with a subtitle that shows how keenly Turner kept his ears as well as his eyes open as he walked on the sea shore, catching snatches of conversation that travelled across the wide sands: *"I've lost my Boat, You shan't have your Hoop"*.

From Margate, the steam packet service ran on round the North Foreland to Ramsgate, and then on down past Deal, St Margaret's-at-Cliffe, and round to Dover. Folkestone and Hastings were an hour or more away. This coastal journey, by now so easy to take, was one which Turner made at will. As his sketchbooks and oil studies show, he haunted the coastline both in fact and in his recollections, driven by the kind of imaginative power that made him paint *Sunrise with Sea Monsters*. With only a small further imaginary step this painting can be read as Jarvis's Landing Place, Margate, with a paddle steamer transformed into, or devoured by, two or three huge fish.

The culmination of the late 1830s series of sea studies is *Rockets and Blue Lights (close at hand) to warn Steam-Boats of Shoal-Water*. Despite the variations in detail of the pier and tower, this may also be a hint of Margate, because no other English harbour that Turner was so familiar with at this time has rocky shoal water, indicated bottom right, so close to the pier. Like *The New Moon* this was exhibited at the Academy in 1840, and together the paintings demonstrated the constant dangers of rocks in shallow waters, the real sea monster which waits constantly offshore. In *Rockets and Blue Lights* Turner brings nature and technology together, and though it is by no means certain here that nature will swamp the two steamboats, the blue signal lights do nevertheless mean "not under command". The predominant colours in the painting, creamy white and blue, not only reflect the natural conditions, but also echo the narrative in the work and its long title which spells out precisely what Turner is trying to say.

At Margate, Turner now had Sophia Booth as a permanent companion. They both found a perfect symbiotic companionship in each other. For Turner, Sophia replaced the mothering side of his father. John Booth had left his widow £1,200 and some other income when he died.[41] Her one surviving child, Daniel Pound, her son from her first marriage, was now grown up. Her house was her own, and although she may have needed companionship, she did not need support. She had already had two husbands, so marriage held no mysteries for her. Turner would never marry, though his need for warmth, companionship and love was as great as anybody's. If left alone to work, and to come and go as he pleased, Turner was a most undemanding man, generous and companionable, in a gruff, improvised kind of way.

For her part, Sophia was an understanding and welcoming hostess. "I have ... set a sandwich and some sherry on the table," she said to a wandering artist a few days after Turner's death, "and I hope you will sit down, and refresh and rest yourself, after being so long in the cold."[42] The number of oil paintings, a dozen or more, which emerged with a Booth/Pound provenance in 1865 suggests that Turner must have given some of them at least to his Margate companion, and given them with kindness.[43] Whatever it was that brought Sophia Booth and Turner together, kept them together in a loose affection for more than fifteen years. Of course, it was the position of the house that first drew Turner to Sophia Booth. If her house had not had the best view in Margate, he would not have looked at her twice. Turner's first mistress was his painting; Sarah Danby and Sophia Booth fell into the second rank. "Mr Turner used to say I am the handmaid of Art, and I have the right to take some freedoms with her sons," Sophia recalled.[44] Sophia followed Turner around the coast of Kent, though she did not give up her house in Margate. She said in 1852 that Turner had had a house in St Margaret's-at-Cliffe, north of Dover, and according to Turner's doctor's affidavit, he had one in Deal also.[45]

There is an apocryphal story that Turner was spotted coming home from Margate to London on 23rd September 1838, by an unknown artist who cut his silhouette portrait on the deck of the *City of Canterbury* steamer. This may have been one of many journeys back to London that summer, and on this, as on others, Turner will have seen, on the north shore of the Thames at Wapping, the flight of steps down to the river at New Crane Wharf. Less than one hundred yards beyond, along New Gravel Lane, was Turner's inn. At this same spot on the river, the jetties and lighters supplying Brunel's Thames Tunnel were busy again, as work had resumed in 1835. In late September, however, if he looked to the left, downstream, opposite New Crane Stairs to the wharves at the head of the Grand Surrey Canal on the Rotherhithe bank, Turner would have seen the hulk of the former man o'war *Téméraire* tied up at John Beatson's wharf, where for the past two weeks it had been gradually broken up. *Téméraire*, which had played a heroic part in the Battle of Trafalgar, and which Turner had already depicted in his two paintings of the battle, had been sold out of the navy the month before and towed to the breakers from Sheerness, nosing her way through the spoil barges and brick lighters around the Tunnel entrance. If he had gone down to the Ship and Bladebone any time that autumn, Turner would have seen her, and, just upstream, the brick structures at the mouth of Brunel's tunnelling works. Turner's first view of the *Téméraire* from across the river was broadside on. By now she had no masts, no superstructure, and her upper timbers were being removed bit by bit. A lithograph of the hulk by William Beatson may well have been drawn from a boat near New Crane Stairs. As Beatson made his drawing in September 1838,[46] Turner thought about a painting.

*The Fighting Téméraire, tugged to her last berth to be broken up, 1838* is the full title of the picture Turner exhibited in the 1839 Academy exhibition. It has since become one of the best known and best loved paintings of all time.[47] It brings and balances facts together: sail and steam, air and water, past and present, setting sun and new moon; it balances qualities: old age and the new, dignity and presumption, silence and noise, steadiness and urgency, the temporal and the eternal; and it balances geometrical forms: the horizontal, the vertical and the diagonal. Where these lines rush towards the setting sun, the black tug and its ghostly white charge move inexorably out into our space.

*The Fighting Téméraire* redirected Turner's switchback reputation with the press. Having been dismissed as "a talent running riot into frenzies" in 1838, Turner was raised up again like an artist-hero, the creator of a "furnace-like blaze of light, making the river glow with its effulgence, and typifying the departing glories of the old Temeraire."[48] In *Phryne* he had been speaking in his own internalised language, making allusions that no one could see. In *The Fighting Téméraire* the allusions were clear, and Turner was the representative of the ordinary Briton at the final pageant for the Napoleonic Wars, now part of history. Though he waited a while for offers, Turner never sold *The Fighting Téméraire*. It was one of the personal, elegiac paintings that thread his career, such as *Frosty Morning, England – Richmond Hill* and *"Interior at Petworth"*. In his personal hierarchy of affection Mrs Booth was the "handmaid of Art", his paintings were his "children", his "family"; but *Téméraire*, as he put it in a draft letter in a sketchbook, was "my Darling".[49] *Téméraire* became Turner's Pygmalion. He had made it; he fell in love with it; and it also reflected one aspect of himself, the old warrior artist being tugged away to die alone and in utter silence.

Turner himself would sit for long periods on his own in silence in these years. He became a fixture at the Athenaeum, where he would inhabit a dark corner with a bottle of sherry; and at the Yorkshire Stingo, an ale house at the Lisson Grove end of Shillibeer's omnibus service that ran to the Mansion House and the Bank, convenient for Wapping.[50] He would quickly move off if anybody recognised and approached him, and disappear. But Turner the silent, reclusive old body was only one aspect of the man in the late 1830s and beyond. Periods of withdrawal were a necessity for him now as they had always been. When his father was alive he would retreat to be with him at Sandycombe or Queen Anne Street. But now, in a gloomy corner of a club or public bar, he could observe the world and overhear conversations, re-forming himself the while in his chrysalis. Then the butterfly would appear, sometimes with a magnificent vanity, at others with an affecting modesty. Spending one evening about 1840 with C. R. Leslie and his family, Turner went into the painting room where the robes, wig and so on of the Lord Chancellor, whose portrait Leslie was painting, were arranged upon a lay figure. After a little joking, Turner "was persuaded to put on the Lord Chancellor's wig, in which ... [he] looked splendid, so joyous and happy, too, in the idea that the Chancellor's wig became him better than anyone else of the party."[51]

There are few Turner stories that are not balanced by an opposite, reflecting not that reports are wrong, but that Turner's character encompassed so many contradictions. John Ruskin had been thinking, no doubt dreaming, about his hero for eight years or more before he at last met him on Thomas Griffith's lawn before dinner on 2nd June 1840. Ruskin was not known to Turner; he could not connect him with the "J. R. Esq." who had tried to champion him four years earlier. He spoke politely to the young man, but seems to have taken no particular notice of him that evening.[52] Ruskin, however, like a watchful lover, observed Turner intently. When he got home he reached for his diary and wrote the clearest and sharpest brief account of Turner there is:

> Introduced today to the man who beyond all doubt is the greatest of the age; greatest in every faculty of the imagination, in every branch of scenic knowledge; at once *the* painter and poet of the day, J. M. W. Turner. Everybody had described him to me as coarse, boorish, unintellectual, vulgar. This I knew to be impossible. I found in him a somewhat eccentric, keen-mannered, matter-of-fact, English-minded-gentleman: good-natured evidently, bad-tempered evidently, hating humbug of all sorts, shrewd, perhaps a little selfish,

highly intellectual, the powers of his mind not brought out with any delight in their manifestation, or intention of display, but flashing out occasionally in a word or a look.[53]

Ruskin encouraged his father to buy Turner's paintings; and the father indulged the son. The first oil painting by Turner that Ruskin owned was *Slavers throwing overboard the Dead and Dying – Typhon coming on*. This had been exhibited at the Academy in 1840, along with *Rockets and Blue Lights* and *The New Moon*. *Slavers* and *Rockets and Blue Lights* are of precisely the same size, but of opposing palettes, the former having dominant red, the latter dominant blue. Two specific factors have led *Slavers* to become one of the greatest Turner paintings outside the Bequest, while *Rockets and Blue Lights* is little known. The first is the horror and clarity of its subject, the second is that one of Ruskin's most famous descriptive passages is devoted to *Slavers*, and was published in the first volume of *Modern Painters* in 1843. While *Slavers* was lost from public sight in Ruskin's collection until 1872 and then hung in an American private collection until 1899, it lived in the public mind through Ruskin's words: "... the noblest sea that Turner ever painted ... the fire of sunset falls along the trough of the sea, dying it with an awful but glorious light, the intense and lurid splendour which bathes like gold and burns like blood."[54] These words became, effectively, a surrogate for the painting for more than fifty years,[55] but unlike Ruskin's words about *Juliet and her Nurse* they were written from a profound knowledge of the picture.

In the 1840 Academy exhibition *Slavers* and *Rockets and Blue Lights* were hung in "conspicuous places", according to Eagles in *Blackwood's*.[56] Eagles maligned them both, while other critics generally dismissed them. Once again the switchback of Turner's public reputation had twisted against him. To the newspaper critics he seemed to be, as a modern sportsman will know, only as good as his last game. But when we put *Slavers* and *Rockets and Blue Lights* together, as they should be, we may see that Turner had a balanced intention. Both paintings warn of grave dangers at sea. In *Slavers* the worst (for the ship) is over. Signified by the small patch of blue sky at the top right, and the direction of the wind in the well-reefed jib, the storm is passing, despite the assertion of the title. In *Rockets and Blue Lights*, however, the storm is at its height. Though the slaves drown or are devoured by fish, they raise their hands in gestures of triumph,[57] and their chains float free. When Turner subtitled this painting *Typhon coming on* and published the following lines from "The Fallacies of Hope" in the exhibition catalogue, he was referring not just to the furious weather but also to the continuing public fury against slavery, which was still being carried on by Spain:

Aloft all hands, strike the top-masts and belay;
Yon angry setting sun and fierce-edged clouds
Declare the Typhon's coming.
Before it sweeps your decks, throw overboard
The dead and dying – ne'er heed their chains
Hope, Hope, fallacious Hope!
Where is thy market now?

The wind-driven slaver, the *alter ego* of *The Fighting Téméraire* is a ship of the past, while the steamships in *Rockets and Blue Lights* are the machines of the future. And, increasing the insistence of hope in this pair of paintings, there is Turner's certain knowledge that in the future there would be no steam slaveships. *Slavers* and *Rockets and Blue Lights* remained together as a pair for over three years with Thomas Griffith, when Ruskin advised a King's Lynn collector, William Wethered to buy both. Wethered bought neither, and eventually the paintings went their separate ways.

The attention that was being focused publicly on Turner in the late 1830s and early 1840s had a comic aspect to set beside the artist's own earnestness and the uncertainty of the press. Even Eagles had his moments of light-heartedness. "Is it an allegory?" he asked of *Slavers*. "Between the vessel and the fish there is an object that has long puzzled us. We may be wrong; but we have conjectured it to be a Catholic bishop in canonicals gallantly gone overboard, to give benediction to the crew, or fish."[58] Thackeray, writing in *Fraser's Magazine* as "Mr Michael Angelo Titmarsh" suggested that if Samuel Joseph's statue of Wilberforce, which was also in the exhibition "were to be confronted with this picture, the stony old gentleman would spring off his chair and fly away in terror."[59]

It was not long before the new humorous magazine *Punch* began to poke fun at Turner. In its first volume (1841) it drew a picture of Academicians preparing to give Prince Albert a sketching lesson in St James's Park:

> The most rabidly-engaged gentleman was Turner, who, despite the remonstrances of his colleagues upon the expense attendant upon his whimsical notions, would persist in making the grass more natural by emptying large buckets of treacle and mustard about the ground.[60]

Even on the stage Turner was not left alone. A pantomime scene of about 1841 was set in an art shop where a crowd gathers to look at a Turner in the window. A baker's boy enters with a tray of jam tarts. He trips and falls through the window and then through the painting. The canvas is ruined, red and yellow jam tarts lie everywhere. The dealer runs in angrily, sees the tray, picks it up, scatters the jam tarts back on it, dusts the lot with flour, puts the frame round it, and immediately sells the mess as a Turner for £1,000 to a connoisseur.[61]

Turner took himself away from raucous London in August 1840 on a journey along the Rhine and Mosel, and on to Venice. He travelled part of the way with a young man who may have been the architect Edward Hakewill, the nephew of James Hakewill, with his wife.[62] When he arrived in Venice on 20th August,[63] he booked into the Hotel Europa, once the Palazzo Giustiani, taking rooms on an upper floor looking out north over the city. The Europa was – is still – at the end of the Grand Canal directly opposite Santa Maria della Salute. Turner's rooms on this visit had an urban view, but from the roof he could see and paint almost all that lay around him. Even at sixty-five he could still be excited like a child on waking up on his first holiday morning – a dawn view of the city and three towers is inscribed happily: "From my Bedroom, Venice."[64] The room was spacious and airy, a room of the kind he had last stayed in at Petworth. Like the Petworth rooms it was light and inspiring enough for him to paint an interior, which he did.[65]

A fellow guest at the Europa was the painter William Callow (1812–1908). They talked quietly together at meals, but Turner painted alone. Callow recalled how intensively Turner worked: "One evening while I was enjoying a cigar in a gondola I saw in another one Turner sketching San Giorgio, brilliantly lit up by the setting sun. I felt quite ashamed of myself idling away the time whilst he was hard at work so late."[66]

On this visit to Venice Turner did not work so late into the night as he had in 1833, when he painted fireworks, theatres and dark, narrow canals. This may be a reflection of his increasing age and a natural tendency to tire easily, or indeed it may suggest that to capture the fugitive tones of these last watercolours of Venice he wanted to get up early this time. This was to be Turner's final visit to Venice. He may have known he would not come again, or may certainly have feared it, even though later he made plans to return.[67] On the back of the watercolour Venice from Fusina[68] he wrote a brief, practically illegible verse. If it is correct to read in the first line the words "... gleam the last of the [..?..] ray" we are perhaps witnessing Turner's final farewell to the crumbling city.

Turner arrived back in London on 6th or 7th October and within a few hours was writing to his solicitor George Cobb about two separate tenancy agreements that were troubling him: "Wally Strong shall be paid but confound him he will not move about the piece of ground, so things remain (as they were). What Young has built and paid his rent for Heaven alone knows, for I do not."[69] Turner the interfering landlord is an area of his life that still has deep mysteries which have not yet revealed. In 1840 he owned property in Twickenham, Lee Clump, Wapping, Barkingside, Queen Anne Street, at St Margaret's-at-Cliffe and Deal in Kent, probably also in Epping, and perhaps elsewhere, both freehold and leasehold. He kept an active and insistent interest in the management of his property. There is a suggestion, such was his entrepreneurial instinct, alive since his youth, that he bought property unseen, just because he spotted a bargain, and had his fingers burnt as a result.[70]

This is all evidence of the irradicability of Turner's desire for control, through which he risked ending up a figure of fun. Learning from the Tilt affair, he stepped in at the last minute just as the entire stock of his engravings and copper plates from *England and Wales* was about to be auctioned in 1839, and bought the lot for £3,000. He presented a drab, lonely figure as he trawled incognito among the print shops for his work. One printseller revealed that she thought she had a country farmer in her shop when a weather-beaten old man came in and demanded to buy her entire stock of Turner prints. He paid her asking price without a quibble,

> and took out his handkerchief, a cotton print, and not too clean, and began bundling them up into it, and tying the corners. I offered to do them up in paper, and send them, but he wouldn't; and put his stick through the tie of the handkerchief, and clapped them over his shoulder, and went off.[71]

The losses of friends that Turner suffered early in the 1830s was mirrored at the end of the decade by a clutch more deaths of people close to him – William Wells in 1836, John Soane and Egremont the following year, and then, hard on each other's heels, David Wilkie and Francis Chantrey in June and November 1841. Wilkie had died of malaria contracted in the Middle East when he was returning home, and his body was buried at sea off Gibraltar. At the following Academy exhibition, Turner exhibited a small, sombre picture *Peace – Burial at Sea*, in memory of his friend. Fireworks from the shore, last seen in Turner's exhibited work as a motif of celebration in *Juliet and her Nurse*, echo the grim torchlight as Wilkie's coffin is slowly lowered into the water. Questioned about the extreme darkness of the paddle steamer's sails, Turner replied: "I only wish I had any colour to make them blacker."[72]

This threnody for Wilkie drew Turner to present the theme of *Peace* beside a companion painting, *War – The Exile and the Rock Limpet*. The exile of the title was Napoleon, who stands on St Helena in the ruinous visionary landscape that Turner has conjured up around him. He is watched over by a sentry, and he in turn watches a tiny mollusc forever tied to his home, yet free to move. The mollusc, its shell a metaphor for a soldier's bivouac, may move in whichever direction he chooses, and as far as he is able, in stark contrast to Napoleon himself. Both paintings turn to noble effect compositional and narrative themes that had preoccupied

Turner throughout his life – marine subjects in the one, and massed architecture dominating the edges of the painting in the other. In making paintings which express his own private thoughts and feelings – and these are bitter works – Turner quarries the vast bank of imagery which he had in portfolios, sketchbooks or as metaphors quietly lodged in his head.

During the previous year or two Turner had read Eastlake's English translation of Goethe's *Farbenlehre*, published in 1840 as *Theory of Colours*, and annotated the margins of his copy. Undoubtedly he and Eastlake had discussed Goethe's controversial ideas and rival theories while the translation was in progress, and indeed Goethe's proposals about the polarity of colour found common ground with Turner. Goethe proposed that Yellow had the characteristics of action, light, brightness, force, warmth, proximity, repulsion; while Blue had negation, shadow, darkness, weakness, coldness, distance and attraction. Turner had already painted pairs of pictures which opposed hot and cool colours – *Slavers* and *Rockets and Blue Lights* for example – but *Peace* and *War*, yellow-red and blue-green respectively, may be deliberate exercises in the polarities of "attraction" and "repulsion".[73] If this is the case, it was an exercise driven by passing curiosity, for Turner was not long seduced by rules or theories. The painter William Henry Hunt (1790–1864) had "frequent opportunities of conversing with Turner," as Ruskin reported, "but never heard him utter a single rule of colour, though he had frequently heard him, like all great men, talk of 'trying' to do a thing."[74]

Turner's contribution to the Royal Academy in 1842 was a sombre group of five paintings. It included *Peace* and *War*, a pair of low-toned, melancholy Venetian subjects, and the turbulent *Snow Storm*. This was exhibited with the full title *Snow Storm – Steam-Boat off a harbour's mouth making signals in shallow water, and going by the lead. The author was in this storm on the night the Ariel left Harwich.* In the unrelieved chaos of the subject, this picture follows in the spirit of the sea paintings Turner made at or about Margate in the late 1830s. There is the same overwhelming power in the waves, pitted against the frail steamer as it fires a distress rocket. The flowing forms of the vortices, their rushing lines, curves and peaks reflect the forms of magnetic lines of force revealed by Michael Faraday and Mary Somerville when they placed magnets under sheets of paper scattered with iron filings: this is a design source which *Snow Storm* shares with *Rockets and Blue Lights*. The long title of the painting, with its technical and apparent autobiographical detail, has confused many writers, as, probably, Turner intended. He himself muddied the waters by saying roughly to the Rev. William Kingsley, who had asked him about the painting: "I did not paint it to be understood, but I wished to show what such a scene was like; I got the sailors to lash me to the mast to observe it; I was lashed for four hours, and I did not expect to escape, but I felt bound to record it if I did."[75]

We need not take Turner's story literally. If a sixty-seven-year old man with a chronic illness had been lashed to a mast in a violent storm for four hours, he would have been found dead from exposure when they came to take him down. No, the story is a deliberate invention, intended both to confuse and impress, but there is nevertheless a grain of truth. The fundamental rule for sailors in a storm is "one hand for yourself and one for the ship". For an artist to record a storm, he must have both hands free, and so be lashed to something. Even if it is not the whole truth, the story does reflect Turner's strong identification with Ulysses the heroic traveller, and it reflects Turner's compulsion to paint what he knows, despite the fact that others would be baffled. He had certainly seen storms of that ferocity, and at some point during his life must have been lashed to a mast to draw. The steamboat *Ariel* of Harwich is another invention, though it may be a misremembering of the report of the loss of the steam-ship *Fairy* out of Harwich with all hands in 1840.[76] On the other hand, Turner may be referring to Shakespeare's Ariel who "put a girdle round about the earth in forty minutes." This same metaphor, relating swift coastal steam-ships to Ariel, was published in *Blackwood's* in 1841 in the preamble to the ballad "The Margate Voyage", quoted above.[77]

When Turner was exhibiting *Snow Storm*, *Peace* and *War*, another of his closest friends fell mortally ill. Edward Daniell had resigned from his curacy in Mayfair in 1840 to travel to the Middle East to paint and to record antiquarian remains. Before he left, he commissioned John Linnell to paint a portrait of Turner surreptitiously, by sitting the two men opposite one another at dinner. Linnell's job was to watch Turner carefully, and to draw a portrait from memory afterwards. The portrait was finished, but never delivered, for Daniell contracted malaria in Lycia and died in September 1843. Daniell's death was a grievous blow for Turner, removing a bright, young, enquiring friend from his life, and reminding him of his catalogue of bereavements. As he mourned, he talked about Daniell repeatedly to David Roberts, saying that he would never form such a friendship again.[78]

# FOURTEEN

## "The great lion of the day"

### 1843–1851

"Heaven grant that he may not be mortally offended with the work!" Ruskin wrote in his diary a few weeks before the first volume of *Modern Painters* was published.[1] He had just called on Turner at Queen Anne Street, and found him "panting with exertion" heaving engraved plates – perhaps the copper plates from *England and Wales* – into a cupboard with John Griffith. "Insisted on my taking a glass of wine, but I wouldn't. Excessively good-natured today." Ruskin now visited Turner regularly, and brought friends with him from time to time to see the gallery. His quiet manner allowed him to slip in and out of 47 Queen Anne Street, and Turner's acceptance of his presence was probably left unsaid. He may have had the rare privilege of being allowed into Turner's studio, for that was where the cupboards were.[2]

On the other side of this mute bargain, Turner found open house with the Ruskins. They were endlessly hospitable, proud, no doubt, to have the great man with them, while he made full use of their kindness. Whether tetchy, irritated or in good spirits, he would sit at their fireside, drink their sherry and touch obliquely on his work. Ruskin was always there to catch Turner's thoughts and attitudes and note them in his diary. Turner was with them in May 1842 when he brooded over ridicule of *Snow Storm – Steam-Boat off a Harbour's Mouth*. He had heard somebody say that it looked as if it had been painted in "soapsuds and whitewash". That cut Turner to the quick, and he sat muttering to himself in the armchair by the fire. "Soapsuds and whitewash! I wonder what they think the sea's like? I wish they'd been in it."[3] On another evening, Turner's buoyancy contributed to the success of Ruskin's twenty-fourth birthday party. "Turner happy and kind," Ruskin wrote.[4]

The author Mary Russell Mitford described Ruskin in the 1840s as a very elegant and distinguished-looking young man, tall, fair and slender – too slender, for there is a consumptive look, and I fear a consumptive tendency ... He must be, I suppose, twenty-six or twenty-seven, but he looks much younger, and has a gentle playfulness that is quite charming.[5]

It was this gentleness in Ruskin, his fresh looks, boyish playfulness and intuitive understanding of what Turner was about that attracted the painter to him. Though in his old age Turner had become gruff and shabby, with rough hands and nails ingrained with paint, he warmed to its opposite; he had been natty and energetic himself once. Having somebody so deeply interested in him as Ruskin seemed to be, asking intelligent questions, always understanding, or appearing to understand, the *reason* behind this picture or that, this was all flattering and heart-warming to the old man, who now only had Hannah and her cats as company at Queen Anne Street.

But sometimes even Ruskin failed to understand a point Turner was trying to make. Turner showed him *War: The Exile and the Rock Limpet* before it went off for exhibition at the Academy. "He tried hard one day, for a quarter of an hour, to make me guess what he was doing in the picture of 'Napoleon', ... giving me hint after hint, in a rough way; but I could not guess, and he would not tell me."[6] This was Turner's manner. For him, the painting carried all the information required for its full comprehension on the surface; the clues were there for all to see. It is possible that what Turner was trying to get at when he poked questions at Ruskin was not Ruskin's understanding of the iconography of *War*, which is straightforward enough, but his knowledge of Goethe's theory of colour. Although it does not feature in the story, *Peace* may very well have been included for comparison in the discussion. Turner's manner of teaching had always been to lead, even seduce, rather than direct. Ruskin was stimulated by this, but some of Turner's less analytical friends, David Roberts for example, found it annoying:

It was mysterious, and nothing seemed so much to please him as trying to puzzle you, or make you think so; for if he began to explain, or tell you anything, he was sure to break off in the middle, look very mysterious, nod, wink his eyes, saying to himself "make that out if you can."[7]

Ruskin's chosen title for *Modern Painters* was *Turner and the Ancients*, but although the publishers Smith, Elder & Co. objected to this and gave it the title we know, Turner's name appeared conspicuously on the title page of the first edition in a long abstract of the author's intentions. There could be

# MODERN PAINTERS:

## THEIR SUPERIORITY

### IN THE ART OF LANDSCAPE PAINTING

#### TO ALL

## THE ANCIENT MASTERS

#### PROVED BY EXAMPLES OF

## The True, the Beautiful, and the Intellectual,

#### FROM THE

## WORKS OF MODERN ARTISTS,

#### ESPECIALLY

## FROM THOSE OF J. M. W. TURNER, ESQ., R.A.

### BY A GRADUATE OF OXFORD.

"Accuse me not
Of arrogance,
If, having walked with nature,
And offered, far as frailty would allow,
My heart a daily sacrifice to Truth,
I now affirm of Nature and of Truth,
Whom I have served, that their Divinity
Revolts, offended at the ways of men,
Philosophers, who, though the human soul
Be of a thousand faculties composed,
And twice ten thousand interests, do yet prize
This soul, and the transcendent universe
No more than as a mirror that reflects
To proud Self-love her own intelligence."
WORDSWORTH.

### LONDON:
SMITH, ELDER AND CO., 65, CORNHILL.

1843.

Title page of *Modern Painters*, by "A Graduate of Oxford" [i.e. John Ruskin], 1843. University of Birmingham Library.

no doubt from the first that this was a pioneering polemic, intended to direct public taste and dispel misunderstanding. "It was written," Ruskin wrote pointedly to Samuel Prout, "for the class of people who admire Maclise; for the paid novices of *The Times* and of *Blackwood*, not for *you*, or for any like you."[8] In a direct riposte to the Rev. John Eagles, whose criticism had prompted Ruskin to leap for his pen in the first instance, Ruskin's preface opens with the words: "The work now laid before the public originated in indignation at the shallow and false criticisms of the periodicals of the day on the works of the great living artist to whom it principally refers."

Ruskin sent Turner a copy when *Modern Painters* was published in May 1843, but heard nothing from him on the subject until Turner quietly thanked Ruskin when the two met at dinner more than a year later with Griffith and William Windus.[9] There is no doubt that Turner had read it, in part at least, for he confided to Mary Lloyd: "Have you read '*Ruskin on Me*'? I said 'No.' He replied 'But you will some day,' and then added with his own peculiar shrug, 'He sees *more* in my pictures than I ever painted!' But he seemed very much pleased."[10]

The coming of summer raised Turner's spirits, and even in his late sixties he looked forward to crossing the Channel again. He went indefatigably to Switzerland in the four summers 1841 to 1844, taking younger companions on two of the tours at least. On one trip he was spotted on a Lake Como steamer by the painter and photographer William Lake Price who wrote:

> Turner held in his hand a tiny book, some two or three inches square, in which he continuously and rapidly noted down one after another of the *changing* combinations of mountain, water, trees etc ... until some *twenty* or more had been stored away in the hour-and-a-half's passage.[11]

The key point here is that in forty or fifty years of travelling Turner's methods of gathering information as it slowly passed by him had not changed in the slightest, and he was still using the books that he could safely hold in the palm of his hand and stuff away in his coat pocket. As an old hand at the game, he had learned to travel light, was completely self-sufficient and knew that the old tried methods were best. He travelled to *look* rather than to paint; painting took place in the inn at the end of the day, as it always had.

> Turner used to walk about a town with a roll of thin paper in his pocket, and make a few scratches upon a sheet or two of it, which were so much shorthand indication of all he wished to remember. When he got to his inn in the evening, he completed the pencilling

rapidly, and added as much colour as was needed to record his plan for the picture.[12]

This observation must have come to Ruskin in conversation with Turner himself, because although he went to the continent in Turner's footsteps, he did not accompany the master.

On many Swiss watercolours of this period, Turner used pen and red ink for highlights or to emphasise the presence of distant buildings. In some cases these markings stand proud of the paint surface like etching ink. Despite his reservations about drawing with pen and ink because he found pens to be apt to sputter,[13] these little criss-crosses or hieroglyphics recall Turner's vignette manner and the calligraphy in *Fairfaxiana*. They are the same kind of calligraphic markings which he had long used on many of his exhibition oil paintings, for example in the window frames of Greenwich Hospital in *London*, or the foreground figures of soldiers in *Hannibal*.

In many oil paintings of the 1830s and 1840s Turner mixed his media yet more drastically by painting watercolour detail onto the dried surface of oil paint. The tiny detail of the rope pulling the lifeboat towards the shipwreck in *Life-Boat and Manby Apparatus* (1831) is pure watercolour, the line having broken up into dots by the resistant action of the oily paint surface. Two unnamed painter friends of Turner were caught out by this technique. Left alone in the Gallery, and thinking that Turner himself was away, one said to the other looking at an oil painting "I'm certain that's watercolour." He wet his finger and rubbed it along a detail of masts and rigging, which immediately disappeared. Turner was watching them through his peep-hole, for he growled from the next room, and the visitors fled in panic.[14]

Though constantly experimenting with techniques that pleased him, Turner was nevertheless dismissive and aggressive when he disapproved of new developments rationally chosen by others. During one evening, probably in the late 1840s, he and other artists were discussing the use of opaque white in watercolour as an alternative to creating lights through scraping the paper or leaving it blank:

> Turner was generally a reticent talker, but on this occasion he wound up a strong speech by shaking his fist at Harding, Roberts and some others, who were supporting feebly the *convenience* of the vulgarising material in question, and saying quite fiercely "if you fellows continue to use that beastly stuff you will destroy the art of water-colour painting in our country."[15]

In his old age Turner found he had a web of interlocking friendships, which, as a whole, filled the spaces left by the loss of Fawkes and

Egremont. Some, such as his friendships with Hawkesworth Fawkes, Henry Trimmer and Clara Wheeler, had deep roots in his life. Another was unique and serendipitous. Hearing that Turner was in the vicinity in the autumn of 1845, King Louis Philippe invited the artist to his château at Eu on the Normandy coast. They dined and talked, spending "one of the pleasantest of evenings" together.[16] This, Turner's last journey to the Continent, was given its own unexpected royal benediction. Other friendships, interlocking through profession, marriage and geography, included John Ruskin, Thomas Griffith and Elhanan Bicknell, a businessman and whaling entrepreneur who lived with his populous family in a large house in Herne Hill. Bicknell was the representative of the new breed of Turner patrons in just the same way that Fawkes and Egremont had been types of two earlier breeds of collector rooted in the eighteenth century. By the late 1830s Bicknell had made his fortune through investment in the whaling industry and in refining spermaceti at his works in London, and had begun to lay the foundations of a large collection of modern English art. By the time Turner came to know him, Bicknell had married his third wife, Sarah, the sister of "Phiz" Dickens's illustrator Hablôt Knight Browne. His son by his second marriage, Henry, had married David Roberts's daughter Christine in 1841, and by the same year Elhanan and Sarah had had six children of their own. In its size, age range and interests, the Bicknell family was directly comparable to the Fawkeses and the Egremonts, and, like Fawkes, Bicknell found it impossible to remain a widower for long.[17]

Bicknell's hospitality was as generous as his collection was wide, and Turner was a regular guest at his table. The Bicknell circle overlapped with others of which Turner was a member – the Ruskins were neighbours in Herne Hill and, from 1843 nearby in Denmark Hill; Griffith lived in Norwood – and through this geographical accident home comforts were freely available to Turner within a very small area of south-east London. Turner could be the life and soul of many of the parties he attended, charming the women, making speeches, but he was also apt to sulk quietly, apparently unable to mask the expression of his moods. "Turner was not in spirits," Christine Bicknell wrote in her diary.[18] At another time, "Turner was particularly talkative to me about Devonshire & an unfortunate trip he made to the Channel Islands." And another: "Turner was in very good humour & returned thanks [at a fiftieth wedding party] for the toast 'the single married & the married happy' with a great many ah-ah-ahs."[19] Turner's many long absences from Queen Anne Street in the 1840s may be explained not only by his slipping off to Mrs Booth in Margate or Deal, but by his putting up at Herne Hill or Denmark Hill with the Bicknells or the Ruskins.

Bicknell did not buy in small measures. In 1844 alone he bought eight Turners, including *Palestrina*, *Wreckers* and *Ehrenbreitstein*, an act that caused Ruskin to become "quite beside myself with joy."[20] Talking with Turner as he must have done about the whaling industry, Bicknell suggested, and possibly commissioned, Turner's four whaling subjects. Whaling was a natural subject for Turner, though not one that might have struck him had he never known Bicknell. Epitomising massive animal force living in an element hostile to man, whales were a rational evolution from the monster subjects of Turner's young manhood, and from the writhing serpent allusions of his early poems. Whalers, whale hunts and sea monsters haunted Turner's late sketches and watercolours, as much as the industrial processes for exploiting their carcasses fascinated him. Although he might have seen whales – one caught off Deptford was displayed there in October 1842[21] – he had not witnessed a whale hunt, nor had he ever sailed where he might have seen them swimming freely. Turner's whaling pictures, unlike any other of his subject groupings which were all based on direct experience, were the unique group in his *œuvre* which he treated entirely from hearsay, reading, other men's pictures and from his imagination. He had caught many fish, from minnows to pike, but whales were another thing entirely and, as *Sunrise with Sea Monsters* indicates, they drew his mind further towards imagination, fantasy and suggestion. Bicknell did not in the event acquire a whaling subject. If they had been commissioned it will have been through the open, easygoing contract that Turner observed with his friends in the latter years.

Turner's relationship with Bicknell differed from that with Fawkes and Egremont in one major respect. Neither of the two earlier patrons engaged in business with Turner. Bicknell, however, natural businessman that he was, made the mistake of doing so by becoming involved in 1845 with a plan to engrave *The Fighting Téméraire*. Turner demanded fifty proofs of the engraving, while Bicknell offered eight, and as a result they quarrelled.[22] The quarrel was exacerbated when Bicknell found watercolour detail on Turner's *Whalers*[23] "and rubbed out some with Handky. He went to Turner who looked daggers and refused to do anything, but at last he has taken it back to alter."[24]

Other industrialist patrons who bought from Turner in the 1840s included the Manchester cotton-spinner Henry McConnel, the Birmingham ironfounder Edwin Bullock and the pen manufacturer, also from Birmingham, Joseph Gillott. The shift in wealth from London to the large English cities, combined with Turner's legendary status and high prices, made approaches to him from rich men in the provinces inevitable.[25] Though there are stories, principally written by Thornbury,[26] which caricature some of them, these industrialist collectors had extreme sensibility, and a determination to fill their galleries with the best. For his part Turner behaved professionally towards his clients; it was his business and his practice to do so. When Edwin Bullock came to town Turner wrote a formal note to him responding to his call and saying that "Mr T. will do himself the honour of waiting upon Mr Bullock immediately."[27]

Turner's sense of the value and irreplaceability of time still drove him, even as he approached seventy. While he had the bodily strength he did not let up. Writing to Clara, who more than anybody knew what it was like to be Turner, he said in his decoratively elliptical way:

> I had intended to call [on you] in G[race] Church St yesterday but the Enemy beat me. Time always hangs hard upon me, but his auxiliary, Dark weather, has put me quite into the background, although before Xmas I conceived myself in advance of Mr Time.

He told Clara how despite the cold he was determined to continue some work he had set himself at the Academy.

> I have got a Macintosh and with some fur round the shoulders I hope to fare better betwixt heat and the cold. If not I will give in for everyone feels the variety of the temperature of the Life Academy to be very bad ... I have been to the RA to study. It is equal hot and cold like Death.[28]

The force that drove Turner in these years came from his sense of responsibility that, since the 1810s at least, had never left him. He was a chronically sick man, and though he could sustain his activities by will power, he remained susceptible to infection and fear of the cold. His responsibilities expressed themselves in three ways – to the young in particular, to the Royal Academy, and to the British public in general. He may have been approached many times during his maturity by people seeking his help and advice in educating their children as artists, but evidence of only one instance survives. John Hammersley of Stoke-on-Trent wrote in 1838 to ask Turner for advice, though probably not direct tuition for his son. Turner drafted and redrafted a reply with a clear anxiety that the advice he would give for the son of a total stranger should be right:

> I have I truly must say written three times and now hesitate, for did I know your son's works or as you say his *gifted merit*, yet even then I would rather advise you to think well and not be carried away by the admiration ... which ardent friends to early talent may assume. They know not the difficulties ... in regard to yourself it is you alone can judge how far you are inclined to support him during perhaps a long period of expense, and particularly if you look towards tuition the more so – for it cannot ensure success, (however it may facilitate the

practice) and therefore it behoves you to weigh well the means in your power before you embark him in a profession which requires more care, assiduity and perseverance than any person can guarantee.[29]

This letter has echoes of the words of understanding Turner spoke to his students from the lecturer's podium at the Academy, in which he assured the students that they were not alone, earlier generations of artists were with them, and that "the joint endeavours of concording abilities ... [would] ... irrevocably fix the united standard of the arts in the British Empire."[30]

Turner was equally free with advice of incomparable sense and clarity for those who pleased and amused him, and listened to his stories. Mary Lloyd met him three or four times a week at gatherings with the Eastlakes, Carrick Moores and Rogerses, and when Mary married, the "small bent figure" with the "kind, shy manner [and] ... grey glittering eyes" used to dine with her and her husband in Hertford Street off Piccadilly. Some of Mary Lloyd's memories of Turner have already been quoted, but the most direct advice came to her in words which every painter should pin up in the studio:

First of all, respect your paper! Keep your corners quiet. Centre your interest. And always remember that as you can never reach the *brilliancy* of Nature, you need never be afraid of putting your brightest light next to your deepest shadow, in the *centre*, but not in the *corners* of your picture.[31]

To the Royal Academy he remained loyal to his death, expressing his fury on its behalf when told by Daniel Maclise in 1846 that Haydon had shot himself. Remembering the cruelty of Haydon's attacks on the Academy Turner growled, but did not look up from his painting. "He stabbed his mother! He stabbed his mother!" he repeated over and over again as Maclise walked out of the studio, out of the house and into the street.[32]

The worldly status of President of the Royal Academy that might have been Turner's in 1830 after Lawrence died did eventually come to him, but in a faint echo of the real thing. The President Martin Archer Shee was seriously ill in the mid-1840s, and George Jones and Turner between them shared the work of President and Deputy President. But it gave Turner no pleasure now; he was too ill for the task and careless of the honour of Deputy President. "Happy New-Year when it comes," he wrote to Hawkesworth Fawkes:

– in regard to my health sorry to say the tiresome and unpleasant duties of [presiding] during the continued illness of our President for two years ... it distroyed my happiness and appetite [so] that what with the business and weak[ness] I was oblidged to give [up] my Summer's usual trip abroad – but thank Heaven I shall be out of office on Thursday the 31 of this month.[33]

To the British public he felt a profound responsibility to articulate a sense of national history and social progress. The historical undertow that he had given to his *Southern Coast* and *England and Wales* series runs through the imagery like the warp in a tapestry, underpinning the entire structure yet sometimes remaining elusive to view. *The Fighting Téméraire* is one of the clearest examples of Turner speaking for Britain; another, equally resonant in its meaning, is *Rain, Steam and Speed – the Great Western Railway*, exhibited at the Royal Academy in 1844.

Rushing out of wind-blown torrential rain, the steam engine pounds across Brunel's new bridge over the Thames at Maidenhead, rapidly catching up on a hare which runs away in front. That is one reading; another is that the train will never catch the hare. To the side of this apparent ambiguity are passengers in a boat and a group of figures like angels waving from the river bank, drenched to the skin, at the magical apparition passing above their heads. Had Turner wanted to show what it felt like to be in a train, or what the train looked like, he would have done so. Instead, he paints a blur, and gives us the retinal after-image of the great machine that has just this second passed by out of sight. The suggested reading that the hare is beating the train can be dismissed when we notice the three well-spaced puffs of smoke that run horizontally along the line of the train. That all too clearly indicates so high a speed that the hare could never attain it. *The Times* critic of 1844 put his finger on the central paradox of the painting: "Whether Turner's pictures are dazzling unrealities, or whether they are realities seized upon at a moment's glance, we leave his detractors and admirers to settle between them."[34]

Other artists who made paintings and prints of railway subjects during the "Railway Mania" period of the late 1830s and 1840s conveyed the prosaic mechanics of the railway engine or the grandeur of the landscape it could conquer. Turner, however, takes us back to the four elements, succinctly graded in their status to reflect the social change that the railway has brought. Water pervades the painting – in the rain that the engine ignores, the steam that drives it and the river that it flies across. Fire heats the water to make the steam; the train flashes through the Air, from nothing to nothing, while the angelic figures can only wave at it *from below* as it passes by. Earth is here too – in the figure of the lone ploughman low down on the right labouring with the old technology, trudging hopelessly in the filthy weather and in the opposite direction.[35]

Turner was now regarded by a wide circle of artists, his own circle certainly, and others far beyond his own acquaintance, as "the greatest living Englishman," "the greatest man living" and "the world's greatest genius". J. C. Horsley RA described him at the gathering where he railed against opaque white as "omnipotent, and standing completely alone".[36] The meaning of this can truly be extended to the position that Turner held in the world. And how well he knew it – one evening, having had too much to drink in a London hotel with Hawkesworth Fawkes, he staggered about exclaiming: "Hawkey, I am the real lion, I am the great lion of the day, Hawkey,"[37] as fellow diners looked away.

On the other hand, there were many highly intelligent men and women who thought otherwise. Robert Browning wrote to Alfred Domett in 1843, after he had seen *Shade and Darkness* and *Light and Colour* at the Academy exhibition, "Turner is hopelessly gone."[38] His *Opening of the Walhalla*, 1842, though exhibited in London to wide praise in 1843, was dismissed and ridiculed when he sent it to the Congress of European Art exhibition in Munich in 1845. The difficulty it faced in Germany was a direct result of the success of Turner's work as a creator of imagery for engraving. Ironically, where Turner's engravers had done him the greatest justice, his own painting, among an audience unfamiliar to it, was misunderstood, and thought to be an insult: "One knew Turner from the lovely steel engravings after his drawings and imagined, therefore, that one had been honoured by a lampoon by him ... For his contribution to the Munich art exhibition he goes down in history ... as a dauber."[39]

The easiest laughs came from those critics who used culinary metaphors to describe Turner's painting. There were many of them published in the 1840s, as if one critic after another seemed to compete to squeeze the metaphor to death at Turner's expense. Of *Snow Storm*, for example, the critic of the *Athenaeum* wrote: "This gentleman has, on former occasions, chosen to paint with cream, or chocolate, yolk of egg or currant jelly – here he uses his whole array of kitchen stuff."[40] Turner appreciated the inventive side of some of these remarks, for at a dinner party he looked at the salad and said to his neighbour: "Nice cool green that lettuce, isn't it? and the beetroot pretty red – not quite strong enough; and the mixture, delicate tint of yellow that. Add some mustard, and then you have one of my pictures."[41]

For all the reports of Turner at this soirée and that gathering in the 1840s we might believe he was forever enjoying a party and the company of ladies. "None but the brave deserve the fair," he said to Mary Lloyd when, rowing her and some girl friends across the river at Hampton Court, he tried with his uncertain legs to land the party on a sedgy bank. Mary Lloyd thought he was about eighty at this time; he did not live that long, but he will certainly have been seventy. Even at seventy his creative sexual appetite did not desert him; there are drawings of female genitalia and copulation in the "Dieppe and Kent" sketchbook of 1845.[42]

There are few dateable traces of Turner's visits to Margate and the Kent coast in the mid-1840s, but the sketchbooks suggest that he was backwards and forwards regularly. While making such visits to Sophia Booth, he was also arranging for them both to share a small house beside the river at Chelsea. Probably by the autumn of 1846 he and Sophia had taken 6 Davis Place, a two storey cottage near the end of a terrace at the further edge of Chelsea, looking across at Battersea. Sophia Booth, and not Turner, was the lessee. This placid stretch of water upstream of the bridges was totally different in character to the other stretch of the river in which Turner had an interest, Wapping and the Docks. At Davis Place he was not, to the world, J. M. W. Turner RA. That distinguished gentleman lived with his housekeeper in a substantial if dilapidated town house, with adjacent gallery, in the Portland Estates. The gentleman who first handed Sophia Booth across the doorstep at Davis Place, short, with grey, glittering eyes, dressed to the edge of shabbiness with a top hat and umbrella, that was "Mr Booth".

There was no concerted intention to deceive in this curious domestic arrangement, or to run a double life. Hannah Danby had had to get used to Turner's disappearances for long periods, while Sophia Booth was a respectable widow, and encouraged the "Mr Booth" nonsense. But she knew exactly who "Mr Booth" was, and went so far as to tease local people in Chelsea by saying that her "husband" was a great man. Sophia and Turner went out on the river together, as Turner himself had done at all stages of his life, but now the pair were rowed about by watermen. There are anecdotal stories about Turner drinking from a bottle of gin as the boatmen rowed "the Booths" along, and of his being referred to as "the Admiral" or "Puggy Booth".[43] Among some of the locals Turner's disguise held, and, despite Sophia's heavy hints, few tumbled to the fact that this was the creator of *The Fighting Téméraire*.

His disguise, however, was thin, and was put at risk when he went regularly to a Chelsea barber's shop for a haircut or shave. Now the wheel was coming full circle, and Turner evidently revealed himself in this busy Chelsea information exchange; the paint ingrained into his hands and scalp most probably betrayed him. As Turner's own father had done sixty years earlier, the barber told his customer something to the effect of "my young brother is going to be a painter." "Let me see his drawings," Turner growled. So Francis Sherrell arrived at 6 Davis Place with a portfolio. The drawings impressed Turner, who took Sherrell on as a studio assistant in return for painting lessons.[44] Once, a retired barber had been Turner's assistant; now that place was taken by a barber's younger brother.

Turner had a small roof terrace built behind the parapet of 6 Davis Place where he could sit and watch the sun and the river. The view to the right, looking west up the river he called the English view; down river to the east was the Dutch view. J. C. Horsley recalled how Turner possessed the faculty ... of awakening at any hour he mentally fixed on going to bed, and in turning out he would swathe himself in one of the blankets on his couch, then ... he would ascend [to the roof] just before sunrise, and if there was a fair promise of an effective rising he would remain to study it, making pencil notes of the form of clouds, and writing in brief their tints of colour.

Then he would go back to bed and paint on rising again.[45] "There are times, sir," Sophia told the picture dealer Vokins, "when I feel he must be a god."[46]

None of Turner's painter friends knew where he went when he left them after an evening at the Academy or the Athenaeum. They knew it was not to go to Queen Anne Street, because they could check up on that at any time. Curious to find out his destination they would try tricks like bouncing Turner into giving an address to direct the cabbie, but all he would say was "Along Piccadilly, and I will then tell him."[47] At other times, knowing he was being followed he might leap onto a passing omnibus going anywhere, or slip into dark corners or double back to confuse the eager young men trying to follow him. Once, however, he was caught out; it was only a matter of time. He was spotted by an acquaintance and his son early one morning on a steam boat leaving Chelsea pier for the City. He was bright and clean shaven, with shiny boots, and had patently just left home. His friend said that he must live in the area now; but all Turner would say in reply was "Is that your boy?"[48]

Turner's attitude to his privacy varied with his mood. He welcomed his neighbour the painter John Martin into his house, having walked him over from Queen Anne Street.[49] Close though he instinctively was about his private affairs, it may be that he never expected "Mr Booth" to come back to live in London. Far away in Margate or Deal "Mr Booth" was an amusing enough cover; and he could walk up and down the sands at Margate with Mrs Booth on his arm and his sketchbook in his pocket. But things change. When Turner became seventy he wanted to be in sight of the Thames in his last few years, not a mile from the river north of Oxford Street. That is the motive for the move given by Sophia in conversation with J. W. Archer.[50] There was no possibility of his setting up house on his own at his age, so Sophia insisted on coming with him.

Sophia Booth gave Turner a new lease of life, tidied him up, fussed over him, and mothered him as his father had done. Turner did not give her a penny towards his keep, but she was prepared to do it, and in return he was Sophia's hero figure, a "great man", a "god" for her to adore and tend. When David Roberts called at the Chelsea house the summer after Turner died, he described Mrs Booth as a "tall, lusty woman" who kept the cottage "clean to a nicety".[51] There was a small garden behind railings at the front, and another at the back where Turner sat and walked. He caught a starling in the garden, and kept it in a cage in the porch, and made a fuss of it.[52]

Meanwhile, at Queen Anne Street, the house was becoming more and more dilapidated, and the gallery falling to bits. The glass in the skylights was broken, the floor wet and stained with rainwater, the rich red wall-covering faded, torn and hanging off in rags. Hannah's half dozen or more Manx cats roamed free about the house, padding over drawings left lying about, jumping up onto the picture frames, bedding down where they wished, and giving the place the nauseating smell of cat. They came and went through a hole in a window partly covered by an old canvas – this canvas cat-flap was in fact Turner's painting *Fishing upon the Blythe-Sand* of 1809. The slippage of standards from the neatness and order that Turner had built devoutly into his life in the 1820s had already begun as early as 1842 when the young painter William Leighton Leitch came to see Turner's pictures. It was raining, and Leitch had to keep his umbrella up: "I walked backwards and forwards in the gallery ... feeling cold an uncomfortable – no sound to be heard but the rain splashing through the broken windows upon the floor." He looked at the pictures in their melancholy state. The sky in *The Building of Carthage* "was cracking – not in the ordinary way, but in long lines, like ice when it begins to break up. Other parts of the picture were peeling off – one piece, I recollect, just like a stiff ribbon turning over."

Then Leitch felt something warm and soft moving across the back of his neck, and over onto his shoulder. He turned his head and found himself face to face with the pink, glaring eyes of an enormous cat, of a dirty white colour with the fur sticking out. He pushed the animal away, dropping his umbrella as he did so. This disturbed four or five more cats which rushed up to him and curled about his legs. Leitch ran out of the room, down the stairs and out of the house, shutting the door behind him with a bang.[53]

Although Turner might appear without any warning at Queen Anne Street, Hannah was normally the only soul living there. At some time during her years with Turner the debilitating skin condition which she suffered had spread to her face. This caused her to cover herself in embarrassment when visitors called, and led to her being dismissed with revulsion, most cruelly by Elizabeth Rigby, Lady Eastlake, who called her "a hag of a woman, for whom one hardly knew what to feel most, terror or pity."[54] She was in no condition to make any impression whatever on the state of the house or gallery, and Turner would probably not have wanted her to touch anything. Opposing forces in Turner's character impelled him both to show intense anger if anybody tried to help him even with the most minor repairs to his paintings, and a pathetic attitude of fatalism which led him to allow his house, his gallery and his great pictures to fall into rack and ruin. A contemporary described the house as having, from the outside, the appearance of a place in which some great crime had been committed.[55]

One attitude reflects the proud artist, self-sufficient, omnipotent; the other is a microcosm of the inevitable decay of empire which he had played out on canvas and was now expressing through his life. Though he might cruelly neglect the physical condition of his masterpieces, while wanting the nation to honour them, he had for years been ensuring that his paintings became more and more widely known through engravings. If there was a trace of madness in Turner in his last years, it was not expressed through his chromatic achievements on paper and canvas, but in his domestic life. Having created one dung-hill, he could only remove himself from it and start again somewhere else. The decay at Queen Anne Street reflects as much on Hannah's decline as on Turner's, and one might hazard that had Hannah died in the 1840s Turner would have gingerly introduced Sophia to Queen Anne Street in the hopes that she might clean that to a nicety too. His loyalty and fondness for Hannah, however, who in late letters he was referring to as "my Damsel", and remembering "the olden time" of her "culinary exploits",[56] made any changes in the arrangements at Queen Anne Street unthinkable.

Sophia was probably Turner's companion on one of his visits to the studio of the photographer J. J. E. Mayall, who had set up shop under the name of "Professor Highschool" in West Strand in 1847. Mayall wrote a long account of meeting the man whom he later knew to be Turner, although he was led at the time by "the inquisitive old man" and his lady to believe that he was a Master in Chancery.[57] The remarkable gentleman came again and again to Professor Highschool's shop, and Mayall took "several admirable daguerreotype portraits of him, one in the act of reading. ... I recollect one of these portraits was presented to the lady who accompanied him." On one of the visits, Turner stayed for "some three hours, talking about light and its curious effects on films of prepared silver. He expressed a wish to see the spectral image copied, and asked me if I had ever repeated Mrs Somerville's experiment on magnetising a needle in the rays of the spectrum. I told him I had."

On other visits, "always with some new notion about light", he was fascinated by Mayall's daguerreotypes of the Niagara Falls. Turner evidently gave his name to Mayall because his visits were so frequent that he became known in the shop as "our Mr Turner". One wonders, having met him over so long a period, talked very intelligently with him about light and colour and known his name to be Turner, why Mayall was so bone-headed as to continue to think he was a Chancery lawyer.

Turner went back to Queen Anne Street on routine visits from time to time, to show people round the gallery, to collect his post, to put a pathetic brave face on his gathering infirmities and signal to Hannah that every-thing was in order. It is unlikely, however, that he painted there much after the end of 1846. His exhibit at the 1847 Academy was an old canvas, taken presumably from the untidy stacks of such paintings in his studio or the store at the back of the gallery. As had become his practice, he now worked extensively on his exhibits on the Varnishing Days, and given the nature of the 1847 painting, this must have happened again this year. The painting he sent was a gloomy brown and green interior of a water-powered foundry, which he had made at least forty years earlier. He knew exactly what he was doing when he heaved it out; he remembered he had it, and this was the one he wanted. On the Academy wall he dusted it off, looked over the foundry wheels with the woman sitting beside them and the scattered still life in the foreground, and painted in large gestural strokes of red, yellow and white the vision of a giant equestrian statue of the Duke of Wellington emerging from the furnace on casting.

Of course, the idea is preposterous, the statue by Matthew Wyatt was cast in sections, not in one piece, but the proud contour of the Duke on his charger Copenhagen is unmistakable. The statue, which had been seven years in the making, was installed at Hyde Park Corner in 1846 to great public controversy. By rekindling such a topical subject on canvas at the Academy, and giving the heroic Duke the aspect of an angel of the Apocalypse, Turner was once again touching on a controversial issue as he had so often throughout his career. Only the old foundry, juxtaposed with the ducal apocalypse, could convey the message that the Duke of Wellington, who was born in the era of water powered mills and foundries, had come to glory in the new Victorian age as *The Hero of a Hundred Fights*.

The young artist Charles Hutton Lear saw Turner at the Academy in May 1847. He wrote:

> There is no evidence of unhealthy biliousness in his face. It is red and full of living blood, and although age has left its mark upon him it does not seem to have taken the energy of his mind, for that lives in the observant eye and that compressed mouth, the evidence of an acute, penetrating intellect, which I may mention is seen in the whole contour of his face. He is a great little man – and all acknowledge it.

Turner walked about the galleries giving his advice on Varnishing Day as he always did, "a little man dressed in a long tail coat, thread gloves, big shoes and a hat of a most miserable description made doubly melancholy by the addition of a piece of broad shabby dingy crape encircling two thirds at least."[58]

Sophia took Turner to Margate in the summer of 1847, and to Deal early in 1849. By the autumn of 1848 another cholera epidemic was killing hundreds of people daily throughout the country. This time the newspapers carried advice about what to do if stricken,[59] and published lists of the numbers of the dead. Chelsea, then a poor area of London with bad drains and prone to flooding, was listed as having one of the highest rates of mortality from cholera north of the river.[60] Despite Sophia's efforts to protect him, Turner caught the disease. Ironically, he would have been less likely to have done so had he been living in 47 Queen Anne Street with its rudimentary water closet, reasonable drains and well paved streets. In the good air beside the sea in Deal Sophia and her doctor, David Price of Margate, treated him. Dr Price had looked after Turner when he had been in Margate since the late 1830s, though he did not seem to know until much later who his patient was. He claimed he prescribed to "Mr Smith or Thompson or whatever name he called himself". The doctor's opinion was that Turner's bout of cholera in 1848/49 should have killed him: "had he not had the most extraordinary constitution, with his habits as [Dr Price] termed it, he could never have got over it." The real credit for Turner's survival goes to Sophia, who gave him unstinting love and care, her attention to him "most unwearied, being up night & day, indeed ... he wanted for nothing."[61]

Incredibly, this iron man made a total recovery and started painting for exhibition again. Turner had showed nothing at the 1848 Academy, but in 1849 returned with two earlier canvases one of which he reworked. This was *The Wreck Buoy* which he had sold perhaps ten years earlier to Munro of Novar. Munro had taken it home to Scotland, but at Turner's irresistible request he sent it down to London again especially for the exhibition. What he did not expect, however, was that Turner would first put the canvas up on his easel and spend six days repainting it.[62]

Instantly returning to full control of his life, Turner snatched back his physical strength, his lucidity and his social poise. The great lion of the day would not be taken so easily. Francis Palgrave met Turner at a soirée "within a few months before we lost him", and found him "talking with eminent sense and shrewdness". Their host had shown the party a copy of an early printed book, and

Turner talked of the mysteries of bibliography and the tangle of politics neither wittily, nor picturesquely, nor technically; but as a man of sense before all things ... He appeared as secure in health, as firm in tone of mind, as keen in interest, as when I had seen him years before; as ready in his dry short laugh, as shrewd in retort, as unsoftened in that straightforward bearing which seems to make drawing room walls start and frightens diners-out from their propriety.

He was the centre of the conversation, and when he left the party, laughing and talking freely, "he stepped sturdily through the door, and turned down the few steps into Piccadilly from our sight."[63]

Though poignantly chipper in his bearing at gatherings such as this, Turner nevertheless had great physical pain which he could only dull through drink. He was drinking at the Athenaeum or the Academy with a fellow Academician who had had too much, and who complained as he was leaving of seeing two cabs. "That's all right, old fellow," said Turner. "Do as I do. Get into the first one." By 1850 Turner had his own regular cabman, "a little bandy legged dwarf about two heads shorter than himself, with whom he seemed to be on intimate terms and spoke of putting him in a livery."[64]

Sophia's care made Turner keep appearances up, though he did reveal himself to Ruskin. "A man may be weak in his age," he said, "but you must not tell him so." And finding that his hands would not obey him, he burst into tears in Ruskin's presence.[65] His teeth gave him increasing trouble, and in his last year he had to have them all removed and be fitted with false teeth which probably made things worse. He could not bite, and with raw gums had to suck meat to sustain himself. A local surgeon dentist, William Bartlett, under Dr Price's orders, put him on a diet of rum and milk, of which he would drink up to eight pints a day.[66]

Despite the onset of this painful and humiliating decay, Turner made four final paintings for the Royal Academy exhibition of 1850. They returned to his lifelong theme of the story of Dido and Aeneas, and knowing how lucid Turner was by Palgrave's report in his last few months, these pictures with their fluttering brushstrokes are his final messages to humanity from the edge of the grave rather than the efforts of a tired old man returning in senility to his old haunts. He worked on the paintings at Chelsea, the canvases being propped up on easels around him, going from one to the other in the production line method he had used at Queen Anne Street.[67]

Sophia took him to Margate and Deal for the summer and autumn of 1850. Turner's last broad watercolours, wide washes with highlights of colour dabbed with instinctive artistry, may have been done at this time as he looked out over the sea. He would, however, keep his finger on the pulse of current affairs at the Academy, as if everything was perfectly all right with him. He was invited by C. R. Leslie to a discussion about the successor to Shee as President of the Academy at a meeting that cannot have taken place before the autumn of 1850. There he enjoyed his hot grog and flirted with Leslie's two daughters with "the indescribable charm of a sailor both in appearance and manners." He also spruced up the appearance of his house in Queen Anne Street by getting the windows cleaned, as an *Observer* correspondent noticed.[68]

From May 1850, Turner was under the more or less constant attention of Dr Price or William Bartlett. According to Dr Price's affidavit it was usually Turner, not Sophia, who took the initiative to call the doctor. This he did daily in May, and intermittently from June to September, running up a large bill. He knew now that he faced the end. Dr Price travelled backwards and forwards to see him between Margate and Chelsea, while William Bartlett acted as Price's locum. He touched on his "want of health" in late letters,[69] and calling on David Roberts put his hand on his breast and said: "There is something wrong here; it is no use hiding it but I feel something here is all wrong."[70] Nevertheless he kept moving, maintaining through his will power the pressure on his body to seek out the new and the inspirational both in art and life. He and Dr Price may have spoken about whales, for a 56 feet long Rosqual whale had been landed at Margate in February 1850, prompting Price to write to Richard Owen about it.[71] He went twice to South Kensington to see how the building of the Crystal Palace was progressing, reporting back by letter on both occasions to Hawkesworth Fawkes: "The Crystal Palace ... looks very well in front because the transept takes a centre like a dome, but sideways the ribs of Glass framework only Towering over the Galleries like a Giant."[72]

During these same months he kept up his social calls. One was to visit his fellow painter William Powell Frith and his family. Frith's daughter, Jane, then aged barely three, could "just recollect a little bent old man and being told his name, and having to thank him for a Madeira cake he brought for us children."[73]

Three months before Turner died, Dr Price knew that

> his heart was very extensively diseased and that life was fast ebbing. I then told him that he must prepare for the worst, that his days were numbered, and that he [had] better arrange any thing he had to do in this world and prepare for the next. He seemed at first staggered, but soon recovered and, looking hard at him with his little lustrous eye, said "Had you not better take a glass of sherry?"

The doctor did as he was asked, and Turner told him to come upstairs again when he had had it. A few minutes later Price returned. "Well, have you got another opinion?" Turner asked. Price shook his head gravely, and Turner replied, stuttering, "So I am to become a nonentity, am I?"

"I do not exactly understand what you mean by a nonentity – but it is as I tell you, your days are numbered and you are under sentence; I cannot state the day, but it is as I tell you."

"I think you had better go and have another glass of sherry," Turner replied.[74]

For much of his last three months Turner was in or near his bed in his room overlooking the river. Sophia set his brushes, paint and paper beside him, tidied his hair and plumped up his pillows, but he was restless and would never be still for long.

Looking out of the window he watched as some policemen pulled the body of a drowned girl out of the river, and insisted on going out to draw her face.[75] Moving in and out of lucidity, Sophia heard him repeating Lady Eastlake's name, and in an eagerness to see the sun again he dragged himself out of bed and crawled to the window, where Sophia found him collapsed, too weak to get back to bed. A few weeks before he died Turner remarked "the sun is God,"[76] but remembering his own mortality, and the religious perceptions that had floated lightly in the background of his life over the past twenty years, he may equally have said "the Son is God."

A figure unfamiliar to the streets of Chelsea found her way to Davis Place in early December. Hannah Danby had come across a note from Sophia Booth, with the address "Chelsea" on it, in a pocket of a coat Turner had left at Queen Anne Street. She had not seen hide nor hair of him for months, and though normally fearful of going out of the house, now found the courage to try to seek her old companion out. With a neighbour, Hannah went to Chelsea and walked up and down asking for Mrs Booth. At a ginger beer shop in Davis Place they were told that two very quiet *respectable* people called Booth lived next door, but that the old gentleman had been very ill and was supposed to be dying. Hannah then melted back with her friend to Queen Anne Street, and contacted Turner's executor, his cousin Henry Harpur of Islington. On 17th December Harpur took a cab to Chelsea, found the house, and was, reluctantly, admitted.[77]

Dr Price travelled from Margate to see his patient almost weekly during the last three months of 1851. He called as usual on 18th December, took Turner's pulse, measured his breathing, looked into his eyes, whispered quietly to Sophia. The following morning began gloomily, with thick clouds masking the sun. The river in that kind of December weather is dark browny green, flat, sombre, with none of the sparkling lights that it will always reflect from a morning sun. But just before nine o'clock the clouds began to break up and the sun came through and filled Turner's bedroom and shone directly and brilliantly upon him. William Bartlett and Sophia were beside him in that hour, and at ten o'clock, in silence, he died.

# Abbreviations given in Notes

| | |
|---|---|
| Alaric Watts | Alaric Watts: "Biographical Sketch of J. M. W. Turner Esq., RA" in *Liber Fluviorum*; H. G. Bohn, 1853. |
| Archer | "Reminiscences of J. M. W. Turner" by J. W. Archer; *Once a Week*, 1st February 1862, pp. 162–6. Reprinted *TS*, vol. 1, no. 1, pp. 31–7 (ed. Eric Shanes). |
| B&J | Martin Butlin and Evelyn Joll: *The Paintings of J. M. W. Turner*; Yale, 2 vols, revised edn, 1984. |
| DNB | *Dictionary of National Biography* |
| Falk | Bernard Falk: *Turner the Painter – His Hidden Life*; Hutchinson, 1938. |
| FD | *The Diary of Joseph Farington RA 1793–1821* (ed. Kenneth Garlick, Angus Macintyre & Kathryn Cave); 16 vols, Yale, 1978–84. |
| Finberg | A. J. Finberg: *The Life of J. M. W. Turner*; Clarendon Press, Oxford, 1939; revised edn 1961. |
| Gage | John Gage: *Collected Correspondence of J. M. W. Turner*; Clarendon Press, Oxford, 1980. |
| Gage: *CinT* | John Gage: *Colour in Turner – Poetry and Truth*; Studio Vista, 1969. |
| Gage: *WRM* | John Gage: *J. M. W. Turner – "A Wonderful Range of Mind"*; Yale, 1987. |
| *Gents Mag.* | *The Gentleman's Magazine* |
| Haydon: *Autobiography* | Tom Taylor (ed.): *The Autobiography and Memoirs of Benjamin Robert Haydon*; 1853. |
| Haydon: *Diaries* | W. B. Pope (ed): *The Diary of Benjamin Robert Haydon*; 5 vols, 1960. |
| Horsley | J. C. Horsley: *Recollections of an Academician*; Murray, 1903. |
| Jones | "Recollections of J. M. W. Turner" by George Jones. Published in John Gage: *Collected Correspondence of J. M. W. Turner*; Clarendon Press, Oxford, 1980, pp. 1–10. |
| C. R. Leslie | C. R. Leslie (ed. Tom Taylor): *Autobiographical Recollections*; 2 vols, 1860. |
| Lindsay | Jack Lindsay: *J. M. W. Turner – a Critical Biography*; Cory, Adams & Mackay, 1966. |
| OED | *Oxford English Dictionary* |
| PHA | Petworth House Archives. Administered by the West Sussex County Record Office, Chichester. |

| | |
|---|---|
| RA | Royal Academy, London. |
| Raimbach | M. T. S. Raimbach (ed.): *Memoirs and Recollections of the late Abraham Raimbach Esq*; F. Shobeel, 1843. |
| Redgrave | Richard and Samuel Redgrave: *A Century of Painters of the English School*; 2 vols, 1866. |
| RIBA | Royal Institute of British Architects, London. |
| Roberts | Helen Guiterman: "The Great Painter – Roberts on Turner"; *TS*, vol. 9, no. 1, pp. 1–9. |
| Ruskin: *Diaries* | J. Evans and J. H. Whitehouse (eds): *The Diaries of John Ruskin*; 3 vols, Oxford, 1956–59. |
| Ruskin: *Works* | Sir E. T. Cook and A. Wedderburn: *The Works of John Ruskin* (Library Edition); 39 vols, 1903–12. |
| Shanes: *THL* | Eric Shanes: *Turner's Human Landscape*; Heinemann, 1990. |
| *Sunny Memories* | "M. L." [Mary Lloyd]: *Sunny Memories*; privately printed, London, 1880, pp. 31–8. Republished as "A Memoir of J. M. W. Turner RA by "M. L.", *TS* vol 4, no. 1, pp. 22–3. |
| TB | Turner Bequest, Clore Gallery for the Turner Collection, Tate Gallery, London. |
| TFP | Turner Family Papers; Private Collection. |
| Thornbury | Walter Thornbury: *The Life and Correspondence of J. M. W. Turner RA*; 1862. The edition cited here is the revised edition, Chatto and Windus, 1897. |
| *TS* | *Turner Studies*; 11 vols, 1981–93. |
| *TSN* | *Turner Society News* |
| Uwins | Sarah Uwins: *A Memoir of Thomas Uwins RA*; 1858. |
| *Verse Book* | Andrew Wilton & Rosalind Mallord Turner: *Painting and Poetry – Turner's "Verse Book" and his Work of 1804–1812*; Tate Gallery, 1990. |
| Whitley | William T. Whitley: *Art in England 1800–1820*; 1928 and *1821–1827*; 1930. |
| Whittingham: *GMD* | Selby Whittingham: *Of Geese, Mallards and Drakes – Some Notes on Turner's Family 1 – The Danbys*; J. M. W. Turner RA Publications, 1993. |
| Wilton | Andrew Wilton: *Turner in his Time*; Thames and Hudson, 1989. |
| WYAS | West Yorkshire Archaeological Society, Leeds. |

# Notes

## PROLOGUE
### 27th April 1775

1 *Annual Register* 1775, p. 110.
2 May 1775, p. 251.
3 *Annual Register, loc. cit.*

## ONE
### MAIDEN LANE AND BRENTFORD

1 Two apprentice indentures, dated 1743 and 1757, name John Turner "Peruke Maker" and "Barber" of South Molton. North Devon Record Office. 814A/PO 472 & 648.
2 Will proved 6.7.1765; destroyed; draft TFP. The will named John Turner as a saddler, a trade he may have adopted late in life.
3 Apprentice indentures dated 1769 names a John Turner "sadler" [*sic*], and another, 1783, names a John Turner "woolcomber". North Devon RO, 814A/PO 811 & 970. Similarities in the signatures suggest that these are one and the same.
4 John Edmunds: *A History of South Molton*; 1986, p. 54ff.
5 Will proved 26.11.1741, TFP.
6 TFP.
7 Kenelm Foss: *The Double Life of J. M. W. Turner*; 1928, p. 18.
8 Thornbury, p. 5.
9 *ibid*, p. 4.
10 Adrian Room: *The Street Names of England*; Stamford, 1992, p. 48.
11 Exhibition catalogues, V&A, National Art Library, 200.B.168A.
12 *Adventures Underground*, quoted Lindsay, p. 12.
13 J. Timbs: *Anecdotal Biography*, 1863. In this passage Timbs was remembering the place as it was c. 1810.
14 John Gay: *The Beggar's Opera*, Act 1., Sc. 4.
15 Mallord (or possibly "Mallard") was misspelt "Mallad" in the Register.
16 JMWT's address in the 1790 RA catalogue is given as Maiden Lane, Covent Garden; in the 1791 as 26 Maiden Lane.
17 There is a tradition that a child, Mary Ann, baptised at St Paul's Covent Garden on 6th September 1778 as the daughter of William Turner by Mary his wife, was JMWT's sister. There is no further evidence that this is our family, beyond the strong coincidence of names, place and date. A further tradition that the family moved to St Martin's-in-the-Fields descends solely from the entry dated 20th March 1786 in the St Paul's Covent Garden Register which records the burial of "Mary Ann Turner from St Martin's in the Fields". It is supposition that this is the same Mary Ann Turner who was baptised at St Paul's on 6th September 1778, as is Mary Ann's ascription to William and Mary Turner.
18 R. B. Sheridan: *The Rivals*, Act 1 Sc. 1.
19 *The Times*, 6.1.1785.
20 F. A. Pottle (ed.): *Boswell's London Journal 1762–63*; Heinemann, 1950, p. 336.
21 A. R. Ellis (ed.): *The Early Diaries of Frances Burney 1768–1778*; Bell, London, 1913, vol. II, p. 289. A further corroboration: "Hair combed Coat 6d." *The Manhood Diary*, 17.8.1778; Catholic Record Society, 1956, vol. 50.
22 *The Works of the late Edward Dayes*, 1805, p. 353.
23 Sir Ambrose Heal: *London Goldsmiths 1200–1800*, 1935, p. 255.
24 *Notes and Queries*, 2nd series, vol. 128, 12.6.1858, p. 475. See also letter Samuel Johnson to Mr Tomkison of Southampton St, 1.10.1783; *The Letters of Samuel Johnson* (ed. Bruce Redford), vol. IV, 1782–84; Clarendon Press, Oxford, 1994.
25 Thornbury, p. 11. See also note 17 above.
26 *Victoria County History of Middlesex*, 1982, vol. VII, p. 116.
27 Macleod Yearsley (ed.): *Diary of the Visits of John Yeoman to London in the Years 1774 and 1777*; London, Watts & Co., 1934, p. 41.
28 *Victoria County History, cit.*, p. 165.

29 Doris Yarde: *Sarah Trimmer of Brentford and her Children*; Hounslow and District History Society, 1990, p. 83.

30 Subscription list, Greater London RO, Acc 728/1.

31 Kirby and Zoffany are known to have worked together in the 1770s. Zoffany painted the figures in Kirby's *Monk's Kitchen, Glastonbury*, exhib. Society of Artists 1770.

32 H. S. Trimmer (ed.): *Some Account of the Life and Writings of Mrs Trimmer*; Rivington, London, 3rd edn 1825, p. 7. Sarah won an award twice, in 1757 and 1758, with two ornamental pencil drawings, both of which are now in the Library of the Royal Society of Arts, B 45 & 46.

33 Mrs [Sarah] Trimmer: *Reflections upon the Education of Children in Charity Schools with the Outlines of a Plan of Appropriate Instruction for the Children of the Poor*; London, 1792, p. 10.

34 Thornbury, p. 8.

35 Fred Turner: *History and Antiquities of Brentford*; Pearce, Brentford, 1922, p. 126.

36 *Sunny Memories*.

37 Doris Yarde: *op. cit.*, pp. 17 & 83; and H. S. Trimmer: *op. cit.*, passim.

38 Thornbury, p. 14.

39 *ibid.*, p. 25; Ruskin: *Modern Painters*, vol. III, iv, 18, 31n. For an insight into Lowe's life see also: *Diary and Letters of Madame d'Arblay*; 1854, vol. II, pp. 27–8.

40 TB II, "Oxford" sketchbook, p. 26a.

41 Thornbury, p. 30.

42 Susan Morris: "Two Perspective Views: Turner and Lewis William Wyatt"; *TS*, vol. 2, no. 2, p. 34ff.

43 Thornbury, p. 32.

44 *Notes and Queries*, 2nd series, vol. 128, 12.6.1858, p. 475.

45 Thornbury, p. 30.

46 RIBA Library, SaT/1/1.

47 Redgrave, vol. 2, p. 83–4.

48 Thornbury, p. 27. Thomas Malton moved from Conduit St to Great Titchfield St in 1791, and in 1796 to Long Acre, where he died in 1804. DNB.

49 William L. Pressly (ed.): "Facts and Recollections of the XVIIIth Century in a Memoir of John Francis Rigaud Esq., RA by Stephen Francis Dutilh Rigaud"; *Walpole Society*, L, 1984, p. 105.

## Two
### "... AN EYE FOR NATURE ..."

1 Ref. Ann Dart's account of JMWT as a boy in the early 1790s, as reported to Ruskin in 1860. Ruskin, *Works*, XIII, p. 473. Turner's height was calculated from his trouser measurements which turned up in the 1870s. Ref. Walter Goodman: "Turner's Trousers"; *The Athenaeum*, 23.2.1878, p. 259.

2 *First Discourse*, 2.1.1769.

3 As counted by Finberg. The register for November 1792 to March 1793 is missing.

4 *Second Discourse*, 11.12.1769.

5 Samuel Rogers: *Table-Talk*; Moxon, London, 1856, p. 20; James Northcote: *Life of Reynolds*; vol. ii, 1819, p. 236.

6 JMWT's Perspective Lectures BM Add MS 46151, K, fo. 2.

7 DNB.

8 See M. Kirby Talley, Jr: "'All Good Pictures Crack' – Sir Joshua Reynolds's Practice and Studio"; *Reynolds* (exhn cat.) ed. Nicholas Penny; Royal Academy, 1986, pp. 55ff.

9 TB XXVII-K.

10 Rev. John Selby Watson: *The Life of Richard Porson*; 1861.

11 Parish records. There was a John Narraway, leather dresser, in Barnstaple in the late 1760s. North Devon RO, B1/3024; affidavit and warrant, 1767.

12 R. G. Sullivan: *Observations Made During a Tour Through Parts of England, Wales and Scotland*; London, 1780, p. 92. Quoted P. T. Marcey in P. McGrath (ed.): *Bristol in the 18th Century*; David and Charles, 1972, p. 28.

13 "Bristol and Malmesbury" sketchbook, TB VI, p. 20a.

14 Finberg, p. 20.

15 Turner's watercolour *St Mary Redcliffe*, Bristol City Museum and Art Gallery, was inscribed on the back of the frame, allegedly in Narraway's hand: "NB. he has crooked legs." Ref. [Beavington Atkinson]: "Turner at Bristol"; *Portfolio*, 1880, pp. 69–71.

16 David Roberts. Quoted *Athenaeum*, 10.7.1852, p. 754.

17 *Annual Register*, 1851, p. 366.

18 G. R. Corner: "The Panorama – With a Memoir of its Inventor Robert Barker and his son the late Henry Aston Barker," *Art*

*Journal*, Feb 1857.

19 *The Times*, 17.3.89.

20 G. R. Corner, *op. cit.*

21 Curtis Price: "Turner at the Pantheon Opera House 1791–92'; *TS*, vol. 7, no. 2, pp. 2ff.

22 *Gents Mag.*, Feb 1792, p. 85.

23 Curtis Price, *op. cit.*

24 Castle Museum, Norwich.

25 "Bristol and Malmesbury" sketchbook, TB VI.

26 TB XIII – N.

27 "Matlock" sketchbook, TB XIX.

28 "South Wales" sketchbook, TB XXVI.

29 TB XVII – Q.

30 TB VI, p. 13.

31 TB XXI–X; Also XXI–O&Q; XXII–A&S and others.

32 Gage, pp. 11ff. This attribution was later withdrawn. John Gage: "Further Correspondence of JMWT"; *TS*, vol. 6, no. 1, p. 2.

33 RSA Minutes, 27.3.1793.

34 C. W. Carey: "Discovery of a New Turner Relic"; *Connoisseur*, Feb. 1923, pp. 79ff; and John Gage: "Turner and the Society of Arts"; *RSA Journal*, vol. CXI, 1962–3, pp. 842ff.

35 Classes published in *Gents Mag.*, April 1792, pp. 393ff.

36 Inventory, Wilton, p. 243: ["1 Prize Palette in Case."]

37 *The Works of James Barry*, 1809, vol. I, p. 555. See also letter JMWT to James Holworthy, 21.11.17; Gage, 70.

38 FD, 12.11.98.

39 FD, 30.12.94.

40 FD, 12.11.98. See also Andrew Wilton: "The 'Monro School' Question: Some Answers"; *TS*, vol. 4, no. 2, pp. 8ff.

41 13.5.1794. Quoted Whitley, vol. ii, p. 182.

42 24.5.1794.

43 V&A, Dept. of Paintings, Prints and Drawings.

44 British Museum, 1958-7–12–402.

45 National Museum of Wales.

46 TB LX(a) – A.

47 TB XXXIII – a.

48 From a letter written in 1857 by the nephew of James Douglas's son-in-law, who was then the owner of the painting titled by B&J *Rochester Castle with Fishermen Drawing Boats Ashore in a Gale*, c. 1794 [B&J,

21]. Letter quoted by J. W. Archer: "Reminiscences", *Once a Week*, 1.2.1862, pp. 162–6; reprinted *TS*, vol.1, no. 1, p.31–2.

49 5.5.1797. The composition of this painting is known through Turner's *Liber Studiorum*.

50 20–23.5.1797. Quoted Finberg, p. 43.

51 *Gents Mag.*, Jan 1825, p. 85.

52 Thomas Green: *Extracts from the Diary of a Lover of Literature*; Ipswich, 1810. These entries are for 2.6.1797 and 3.6.1799 respectively.

53 Postmark ?1798. Tate Gallery, TBA 941–1.

54 FD, 24.10.98.

55 TB XLVI, p. 120.

56 FD 28.11.98. Thornbury quotes the same sum on p. 86, but gives 10 shillings a lesson on p. 78.

57 Thornbury, p. 235.

58 *ibid*, p. 234.

59 This story is third or fourth hand, having been told to Samuel Palmer by Joshua Cristall, who was not present, and published by Byron Webber: *James Orrock R. I.*; 1903, vol. 1, p. 81.

60 Thornbury, p. 236.

61 *New Grove Dictionary of Musicians* and Philip H. Highfill: *Biographical, Dictionary of Actors ... Musicians ... and other Stage Personalities in London 1660–1800*; S. Illinois University Press, 1975.

62 TB LXXVIII "Swiss Figures" sketchbook, inside back cover. *Merry Sherwood* was performed at Covent Garden from Dec. 1795.

63 Falk, p. 40.

64 Obituary, *Catholic Record Society*, vol. 12 (1913), p. 65.

65 This is the traditional view. Some authorities speculate that Turner's father was Sarah's lover, and the father of Evelina and Georgiana.

66 FD, 1.10.02.

67 FD, 5.1.98.

68 23.4.98.

69 Letter JMWT to F. H. Fawkes, 27.12.1847, Gage, 307.

70 FD, 26.9.98.

71 FD, 24.10.98.

72 *ibid*.

73 FD, 6.11.98.

74 The Pantzer Collection at the Indianapolis Museum of Art has what is widely held to be

a *Self Portrait* of Turner, *c.* 1793. Its provenance and the arguments in favour of the attribution, and some of the doubts, are given in B&J, 20. Though it is likely to be *of* Turner, the present writer feels that the face is too prettified to be by so uncompromisingly objective a painter as Turner.

### THREE
#### "TURNER, A YOUNG ARTIST ..."

1 RA Council Minutes, 22.12.96
2 RA Council Minutes, 11.7.98.
3 Abraham Raimbach: *Diaries*; 1843, pp. 26–7.
4 *ibid.*, pp. 21–2.
5 FD, 4.6.95.
6 FD, 6.7.99.
7 FD, 24.10.98.
8 FD, 10.7.96.
9 David Hill: " 'A Taste for the Arts' – Turner and the Patronage of Edward Lascelles of Harewood House, 1 & 2"; *TS* vol. 4, no. 2 & vol. 5, no. 1.
10 DNB.
11 FD, 28.3.04.
12 FD, 27.5.99.
13 Letter John Constable to John Dunthorne, nd [?Winter 1799]. Quoted C. R. Leslie: *Memoirs of the Life of John Constable*; Phaidon, 1951, p. 9.
14 FD, 6.7.99.
15 This William Turner has been confused with JMWT, who was for some years assumed to be the developer of the Naumachia. The identity of the coachmaker Turner has been satisfactorily separated from JMWT by Richard Spencer in " 'Mr Turner' and the Naumachia"; *TS* vol. 6, no. 1 (1989), pp. 27ff.
16 29.4.–1.5.99. Quoted at B&J 10.
17 Thornbury, p.8.
18 29.4.99.
19 *ibid.*
20 RA Council Minutes, vol. III, 1798–1806, 29.7.1799. Sums taken: Admission: £3,051. 7s.0d [at 1 shilling per head]. Catalogues: £701.6s.0d [at 6 pence each].
21 Andrew Caldwell to Bishop Percy, 14.9.02. Quoted John B. Nichols: *Illustrations of the Literary History of the Eighteenth Century*; London, 1817–58, vol. VIII, pp. 41–3.
22 Reconstructed from Jones, p. 4.
23 FD, 27.5.99.
24 FD, 8.5.99.
25 FD, 21.7.99.
26 FD, 16.11.99.
27 Quoted Boyd Alexander: *England's Wealthiest Son – A Study of William Beckford*; London, 1962, p. 166.
28 TB XLVII–1 & 5; XLVIII–1; XLVII–10.
29 The painting actually represents the Seventh Plague, of hail and fire.
30 "Smaller South Wales" sketchbook, TB XXV, p. 1.
31 "Dinevor Castle" sketchbook, *c.* 1798. TB XL, pp. 60a–61 & 67.
32 FD, 12.10.99.
33 FD, 30.10.99.
34 St Luke's Hospital, Admission Registers; Camden and Islington NHS Trust Archives.
35 W. Wickstead of 8 Cecil Court and Richard Twemlow of 2 Air Street. *ibid.*
36 FD, 16.11.99.
37 Field is named in the Deed of Separation, in which it was to be fully understood "that the only reason for the separation ... is the differences in the Tempers and dispositions and not from any Conjugal infidelity on the part of the said Olive." (Warwick CRO, CR1886/Box 677/8.) That this was simply a legal gag to prevent Olivia's affairs being discussed publicly by those involved was later made clear in Serres's will, in which he disinherits Olivia: "In the first place my wish is to prevent my wife Olivia Serres for whose misconduct I was separated from by legal deeds of agreement in 1803 having any claim as my Widow to the least portion of whatever I may be possessed of at the time of my Death, she having repeatedly committed adultery with several persons, given birth to illegitimate children, and has unnaturally deserted them to be supported by others." (Warwick CRO CR1886/Box 676.)
38 Whittingham: *GMD*, p. 30 and *passim*. This is based on the considerable evidence of the baptism record at Guestling, Sussex, of Evelina, daughter of William and Sarah Turner, 19.9.01. Despite the convincing coincidence of names, however, we should remember that this may be an entirely different family.
39 "Salisbury" sketchbook, TB XLIX, inside

front cover. See Andrew Wilton: *Painting and Poetry – Turner's Verse Book and his Work of 1804–1812*; Tate Gallery, 1990. The transcriptions from Turner's poetry are by Rosalind Mallord Turner.

40 Address given in letter dated 3.3.1811; TFP.

41 Bethlem Royal Hospital Archives and Museum.

42 Dr Thomas Monro: *Observations ... upon the Evidence Taken before the Committee of the Hon. House of Commons for Regulating Mad-Houses*; 1816, pp. 13ff.

43 E. G. O'Donoghue: *The Story of Bethlem Hospital from its Foundation in 1247*; 1914, pp. 286ff.

44 TB XL p. 6a–7.

45 TB LXVI, p. 127a.

46 "Marford Mill" sketchbook, TB XX, p. 35.

47 Gallery plan, FD, 5.5.02.

48 Eric Shanes's suggestion in his review of B&J, *TS*, vol. 1, no. 1, p. 46.

49 June 1801.

50 Quoted B&J, no. 14.

51 Richard Wilson's *Landscape with the Story of Niobe* was exhibited at the Society of Artists in 1760. FD, 10.6.01.

52 *Porcupine*, 28.4.01.

53 8.5.01

54 *Reflector*; 1811. Jerrold Ziff suggests the author was Robert Hunt, art critic of the *Examiner*.

55 FD, 10.6.01.

56 FD, 19.6.01

57 *ibid.*

58 Further insight into the circumstances of Turner's 1801 trip can be found in Francina Irwin: "Turner the Tourist", and Andrew Wilton: "Turner in Scotland: The Early Tours", collected in *Turner in Scotland* (exhn cat.), Aberdeen Art Gallery and Museums, 1982.

59 T. M. L. Wigley and N. J. Huckstep: "An Account of the Weather Conditions During Turner's tour of ... 1801", *loc. cit.*, pp. 26–7.

60 TB LVIII.

61 FD, 6.2.02.

62 "... I have not sent to London, nor shall I. It was expensive enough last Summer." Jonathan to Price Turner, 24.4.02. TFP.

63 Verso of joint letter from Joshua and

William to Price Turner, 24 & 27.5.02. TFP.

64 Letter from William Turner, 27.5.02. TFP.

65 FD, 14.2.02.

## FOUR
### ROYAL ACADEMICIAN: "CONFIDENT, PRESUMPTUOUS – WITH TALENT"

1 FD, 13.2.02.

2 *loc. cit.*

3 John Gage: *Colour in Turner*; 1969, pp. 33f. See also: Fletcher (ed.): *Conversations of James Northcote with James Ward*, 1901, p. 235, and FD, 30.3.1797.

4 Society of Arts *Transactions*; vol. XXIV (1806), pp. 85–9.

5 "Turner I called upon. Grandi being there laying some absorbing grounds. He uses white, Yellow Oker, Raw & Burnt Terre de Siena, Venetian Red, Umber, prussian blue, blue black, Ultramarine." FD, 27.2.02.

6 "On a Lee Shore – 1" sketchbook, TB LXVII, ff. 1, 2, 5, 6.

7 Louvre, Paris. Engraved in 17th century.

8 TB XLVI, 3 1/8" × 5 1/4".

9 RA Council Minutes, 30.2.1802.

10 Admitted 24.7.1795. RA Council Minutes.

11 Admitted 28.2.1801. RA Council Minutes.

12 RA, 1792.

13 Society of Artists, 1791.

14 Sunningwell Parish records, 17.6.1820.

15 Gage, 329.

16 Ref. letter Jonathan to Price Turner, 24.4.02. TFP.

17 Verso joint letter Joshua and William to Price Turner, 24 & 27.5.02. TFP.

18 Letter Jonathan to Price Turner, 24.4.02, TFP.

19 *ibid.*

20 Letter William to Price Turner, 27.5.02. TFP.

21 Letter John to Price Turner, 21.6.02. TFP.

22 Raimbach, pp. 37ff.

23 FD, 14.7.02.

24 Cecilia Powell: "Turner's Travelling Companion of 1802 – A Mystery Resolved?" *TSN*, 54, Feb. 1990, pp. 12ff.

25 *Art Treasures ... at Manchester in 1857*; 1857, p. 88. Passport ref. PRO FO/610/1.

26 Raimbach, *loc. cit.*

27 "Calais Pier" sketchbook TB LXXXI, pp.

58–9. The inscription "Our landing ..." is in the same pen and ink as other page inscriptions, and, by internal evidence, these were written much later than 1802.
28 FD, 22.11.02.
29 FD, 30.9; 1.10; 22 & 23.11.02.
30 FD, 30.9.02.
31 "France, Savoy and Piedmont" sketchbook TB LXXIII.
32 ibid., p. 19. Wrongly inscribed "Macon". Ref. David Hill: Turner in the Alps ... 1802; Geo. Phillip, 1992, pp. 28–9.
33 FD 22.11.02. One livre was about 1s 8d in 1800, i.e. about £5 in 1990s money.
34 FD, 30.9.02.
35 FD, 22.11.02.
36 "Swiss Figures" sketchbook, TB LXXVIII, p. 1.
37 ibid., inside back cover. A "warden" is a type of pear.
38 FD, 23.11.02.
39 FD, 23.11.02.
40 FD, 1.10.02. This may mean Paris to Lyons, and Strasbourg back to Paris, including the Burgundian Hills and the flat land of the Île de France.
41 FD, 30.9.02.
42 FD, 1.10.02.
43 Raimbach, p. 43.
44 ibid., p. 46.
45 ibid, pp. 47ff.
46 "Studies in the Louvre" sketchbook, TB LXXII.
47 ibid, pp. 31ff.
48 FD, 5.10.02.
49 Raimbach, p. 50.
50 FD, 3.10.02.
51 OED.
52 Gage, 5.
53 Thornbury, p. 61.
54 ibid.
55 FD, 18.4.1800.
56 Tate Gallery.
57 25.8.02.
58 Thornbury, loc. cit.
59 Thornbury p. 71.
60 Thornbury.
61 FD, 9.2.99.
62 FD, 3.5.03.
63 FD, 3.5.03.
64 FD, 6.7.09.
65 FD, 21.10.12.
66 FD, 24.12.03.
67 FD, 30.4.03 & 13.5.03.
68 FD, 13 & 15.5.1803.
69 Alaric Watts, p. xvi.
70 For The British School see also John Gage: George Field and his Circle; Fitzwilliam Museum, Cambridge, 1989, pp. 9ff.
71 Warwick CRO, CR 1886/Box 677/S. See also FD, 20.6.04.
72 "There being three new elected Academicians, viz W. M. Turner, Jno Soane, & Cha. Rossi, they must with the One in rotation on the old list viz Sir F. Bourgeois, be the Four new members in the ensuing Council according to His Majesty's commands." RA General Assembly minutes, 14.12.02.
73 Finberg, p. 267.
74 Westminster RO. Listed as "Joseph William Turner".
75 FD, 19.4.04.
76 The plans are held in the Howard de Walden Estate Office, which, by a serendipitous intervention, is on the site of Turner's house and gallery. Plans vol. 1, no. 138. Farrington's "seventy" could be a mishearing for "seventeen".
77 One at least of his works for the 1804 Academy exhibition was painted there. FD, 16/17.4.04.
78 Finberg's estimate, p. 107, based on Farrington's measurements, suggested at least twenty or thirty large paintings.
79 There is no record of her name in the St Paul's Covent Garden burial register at this period.
80 Letter Mary Eliza Turner to Jabez Tepper, 16.4.1853. TFP.
81 Gage, 4.
82 Gage 5, 6, & p. 248.
83 Gage, 3.
84 FD, 22.5.04.
85 FD, 17.7.04.
86 Westminster RO: rate returns for 75 Norton St – 1803: "William Turner; Empty MidS[ummer]." 1804: "William Turner; 1/2 empty." 1805 et seq: "Alexander Hood."
87 True Briton, 9.5.03.
88 FD 11.5.04.
89 "Studies for Pictures, Isleworth" sketchbook, TB XC, pp. 1, 49a, 52a, 55a, 59 & passim.

90 Trimmer's move to Heston was listed in *Gents Mag.*, Oct. 1804.

91 See Linda Colley: *Britons*, 1992. *Passim*, esp. chap. 7.

92 A. G. H. Bachrach: *Turner and Rotterdam*; 1974, p. 14.

93 10.5.04.

94 *British Press*, 8.5.04.

95 Andrew Wilton: *Turner and the Sublime*; 1980, pp. 136–9.

96 See Selby Whittingham: "A Most Liberal Patron: Sir John Fleming Leicester Bart ..."; *TS*, vol. 6, no. 2, pp. 24ff.

97 R. R. M. Sée: *Masquerier and his Circle*, 1922, p. 18.

98 e.g. RA Council Minutes 19.4.1796 (*True Briton; Public* or *Oracle* [sic]; *Herald; Telegraph; Times; Morning Chronicle; Daily Advertiser*) and 3.1.1804 (*Morning Post; Morning Herald; True Briton; Times; Sun; Courier; Oracle.*)

99 Gage, 9.

100 "Victory" sketchbook, TB LXXXIX.

101 FD, 3.6.06.

102 A. Freemantle (ed.): *The Wynne Diaries*, OUP, 1940, vol. III; 6.5.06.

103 The painting had subsequently become known as *The Victory Returning from Trafalgar in Three Positions*, but Eric Shanes has shown that the painting cannot represent the flagship's return. See his "Picture Note", *TS* vol. 6, no 2, pp. 68ff. Fawkes exhibited it at the Northern Society in Leeds in 1823 under the title given in the main text. See David Hill: *Turner's Birds*, 1988, p. 10.

104 Quoted R. G. Thorne: *History of Parliament: The House of Commons, 1790–1820*; London, Secker & Warburg, 1986. vol. 3, "Members A–F", pp. 730–1.

105 *ibid.*

106 The cost of this distant benefactor's funeral, over £700, reflects the extent of the inheritance, and included the purchase of 50 women's silk bonnets, 39 mourning cloaks, 90 yards of black wildbore, 200 yards of mourning crepe and 100 yards of bombazine. Bills in WYAS, DD146/5/1/17.

107 Letter Francis to Hawkesworth Fawkes, 25.8.1774. Francis Fawkes's Letter Book, p. 26. WYAS, D/146/5/1/16.

108 Turner's "Verse Book", p. 7. Transcribed in A. Wilton and R. Turner: *Painting and Poetry*; Tate Gallery, 1990, pp. 30 & 149.

109 The Goddess of Discord, Eris, is the sister of Ares and daughter of Jove; the wedding, to which she was not invited, was of Thetis, not Psyche, to Peleus.

110 Fawkes to Creevey, n.d. (?Feb 1806). Quoted *History of Parliament*, loc. cit.

111 Walter Fawkes: *The Englishman's Manual, or, A Dialogue Between a Tory and a Reformer*; London, 1817, 2nd edn, p. 37.

112 Fawkes to Lascelles, 18.10.06; and reply, 18.10.06, 6p.m. Leeds RO, Harewood Papers, Local Affairs 9.

113 Ref. Anon. letter, Wakefield, 17.11.06. Election Bills, Leeds RO, Harewood Papers, loc. cit.

114 Letter Clara Wheeler (née Wells) to H Elliot, 27.7.1853. Quoted Finberg p. 128. The best account of the evolution of the *Liber Studiorum* is Gillian Forrester: *Turner's "Drawing Book"*; Tate Gallery, 1996.

115 His designs and costings for a sailing boat appear in the "River and Margate" sketchbook, TB XCIX, p. 86.

116 F. G. Stephens, quoted W. T. Whitley: *Artists and their Friends in England, 1800–1820*, p. 195.

117 FD, 9.5.04.

118 Finberg, p. 133.

119 I. Faulkner: *Hammersmith*, 1839, pp. 339–40; Philip D. Whiting: *History of Hammersmith*, 1965, p. 126.

120 Auction particulars and deeds in TFP. A note in Turner's "Finance" sketchbook, TB CXXII, p. 8, reads: "Paid for the freehold Lee Common ... £119 5s."

121 GLRO Acc 1379/122/2.

FIVE

VARIOUS DEGREES OF FRIENDSHIP

1 Scone Palace, Perthshire.

2 Haydon: *Autobiography*, vol. I, p. 36.

3 *ibid.*

4 *ibid.*

5 1.6.07.

6 FD, 5.4.06.

7 FD, 3.6.06.

8 FD, 20.7.07.

9 "Mercury and Herse" sketchbook, TB CXI, p. 65a. "Bird" is the painter Edward Bird.

10 C. R. Leslie: *Memoirs of the Life of John Constable*; Phaidon, 1951, p. 114.

11 Quoted David Blayney Brown: *Augustus Wall Callcott*; Tate Gallery, 1981, p. 24.

12 FD, 8.6.11.

13 Wilton, p. 247.

14 "Tabley no. 3" sketchbook, TB CV, p. 24 and *passim*.

15 Isaak Walton: *The Compleat Angler*, pt I, ch. i.

16 FD, 11.2.09.

17 "Tabley no. 2" sketchbook, TB CIV p. 88.

18 William Jerdan: *An Autobiography*, 1852, vol. II, p. 260.

19 23.10.06. Leeds RO, Harewood Papers, Local Affairs, 9.

20 DNB.

21 William Marshall: *The Rural Economy of the Southern Counties ...*, 1795, p. 195. See also Ian Warrell: "'Lord of the Soil': a re-appraisal of Turner's Petworth Patron", *Turner at Petworth*, Tate Gallery, 1989, pp. 105ff.

22 Bill from Thomas Taylor dated August 1808 lists payments for extensive decorations, including "Painting the Entrance Hall at Farnley three times over also the New Wood Work, £16.0.0; Decorating the Hall in Chiaro Scuro £126.0.0; ... Repairing the painting on the wall in the Drawing Room & Library ... £2.10.0; ... Painting the Landscape in the Bath £31.10.0; Two Views of Farnley £10.10.0." Fawkes Papers, WYAS, DD146/5/1/13.

23 Fawkes Papers, WYAS, DD 146/5/1.

24 Bills dated 1788–90 for construction, plastering and erecting marble fireplaces are among the Fawkes Papers, WYAS, DD 146/5/1/13.

25 Quoted Lindsay, p. 172.

26 RA Council Minutes, 19.12.08.

27 RA Council Minutes, 17.10; 15.12.09.

28 Quoted B&J, no. 86.

29 TB CVIII.

30 *ibid.*, p. 13.

31 *ibid.*, p. 20.

32 TB CCCLXV-A. The rest, "a large number" according to William Rossetti (*Rossetti Papers 1862–70*, 1903, p. 383) were burnt by Ralph Wornum, Keeper of the National Gallery, and John Ruskin when the latter made the first list of the Turner Bequest.

33 "Academies" sketchbook, TB LXXXIV, pp. 11, 22–4, 28, 31, 56. See also Selby Whittingham: *GMD*, p. 5; and Ann Chumbley and Ian Warrell: *Turner and the Human Figure*; Tate Gallery, 1989, pp. 13–14.

34 TB CVIII, p. 29–31a.

35 "Lowther" sketchbook, TB CXIII, p. 59.

36 "Mrs Danby, widow of a Musician now lives with [Turner]. She has some children." FD, 11.2.09.

37 There is a draft advertisement written out by JMWT very scrappily in pencil in TB CXI, pp. 62a–63, the text suggesting composition rather than transcription. The advertisement is dated "Thursday Aug–9". 9th August fell on a Thursday in 1810.

38 TFP.

39 Buckinghamshire CRO, Q/RPL/2/1–53.

40 Royal Society of Musicians Claimants' Registers, 1810–38, and miscellaneous additional papers. Ref. Jean Golt, *TS* vol. 9, no. 2; and Whittingham: *GMD*, *passim*.

41 Royal Society of Musicians. Whittingham, *GMD*, p. 31 suggests that Georgiana Danby was born in Surrey between 7 June 1811 and 29 January 1812.

42 Whittingham, *GMD*, pp. 51ff. The approximate date of Hannah's arrival at Harley Street is calculated from the statement in the *Literary Gazette* (27.12.51, p. 924) that she had lived with JMWT for forty-two years to the day of his death.

43 TB CXIV.

44 TB CXI, *passim*, and TB CXIII, p. 13.

45 23.11.1809; Gage, 26.

46 Museum of Fine Arts, Boston. Quoted Anne Lyles and Diane Perkins: *Colour into Line – Turner and the Art of Engraving*; Tate Gallery, 1989, p. 45.

47 Letter C. Turner to Colnaghi's, 14.2.1852. Ref. Gillian Forrester: *Turner's Drawing Book*; Tate Gallery, 1996, p. 12.

48 27.7.10, Gage 35.

49 17.11.09; Gage, 24.

50 21.11.09; Gage, 25.

51 9.12.09; Gage, 27.

52 Letters: postmarked 25.12.09; Gage, 28. 4.2.10; Gage, 29. 14.3.10; Gage, 31.

53 Letter 28.2.10; Gage, 30.

54 Letter 14.3.10, Gage 31.

55 Letters late March 1810, Gage 32; 6.4.10, Gage 33.

56 Postmarked 6.4.10; Gage, 33.

57 Admiral Bowles, quoted B&J, no. 210.

58 B&J, 54.

59 "Greenwich" sketchbook, TB CII 1808–9, p. 3a.

60 1812 RA catalogue.

61 Andrew Wilton and John Russell: *Turner in Switzerland*, 1976, p. 17.

62 Weather information from J. M. Stratton and Jack Houghton Brown (ed. Ralph Whitlock): *Agricultural Records AD 220–1977*; John Baker, 1978.

63 Haydon: *Autobiography*; vol. I, p. 40.

64 Ref. letter Arthur Young to Mrs Oakes, 9.4.1810 in M. Betham-Edwards (ed.): *The Autobiography of Arthur Young; 1*898, pp. 449f.

65 R. G. Thorne: *loc. cit.*

66 Walter Fawkes: *Speech on the Subject of Parliamentary Reform ... Delivered at the Crown and Anchor Tavern May 23rd 1812*; London, 1813, pp. 5–6.

67 R. G. Thorne: *loc. cit.*

68 A bill for 7 guineas to George Burley "to 14 lessons given to the young Family ... from Oct 22nd to Dec 3rd 1813 at 10s 6d per lesson." Fawkes Papers, WYAS, DD146/5/1/15.

69 Tax bill dated 24.12.1802: £67 6s 10½d. Fawkes Papers, WYAS, DD146/6.

70 M. H. [Marcus Huish?]: "The Early History of Turner's Yorkshire Drawings". *Athenaeum*, 8.9.1894, pp. 326–7. Reprinted *TS*, vol. 5, no. 2, pp. 24ff. See also E. M. Fawkes typescript "Turner at Farnley", Clore Gallery.

71 Thornbury, p. 239.

Six
"The difficulty great ..."

1 According to the *Sun* 8.1.1811. The Great Room, the largest of Somerset House exhibition galleries, was not the usual venue for Academy lectures.

2 TB CVI, p. 67a.

3 *ibid*, p. 68.

4 British Library, MS B f. 2r.

5 British Library MS K f. iv.

6 British Library MS P ff. 19v–20r.

7 TB CXIV, p. 50a and passim.

8 8.1.11.

9 FD, 8.1.11.

10 FD, 14.1.11.

11 FD, 1.1.95 & 12.3.13.

12 W. P. Frith: *My Autobiography*; 1887, i, pp. 137–9.

13 Leslie, vol. I, p. 206.

14 Redgrave, vol. II, p. 95.

15 *ibid*.

16 *ibid*.

17 This is on one of two surviving leaves from a sketchbook, with sketches also of Fuseli, Flaxman and Soane. It is dated 1810, evidently an error. NPG 4913–1.

18 "Chemistry and Apuleia" sketchbook, TB CXXXV, p. 54a.

19 Gage, 41.

20 See Patrick Youngblood: "The Painter as Architect – Turner and Sandycombe Lodge"; *TS*, vol. 2, no. 1, pp. 20ff.

21 "Windmill and Lock", TB CXIV, *c.* 1810–11; "Sandycombe and Yorkshire", TB CXXVII, *c.* 1812; "Woodcock Shooting", TB CXXIX, *c.* 1810–12.

22 Letter JMWT to A. B. Johns, 4.11.15; Gage, 59.

23 Thornbury, p. 118.

24 Gage, 52.

25 See Patrick Youngblood, *op. cit.* Youngblood suggests *inter alia* that the Sandycombe entrance hall is loosely based on the vestibule of Soane's Pitzhanger Manor at Ealing.

26 The house was extended in the 1890s by the raising of the two wings to make an additional bedroom on each side of the house.

27 "Woodcock Shooting" sketchbook, TB CXXIX, p. 122.

28 *Gents Mag.*, vol. LXI (1807), pp. 624 & 988. An engraving of the willow was published *ibid.* supplement for 1807.

29 John Britton: *The Fine Arts of the English School*, 1812. Turner's comments on the text are at Gage, 43. See also Shanes, *THL*, pp. 24–6.

30 *Verse Book*, p. 11.

31 See elevation by Peter Tillemans, 1719–20. Repr. Terry Friedman: *James Gibbs*; Paul Mellon Foundation, Yale, 1984, fig. 148.

32 RA Council Minutes, 24.4.11.

33 FD, 27.4.11.
34 *ibid.*
35 FD, 8.6.11.
36 TB CXI, p. 68a.
37 Thornbury, p. 123.
38 TB CXI, pp. 2a & 8a–8.
39 *ibid.*, p. 17.
40 *ibid.*, p. 66a.
41 "Come Oh Time nay that is stuff/Gaffer, thou comest on fast enough ..." TB C, "Spithead" sketchbook, 1807, inside front cover.
42 Letter Joseph Crompton to his son Rookes, 19.5.11. Crompton Papers, North Yorks CRO.
43 "Devonshire Coast" No. 1 Sketchbook [a copy of *The British Itinerary*], TB CXXIII, p. 30a.
44 *ibid.*, p. 110a.
45 *ibid.*, p. 149a.
46 "Vale of Heathfield" sketchbook, TB CXXXVII, p. 1.
47 Sir C. L. Eastlake: *Contributions to the Literature of the Fine Arts* (2nd Series); London, 1870, p. 23. Quoted Sam A. Smiles: "Turner in Devon ...", *TS*, vol. 7, no. 1, p. 11. (George was Charles Eastlake's brother.)
48 "Plymouth, Hamoaze" sketchbook, TB CXXXI, p. 43a.
49 Letter Jonathan to John Turner, 5.3.11. TFP.
50 *ibid.*
51 Our evidence for knowing that Turner himself called on his Uncles John and Price in 1811 appears in an affidavit sworn by Mary Matthews, Price's daughter, in 1853. Mary Matthews recalled that Turner had twice visited her father in Exeter about his grandmother's effects. TFP.
52 Falk, p. 113.
53 13.11.1820. Gage, 89.
54 Thornbury, pp. 235–6.
55 W. G. Rawlinson: *Turner's Liber Studiorum*, 1906, pp. xii–xiii.
56 See Gage, 1980, p. 295, and letter 56.
57 Letter H. Elliott to Robert Finch, 1814. Oxford, Bodleian Library MS. Finch c.2.d.5, fo. 284, quoted Gage, 1980, p. 294.
58 *ibid.*
59 *Art Journal*, 1863, pp. 87ff. Quoted Gage, p. 299.
60 Gage, 265.
61 Thornbury, p. 122.
62 *ibid.*, p. 123.
63 *ibid.*, p. 116.
64 See *Gents Mag.* 9.1811, p. 280; 10.1811, p. 381. Also *Examiner*, 1811, 616, 627, 665, 676, 691, and M. A. Sellon: *The Caledonian Comet Elucidated*, 1811.
65 Thornbury, p. 224.
66 Thornbury, p. 269.
67 *ibid.*, p. 271.
68 RA Council Minutes, 10.12.11.
69 FD, 8.1.11.
70 Redgrave, vol. II, p. 94.
71 Oct. 1811, p. 89.
72 Forster's *Pedigree of West Riding Families*, vol. I, 1874.
73 FD, 10.3.12.
74 W. T. Whitley: "Turner as a Lecturer", *Burlington Magazine*, XXII, 1913, p. 206.
75 FD, 10.4.12.
76 Reconstructed from FD, 11.4.12.
77 There is a study for an early idea of Hannibal in the "Calais Pier" sketchbook of 1802–3, TB LXXXI, p. 38.
78 Walter Fawkes: *op. cit.*, p. 4.
79 Leslie, II, p. 12.
80 *Repository of Arts, Literature and Commerce*, 12.6.12.
81 T. Sadler (ed.): *Henry Crabb Robinson's Diaries*; Macmillan, 1872, vol. I, p. 198.
82 FD, 4.11.12.
83 TB CXXXV, "Chemistry and Apuleia" sketchbook, p. 1.
84 Joyce H. Townsend: "Turner's Writing on Chemistry and Artists' Materials"; *TSN* no. 62 (Dec. 1992) pp. 6ff.

## SEVEN
### "... THE FIRST GENIUS OF THE DAY ..."

1 Letter Constable to Maria Bicknell, 6.5.1812; R. B. Beckett (ed.): *John Constable's Correspondence II*; Suffolk Records Society, vol. VI, 1964, p. 66.
2 Constable to Maria Bicknell, 30.6.1813. *ibid.*, p. 110.
3 Letter John Fisher to Constable, 14.6.1813, quoted to Maria Bicknell, *ibid.*
4 Thornbury, p. 121–2.
5 For an alternative reading of the painting

see David Hill: "A Frosty Morning – Turner in Yorkshire'; *Country Life*, 25.12.1980, pp. 2402–3; and the same author's *In Turner's Footsteps*; Murray, 1984, p. 22.

6 £6 6s 6d per quarter. Stratton and Brown, p. 96.

7 Walter Fawkes: *op. cit.*

8 Thornbury, p. 122.

9 Gage, 73.

10 Thornbury, p. 432.

11 British Library Add Ms 46151 BB, f. iv. See also Jerrold Ziff: "Turner as Defender of the Art, 1810–20"; *TS*, vol. 8, no. 2, pp. 13ff.

12 FD, 8.6.11.

13 FD, 21.10.12.

14 Annotation by Hugh Munro in Prof. Francis Haskell's copy of Thornbury, vol. 1, p. 269.

15 FD, 8.4.13.

16 FD, 24.5.13.

17 Letter Clarissa Wells to Robert Finch, 22.7.1813. Finch Papers, c.2 d.16 ff. 315–16; Bodleian Library, Oxford.

18 27.7.1813, *ibid*, f. 270

19 Thornbury, pp. 118–19.

20 *ibid*. p. 120.

21 Letters JMWT to William Turner of 1827, Gage, nos 123–5.

22 Thornbury, p. 116.

23 *ibid*., p. 117–18.

24 Cyrus Redding: "The Late J. M. W. Turner"; *Fraser's Magazine*, Feb. 1852, pp. 150–6.

25 Thornbury, p. 153.

26 *ibid*.

27 Redding, *op. cit.*

28 See Sam Smiles: "Turner in Devon"; *TS*, vol. 7, no. 1, pp. 11ff.

29 Diary 24.8.1813. Quoted Gage, p. 301.

30 Andrew Wilton: *The Life and Work of J. M. W. Turner*, 1979. Catalogue of Watercolours, pp. 297ff.

31 Francis's surname was Hawkesworth; he had not followed Walter in assuming the name Fawkes.

32 See Anne Lyles: *Turner and Natural History – The Farnley Project*; Tate Gallery, 1988.

33 The present writer has serious doubts about the authenticity of the following "Turner" birds, traditionally ascribed to the artist: Cuckoo, Goldfinch, Robin, Hen Pheasant, Partridge, Woodcock. All, how-ever, have been generally accepted on the strength of the fact that Turner, as an old and sick man about thirty-five years later, gave a vaguely worded approval of a list of his work at Farnley, which had been compiled by the Fawkes family. See David Hill, *Turner's Birds*; Phaidon, 1988, p. 18.

34 Anne Lyles, *op. cit.*

35 Ashmolean Museum, Oxford.

36 John Cam Hobhouse: *Recollections of a Long Life*; 1865, vol. 1, 1786–1816, iii 28, 1910–11.

37 Jan Piggott: *Turner's Vignettes*; Tate Gallery, 1993, pp. 32ff.

38 Gage, 47, 48, 49, 51, 53, 54.

39 16 or 23.11.13, Gage, 47.

40 William Combe to W. B. Cooke, published Thornbury, pp. 189–90.

41 JMWT to W. B. Cooke, 16.12.1813. Gage, 49.

42 Tate Gallery, TO05382.

43 5.1.14. Quoted Finberg, p. 206.

44 10.8.28. Oxford, Bodleian Library. MS Finch, c.2.d. 17 f. 205.

45 Michael Kitson: "Turner and Claude"; *TS*, vol. 2, no. 2, p. 10

46 13.2.14. Quoted B&J, p. 92.

47 FD, 3.5.03.

48 Note to Holworthy quoted Finberg, p. 212; lease on 44 Queen Anne St West: Howard de Walden Estate Office, Contracts vol. 2, no. 227, 7.8.1813. Renewed to 35 years from 1818, on 21.6.1817.

49 Gage, 56.

50 Quoted Michael Marrinan. *Painting Politics for Louis-Philippe*; Yale, 1988, pp. 3–4.

51 Virgil's *Aeneid*, Book 1, lines 597–610.

52 One survives at Morwhellham Quay near Tavistock.

53 Ref. letter JMWT to James Holworthy, n.d. (27.6.1815), Gage, 55.

54 Letter MS untraced JMWT to H. S. Trimmer, 1.8.1815. Gage, 56.

55 Letters JMWT to William Turner of 1827; Gage, 123–5.

56 Haydon: *Diaries*, vol. I, p. 484 (28.11.15).

57 Rome, Academy of St Luke, MS *Congregazioni*, vol. 59, fos. 87v–88; 24.11.1819. Quoted Gage, 86, n. 1.

58 C. J. Feret, *Isle of Thanet Gazette*, 23.9.1916.

59 Letters JMWT to H. S. Trimmer, 1.8.1815;

and to A. B. Johns, 26.10.15. Gage, 56 & 58.
60 Letter JMWT to James Holworthy, postmarked 11.9.1816. Gage, 68.
61 FD, 15 & 17.5.16; amended to 2,000 guineas plus expenses, FD, 20.12.17.
62 Ref. letter JMWT to W. B. Cooke, 28.8.1816. Gage, 66.
63 Letter, Thomas Uwins to Mr Townshend, 19.5.1815. Sarah Uwins: *Memoir of Thomas Uwins RA*, 1858, pp. 37ff.
64 7.5.1816.
65 *The Annals of Fine Art*, quoted B&J, no. 135.
66 FD, 5.6.15.
67 *ibid*.
68 FD, 5.6.15.
69 *Catalogue Raisonée of the Pictures now exhibiting at the British Institution*, 1815, p. 66.
70 Finberg, p. 226. See also Peter Fullerton: "Patronage and Pedagogy: the British Institution in the early nineteenth century"; *Art History*, vol. 5, no. 1 (March 1982), pp. 59ff.
71 FD, 21.6.15.
72 FD gives seating plans showing that Turner and Fawkes sat together in 1813, 1814, 1815, 1818 and 1821.
73 FD, 21.6.15.
74 William Hazlitt: *Complete Works*; Centenary edn, vol. 18, p. 95.
75 B CLIX "Itinerary Rhine Tour".
76 Letter R. R. Reinagle to Dawson Turner, 21.11.15 Trinity College Library, Cambridge, 0.13.11/193.

### Eight
### Into Europe: I

1 TB CLIX.
2 "Waterloo and Rhine" sketchbook, TB CLX, pp. 21a & 24a.
3 See A. G. H. Bachrach: "The Field of Waterloo and Beyond"; *TS*, vol. 1, no. 2, pp. 4ff.
4 TB CLIX, pp. 19, 22, 24, 29.
5 A full account of this journey is given by Cecilia Powell: *Turner's Rivers of Europe – The Rhine, Meuse and Moselle*; Tate Gallery, 1991.
6 "Dort" sketchbook, TB CLIX, p. 100.
7 The view was taken from the bank of the River Nort. TB CLXII, p. 77. See also Bachrach, *loc. cit*.
8 TB CLXII, pp. 58a–59.

9 *ibid*., p. 39.
10 *ibid*., p. 64a.
11 TB CLIX, p. 101a.
12 If this is a correct interpretation of the remark in a letter JMWT sent to James Holworthy, postmarked 21.11.1817: "... Lord Strathmore called at Raby and took me away to the north; ..." Gage, 70.
13 DNB.
14 Letter Lord Darlington to Henry Lascelles, 20.10.1806; Leeds RO, Harewood Papers, Local Affairs 9.
15 TB CLVI, p. 22a.
16 *Literary Chronicle*, 22.6.1818.
17 WYAS, Fawkes Papers, DD/161/7/g.
18 TB CLIV(a), p. 69. The memo reads thus:

| Mr Fawkes: | Bond | 1200 | |
|---|---|---|---|
| | Note | 780 | |
| Dort | | 550 | 7 10 |
| Sir John [?] Leicester's Note | | 400 | |
| | | 2930 | |
| Interest upon Sir John 2 years | | 47 | 10 |
| | | 40 – | |
| | | 3017 | 10 |

I interpret this as meaning that, in addition to any other agreements they may have had between them, Turner gave Fawkes £1,200 on some unknown security; also £780 in cash; also the painting *Dort* ... valued at £550. At the same time he seems to have lent Sir John Leicester £400 cash. The total of this loan is £2,930. The loan to Leicester would be due £47 10s interest over two years, i.e. 12%. The further £40 given may be more interest either on Leicester or Fawkes. Turner's total asset in this transaction would be £3017 10s.
19 TB CXXII.
20 Thornbury, p. 287. The "intimate friend" may have been George Jones. see Jones, p. 4.
21 Finberg, p. 249.
22 FD, 4.5.18.
23 Thornbury, p. 429.
24 So Dupuis claimed in 1853 when he wrote to request the position of custodian of Turner's pictures after the artist's death. Letter Joseph Dupuis to Jabez Tepper, 15.12.1853. TFP.
25 Joseph Dupuis: *Journal of a Residence in Ashantee*, 1824. New ed., Frank Cass Rep-

rints, 1966 (ed. & intro. W. E. F. Ward). See also Whittingham: *GMD*, *passim* & p. 9 for family suggestions that JMWT felt his daughter could do better.

26 For the full circumstances of the commission see Cecilia Powell: "Topography, Imagination and Travel: Turner's Relationship with James Hakewill"; *Art History*, vol. 5, no. 4, 1982.

27 Bachrach: *op. cit.*

28 Documents ref. GLRO MR/DE/TWI. See also Patrick Youngblood: "The Painter as Architect"; *TS*, vol. 2, no. 1, pp. 20ff.

29 Howard de Walden Estate Office, Contracts vol. 2, no. 227, 21.6.18.17; 12.7.1820; vol. 5A, no. 552, 27.2.1822. Maps: vol. 1, no. 138 & vol. 4, nos. 421 & 422.

30 See Gerald Finlay: *Landscapes of Memory – Turner as Illustrator to Scott*; University of California, 1980 for a full account of the 1818 trip, as of much else.

31 20.10.1818; Finlay, p. 50.

32 Letter Walter Scott to James Skene, 30.4.1819; Finlay, p. 55.

33 S. F. L. Schetky: *Ninety Years of Work and Play – The Public and Private Career of J. C. Schetky*; 1877, p. 109.

34 *ibid*.

35 A. Fraser: *The Works of Horatio McCulloch*, 1872, p. 24.

36 See Eric Shanes: *Turner's Human Landscape*; 1990, pp. 11ff.

37 E. M. Fawkes, "Turner at Farnley", TS, Clore Gallery.

38 *ibid*.

39 TB CXCVI – N.

40 Ref. Gage, *CinT*; p. 108 and notes.

41 Gage, 81, postmarked 10.2.1819.

42 W. Carey: *Some Memoirs of the Patronage and Progress of the Fine Arts*; 1826, p. 147. Quoted Gage, p. 254.

43 Jean Golt: "Beauty and Meaning on Richmond Hill ..."; *TS*, vol. 7, no. 2, pp. 9ff.

44 *Times* 14.8.1817, quoted Golt, *loc. cit.*

45 Charles Stuckey: "Turner's Birthdays"; *TSN*, no. 21, Apr. 1981, pp. 4–6.

## NINE
### INTO EUROPE: II

1 Royal Academy of Arts, Lawrence letters, LAW/3/52, Sir Thomas Lawrence to Joseph

Farington 2nd July 1819.

2 Quoted Finberg, p. 260.

3 TB CLXXI, "Route to Rome" sketchbook, p. 45.

4 TB CLXXII, "Italian Guide Book" sketchbook, pp. 17–21a. The engravings were published in Smith, Byrne and Eme's *Select Views of Italy*, 1792 & 1796.

5 See Cecilia Powell: "Topography, Imagination and Travel: Turner's Relationship with James Hakewill": *Art History*, vol. 5, no. 4, Dec 1982, pp. 408ff.

6 TB CLXXII, p. 15.

7 TB CLXXIII, "Paris, France, Savoy 2"; notes inside front cover.

8 *ibid.*, p. 1a.

9 TB CLXXIII, "Paris, France, Savoy 2", *passim* and pp. 22 & 32.

10 TB CLXXIII and CLXXIV, "Turin, Como, Lugarno, Maggiore".

11 TB CLXXV, "Milan to Venice"; and CLXXVI, "Venice to Ancona".

12 TB CLXXVI, "Venice to Ancona" sketchbook, p. 20.

13 *ibid.*, pp. 65–78.

14 TB CLXXVII, "Ancona to Rome" sketchbook, p. 6.

15 TB CLXXIX, "Tivoli and Rome" sketchbook, p. 14.

16 TB CLXXXIX, "Rome C[olour] Studies" sketchbook, p. 41; TB CLXXIX, "Tivoli to Rome" sketchbook, pp. 25a–26.

17 TB CLXXI, "Route to Rome" sketchbook, pp. 13 & 14a

18 TB CLXXX, "Vatican Fragments" sketchbook, p. 2a.

19 Wilfred S. Dowden (ed.): *The Journal of Thomas Moore*, Univ. of Delaware, 1983, vol. 1, p. 257. (15.11.19).

20 *ibid.*, p. 306.

21 Humphry Davy notebook 14e, p. 53. Royal Institution.

22 Humphry Davy notebook 14h, pp. 115–113 [sic]. Royal Institution.

23 Donaldson's and another's name and address is written out in the "Vatican Fragments" sketchbook, p. 81a: "Capt Graham 12 Pozza Mignanelli/Thomas L. Donaldson 46 Via Gregoriana, Trinita de 'Monti".

24 TB CLXXXV, "Pompeii, Amalfi, Sorrento, Herculaneum" sketchbook.

25 J. Holland: *Memorials of Francis Chantrey*; Sheffield, 1851, p. 113.

26 TB CLXXXVII, "Naples, Rome. C[olour] Studies" sketchbook.

27 TB CLXXXIV, "Gandolfo to Naples" sketchbook.

28 TB CLXXXV, "Pompeii, Amalfi, Sorrento, Herculaneum" sketchbook, p. 68.

29 TB CLXXII, p. 14a. Quoted by Turner from J. C. Eustace, *op. cit.*, 1815, vol. III, pp. 91–2.

30 The Correale Museum in Sorrento has an important group of these figures, presented by Giuseppe and Antonio Parlato, 1992.

31 TB CLXXXVI, "Naples, Paestum and Rome" sketchbook, p. 70.

32 Dr J. Percy, MS note of 1885 in his *Catalogue of Drawings*, British Museum Print Room MS 6.7, p. 72. Quoted Gage *WRM*, p. 65.

33 Letter John Soane Jr to his father. Sir John Soane's Museum.

34 Drawings of Lake Albano, south of Rome, dated 9th, 10th and 11th November 1819. TB CLXXXII, "Albano, Nemi, Rome" sketchbook, itself dated "Nov 30th 1819".

35 TB CXCI, "Rome and Florence", and TB CXCIII, "Remarks (Italy)" sketchbooks.

36 TB CXCII, "Return from Italy" sketchbook, p. 2a.

37 City Museum and Art Gallery, Birmingham. The watercolour is inscribed "Passage of Mt Cenis Jan 15 1820".

38 Postmarked 7.1.1826. Gage, 112.

39 Including TB CLXXIV to CLXXVII, CLXXIX, CLXXXII, CLXXXV to CLXXXIX and CXCI.

40 TB CLXXXIII, "Tivoli" sketchbook, p. 72.

41 FD, 2.2.20.

## TEN
### "THE AUTHOR OF GAMBOGE LIGHT"

1 TB CLXXIX, "Tivoli and Rome" sketchbook, pp. 13a–21.

2 Letter JMWT to Clara Wells, postmarked 4.5.20. Gage, 87.

3 Ref. Gage, 87.

4 Letter JMWT to James Holworthy, postmarked 23.12.20, Gage, 90.

5 Jones, "Recollections".

6 Ref. letter JMWT to W. B. Cooke, Gage, 92.

7 Ref. letter JMWT to James Holworthy, early 1821?, Gage, 94.

8 Howard de Walden Estate Office, contracts vol. 2, no. 227, 12.7.1820.

9 TB CCXI, "Paris, Seine and Dieppe" sketchbook, inside cover.

10 Witold Rybczynski: *Home*; Heinemann, 1988, p. 129.

11 Letter JMWT to W. F. Wells, 13.11.20. Gage, 89.

12 Dated 19.3.21. TFP.

13 Letters JMWT to George Cobb, his Solicitor, 28 & 31.10.27. Gage, 126, 127.

14 TB CXCVIII, pp. 2 & 2a.

15 JMWT's instruction to W. B. Cooke, British Library, Add. MS 50118, f. 67, quoted Finberg, pp. 275–6; see also letter S. Lovegrove to JMWT, 19.11.27, Gage, 130.

16 Joseph Dupuis published his account of the West African adventure, and there gives these clues about his private life. Joseph Dupuis: *op. cit.* Also: Cecilia Powell: "Turner's Women: Family and Friends"; *TSN*, no. 62, Dec 1992, pp. 10ff.

17 Gage, 94.

18 Finberg, *loc. cit.* and TB CXCVIII, "Folkestone" sketchbook, inside back cover.

19 TB CCV, "Old London Bridge" sketchbook, pp. 5a–6.

20 RA Council Minutes, 2.8.20.

21 Andrew Wilton: *The Life and Work of J. M. W. Turner*; 1979, catalogued at no. 493; dated there *c*. 1815, but shown by Gage to be 1825. John Gage: "Turner and the Greek Spirit"; *TS*., vol. 1, no. 2, pp. 14ff.

22 C. R. Cockerell Diary, 14.11.21; RIBA.

23 *ibid.*, 14.1.25.

24 *ibid.*, 2 & 16.2.25.

25 Letter Wilkie to Andrew Geddes, quoted David Laing: *Etchings by Sir D. Wilkie*, 1875, p. 14.

26 Wilton, p. 248.

27 Some of the furniture, probably those pieces described in the inventory as "Mahogany Cheffonier with Drawer, Pair of Mahogany pedestals with Vases and five Mahogany hall chairs" were presented by Miss M. H. Turner to Hastings Borough Council in 1944, and are now in the Mayor's Parlour.

28 P. W. Clayden: *Rogers and his Contempor-*

*aries*, 1887, vol. II, p. 127.

29 Quoted by L. G. Fawkes in a letter to D. S. McColl, 23.7.1911. Quoted Gage, *CinT*, p. 162. Plan of gallery: Howard de Walden Estate Contracts, vol. 4, p. 422. The house has been demolished.

30 Quoted Gerald Finlay: *Landscapes of Memory*, p. 61.

31 Cockerell Diaries, 15.8.22.

32 Allan Cunningham: *The Life of Sir David Wilkie*, vol. II, p. 85.

33 Cockerell Diaries, 23.8.22.

34 TB CCI, "King at Edinburgh" sketchbook, inside end cover and p. 43a.

35 Gerald Finlay: *Turner and George IV in Edinburgh 1822*; Tate Gallery and University of Edinburgh, 1981, pp. 25ff.

36 Letter JMWT to J. C. Schetky, 3.12.1823; Gage, 101.

37 Gerald Finlay: *op. cit.*, p. 16, quoting Drummond: *Perthshire in Bygone Days*, p. 257.

38 Diaries, 22 & 24.8.22.

39 Gage, *CinT*, pp. 122ff.

40 *ibid.*, p. 124, gives 1831. See also Thornbury, pp. 138–9 and note.

41 Thornbury, *loc. cit.*

42 James Skene, on "Painting", *The Edinburgh Encyclopaedia* (ed. David Brewster) 1830, vol. 16 pp. 263ff.

43 TB XLVII "Fonthill" sketchbook, p. 10, and TB XXVII-X.

44 Ref. letter Thomas Phillips to Dawson Turner, 13.12.22 referring to the commission. See B&J, no. 252.

45 B&J, *loc. cit.*

46 Thornbury.

47 Ref. Mrs Arbuthnot: *Journal*; eds Bamford and Wellington, 1950, i. p. 313.

48 Haydon: *Diary*; vol. ii, p. 487 (27.5.24).

49 Thornbury, p. 288.

50 From letter Henry Tijou to Sir John Leicester, 22.12.24, quoted Douglas Hall, *Walpole Society*, XXXVIII, 1960–62, pp. 109–10. See also B&J, 252.

51 Thornbury, p. 429. William Huggins (1781–1845) was the Marine Painter to George IV and William IV.

52 TB CXXIII, pp. 203a & 205.

53 TB XXXIV, "North of England" sketchbook, p. 80.

54 See also Eric Shanes: *Turner's England*

*1810–38*; Cassell, 1990 and Shanes: *THL*.

55 Thornbury, p. 183.

56 Thornbury, pp 192–3.

57 *ibid.*, p. 192.

58 See Gage, 47, 48, 49, 51, 53, 54 and *passim*.

59 See Gage, 81, 82, 92, 95, 98, 100, 102.

60 Letter JMWT to W. B. Cooke, 13.6.21; Gage, 95.

61 Letter JMWT to W. B. Cooke, 13.7.21. Gage, 95a. John Gage: "Further Correspondence of J. M. W. Turner"; *TS*, vol. 6, no. 1, p. 3.

62 C. W. Radclyffe: *Catalogue of the Exhibition ... of Engravings by Birmingham Engravers*; Birmingham, 1877, pp. 5–6. Quoted Eric Shanes: *Turner's England*, p. 15.

63 Charles Heath to Dawson Turner, 19.2.25. Dawson Turner Correspondence, Trinity College, Cambridge.

64 Gage, 121.

65 Gage, 120.

66 Thomas Moore: *Memoirs ...*, 1853, vol. III, p. 74. Also ref. A. Gilchrist: *Life of William Etty*, 1855, vol. II, p. 59.

67 *Report of the Commission ... on the Royal Academy*, 1863, p. 65.

68 Given by Dr Pearson. Royal Society Journal Book, 14.12.97.

69 Dr Bence Jones: *Life and Letters of Faraday*, 1870, vol. 1, p. 378.

70 Humphrey Ward: *History of the Athenaeum 1824–1924*; 1926, ch. 2.

71 Ref. letter Chantrey to JMWT, 24.6.29; Gage, 151.

72 Cecilia Powell: " 'Infuriate in the wreck of hope': Turner's 'Vision of Medea'."; *TS*, vol. 2, no. 1, pp. 12ff.

73 Quoted Finberg, p. 274. Diary not seen by the present author.

74 *Sunny Memories*.

75 *ibid.*

76 Letter JMWT to James Holworthy, 5.5.26. Gage, 116.

77 "Statement of Mr Fawkes's Income and Outgoings", 1824. Fawkes Papers, WYAS, DD161/7/9.

78 Maria Fawkes's diary. Finberg, p. 291.

79 E. M. Fawkes: "Turner at Farnley". Typescript, copy in Clore Gallery.

80 Lindsay, p. 251.

81 1.5.26; Gage, 114.

82 Letter JMWT to John Soane, with Soane's note annotated, 8.7.26; Gage, 117.
83 From press cutting sent to Turner by Robert Balmanno, and returned by the artist. Cutting dated 30.4.26. Gage, 115.
84 5.5.26; Gage, 116.
85 4.12.26; Gage, 119.
86 Letters JMWT to Holworthy; Gage, 112, 116, 119.
87 ?.8.27; Gage, 123.
88 C. Fulke Greville: *Memoirs*; 1874–87, vol. 2, p. 337.
89 PHA 3110 & 5274.
90 PHA 3110–3111.
91 *Literary Gazette*, 13.5.26.
92 Thomas Creevey to Miss Ord, 18.8.28. Quoted Butlin, Luther & Warrell: *Turner at Petworth*, p. 75.
93 Thornbury, p. 199.
94 Named in the Act establishing the Portsmouth and Arundel Canal in 1817.
95 This is named for "William Turner", and may refer to JMWT's father. TFP.
96 4.12.26. Gage, 119.
97 21.4.27; part at Gage, 122. The letter is printed in its entirety by Gage in *TS* vol. 6, no. 1, p. 3.
98 Thames Tunnel Minutes of Occurrence, 13.8.25 – 27.5.27. Brunel Collection, University of Bristol Library.
99 28.10.27; Gage, 126.
100 Book 1, lines 814–18.
101 Typescript, V&A, NAL 55.CC. Gage, *CinT*, p. 128, reads this as "no attendance but me".

9 Sir John Gilbert, quoted L. Cust: "The Portraits of J. M. W. Turner"; *Magazine of Art*, 1895, pp. 248–9.
10 Jerrold Ziff: "But why 'Medea' in Rome?"; *TS*, vol. 2, no. 1, p. 19. See also Cecilia Powell: *op. cit.* in *TS* vol. 2, no. 1, pp. 12ff.
11 Whitley, II, p. 159.
12 E. Fuchs: *Geschichte der erotischen Kunst*, 1912. Illustrated Wilton, p. 158.
13 13.10.28; Gage, 141.
14 Letter John Gibson to Thomas L. Donaldson, 5.4.29; RIBA Library, DoT/1/3/1.
15 6.11.28; Gage, 142.
16 15.12.28; Gage, 143.
17 Letter Eastlake to Mrs Callcott, *cit.*
18 2.12.28; Gage, 146.
19 Letter Gibson to Donaldson, *cit.*
20 Leslie, vol. ii, p. 205.
21 JMWT to Eastlake, 16.2.29; Gage, 147, and 11.8.29; Gage, 154.
22 Gage, 154.
23 16.2.29; Gage, 147.
24 Letter to Mrs Callcott, *cit.*
25 Uwins, II, p. 240.
26 Letter Francis Danby to John Gibbons, 24.2.29. Quoted Francis Greenacre: *Francis Danby*; Bristol and Tate Gallery, 1988, p. 29.
27 16.2.29; Gage, 147.
28 Gage, 147.
29 Letter Charles Eastlake to Mrs Callcott, 26.3.29. V&A, NAL, *loc. cit.*
30 19.3.29; Gage, 148.
31 Mary Somerville: "On the Magnetising Power of the more Refrangible Solar Rays." Paper read to the Royal Society, 2.2.26.

ELEVEN
ITALY: "TERRA PITTURA"

1 13.10.28; Gage, 141.
2 JMWT to Charles Eastlake, 23.8.28; Gage, 140.
3 *ibid.*
4 Maria Callcott to her sister, 22.5.28. V&A, NAL. 86.PP.14/IV.
5 Uwins, II, p. 296.
6 Kestner to Mrs Callcott, 10.11.28; V&A, NAL, *loc. cit.*
7 Letter Charles Eastlake to Mrs Callcott, 5.11.28; V&A, NAL *loc. cit.*
8 JMWT to Chantrey, 6.11.28; Gage, 142.

TWELVE
"MY JAUNDICED EYE"

1 *The Steamboat Companion: London to ... Margate*; 1830, p. 25.
2 *ibid.*, p. 33.
3 Clara Wheeler to Robert Finch, 4.11.28; MS Finch, c. 2. d. 17, fo. 201, Bodleian Library, Oxford. Quoted Gage, p. 135n.
4 Leslie, vol. 1, 1860, pp. 207–8.
5 3.1.30; Gage, 159.
6 22.2.30; Gage, 161. Gage takes his text from Thornbury's transcription of the now missing letter. See Thornbury, 1862, ii, 233–4.

7 Haydon: *Diary*, vol. 3, p. 372, 3–16.6.29.

8 Gage, 161.

9 Gilbert, *loc. cit.*

10 Spitting and snuff story: *Farington Diary*; 1923 edn, vol. II, 1802–04, p. 97n. Paper silhouette story: Eric Shanes: "The Mortlake Conundrum"; *TS*, vol. 3, no. 1, pp. 49–50.

11 Lindsay, p. 257; Thornbury (1862 edn), ii, p. 167.

12 A. T. Storey: *James Holmes and John Varley*; 1894, p. 120.

13 Leslie, vol. 1, pp. 201–2.

14 Reconstructed from Jones, "Recollections".

15 The source of this quote has fled. The author read it somewhere; but where?

16 Jones, "Recollections".

17 See Gage, pp. 237–8, 258 & *passim*.

18 Letter J. S. Cotman to Dawson Turner, 8.1.34. Private colln, quoted Gage, p. 258.

19 *Athenaeum*, 1840, p. 893.

20 See Gerald Finlay: *Landscapes of Memory*; University of California Press, 1980, p. 229.

21 16.10.33. Reprinted in Gerald Finlay: *op. cit.*, pp. 229–31.

22 *Sunny Memories*.

23 Ruskin MS, quoted Gage, p. 280.

24 John Taylor, 1827. Quoted Gage, p. 274.

25 Ruskin MS, quoted Gage, p. 279.

26 Dr Bence Jones: *Life and Letters of Faraday*; 1870, vol. 1, pp. 378–9.

27 Roberts, pp. 2ff.

28 TB CCXXXVIII.

29 These have been tentatively titled "Gloucester Cathedral" and even "Boston Stump", TB CCLXIII-246 & 307.

30 Letter Walter Scott to Samuel Rogers, 15.11.30; W. Scott: *Letters*, vol. XI, pp. 459–61.

31 JMWT to Walter Scott, 20.4.31; Gage, 169.

32 Finlay: *op. cit.*, pp. 116ff.

33 Thornbury, p. 139.

34 JMWT to James Lenox, 16.8.45, Gage, 288.

35 Charles Fulke Greville: *Diaries*, 6.4.32, vol. 2, p. 309.

36 25.2.32; Gage, 174.

37 "Berwick" sketchbook, TB CCLXV, p. 42.

38 Gage, 174.

39 A. G. H. Bachrach: *Turner's Holland*; Tate Gallery, 1994.

40 See B&J, no. 259.

41 TB XXXVII.

42 Uwins: vol. II, pp. 251 & 253.

43 Jane Thistlethwaite: "The Etchings of Edward Thomas Daniell"; *Norfolk Archaeology*, xxxvi (1977), pp. 1ff.

44 Roberts, *op. cit.*

45 *ibid.*

46 F. R. Beecheno: *E. T. Daniell – A Memoir*; 1889, p. 13.

47 "Guernsey" sketchbook, TB CCLII, inside back cover; "Brussels up to Mannheim" sketchbook, TB CCXCVI, inside front cover.

48 Delacroix *Journal*, 24.3.55, and Delacroix to Silvestre, 31.12.58, quoted Gage, *CinT*, p. 268n.

49 The dating of Turner's Continental journeys in the 1830s is unclear. See Cecilia Powell: *Turner's Rivers of Europe*, 1991; Anne Lyles: *Turner – The Fifth Decade* and Powell: *Turner and Germany*, 1995.

50 *Arnold's Magazine*, Summer 1833, vol. 1, p. 312–23. The identity of the author has been discovered by Jerrold Ziff. See his "William Henry Pyne's 'J. M. W. Turner RA' – A Neglected Critic and Essay Remembered"; *TS*, vol. 6, no. 1, pp. 18ff.

51 For a full acount of the vignettes and their evolution, see Jan Piggott: *Turner's Vignettes*; Tate Gallery, 1993.

52 B. Webber: *James Orrock R. I.*; 1903, vol. 1, pp. 60–1.

53 Ruskin: *Modern Painters*, vol. V, part viii, ch. 2, para. 15.

54 E. M. Fawkes typescipt, *cit.*

55 This is the absorbing thesis of Eric Shanes, explored in his *Turner's Human Landscape*, Heinemann, 1990.

56 *Art Journal*, 1860, p. 100.

57 Walter Fawkes: *Speech ... on Parliamentary Reform, May 23rd 1812*; London, 1813, p. 15.

## THIRTEEN
## GATHERING MORTALITY

1 *Felix Farley's Bristol Journal*, 19.6.30.

2 *ibid*.

3 *ibid*, Sept. 1829.

4 Thornbury, pp. 446–7.

5 *Blackwood's*, Oct 1836, vol. XL, pp. 543ff.

6 *ibid.*, pp. 550–1.

7 Ruskin: *Works*, vol. III, pp. 635–40.

8 6.10.36; Gage, 202.

9 Letter n.d. [after Nov 1836]; Gage, 205.

10 T. M. Monck Mason: *Account of the late Aeronautical Expedition*; 1836. Gage, pp. 163–4.

11 Letter John Ruskin to his father 22.4.37; *Works*, vol. XXXVI, p. 14.

12 Martha Somerville (ed.): *Recollections of Mary Somerville*; Murray, 1874, p. 269.

13 *ibid.*, pp. 231, 251.

14 *ibid.*, p. 244.

15 Richard Owen: *The Life of Richard Owen*, 1894, vol. 1, pp. 262–4.

16 *loc. cit.*

17 JMWT to Clara Wheeler, 12.3.37; Gage, 207.

18 2.1.37. D. Hill: "A Newly Discovered Letter by Turner"; *TSN*, Winter 1981–2, pp. 2–3.

19 *Spectator*; *Literary Gazette* both 6.5.37.

20 Raymond Lister: *The Letters of Samuel Palmer*; 1974, vol. 1, p. 182.

21 Quoted Gage, p. 242.

22 W. H. Harrison: *University Magazine*, Dublin, ii (1878), p. 705.

23 *The Academy*, 1878, pp. 232ff, 345ff. Quoted Gage, p. 183.

24 B&J 527; dated there "*c*. 1830?"

25 B&J 434; dated there *c*. 1830.

26 Cecilia Powell: "Turner's Women: The Painted Veil"; *TSN*, no. 63 (1993), pp. 12ff.

27 *Times*, 3–26.9.33.

28 B&J 453; dated there *c*. 1830.

29 28.8.37; Gage, 210.

30 Housekeeping Account, 1836–7; PHA 3111.

31 Mary, Lady Leconfield's diary, typescript PHA 5274; and letter from James Clark MD, 7.7.30, PHA 81.

32 Jones, p. 3.

33 Letter Thomas Phillips to Rev. Thomas Sockett, 15.11.37. PHA 728.

34 Patrick Youngblood: "That House of Art – Turner at Petworth"; *TS*, vol. 2, no. 2, pp. 16ff.

35 Corresp. in PHA 1097. Barry's proposals were not in the event carried out.

36 7.12.37 & 20.12.37; Gage, 214 & 215.

37 One view: Andrew Wilton: "Picture Note"; *TS*, vol. 10, no. 2, pp. 55ff. The other: Patrick Youngblood: *op. cit.*, *TS* vol. 10, no. 1, pp. 56–7; and Gage, *WRM*, pp. 167–8.

38 *Athenaeum*, 12.5.38.

39 "Aretino" in *Blackwood's Magazine*, March 1841, pp. 342ff.

40 Alaric Watts, "Biographical Sketch of JMWT"; *Liber Fluviorum*, 1853, p. xxxii.

41 Falk, p. 196.

42 Archer.

43 Christie's sale, 25.3.65.

44 Archer.

45 Eric Shanes (*TS* vol I, no I, p. 37) has suggested that the St Margaret's house is possibly The Hermitage, built 1830, the only house in the village with a sea view. This may be so, but I doubt it. Now called South Sands House, it is an extensive mansion which was owned in the 1930s by J. J Astor. If Turner had lived there it would have been as part of a very large household. Likelier candidates are some of the cottages in the village, despite the fact that they are about half a mile from the sea. Dr David Price's Affidavit is reprinted at Appendix 3.

46 Judy Egerton: *Turner – The Fighting Téméraire*; National Gallery, London, 1995, p. 44

47 Judy Egerton: *op. cit.* is a full account of the painting, in the National Gallery's "Making & Meaning" series.

48 *Spectator*, 11.5.39.

49 British Museum, 1981–12–12–15; p. 1*v*.

50 Thornbury, pp. 305, 352.

51 Robert Leslie, recorded in Ruskin, *Works*, xxxv, pp. 576–7.

52 E. T. Cook: *Life of John Ruskin*; 1911, vol. 1, p. 108.

53 Ruskin, *Works*, vol. XXXV, p. 305.

54 Ruskin: *Modern Painters*, vol. 1, part II, sec. V, ch. III, para 39.

55 Prof. John McCoubrey: "The Slave Ship": unpublished lecture given for the Turner Society at the Tate Gallery, May 1995.

56 *Blackwood's*, Sept 1840, p. 384.

57 Prof. John McCoubrey, lecture *cit*.

58 *Blackwood's*, *loc. cit.*

59 June 1840.

60 Vol. I, 1841, p. 33.

61 Ref. Sir Wyke Bayliss: *Olives: The Reminiscences of a President*, 1906. Lindsay, p. 192.

62 Letter "E. H." to JMWT, 24.8.40; Gage, 236.

63 Ref. *Gazzetta Privilegiata di Venezia*, quoted Robert Upstone: *Turner – The Final Years;* Tate Gallery, 1993, p. 11.

64 TB CCCXVI-3.

65 TB CCCXIV-34.

66 William Callow: *Autobiography;* 1908, pp. 66–7.

67 Christine Bicknell writes in her diary 24.6.45: "Turner going to Venice." There is no record that he ever made this later journey. Quoted Peter Bicknell and Helen Guiterman: "The Turner Collector – Elhanan Bicknell"; *TS*, vol. 7, no. 1, p. 40.

68 TB CCCXVI-25.

69 7.10.40; Gage, 238.

70 Archer

71 *ibid*.

72 Thornbury, p. 324.

73 John Gage: "Turner's Annotated Books: 'Goethe's Theory of Colours'"; *TS*, vol. 4, no. 2, pp. 34ff.

74 Ruskin: *Works*, vol. XII, p. 500.

75 *ibid.*, VII, p. 445n.

76 See B&J, 398.

77 "But to John Bull ... the voyage [to Margate] is second nature; a thing of sport, like Ariel's 'putting a girdle round the earth, and asking but forty minutes to do it in.'" "Aretino", in *Blackwood's*, March 1841, p. 342.

78 David Roberts: *op. cit.*

FOURTEEN

"THE GREAT LION OF THE DAY"

1 Ruskin: *Diaries*, vol. I, 24.2.43.

2 Inventory; Wilton, p. 248.

3 Ruskin: *Works*, XIII, p. 161. The source of the criticism has not been traced.

4 Ruskin: *Diaries*, Vol I, 8.2.43

5 *The Letters of Elizabeth Barrett Browning to Mary Russell Mitford*, vol.2, p. 257n. eds M. B. Raymond & M. R. Sullivan, Wedgestone Press, 1983.

6 Ruskin: *Works* vol. VII, p. 435n.

7 Roberts, p. 4.

8 Letter John Ruskin to Samuel Prout, 7.12.43. Ruskin: *Works*, vol. XXXVIII, p. 336.

9 Ruskin: *Diaries*, vol. I, 20.10.44.

10 *Sunny Memories*.

11 *Photographic News*, 1860, p. 407. Quoted Wilton, pp. 226–7.

12 Ruskin: *Works*, vol.XIII, p. 190.

13 Thornbury, p. 99.

14 Philip Hamerton: *The Life of J. M. W. Turner RA*, 1879, p. 135.

15 Horsley, p. 240.

16 Redgrave, vol. II, p. 86.

17 Bicknell and Guiterman, *op. cit.*

18 25.2.45; Roberts, p. 3.

19 15.2.44; & 6.2.45, Bicknell and Guiterman, p. 3.

20 Ruskin: *Diaries* 27.3.44.

21 Lindsay, p. 192

22 Letter J. J. Ruskin to John Ruskin, 15/19.9.45; quoted B&J, 337.

23 New York, Metropolitan Museum; B&J 415.

24 Ruskin letter, *ibid*.

25 See Julian Treuherz: "The Turner Collector: Henry McConnel, Cotton Spinner"; *TS* vol. 6, no. 2, pp. 37ff; & Jeannie Chapel: "The Turner Collector: Joseph Gillott 1799–1872"; *ibid* pp. 43ff.

26 e.g. pp. 178ff.

27 11.5.43; Gage, 260.

28 13.2.44; Gage, 265.

29 4.12.38; Gage, 219.

30 British Library MS P ff. 19v–20r. Hammersley's father retained his faith in his son, for J. A. Hammersley went on to become Head of the Manchester School of Design. Gage, p. 259.

31 *Sunny Memories*

32 Thornbury, p. 265.

33 26.12.46; Gage, 302.

34 8.5.44.

35 See also: John Gage: *Turner – Rain, Steam and Speed*; Art in Context series, Allen Lane, 1972.

36 Horsley: *loc. cit.*

37 Thornbury, p. 239.

38 15.5.43. Kelley and Hudson (eds): *The Brownings' Correspondence*, Wedgestone Press, 1989, vol. 7, p. 125.

39 From Nagler's *Kunstler-Lexikon*, 1849, quoted B&J, 401.

40 14.5.42.

41 W. P. Frith: *My Autobiography and Reminiscences*; 1887, vol. 1, pp. 130–1.

42 TB CCCLXI, pp. 2 & 5.

43 Thornbury, p. 360

44 Sherrell's reminiscences were collected by C. J. Feret in the *Isle of Thanet Gazette*, 23.9.1916.

45 Horsley, p. 284.

46 *ibid*.

47 John Burnet: *Turner and his Works*, 1852, pp. 34–5.

48 Thomas Miller (ed.): *Turner and Girtin's Picturesque Views Sixty Years Since ...*; 1854, p. 40; quoted Wilton, p. 218.

49 Leopold Martin, quoted Wilton, pp. 218–19.

50 Archer, p. 36.

51 Roberts.

52 Archer

53 A. McGeorge: *William Leighton Leitch Landscape Painter, A Memoir*, 1884, pp. 81–6.

54 Lady Eastlake: *Journal & Correspondance*, 20.5.46.

55 Peter Cunningham, Memoir in Burnet, *op. cit.*, pp. 28–9.

56 Letters JMWT to William Wethered, – ? 12.44; and to F. H. Fawkes, 28.12.44; Gage, 276 & 275.

57 Thornbury, pp. 349ff.

58 From C. H. Lear's diary, 3.5.47; National Portrait Gallery Archive.

59 e.g. *Illustrated London News*, 28.10.48, p. 263.

60 *Gents Mag.*, Oct 1849, p. 410.

61 Roberts.

62 Thornbury, p. 105.

63 Letter F. T. Palgrave to John Ruskin; quoted Finberg p. 434.

64 Roberts.

65 Ruskin: *Works*, vol. XXXVI, p. 595; annotation to letter Ruskin to Frederick Harrison, 1869.

66 Letter William Bartlett to John Ruskin, 7.8.57. Quoted Finberg, p. 437. See also Dr Price's Affidavit, reprinted Appendix 3.

67 Archer, p. 36.

68 G. D. Leslie: *The Inner Life of the Royal Academy*; 1914, pp. 143–4. *Observer* notice: 8.9.50. Cutting in Henry Bicknell's Album, Paul Mellon Center, New Haven.

69 JMWT to George Jones, 2.1.51; Gage 321, and others.

70 Roberts.

71 Letters David Price to Richard Owen, 28.2 and 5.3.50. Richard Owen Correspondence, Natural History Museum Library, London vol. 21, pp. 453–4

72 31.1.51; Gage, 323.

73 J. E. Panton [Jane Ellen Frith]: *Leaves from a Life*; 1908, p. 41. Quoted Bill Ruddick, *TSN*, 53 (oct 1989), p. 9. Jane was born on 18.10.48, so this could not reasonably have taken place before early summer 1851.

74 Roberts.

75 Falk, p. 220.

76 Ruskin: *Works*, vol.XXVIII, p. 147. Ruskin does not say who was with Turner when he said these words.

77 Roberts.

# Appendix 1

## TURNER AND THORNBURY

Though many hundreds of writers and art historians have written about every aspect of Turner's work since his death, there have been only seven significant biographers: Walter Thornbury (1862), P. G. Hamerton (1879), Cosmo Monkhouse (1879), Bernard Falk (1938), A. J. Finberg (1939), Jack Lindsay (1966) and Andrew Wilton (1979 and 1987). The most acute problem which they all faced was the dearth of documentary sources. Turner was an active and lucid correspondent, as revealed by the surviving letters collected by John Gage.[1] He wrote to good friends such as James Holworthy and Ambrose Johns at some length, and with an easy, conversational style. His detailed and careful correspondence with one of his many business partners, James Wyatt, suggests that there would have been many more such relationships by letter with engravers and patrons.

However, his three great friendships, with Henry Scott Trimmer which lasted for nearly sixty years, with Walter Fawkes which lasted for about thirty, and with Lord Egremont which was of about the same length of time, are hardly traceable through correspondence. The reason for this is that the heirs of each of these men decided for whatever reason to destroy their papers, and documented the fact that they had done so. The existence of letters to Holworthy, Johns and Wyatt can only lead us to the conclusion that Turner wrote at length to his closer friends also. In the case of Trimmer, Thornbury writes:

> Mr Trimmer was remarkable for a habit of keeping all letters that he ever received; and the result of this literary accumulation was that, after his death, his son, exhausted by the labour of reading a packet or two of crabbed MS, set to and with ruthless hands burnt some twenty sacksful of original and unpublished letters, including, no doubt, some hundreds of Turner's.[2]

E. M. Fawkes recorded the destruction of Walter's papers in her typescript "Turner at Farnley",[3] although the flotsam and jetsam of this destruction, including Walter's financial accounts of 1824, have found their way into the West Yorkshire Archaeological Society in Leeds.

This loss is compounded by the disappearance of all of Turner's own private papers, those thousands of letters sent to him and otherwise accumulated over the years. They will have been left at Queen Anne Street when he died, probably in some chaos. It took over four years of legal wrangling to settle the ownership of Turner's money and of his paintings and drawings, and in the heat of that battle his papers were either an irrelevance or an embarrassment. Of the very few letters to Turner that do survive, most have sketches or other notes on the back, suggesting that his executors carefully picked over the remaining detritus and took out what they wanted to keep. So until other evidence emerges, we can only assume that the mass of Turner's papers slipped through the net and into the bonfire. Thus, deeper knowledge of both sides of three very important friendships, and much else, has been lost.

The first biographer, Walter Thornbury (1828–76), has been excoriated by his successors one by one. Indeed ever since his *Life and Correspondence of J. M. W. Turner RA* was published Thornbury has been the butt of intense criticism, much, but not all of it, justified. Though it could possibly have been arranged, Thornbury never met Turner, and did not claim to have done so. He was a professional journalist who had worked on the *Athenaeum* and with Dickens on *Household Words*. He had a natural eye for a good marketable story, and in Turner's life, found one. He did claim to have asked around to find out if anyone more qualified than he was writing Turner's life:

> I determined to take no steps in such a scheme until I had ascertained whether Mr Ruskin might not himself have some intention of one day becoming the biographer of that great painter whose genius he had done so much to illustrate ... Encouraged by this certainty that I was neither trespassing nor interfering with anyone, I at once set to work steadily and quietly ...[4]

Thornbury encouraged a number of Turner's friends and acquaintances to write or talk to him about his subject. Some, such as George Jones RA and John Mayall wrote to him at length, and there is no reason for us to doubt their words as published by Thornbury.[5] However, neither Sarah, Hannah, Evelina nor Georgiana Danby, all of whom were living when Thornbury was writing, talked to him, nor did Sophia Booth who lived on until 1868.

The most serious omission among Thornbury's direct sources appears to be Turner's oldest friend the Rev. Henry Scott Trimmer, who lived until November 1859. Thornbury says in the Preface to his first edition that the desire to write a life of Turner first entered his mind "some four years ago", i.e. around 1858. This was before Trimmer's death, and it is surprising that Thornbury seems not to have sought out straight away the man who was Turner's oldest friend. The most likely explanation for these obvious gaps is that Thornbury did approach some or all of them, but they refused to co-operate, knowing that a clever journalist might ferret personal information from them that they, and Turner, would not wish to be revealed. Nevertheless, no day passed, Thornbury claims

> without some search for materials, some noting down of traditions, some visit to Turner's old friends ...[I] resolved not to complete my book, however long it might take me, until I had collected all that patience and enthusiasm could enable me to gather together.

Perhaps as a result of the unwillingness of Turner and his loyal relations and close friends to reveal themselves to Thornbury, there has been a long history of Thornbury-bashing by his successors as Turner's biographer. Bernard Falk, whose *Turner the Painter: His Hidden Life* was published in 1938, called Thornbury's book a "... voluble and shapeless biography, a rag-bag of odds and ends, unassimilated and to a large extent uncorroborated ..."[6] A. J. Finberg, who had been studying Turner for longer than anyone, and was pipped to publication by Falk, wrote of Thornbury:

> To cover up his tracks, [Thornbury] distorted the material he appropriated without acknowledgements, and amplified his distortion with a wealth of fictitious detail. His personal contribution to the *Life* may be best described as the deliberate falsification of current information, legends, and gossip.[7]

However, as a more or less contemporary biographer working within the covers of one book, Thornbury is all we have got. He is the Old Testament of Turner studies – chronologically unreliable, vague, muddled and repetitious, but containing a few searing truths, many inaccuracies and lots of good stories. As an example of the dynamics by which the readers of Thornbury's biography have been misled, I quote the mysterious life of Mary Turner's portrait. There are no surviving portraits of Turner's mother, unless the small pencil profile of a woman in a mob-cap in the "Bristol and Malmesbury" sketchbook of 1791 can be taken to be her.[8] Thornbury, however, draws Mary Turner's picture by describing a portrait supposedly painted by Turner as a boy and which, if it ever existed, is now lost. Thornbury had never seen it. The resulting description from this phantom portrait quoted here in Chapter One, has echoed as the fact of Mary's appearance through the work of Turner's biographers, even though it is hearsay.

Thornbury got his information about the portrait from a source he describes as "the rector of Heston, the eldest son of Turner's old friend and executor". Even this statement is riddled with impossibilities. Turner's "old friend and executor" was the Rev. Henry Scott Trimmer, the vicar of

Heston, Middlesex from 1804 until his death. He had three sons: Henry Syer Trimmer (1806–76) who became Vicar of Marston-on-Dove, Derbyshire; Barrington Trimmer (1809–60) who became his father's Curate at Heston, and only survived his father by a year; and Frederick Edmond Trimmer (1813–83) who became a businessman, landowner and JP. He lived in Heston all his life.

None of Trimmer's sons could have known Mary who died in 1804, though they may have seen the portrait. All these can only have got their information from their father, though to compound the muddle further Thornbury goes on to say that "Mr. Trimmer [sic] ... obtained his facts from an authority no less unquestionable than Hannah Danby, Turner's old housekeeper, who personally had them from the painter's father." To bring Hannah Danby into the chain at this point was in fact unnecessary, as Henry Scott Trimmer had had every opportunity to meet Mary Turner when he was a boy, and thus pass on his own first hand account to his sons.

Thornbury credits the information with a "Trimmer" source as coming from F. E. Trimmer, H. S. Trimmer's third son, who was not born until 1813. So the more trust we put into Thornbury's "Trimmer" material, the more we have to accept that it did, in fact, come directly from the aged Henry Scott Trimmer himself. When Thornbury was beginning the research for his book, the conditions of Turner's will concerning the display of his pictures had not been met. As one of his executors, H. S. Trimmer technically shared responsibility for the state of affairs. In the intense legalistic atmosphere surrounding the proving of Turner's will, Trimmer would have been rash to speak freely about Turner under his own name, particularly to a professional journalist. He could, however, speak of Turner through the mouthpiece of one of his sons, and this, I suggest, is what happened.

In a devastating review of Thornbury's book in *Quarterly Review*, the unnamed reviewer, actually Elizabeth Rigby, Lady Eastlake, pointed out that during the four years in which the author claimed to have been researching and writing Turner's *Life*, he also "enriched our literature with at least nine other separate volumes" as well as reviews in pamphlets and contributions to periodicals. Lady Eastlake described the *Life of Turner* by "this indefatigable gentleman" as "simply the most deplorable piece of bookmaking that has ever fallen our way".[9]

It is significant that nobody else in Thornbury's day took up the challenge to write Turner's life. Ruskin wavered over the matter, but ultimately refused, urging a Frenchman, Ernest Chesneu, to write the life. George Jones, another great friend and executor, had the knowledge and understanding to write at the very least an anecdotal account. So did C. R. Leslie and David Roberts, though both left extensive notes, and may both be excused on the grounds that they had pictures to paint.

Two writers however did have the knowledge and the ability to write Turner's life, but failed to do so. One, the poet and banker Samuel Rogers, was an executor, and had known Turner since the 1790s. They had many mutual friends, and Turner was a regular guest at Rogers's renowned breakfast parties. Rogers was also a useful gossip, inquisitive about the lives, opinions and intentions of his artistic friends, and an easy writer. The other was the demolisher of Thornbury herself, Elizabeth, Lady Eastlake. She had known Turner since 1844 when they had met over dinner with the publisher John Murray in Albemarle Street. She was then the perceptive and inquisitive thirty-five-year-old Elizabeth Rigby, who had already travelled widely, particularly in Germany and Russia, had written a book about the Baltic, and had been a regular contributor to the *Quarterly Review* since 1842. She recorded her first impressions about Turner in her diary: "a queer little being, very knowing about all the castles he had drawn – a cynical kind of body, who seems to love his art for no other reason than because it is his *own*."[10]

Five years after she and Turner met, Elizabeth Rigby married Sir Charles Eastlake, then secretary of the Fine Arts Commission, and, by the time of Turner's death, President of the Royal Academy. Lady Eastlake went on to translate Waagen's *Treasures of Art in Great Britain*, 1854–57, and to publish extensive art criticism. If anybody could have written a reliable and contemporary life of Turner, it was Lady Eastlake. She had known him, she was in a unique position to ferret information out of Turner's surviving friends, she seems to have been an eager seeker out of the truth, and she had a good turn of phrase and publishing contacts. That she failed to take up the challenge, and so let in Thornbury, is a serious matter.

The possible reasons, however, are not hard to find. Turner had a "dark side", as Ruskin had pointed out to Thornbury, that if fully revealed would have upset mid-Victorian propriety. He had had a shadowy unmarried relationship with Sarah Danby, and had had two known children by her; he had recently lived as the husband of a Margate landlady under an assumed name; and he had a highly developed libido which found expression through pornographic drawings which Ruskin and the Keeper of the National Gallery felt he had to burn. Furthermore, Turner was reportedly tight with money, though rich as Croesus, and had run up a bill of more than £500 with his doctor which remained unpaid at his death. His doctor, David Price of Margate, had to take legal action in 1853, naming *inter alia* George Jones RA, Philip Hardwick RA, the Treasurer of the Royal Academy, and John Ruskin, in order to recover the money (see Appendix 3). Turner had a secret life that, by the time Thornbury's book was published in 1861, was common knowledge in the upper reaches of the art world establishment.

It does Lady Eastlake no credit when she says at the beginning of her review of Thornbury's *Life*:

It may appear surprising that the task of writing Turner's life should have been left to an utter stranger, since there must be among those who knew him persons well qualified to do justice to the subject. [Here Lady Eastlake suggests George Jones might have done it.] But it would seem that, for whatever reason, Turner's personal friends have declined the task.

And at the end:

... it is even possible that, by requesting some competent friend to draw up a modest memoir of him, and furnishing the necessary information, he might have saved himself from the worst of his posthumous misfortunes – that of falling victim to such a biographer as Mr Thornbury. Perhaps the appearance of this wretched book may be the means of calling forth some writer qualified, by knowledge of the man and of his art, to investigate the truth and to tell it as it ought to be told.

Had Lady Eastlake taken her own advice, she might have made a greater name for herself. Where angels had feared to tread, however, a fool – no, Thornbury was no fool, but a very canny, opportunist young journalist and an inexperienced biographer – walked right in.

## Notes to Appendix 1

1 John Gage (ed.): *Collected Correspondence of J. M. W. Turner*; Oxford, 1980. See also John Gage: "Further Correspondence of J. M. W. Turner"; *TS*, vol. 6, no. 1 (1986), pp. 2ff.

2 Thornbury, p. 225. After this passage Thornbury adds the Trimmer son's unconvincing palliative that, *inter alia*, Turner "like most artists did not like writing".

3 Copies in the National Gallery and Clore Gallery Libraries.

4 Thornbury, p. xi.

5 The Jones MS is in the Ashmolean Museum, Oxford.

6 Falk, p. 17.

7 Finberg, p. 4

8 TB VI, p. 2.

9 *Quarterly Review*, vol. CXI (1862), pp. 450ff.

10 Lady Eastlake: *Journals & Correspondence*, ed. Smith, 1895.

# Appendix 2

## TURNER'S MEDICAL RECIPES

The recipes which follow were written in his sketchbooks by Turner at different times of his life.

*TB XXX*=Turner Bequest catalogue number. Sketchbook kept in the Clore Gallery, Tate Gallery, London.

"*Swans*" [e.g.] = name given to sketchbook by Ruskin when he first catalogued the Turner Bequest in the 1850s.

*TB XLII "Swans"* c. 1796/97
Inside front cover:
"Receipt for making an Efficable ointment for cut ... [?]
Solomon's Seal leaves and buds
Comfrey do.
Bay
Elder
Valerian
An equal quantity to which may be added a handful of Parsley these herbs must be cut small bruise in a stone mortar boil'd for some hours in a Bell mold kettle over a slow fire in a sufficient quantity of unwashed butter [?] to make the herbs thoroughly moist it must stand ten or 12 days after which strain thro a cloth, the Juice then to be boild and well skimmed and run into small jars or pots.
Given by Miss Narraway of Bristol."

*TB CXI "Hastings and Oxford"* c. 1809–11
p. 2a
"The Herb Stramonium
Smoke 2 or 3 pipes every day
Swallow the saliva."

p. 8a-8
"Dis[solve] Blue Vit[riol] in Spring Water. Precipitate it by six ... Evernescence ... separate it out of a clear spirit. Wash the precipitate in warm water ... decant the liquor ... of salt ... the solution and reserve the precipitate in ... precipitate ... to filter it ...
5 drops of the fluid to an ounce of water ... a dram of the solution to your w ... after ... with x 2 or 3 times day during the ..."

*TB CXXXV "Chemistry and Apuleia' 1813*
p. 1
"Maltese Plague
1. Symptoms: Sickness, debility, shivering, heat, thirst, headache
2. Delirium
3. Darkspots, ulcer.

Emetic: 10 grains Epicacuina
Purge: 5 grains of Calomel, 10 of Jalep
Teaspoonful of Sal Mendaveri every 2 hours. Common drink lemonade –
Head shaved. Vinegar and water applied with a sponge to head and
body."

*TB CLIV(a) "Liber Notes (2)" c. 1816/17*
p. 53a
"Half an ounce of camphor dissolved in a gill of Brandy and taken at three
different times of 3 minutes a remedy for surfit or when the [?rinsing] of
cold water has taken Effect. Dr John ... [?] White [?]"

*Prescription dated December 1827 [Turner Family Papers]*
*This is named for "William Turner" and may refer to J. M. W. Turner's father.*

"Rx Spir Aether Nitrosi z xx
  Liq. Ammon. Acetat. z xx
  Glyn. Scilla z xx
  Aqua Mentha pip. z xx"

*TB CCXXXVII "Roman and French Notebook" 1828*
p. 10a
"Alum Com zp
Zinc Sulphur gr x &
[?] prl Matte x"

*TB CCLII "Guernsey", c. 1830*
Inside back cover:
"1 oz of Cinnamon water
1 grain Epicackuana
35 drops Laudanum          "within an hour
2 drams of Spirits of Lavender    after the attack"
2 dr of Tincture of Rhubarb"

p. 92a
"Soda and ginger
20 gr of carbonate of soda

| | |
|---|---|
| Carbonate of soda | 8 scruples |
| Tartarate of Potash | 3 scruples |
| Nitrous ether | 4 scruples |

distilled 7½oz for 6 or 8 [?] days."

*TB CCLXV "Berwick", c. 1831.*
p. 42
"25 drops of Cajeput oil in glass of Hot Water, if not relieved in 5 min take 50 more. Sir M. Turpey [?] remedy for the Cholera."

*TB CCXCI (a) "Rhine, (between Cologne and Mayence) also Moselle and Aix-la-Chapelle." c. 1835*
p. 14a:
"Said to be an infallible cure for the bite of a mad dog. Leaves of Rue. Bruised Vincu[?] treacle Mithridate, and scrapings of Pewter – each 4 ounces. Boild slowly in 2 quarts of Strongs Hale [sic] until the ale is one quart.
9 table spoonsful 7 mornings fasting. Warm cattle 10 cold dog 5. apply some of the ingredients strained to the wound within 9 days of the bite."

*TB CCXCVI "Brussels up to Mannheim", c. 1837/38*
Inside cover:
"1 oz of Cinnamon water (?)
1 gr Epicachua
25 drops laudenum
2 drams tincture of rhubarb
Q . . .
20 grains of carbonate of soda
Tart[ar] of Potash 8 scruples
N[itrous?] Ether Distilled W[ater] for 6 or 8."

# Appendix 3

## Dr David Price's Affidavit

David Price (1787–1870) practised in Margate from 1826. He was Sophia Booth's doctor, and through her came to be Turner's doctor. He was a consulting surgeon at the Royal Sea Bathing Hospital, Margate, a Justice of the Peace and a member of the Margate Town Council. He attended Turner through his latter illnesses, and claimed through this affidavit that he had not been paid by his patient since May 1850.

The original document is in the collection of the Price family, and is quoted here by permission.

In Chancery
Between Henry Scott Trimmer, George Jones, Charles Turner, Philip Hardwick, Henry Harpur and Hugh Andrew Johnston Munro – Plaintiffs
Hannah Danby, Mary Tepper, William Turner, Thomas Price Turner, Mary Mathews, John Widgery and Mary Ann Turner his wife, John Turner, Sophia Caroline Booth and Her Majesty's Attorney General – Defendants.
And Between Henry Harpur – Plaintiff
Henry Trimmer, Samuel Rogers, George Jones, Charles Turner, John Ruskin the Younger when he shall come within the jurisdiction of the court, Philip Hardwick and Hugh Andrew Johnston Munro. Defendants.

I David Price of Margate in the County of Kent, a Doctor of Medicine, a Fellow of the Royal College of Surgeons of England and also Consulting Surgeon to the Royal Sea Bathing Infirmary at Margate aforesaid where I have practised for twenty-seven years last past, make oath and say, That Joseph Mallord William Turner Esquire Royal Academician deceased the Testator in the pleadings of this cause named, was in his lifetime and at the time of his death and his Estate still is justly and truly endebted to me in the sum of Five hundred and twenty-one Pounds seventeen shillings for professional Journies, and the attendances taken and made by me as consulting Surgeon for and upon the Testator at his request at Margate and Deal in the County of Kent and at Chelsea in the County of Middlesex and for Travelling and other Expenses attendant thereon during the life time of the Testator And I say that I so attended the said Testator at Margate where he was then living in Lodgings and at Deal during a severe attack of Cholera and a serious illness consequent upon it where he resided in a house of the Defendant Sophia Caroline Booth, and also at Davies Place Chelsea in the County of Middlesex where he was also residing in a house belonging to the said Sophia Caroline Booth and that I was on various occasions summoned to Deal and also to Chelsea by messages through the Electric Telegraph And I say that in order to save the expenses of journeys by myself to Chelsea it was arranged by the request of the Testator that Mr William Bartlett of Chelsea aforesaid, Pharmaceutical Chemist, should see him daily and make reports to me of the daily progress of the Testator and of the effect of the Medicines And I visited the Testator personally from time to time only when my attendance was deemed indispensible and particularly requested by him And I further say that the following contains a just and true particular of my Account for the said sum of Five hundred and twenty-one Pounds seventeen shillings, that is to say,

1850
11th May to 6th July: For a daily attendance at Margate on the Testator, from the 11th May 1850 to the 25th May 1850, and for occasional visits from the last mentioned day to the 6th July 1850 ... £10.10.0

1850
August 20, 25 & 26, and September 1st, 4th, 10th, 11th, 12th, 15th and 18th: For Journeys to Deal from Margate specially to visit the Testator by his request, and attendances on the Testator on each of those days (ten in number) including Travelling and other expenses from Margate to Deal and back again ...52.10.0

1851
February 5, March 8, April 9 and 30, May 29, July 2nd, 6th and 15th, September 5, 17th and 29th, October 9th, 23rd and 30th, November 11, 19 and 28, December 9th and 18th: Journeys from Margate to London specially to visit the Testator by his request and attendances on the Testator on each of those days (nineteen in number) and on some occasions attending the Testator on two successive days at Twenty Guineas for each journey, and for numerous letters to Mr Bartlett and prescribing from time to time for the Testator, from the end of the month of June 1851 to the death of the Testator on the 19th December 1851
... 399.00.0

Travelling and other expenses from Margate to Chelsea and back, at Three guineas per journey ... 59.17.0

£521.17.0

And I further say that the aforegoing is a true and just particular of the said Account or claim and that the charges therein made are fair and reasonable and such as are usual or customary in the same profession and under similar circumstances And I further say that neither I nor any person or persons by my order or to my knowledge or belief for any use hath or have received the said sum of Five hundred and twenty-one Pounds seventeen shillings or any part thereof or any security or satisfaction for the same or any part thereof but that the whole of the said sum of Five hundred and twenty-one Pounds seventeen shillings still remains justly due and owing to me on the said Account.

Sworn at Margate in the County of Kent this 17th day of December 1853.
Before me
  John Hawly Boys
  A Commissioner for administering Oaths in Chancery in England

  David Price.

# Index

Page numbers in **bold** indicate illustrations in the text.
* Asterisked entries show an item is included in the sections of illustrations.